Foreign Relations of the People's Republic of China

Foreign Relations
of the People's Republic
of China

JOHN W. GARVER
School of International Affairs
Georgia Institute of Technology

 PRENTICE HALL, Englewood Cliffs, New Jersey 07632

Library of Congress Cataloging-in-Publication Data

GARVER, JOHN W.
  Foreign relations of the People's Republic of China/John W.
Garver
    p. cm.
  Includes bibliographical references and index.
  ISBN 0-13-326414-9
  1. China—Foreign relations—1949– I. Title.
DS777.8.G37 1992
  327.51—dc20   92-31663
                                                    CIP

Editorial/production supervision,
  interior design, and page makeup: Kari Callaghan Mazzola
Acquisitions editor: Julie Berrisford
Cover design: Patricia Kelly
Prepress buyer: Kelly Behr
Manufacturing buyer: Mary Ann Gloriande

© 1993 by Prentice-Hall, Inc.
A Paramount Communications Company
Englewood Cliffs, New Jersey 07632

Printed in the United States of America
10 9 8 7 6 5 4 3 2

ISBN   0-13-326414-9

PRENTICE-HALL INTERNATIONAL (UK) LIMITED, *London*
PRENTICE-HALL OF AUSTRALIA PTY. LIMITED, *Sydney*
PRENTICE-HALL CANADA INC., *Toronto*
PRENTICE-HALL HISPANOAMERICANA, S.A., *Mexico*
PRENTICE-HALL OF INDIA PRIVATE LIMITED, *New Delhi*
PRENTICE-HALL OF JAPAN, INC., *Tokyo*
SIMON & SCHUSTER ASIA PTE. LTD., *Singapore*
EDITORA PRENTICE-HALL DO BRASIL, LTDA., *Rio de Janeiro*

To my mentors,
Allen S. Whiting and Lawrence W. Beer

Contents

Figures

Tables

Abbreviations

ABM	Anti-Ballistic Missile
ASEAN	Association of South East Asian Nations
CCP	Chinese Communist Party
CIA	Central Intelligence Agency
COCOM	Coordinating Committee for Multilateral Export Controls
CPSU	Communist Party of the Soviet Union
DRV	Democratic Republic of Vietnam
ICBM	Inter-Continental Ballistic Missile
IRBM	Intermediate Range Ballistic Missile
KM	Kilometers
KT	Kilotons (1,000 tons TNT equivalent)
KMT	Kuomintang, Nationalist Party of China
MFA	Ministry of Foreign Affairs
MFN	Most Favored Nation
MIRV	Multiple Independent Reentry Vehicle
MT	Megaton (1 million tons TNT equivalent)
NIC	Newly Industrialized Country
NPC	National People's Congress

NLF	National Liberation Front of South Vietnam
PLA	People's Liberation Army
PLAN	People's Liberation Army, Navy
PRC	People's Republic of China
ROC	Republic of China
SEATO	South East Asia Treaty Organization
SEZ	Special Economic Zone
SRV	Socialist Republic of Vietnam
SLBN	Submarine Launched Ballistic Missile
SSBN	Ballistic missile submarine, nuclear
TRA	Taiwan Relations Act
UN	United Nations
U.S.	United States
USSR	Union of Soviet Socialist Republics
VWP	Vietnamese Workers Party

Preface

This book is intended as a comprehensive general survey of the foreign relations of the People's Republic of China (PRC) from 1949 to 1992. PRC foreign relations are broken down into six interrelated dimensions, presented in six parts of the book representing, I believe, the major aspects of China's foreign relations. Part One deals with pre-1949 experiences and traditions that influenced significantly China's post-1949 foreign relations. Part Two explores China's attempts to cope with the American and Soviet superpowers that dominated the post–World War II era and, more importantly for our purposes, the attention of China's foreign policy decision makers. Part Three probes the implications and significance of the PRC's revolutionary origins, ideology, and aspirations. Part Four looks at the international implications and components of China's quest for economic development. Part Five dwells on China's national security and on its employment of military force as an instrument of foreign policy. Part Six engages in a bit of futurology and speculates about China's future as a major power.

As a general survey, this book is synthetic. It draws on a plethora of more specialized studies by other scholars, summarizes those studies and their conclusions, and uses them to create a broad mosaic of modern China's foreign relations. On occasion newly available primary material is integrated into the narrative, or my own interpretation of events, based on that evidence, is presented. By and large, however, I have attempted to synthesize and integrate the work of numerous other scholars who have dealt in greater detail with particular aspects of China's foreign relations.

I have tried to cover in this book virtually all the major aspects of modern China's foreign relations—from China's relations with ethnic Chinese communities in Southeast Asia, to the wars China has fought, to its efforts to acquire foreign technology, to its role in the United Nations and its relations with foreign revolutionary movements. When there are important differences of interpretation among scholars on various points, I have also tried to describe the contours of those debates. The danger of attempting such a panoramic view, especially when confined to a single, fairly concise text, is superficiality. The author must walk a narrow line: He must generalize, but also delve deeply enough into the complexity of issues to avoid simplification. He must avoid excessive detail, but present enough detail to give a sense of the issues involved. It is not my place to judge whether or not I have avoided this pitfall. I can only acknowledge that I was aware of it and plea that I tried to avoid it.

Disaggregation of China's foreign relations into six dimensions facilitates accomplishment of a broad overview. By providing a non-historical way of organizing relevant information, it encourages students to think in terms of the broad categories of influences on China's foreign relations. This form of organization risks either redundancy or artificial separation of closely related topics, however. Avoidance of redundancy requires consignment of a particular topic to one dimension or another when at all possible. Yet since various dimensions are often closely interrelated, discussions of closely related topics separated by several pages may be inconvenient. Moreover, consignment of a particular topic to one dimension rather than another is often somewhat arbitrary. China's support for Hanoi's drive to unite all of Vietnam under its rule in the late 1960s, for example, is discussed in Part Three dealing with China as a revolutionary power. It could as sensibly be discussed in terms of Chinese relations with the United States or in terms of China's national security. Usually topics have been consigned to one section or another on the basis of my subjective determination of which aspect was probably more important. For example, because of the prominent role Hanoi's drive played in Chinese revolutionary diplomacy in the 1950s and 1960s, Chinese relations with Vietnam during that period is consigned to Part Three. Chinese support for Hanoi after 1964, on the other hand, is discussed in Part Five because the Americanization of the Vietnam war brought national security considerations to the fore. In other cases, discussion of different aspects of a single phenomenon in different parts of the book simply cannot be avoided. Thus the Sino-Soviet alliance of the 1950s is discussed in terms of triangular diplomacy in Part Two and in terms of the economic dynamics of that alliance in Part Four.

The notes at the end of each chapter are mainly intended as guides for further reading. The reader will find in them the major scholarly sources dealing in greater depth with particular topics and debates discussed in general terms in the text. Except for direct quotations, citations of factual information have usually been avoided. Citations are provided, however, for new information drawn from recently published Chinese memoirs. Aside from these latter sources, all notes refer to English-language sources. Students interested in conducting research may consult the list of English-language sources provided below:

MAJOR ENGLISH LANGUAGE SOURCE MATERIALS

CHRONOLOGIES AND HANDBOOKS

Asian Recorder, New Delhi, India.

Asia Yearbook, Far Eastern Economic Review, Hong Kong.

Keessing's Record of World Events, London: Longman.

NEWSPAPERS AND NEWS MAGAZINES

Asian Wall Street Journal, Hong Kong.

Beijing Review (Beijing, China). Known as *Peking Review* prior to 1979.

China Business Review, National Council on U.S.-China Trade, Washington, D.C.

China Daily, Beijing, China.

Far Eastern Economic Review, Hong Kong.

Japan Times Weekly, Japan Times, Inc., Tokyo, Japan.

The New York Times, New York City.

South China Morning Post, Hong Kong.

Survey of the Regional Press, Institute of Regional Studies, Islamabad, Pakistan.

TRANSLATIONS OF CHINESE MATERIALS

Chinese Law and Government, Joint Publications Research Service, Arlington, Virginia.

Foreign Broadcast Information Service, Daily Report, China, National Technical Information Service, Springfield, Virginia. Began publication 1971.

JPRS Report, China, National Technical Information Service, Springfield, Virginia.

Survey of the China Mainland Press, U.S. Consulate, Hong Kong. 1950–1977.

MAJOR JOURNALS

Asian Survey, University of California Press, Berkeley, California.

China Report, Center for the Study of Developing Societies, Delhi, India.

The China Quarterly, School of Oriental and African Studies, University of London, London. Each issue contains a chronology of developments during the previous quarter.

Current Scene; Developments in Mainland China, U.S. Information Service, Hong Kong. 1961–1973.

Far Eastern Affairs, Institute of the Far East, USSR Academy of Sciences, Moscow.

Issues and Studies, Institute of International Relations, Taibei, Taiwan.

Japan Review of International Affairs, Japan Institute of International Affairs, Tokyo.

Journal of Asian Studies, Association of Asian Studies, Ann Arbor, Michigan.

Journal of East Asian Affairs, The Research Institute for International Affairs, Seoul, Korea.

Journal of Northeast Asian Studies, Institute of Sino-Soviet Studies, George Washington University, Washington, D.C.

Problems of Communism, U.S. Information Service, Washington, D.C.

WRITINGS OF MAO ZEDONG AND DENG XIAOPING

Deng Xiaoping, *Selected Works of Deng Xiaoping (1975–1982),* Beijing: Foreign Languages Press, 1984.

———, *Speeches and Writings—Deng Xiaoping,* New York: Pergamon, 1984.

———, *Build Socialism with Chinese Characteristics,* Beijing: Foreign Languages Press, 1985.

———, *Fundamental Issues in Present Day China,* Beijing: Foreign Languages Press, 1987.

Mao Zedong, *Selected Works of Mao Tse-tung,* 4 volumes, Beijing: Foreign Languages Press, 1967.

———, *Miscellany of Mao Tse-tung Thought, (1949–1968)*, 2 parts, Joint Publications Research Service, Arlington, Virginia, 1974.

———, *The Secret Speeches of Chairman Mao*, Roderick MacFarquhar, Timothy Cheek, Eugene Wu, ed., Cambridge, MA: Harvard University Press, 1989.

———, *The Writings of Mao Zedong*, Michael Y.M. Kau, John K. Leung, ed., vol. 1, 1949–1953, vol. 2, 1956–1957. New York: M.E. Sharpe, 1991.

BIBLIOGRAPHIES

Bibliography of Asian Studies, Association of Asian Studies, Ann Arbor, Michigan.

ACKNOWLEDGMENTS

My thanks are due to a number of individuals who provided help at various stages in the writing of this book. Dr. Daniel S. Papp, Director of our School of International Affairs at Georgia Tech, facilitated approval of various leaves during which large pieces of this book were written. Dr. Michael H. Hunt of the University of North Carolina at Chapel Hill and Dr. Morris Rossabi of City University of New York and Columbia University read and critiqued the chapters on historical influences on China's foreign relations. Dr. David Zweig of Tufts University, Dr. Carol Lee Hamrin of the U.S. State Department, and Dr. Samuel S. Kim of Princeton University critiqued the chapters on China as a revolutionary power. Dr. Penelope B. Prime of Kennesaw State College reviewed the chapters dealing with China's international economic relations. Dr. June T. Dreyer of the University of Miami at Coral Gables and Dr. Paul H. B. Godwin of the U.S. National Defense University read and critiqued the chapters on China's national security. Dr. James C. F. Wang of the University of Hawaii at Hilo and Dr. Lawrence Ziring of Western Michigan University also reviewed several chapters and offered constructive criticisms and insights. Any errors that remain are, of course, entirely the responsibility of the author. Colleagues who detect errors or who have suggestions for making the book more useful as a text are urged to write me directly at Georgia Tech.

John W. Garver
Georgia Institute of Technology

Part One

Historical Influences on China's Foreign Relations

Chapter One

The Legacy of the Past

THE ROLE OF HISTORY IN CHINA

Although our concern in this text is with the foreign relations of the People's Republic of China (PRC), we must begin with a consideration of China's earlier history, for that history exercised a significant influence on China's post-1949 foreign relations. Events long past influence subsequent generations through shared recollections of those events and beliefs about their meaning. Frequently such shared memories and beliefs assume mythic proportions: mythic not in the sense that they have no grounding in fact, but in the sense that the shared belief itself is in many ways more important than what actually happened in the past.

Shared memories and beliefs shape the international relations of all countries. In the United States, for example, recollections of more than a century of deliberate non-involvement in the affairs of Europe, of reliance on the two great oceans flanking North America that made such isolationism possible, and memories of a long period of self-absorption focused on the creation of a new civilization still exert powerful influences on U.S. foreign policy in the late twentieth century. Comparable shared recollections play an arguably even greater role in shaping the foreign policy of the PRC.

One of the ways that memories of events are passed from generation to generation is via the writing and interpreting of history. In few countries does history play a greater role than in China. For more than two millennia, successive imperial dynasties and generations of Confucian scholar-officials found in the history of earlier eras explanations of the moral waxing and waning of society and its institutions. From this they drew conclusions about how the affairs of their own era ought to be governed. The legitimacy of each dynasty was closely tied to this historical explanation, and each dynasty produced an orthodox history justifying its rise to power. This official history invariably demonstrated that the decline of the previous regime was caused by moral decay and the establishment of the present regime resulted from its superior virtue. History, and the writing of history, thus revealed the moral basis of the existing state.

Marxism, with its search for historical "laws," coincided with and reinforced China's hoary concern with the past. In Marxism, as in Confucianism, the fundamental workings of society and the relationship between power and morality is revealed through a study of history. Just as Confucianism postulated a direct link between the virtue of the ruler and his claim to power, Marxism found a similar link between the moral quality of a social class and its rule of society. Marx found a moral progression in human history, with each succeeding ruling class and form of social organization reflecting the interests of that class representing a moral advance over the previous ruling class and social organization. The proletariat had the most genuinely moral claim to power, for only it would lead humanity to the abolition of the exploitation of labor. Lenin took this idea one step further by claiming, again like Confucius, that the right to rule lay with the handful of people who understood the true principles of history.

The propensity of both Confucianism and Marxism to explain and justify policy in terms of historical principles probably contributed to the intellectual appeal of various grand theories of international relations to the leaders of the PRC. The PRC's leaders have usually felt a need to frame their foreign policies in terms of broad historical epochs and categories. In 1949 New China was seen as standing with the socialist camp led by the Soviet Union, and struggling to defeat the efforts at domination by the imperialist camp led by the United States throughout a vast intermediate zone of countries between the socialist and imperialist camps. By 1958 Beijing was advocating a united front of all possible forces to defeat U.S. imperialism and usher in the new, post-imperialist era of history. By 1972 Beijing had formulated a new grand scheme, the Three Worlds Theory, in which the United States and the USSR made up the First World, the economically developed capitalist and socialist countries other than the United States and the USSR made up the Second World, and the developing countries constituted the Third World. Historical necessity and progress required, according to this theory, that the Second and Third worlds unite against the First World. This Three Worlds theory was flexible enough, however, to be directed primarily against one or the other of the two superpowers, and during the period from about 1977 to 1982 it took the form of advocacy of a united front against the Soviet Union. Then in about 1985, as China integrated itself into the world capitalist economy and modified the centralized forms of economic organization that it had previously taken as the sine qua non of socialism, Beijing developed a new scheme of history to frame its current foreign policy—the theory of the "initial stage of socialism." According to this theory, Chinese socialism was in its initial historic phase, during which accommodations with global capitalist markets and acceptance of "lower," more capitalist-like forms of economic organization were necessary.

While these various historical schemes were rooted in China's immediate political situation and needs, they also reflected traditional Chinese notions about the appropriate relationship between power and morality. Power had to serve a moral purpose, which was derived from a study of history. The legitimacy of political power in contemporary China is still rooted squarely in interpretations of history, just as it was in traditional China.

THE MYTH OF NATIONAL HUMILIATION

The central aspect of recent Chinese history, as interpreted by the Chinese Communist Party (CCP), is the Chinese people's struggle against the "humiliation" of China by foreign imperialism during the 110 years between 1839 and 1949. To the CCP, the era between the first opium war and the establishment of the People's Republic of China is essentially a chronicle of wars imposed by aggressive and arrogant imperialist powers, and of increasingly harsh terms forced on China in consequence of its defeat in those wars. Heavy indemnities were imposed on China because of its supposed responsibility for provoking various conflicts by being so unreasonable as to refuse to accept imperialist demands in the first place. Those indemnities then seriously constrained the finances of China's government and limited its ability to strengthen its military defenses or develop its economy. The imperialist powers forced China to fix its tariffs at a nominal level (5 percent), thereby precluding the protection of China's infant industry from foreign competition and limiting the government's ability to raise revenues that might be used to strengthen China against the foreign threat. Against great official and popular resistance, China was forced to allow Christian missionaries to proselytize in China's interior and to legalize the import of opium—events that some Chinese saw as interrelated, both being intended to make Chinese lose self-confidence and self-respect as well as become psychologically dependent on the foreigners. And throughout the century of National Humiliation there were repeated episodes of foreign barbarism, such as the Anglo-French burning of Beijing's beautiful Summer Palace in 1860.[1]

During the decades after the end of first opium war in 1842, imperialist influence rapidly penetrated deep into China. More and more ports were opened by the terms of various treaties forced on China's beleaguered government. By the early twentieth century there were over fifty so-called treaty ports in which foreigners enjoyed special rights. Foreigners were removed from the jurisdiction of Chinese law and courts and placed under the jurisdiction of the consuls of their native country or of specially constituted foreign courts. Large districts of major commercial centers, along with the Chinese and foreigners residing in those districts, were placed under exclusive foreign jurisdiction. These foreign-controlled districts were called *concessions*, and the whole practice of placing parcels of the land and population of China under foreign jurisdiction was referred to as *extraterritoriality*. Other pieces of Chinese territory were leased for long periods of time. Foreign troops were stationed in the foreign concessions and leaseholdings. Foreign warships patrolled the rivers and coasts of China to protect foreign interests. As the superiority of foreign military and economic power became clear, the imperialist powers found many Chinese willing to cooperate with them for one reason or another. As the authority and effectiveness of China's central government waned, the autonomy of foreign-supported local governments often increased. By the end of the nineteenth century the various imperialist powers were on the verge of dividing China among themselves into outright colonies. They were prevented from doing so largely because they realized that such a partition would probably lead to war among the major powers. Yet they did carve out informal spheres of influence, regions guarded by the military might of a particular power and within which the interests of that power were paramount (see Figure 1–1). Britain's sphere of influence was the vast Yangtze valley. Japan's lay in southern Manchuria and Fujian. Taiwan was ceded outright to Japan in 1895. France's sphere of influence was southern Guangdong and Guanxi. Germany's was in Shandong, and Russia's in northern Manchuria, Outer Mongolia, and Xinjiang. The United States used its influence to prevent the partition of China, favoring instead an Open Door policy in which all areas of China would remain open to the commercial activity of all foreign powers.

Still another component of China's National Humiliation was its loss of extensive territory and the destruction of Chinese influence in broad areas of Asia. Russian imperialism seized vast tracts along the left and right banks of the Amur River, Sakhalin Island, Outer Mongolia, and central Asia. The British took over Hong Kong and large parts of what is today northern Myanmar (Burma) and northeast India, which

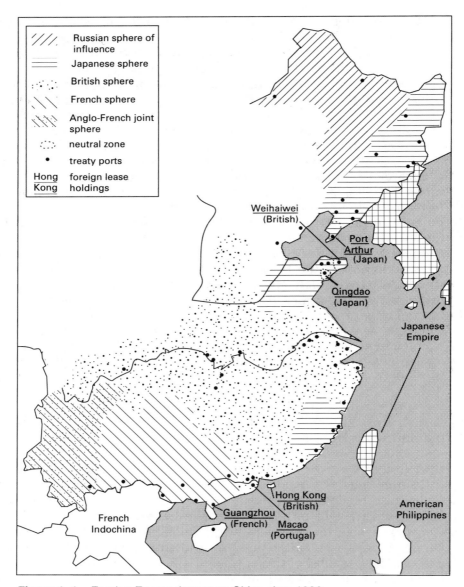

Figure 1–1   Foreign Encroachment on China circa 1920

China's government felt was Chinese territory. Japan seized Taiwan and later Manchuria. In other non-Chinese areas of Asia, China had traditionally enjoyed a degree of status and influence—in Korea, the Ryukyu Islands, in most of continental Southeast Asia, and in the small kingdoms in the Himalayan Mountains. These areas too were seized by foreign imperialism and Chinese influence extirpated.[2] Figure 1–2

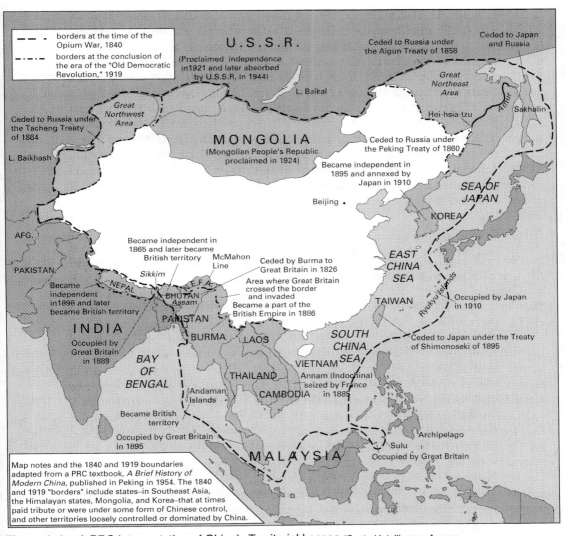

Figure 1–2 A PRC Interpretation of China's Territorial Losses (Central Intelligence Agency, *People's Republic of China, Atlas*, 1971)

presents one authoritative Chinese interpretation of the territorial losses inflicted on China during the century of National Humiliation.

The century of National Humiliation can be termed a myth, but not because the episodes pointed to by Chinese scholars did not occur. Indeed, most of them did, though not always with the utterly sinister nature and motivation imputed to them. It is mythic, rather, in the sense that the fact of belief is more important than what actually occurred. The story of National Humiliation is constantly told and retold in Chinese schools, in the mass media, and in countless mandatory study sessions attended by Chinese citizens. Contrary interpretations or evidence are not allowed. Belief in the century of National Humiliation is virtually universal in China; even most dissidents share it. For our purposes, what is of primary importance is that Chinese believe in the century of National Humiliation.

The myth of National Humiliation stands at the center of the political culture of the People's Republic of China. It has greatly influenced China's approach to the world by giving rise to an ardent determination to end all aspects of China's "humiliation," to blot out all remnants of China's past weakness and degradation, and to prevent its recurrence. Mao Zedong expressed those sentiments in September 1949, just before the establishment of the People's Republic, when he said:

> The Chinese have always been a great, courageous, and industrious nation; it is only in modern times that they have fallen behind. And that was due entirely to oppression and exploitation by foreign imperialism and domestic reactionary governments....Ours will no longer be a nation subject to insult and humiliation. We have stood up.[3]

Scholars differ regarding the actual impact of the foreign influence on China in the century between 1839 and 1949. Some argue that the real foreign impact was marginal and that the essential dynamics of Chinese development during that century had more to do with such endogenous variables as population growth, exhaustion of available arable land, and the emergence of new social elites and classes. Others, more representative of mainstream scholarly opinion, maintain that foreign influence had a great effect on China, interacting with and shaping the evolution of endogenous factors. CCP historiography belongs to the latter camp. In the CCP's view, during the century of National Humiliation, foreign, imperialist influence was decisive. China was reduced to a "semi-colony," with its independence and sovereignty becoming an empty formality. Imperialism became, according to the CCP, one of the two "mountains" oppressing the Chinese people. "Feudalism" was the other.

The experience of National Humiliation was a major factor impelling many young Chinese to embrace the doctrine of Marxism-Leninism in the early twentieth century. Lenin's theory about the evolution of industrial capitalism into imperialism and his observations about the rapacious nature of imperialism seemed to fit with the facts as seen by many young Chinese. Lenin's theory of imperialism not only provided a systematic and seemingly cogent explanation of Western and Japanese pressure against China, but also provided a damning moral condemnation of that pressure as well as a programmatic response. Stated simply, the anti-imperialism of post-1949 China was a function of China's experience of National Humiliation.

THE TRADITIONAL CHINESE WORLD ORDER

Perhaps the most bitter aspect for Chinese of growing contact with the West was not military defeat, intrusive foreign presence, or territorial losses, but an awareness that China was, in fact, inferior to the foreign powers in the very areas that Confucianism had long held to be the proof of China's superiority over others.[4] Confucianism had held that skill in the art of governance and superior material well-being were proof of China's higher level of civilization. Yet China's experience during the years from 1839 to 1949 made it steadily clearer that it was precisely in those areas that the Western countries were superior to China. The inability of Chinese governments to cope with Western demands became increasingly obvious. Moreover, the orderly, well-administered extraterritorial concessions in the treaty ports increasingly stood in contrast to the disorder, corruption, and incompetence of Chinese governments ruling adjacent areas. And the more Chinese learned about the Western countries, the clearer it became that China was abjectly poor.

To understand the full psychological depth and intensity of Chinese bitterness over this realization of its humiliation and inferiority, one must go back a bit further and probe another important memory shared by most Chinese: the memory of China's ancient and medieval grandeur.

China was, of course, one of several dozen vast, powerful, and wealthy empires built during pre-modern history. In terms of longevity, size, and brilliance of its achievements, it was arguably one of the greatest. Along with the Nile, Mesopotamian, and Indus river valleys, the middle valley of the Yellow River was one of the earliest cradles of human civilization. In each of these regions, humans settled into agricultural communities several thousand years before Christ. The social revolution that came with settled agriculture brought urban centers, architecture and engineering, complex forms of government and warfare, writing, and many other accoutrements of civilization. What is remarkable in the case of China is that the civilization created several millennia ago continued into the early twentieth century, while the other great civilizations experienced radical discontinuities. It is as if Egyptians at the beginning of the twentieth century still wrote in hieroglyphics, studied in their schools a variant of the ancient cults of Isis and Ra, and were still ruled by a dynasty modeled after that of the Pharaohs. Chinese civilization is not the oldest; those of Egypt and Mesopotamia developed somewhat earlier. But China holds an unchallenged record for longevity and continuity. This unsurpassed continuity is the first basis of Chinese pride in their history.

Size and power are the second basis for Chinese pride. In those terms, other great empires—e.g., those of Hellenistic and Byzantine

Greece, Rome, Mughal India, Persia, the Ottoman Turks, the Arabs, and the Mongols, to name only a few—equaled the Chinese. But again China was exceptional in its longevity. The other great empires waxed, waned, and then disappeared. Various Chinese dynasties collapsed as well, sometimes to be followed by long periods of political disunity, but a new dynasty always arose to reunite the vast cultural area of China. The reasons for this exceptional political cohesion are extremely complex. Suffice it to say that by the time of the Tang dynasty (618–907 A.D.), educated Chinese generally accepted the idea that lands populated by Chinese and making up the Chinese cultural area ought to be united under a single ruler. This idea was handed down from generation to generation, and still has a significant influence on the behavior of China's leaders.[5]

The brilliant achievements of Chinese civilization are a third basis of Chinese pride. Marco Polo, the Genoese merchant explorer who travelled to the court of the great Mongol emperor Kublai Khan in the thirteenth century, was astounded by the size, wealth, and sophistication of the cities of Cathay that he visited—a wealth that helped lure various European navigators across uncharted seas in search of new routes to the fabulous East. The humanistic benevolence of China's traditional Confucian autocratic governments contrasted favorably with the brutal forms of government characteristic of much of the world for much of human history. As late as the Enlightenment of the eighteenth century, European philosophers were inspired by what they understood of China's secular and humane system of government.[6] In terms of art and technology, no pre-modern civilization surpassed China. The multitude of ancient discoveries bequeathed by Chinese inventors to mankind are well known. The walls of one of Beijing's subway stations, for example, are adorned with murals depicting China's "four great inventions": gunpowder, paper, printing, and the magnetic compass. Contemporary Chinese remain immensely proud of their ancient heritage and see it as proof that the present technological superiority of the West over China is a temporary aberration.

The proud recollection of this past grandeur has had a profound impact on modern China. In the words of Lucian Pye, "The most pervasive underlying Chinese emotion is a profound, unquestioned, generally unshakable identification with historical greatness. Merely to be Chinese is to be a part of the greatest phenomenon of history."[7] This sentiment has extremely deep roots. The neolithic forebears of the Chinese developed ancestor worship very early on. Gradually this practice evolved into a concept of social order and harmony centering on observance of prescribed roles, a concept that allowed the early Chinese to distinguish very clearly between their own society and that of surrounding peoples. There was no doubt in Chinese minds as to which was superior. Probably by the middle of the second millennium B.C., the

Chinese had added to this notion the idea of a single supreme king within the civilized world. The next step came during the first two centuries A.D., when the Chinese concluded that intercourse with the surrounding "barbarian" peoples ought to take the form of symbolic acceptance by the latter of China's superiority.[8]

By the time of the Tang dynasty, the Chinese were convinced not only of the superiority of their civilization, but even that they were the only truly civilized people in the world. Civilization—that is, Chinese culture—stood literally and figuratively at the center of human affairs, Chinese believed. This was the notion of the "Middle Kingdom"—which is the literal meaning of *zhongguo*, the word translated nowadays as "China." Surrounded by more or less uncivilized peoples, the Middle Kingdom exerted a civilizing influence on those peoples as they interacted with it and partook of civilization—that is, of Chinese culture. Through submissive interaction with the Middle Kingdom, non-Chinese barbarians might gradually become civilized, an idea embodied by the words *lai hua*, "to come and be transformed." In other words, non-Chinese became civilized to the extent that they assimilated Chinese culture.

According to Confucian orthodoxy, China's superiority was based primarily on virtue rather than on material strength. The most important aspect of human existence, according to Confucianism, was to understand and live in accordance with the principles of correct conduct. People of all stations in society ought to strive to live in accordance with the precepts of the five cardinal relationships: between father and son, husband and wife, elder brother and younger brother, friend and friend, and emperor and subject. If everyone acted as they should, society would be orderly and prosperous. The heaviest responsibility of all fell on the emperor, the Son of Heaven or *tian zi*, whose outstanding moral example was the linchpin of the entire social, and indeed cosmological, order. When the emperor was virtuous, his officials would be virtuous. When the officials were virtuous, the people would be virtuous. When the people were virtuous, there would be harmony in human affairs, and between human affairs and the cosmos.

In terms of foreign relations, when there was proper order under heaven, when all was as it should be, foreign barbarians would be awestruck and submissive to China. Traditional Confucian thinkers were aware that barbarians might at times be more powerful than China. Power, however, was not the criterion of civilization. The unparalleled catastrophe of the Mongol conquest of China in the thirteenth century forced a hard reappraisal of the relationship between morality and power, but proper behavior still remained the bedrock of civilization, and proper conduct was still defined in terms of Confucian principles, albeit in a somewhat modernized version.

China was not unique in developing notions about its own

superiority. Many other countries, modern as well as ancient, have done likewise. But in China's case geographic circumstances conspired to allow this idea to develop relatively unchallenged. The other great civilizations of the Middle East, South Asia, the Mediterranean, and Europe were forced willy-nilly by their geography to rub elbows with one another. But China, or more precisely the East Asian area of Sinic civilization, was separated from other areas of great civilization by the vast steppes and deserts of Inner Asia and by the rugged Himalayan Mountains and Tibetan plateau. The non-Sinic societies well known to the Chinese included those of the nomadic peoples of Inner Asia and the tribal peoples inhabiting the mountainous areas to the south of Chinese settlement who practiced slash-and-burn agriculture. These peoples were simply not civilized by Chinese standards; comparison inspired not humility but arrogance. The several important non-Chinese, settled-agricultural, and literate societies within the confines of the East Asian world order—Korea, Japan, Vietnam—drew heavily and more or less consciously from the font of Chinese civilization, further confirming China's own ethnocentrism. Some knowledge of the alien but developed societies of South Asia, the Middle East, and the Mediterranean did seep into China. On occasion China even adopted elements of those alien cultures—Indian Buddhism being the most important example. But a process of intellectual filtration and compartmentalization prevented an awareness of foreign civilizations from calling into question China's assumptions regarding its own superiority.[9]

Gradually a set of practices were developed to institutionalize the "proper" relationship between the Chinese emperor and the emissaries from "barbarian" states. Central to this system were tribute-bearing missions from barbarian rulers to the Chinese emperor. By bearing gifts to the emperor and performing the prescribed rituals in the process (most notably the kowtow before the emperor), the foreign tributaries recognized the grandeur and superior virtue of the emperor. In return for their gifts, they received from the emperor gifts that typically were of greater value than those submitted to him. This was taken to be an indication of the emperor's munificence. In addition, the emperor would confer on tributary rulers a patent and an official seal of office, a rank in the Chinese aristocracy, and a calender—all of which had certain practical utility for foreign rulers. On occasion the Chinese emperor would adjudicate disputes within tributary states—over succession to foreign thrones, for example—or would dispatch armies to help loyal tributary rulers suppress rebellions.[10]

Often rulers of the non-Chinese states of Inner Asia and Southeast Asia, and later of Europe, accepted such Chinese practices only reluctantly or superficially as a matter of practical expediency. Not infrequently they refused to accept them at all. Dealing with such "rebellious" behavior by barbarians, especially militarily powerful ones, was a major diplomatic problem for traditional China. Chinese statesmen displayed considerable flexibility in dealing with such problems, resorting to such means as payments of money, indoctrination via cultural-ideological means (sending Chinese wives or advisers to foreign rulers, for example), maneuvering one barbarian state into conflict with another, or simply accepting the barbarian's refusal to perform prescribed rituals while recording that the necessary acts had, in fact, been performed. It may well be, in fact, that the set of ideals embodied in the tribute system was more a Chinese myth than a reality. Yet that myth reflected deeply ingrained notions about the proper relation between China and other countries—about how the world ought to be.

It is perhaps well to stress that China was not unique in developing notions of its cultural superiority and civilizing mission. Other nations have done likewise. The United States, for example, has typically seen itself as the promoter of liberty and democracy around the world. Britain, France, Japan, the Soviet Union, and India, among others, have also developed strong senses of international mission at one time or another.

The intellectual premises of the traditional Chinese world order were quite different from those upon which the European international order, and the modern world order extrapolated from the European model, was based. The Chinese world order was, in theory, hierarchical and centralized, with China at the apex and centered about the Son of Heaven. The European state system was based on the ideal of equal, sovereign states coexisting without any superior power. In the European system, each state enjoyed exclusive sovereignty over a precisely defined national territory. In the Chinese world order, the territorial limitations were imprecise and the purpose of interaction was the transformation of lesser societies along the lines of the Chinese model. During the nineteenth century, Chinese statesmen had great difficulty handling the discrepancies between the diplomatic practices based on these two systems.

Scholarly opinion differs greatly regarding the contemporary impact of the traditional Chinese world view. Some scholars, such as Mark Mancall and C.P. Fitzgerald, contend that traditional ideas continue to exert great influence.[11] Those scholars point to the many similarities between the behavior of traditional and modern China. In terms of diplomatic style, for example, they point to the persistence of the practice of ritual bestowal of gifts on foreign countries (though now these gifts are bestowed on "the people" rather than on the rulers of those countries), the emperor-like inaccessibility of Mao Zedong and other Chinese leaders, the stylized audiences granted to foreign representatives by China's leaders, and so on. They also point to China's efforts to lead Asia or the Third World, or the moralistic tone of Chinese pronouncements on world affairs—as if other nations have mere interests, while China has principles. Again one hears echoes of Chinese virtue chastising barbarian avarice and cupidity. Nor is it difficult to find post-1949 Chinese statements that reflect traditional notions about China's civilizing mission. For example:

> The Chinese people have elevated their nation to its rightful place as one of the leaders of the world....We have set a new standard for the people of Asia and the Pacific. We have given them a new outlook on their own problems. [Beijing] serves as the birthplace of the new unity of the Asian and Pacific peoples in their struggle for harmony among nations.[12]

The influence of tradition is seen not only in relatively minor matters of style, but also, so these scholars argue, in terms of substantive policy issues. The similarity between China's traditional, hierarchical, universalistic, moralistic world view and the Stalinist approach to international relations in the 1950s was, scholars such as Fitzgerald and Mancall maintain, one factor predisposing the CCP to accept the latter. From a slightly different perspective, whether the CCP was upholding true doctrine (i.e., virtue) against the unprincipled Soviet Communist Party in the early 1960s or pontificating to the Third World on how best to develop and defeat U.S. imperialism, the central idea was the same: China was lawgiver to the foreigners. In most general terms, Chinese remain convinced that their new socialist way, whether Maoist or Dengist, is as superior to all other as they formerly felt that the Confucian empire was superior to those of the barbarians. As Professor Fitzgerald puts it, "The Chinese view of the world has not fundamentally changed; it has been adjusted to take account of the modern world, but only so far as to permit China to occupy, still, the central place in the picture."[13]

Most scholars would not go as far as Fitzgerald and Mancall. While acknowledging that the traditional Chinese world view has some influence on modern Chinese foreign policy, especially on its style and tone, the more mainstream position argues that this influence is slight, and that the discontinuities with tradition are far more important than the similarities. This viewpoint concedes that tradition did have a significant influence on the thinking and policies of some Qing officials during the nineteenth century, and that the smugness, complacency, and rigidity engendered by this traditional perspective contributed to China's difficulty in dealing with the imperialist onslaught of that era. Resorting to previously successful methods of dealing with powerful and aggressive barbarians—such as allowing them to be governed by their own laws and consuls while residing in China—also backfired when applied to the far more powerful seaborne Westerners. Yet as early as the 1830s and 1840s, some Chinese thinkers were beginning to ponder the viability of traditional ways in dealing with China's modern problems, and by the late nineteenth century China's leading statesmen and intellectuals had broken with traditional views.[14]

THE BREAKDOWN OF THE TRADITIONAL WORLD VIEW

As one might expect, Chinese thinkers and leaders in the nineteenth century responded variously to China's National Humiliation. Most initially clung doggedly to traditional views, but a few began to challenge traditional notions quite early on. Shortly after China's defeat in the first opium war in 1842, Lin Zexu, the commissioner whose attempts to suppress the opium trade at Canton had precipitated the war, advanced the radical proposition that China needed to study Western military techniques and acquire Western weapons. At about the same time, some middle-level scholar-officials began informing Chinese about an outside world that differed substantially from the one derived from traditional Confucian assumptions. In 1848 Xu Jiyu, then governor of Fujian province (a position that placed him in frequent contact with Westerners), published a geography of the world informing Chinese readers that their country occupied only one corner of one continent on the globe, and that the Western countries then pressing in on China had long histories and impressive cultural achievements of their own. Xu also gave a positive appraisal of the wealth and power of the Western countries. He further wrote that the international society that China now faced was an amoral order based on power and characterized by constant diplomatic maneuvering. He informed his contemporaries about the European colonization of India, Africa, and Southeast Asia then underway, and warned that such a fate might befall China too if it failed to respond appropriately to the new Western threat. Xu's prescription was that China should hold off the Western powers via diplomatic maneuvers while studying them and borrowing their advanced techniques. When first published, Xu's radical ideas had little impact on top-level Chinese thinking. By the 1860s, however, his book was reshaping the Chinese view of their position in the world.[15]

Regarding the transformation of China's view of the world in the nineteenth century, Michael Hunt makes the important point that intense Chinese self-esteem did not necessarily translate into isolation and chauvinism. While such xenophobia was the common Chinese reaction to the West in the mid-nineteenth century, Hunt says, Chinese pride could also manifest itself in a more cosmopolitan form that welcomed extensive interaction with, and learning from, foreign countries.[16] Chinese intellectuals came to this latter position only reluctantly, however. In the 1840s and 1850s the overwhelming majority of Chinese scholar-officials had only contempt and complacency toward the mounting Western intrusion. There was no need to study the barbarians, they maintained. Indeed, to do so would only further weaken China by giving the barbarians an opportunity to corrupt young Chinese. The true path to national strength, they argued, was to strengthen China's traditional virtues. There is a consensus among contemporary scholars that this conservatism led to an ineptness that greatly exacerbated the difficulties faced by China in dealing with the West in the nineteenth century.

It took the shock of defeat in the second opium war in 1858, the Anglo-French capture of Beijing and the burning of the Summer Palace in 1860, and the growing strength of the Taiping Rebellion at about the same time to overcome this conservatism. In 1860 a group of reformers who styled themselves "Self-Strengtheners" came to power under the auspices of the Manchu Prince Kung, half-brother of the Xianfeng emperor until 1861 and then regent for the new Tongzhi emperor from 1862 to 1874. From 1860 to 1896 the Self-Strengtheners sought to develop new institutions while drawing on Western expertise and technology to strengthen China militarily. Initially the Self-Strengtheners thought largely in terms of military strength, and did not think it was necessary to abandon Confucian political and social institutions. Yet they were ready to modernize within those limited parameters, and under their auspices a Western-style foreign ministry, a customs service, a foreign languages school, two shipyards, and an arsenal were set up. Gradually their understanding of the changes that were necessary to strengthen China deepened. Over time they spoke increasingly of the need for overall economic and industrial development.[17]

The most prominent and farsighted of the Self-Strengtheners were Li Hongzhang and Zhang Zhidong. Gradually, Li and Zhang began to understand that China's weakness was linked to its general poverty. National wealth and power were tied together, they began to argue, and to make China strong it was necessary to develop coal and iron mines, metal smelters and mills, harbors, railways, telegraphs, and so on. Such ideas seemed radical in the 1860s, but by the 1890s they represented the mainstream of thinking among Chinese intellectuals—although not among the imperial court.[18]

By the end of the nineteenth century such seminal thinkers as Kang Youwei and Liang Qichao, men whose ideas exerted a profound influence on Chinese thinking in the twentieth century, had concluded that China's survival demanded rejection of traditional social and political institutions. To ensure the political survival of the Chinese people, and of what they took to be the core values of the Chinese tradition, Chinese society had to be remade, for a very great part of the traditional Confucian order stood in the way of China's advance, Kang and Liang argued. If China was to survive, it had to reject its old complacent attitude and learn from the foreigners. For Kang and Liang,

China had to master not just Western technology, but the entire corpus of Western knowledge, from social philosophies to natural sciences. In short, China had to be remade, they argued. A "New China," and a new type of Chinese person, had to be created. Only in this way could China survive as a nation.[19]

This was the watershed between commitment to tradition and nationalism. For Liang Qichao, especially, the commitment to the societal entity known as the nation took priority over commitment to particular institutions. Liang and later Chinese thinkers still derived solace from a belief in the superiority of China's national past, and could imagine that the core traditional values would be retained in the transition to the future society. Yet "traditional" values covered a very wide spectrum of possibilities, and picking and choosing those for retention was done on the basis of whether they facilitated the search for national wealth and power.[20]

Regarding international relations, Kang and Liang followed the examples of such people as Xu Jiyu and Li Hongzhang in explicitly rejecting the idea that human society was some sort of universal moral order centered around China. Instead they recognized that the international system is made up of competing and frequently hostile nations and that the common denominator of international politics is power. To survive in this competitive and amoral world, China must be powerful and maneuver like other nations.

It is difficult for Westerners to comprehend the full boldness and significance of this shift in viewpoints. The nearest equivalent in the West was, perhaps, the intellectual revolution wrought by Copernican astronomy in the sixteenth century, when the Earth was displaced from the center of the universe to become a mere planet circling one of a great number of stars. Similarly revolutionary, non-traditional ideas fundamentally shaped the thinking of the men and women who created and led the People's Republic of China. This drastic break with China's traditional world view is one reason why most scholars are reluctant to ascribe to traditional attitudes much influence on modern China's foreign relations.

FOREIGN INFLUENCE AND MAINTAINING THE CHINESE ESSENCE

While Chinese intellectuals were led to increasingly radical conclusions about the need for change in Chinese society, they continued to believe that there was a unique, distinctive moral essence at the center of Chinese civilization that should be preserved. As indicated previously, this is an ancient notion, closely tied to the idea that society is a totalistic moral order in which stability and prosperity depend upon maintaining virtue. The problem Chinese faced, as they realized that they would have to adopt many ideas and techniques from the West, was how to assimilate Western things without allowing those foreign things to corrode China's distinctive moral essence?

Michel Oksenberg and Steve Goldstein argue that the spectrum of political debate in modern China has revolved around this question. At one extreme of the Chinese political spectrum dubbed the nativist isolationist pole by Oksenberg and Goldstein, have been those who maintained that the only way to protect China's national essence was isolation from the outside world. At the other extreme of the political spectrum, were people relatively unconcerned about protecting China's unique cultural essence, either because they were confident of the resiliency of that essence or because they viewed its fundamental change as a positive development. People at this end of the political spectrum, whom Oksenberg and Goldstein call Westernizers, were ready to throw open the doors to all sorts of foreign influences without much regard for the subversive impact they might have on the moral matrix of Chinese society. At times people representing one or the other of these extreme points of view were able to determine Chinese policy. Usually, however, a more centrist outlook prevailed. This centrist, mainstream, viewpoint attempted to reconcile the arguments of the two extremes by saying that while foreign technology and techniques should be brought into China and assimilated, undesirable, corrosive values and ideas should be filtered out. By the 1890s China's Self-Strengtheners encapsulated this idea in the slogan "Chinese learning for the essence, Western learning for practical use" (*Zhong xue wei ti, xi xue wei yong*).[21] Ninety years later, this idea remained at the center of the Chinese political spectrum, with Deng Xiaoping characterizing his grand goal as "building socialism with Chinese characteristics." To Deng, this meant extensive assimilation of foreign techniques while firmly upholding the "four cardinal principles" to ensure that China remained socialist.[22]

Both the Maoist and post-Mao regimes have shown great concern about protecting the distinctive moral characteristics of Chinese society. In the PRC, virtue and correct behavior have not been defined in Confucian terms, but in terms of Marxism-Leninism–Mao Zedong Thought. Yet in one regard the underlying notion remains very much the same: Social unity, order, and prosperity depend on protecting the moral basis of society from foreign contamination. Any society must to some degree encourage morality among its members, but the Chinese tradition has placed a special stress on morality as the very basis of social order, and more important for us, has seen foreign influence as a basic source of corruption. China's post-1949 rulers have perennially been concerned that foreign values and ideas might corrode or subvert the essential moral characteristics of Chinese socialism.

During the forty-year history of the PRC, the political pendulum has swung from all-out Westernization in the 1950s, to nativist isolationism in the 1960s, and back to the center of selective assimilation in the 1980s. During the period of close Sino-Soviet cooperation in the 1950s, policies of all-out Westernization were implemented. (Americans should keep in mind that the Soviet Union was, after all, a Western country.) In the 1950s Beijing pushed through a breathtakingly comprehensive effort to remake Chinese society along the lines of the Soviet model. The economy was reorganized according to the Soviet system of centralized, comprehensive planning, complete with material quotas and one-man management of enterprises. Educational institutions were remodeled along Soviet-style lines. Soviet books in virtually all fields of knowledge were translated into Chinese and used as textbooks. The political institutions of the new PRC—from the constitution of 1954, to the system of elections and popular representative institutions, to trade union organization—were modeled after those of the Soviet Union. In virtually all areas, the Soviet Union was held up as China's "big brother," the one China should emulate. The 1950s was perhaps the only period of genuine "all-out Westernization" in the PRC's history.

This period did not last long. By 1957 and 1958 many Chinese chafed at the mimicking of the Soviet Union, and Mao Zedong began searching for a distinctive, Chinese road to socialism. The Great Leap Forward was a bold experiment in this direction, with Soviet-style institutions and policies being replaced by others inspired by an egalitarian and collectivist ethos. The political pendulum moved further toward the nativist isolationist extreme of the political spectrum with the Cultural Revolution decade of 1966 to 1976. Foreign trade stagnated as policies of economic autarky were adopted. Even after the import of advanced foreign technology was resumed in 1971 and 1972, contacts between Chinese people and the outside world remained minimal in order to decrease dangers of ideological-moral contamination.

With the consolidation of Deng Xiaoping's regime in 1978, politics moved back toward the center of the spectrum. Deng's regime opened wide the doors of China to foreign technology, scientific knowledge, and even organizational techniques, but simultaneously waged repeated campaigns to ensure that Western values and ideas did not gain hold in China. Deng explained this orientation to Zimbabwean Prime Minister Robert Mugabe in August 1985:

> By setting things to rights, we mean developing the productive forces while upholding the Four Cardinal Principles. To develop the productive forces, we have to reform the economic structure and open to the outside world. It is in order to assist the growth of the socialist productive forces that we absorb capital from capitalist countries and introduce their technology....In the course of reform it is very important for us to maintain our socialist orientation....The policies of invigorating our domestic economy and opening to the outside world are being carried out in accordance with the principles of socialism.[23]

In other words, while Western science, technology, and organizational methods are welcome, these imports are not to be allowed to erode China's distinctive, superior socialist morality. In line with this, in 1980 Deng authorized suppression of the movement of dissident young intellectuals advocating Western-style liberty. In 1983 there was another campaign against Western-derived "spiritual pollution." Again in 1987 another campaign was launched against "bourgeois liberalism." Finally, in 1989 there was a massive clampdown on all forms of heterodox thinking and activity. These repressive campaigns had complex origins. One of their objectives was to prevent the spread of Western individualistic and liberal values among the Chinese populace.

CHINESE NATIONALISM

Recollections of ancient grandeur combined with outrage at China's century of National Humiliation provides the starting point for modern Chinese nationalism. The common denominator of the leaders of modern China—from Sun Yat-sen, to Chiang Kai-shek, to Mao Zedong and Deng Xiaoping—has been a deep bitterness at China's "humiliation," and a determination to blot out that humiliation and restore China to its rightful place as a great and respected power. Those men no longer thought of China as the Middle Kingdom, but they did harbor a deep conviction that China ought to stand among the front ranks of the nations of the world and that there was something profoundly wrong with a world that denied it this status. This determination to restore China's national grandeur is the crux of Chinese nationalism.

Sun Yat-sen is generally regarded as the father of Chinese nationalism. When systematizing his thoughts on China's struggle into the Three Principles of the People in 1924, Sun stated clearly that the purpose of those Principles was to secure China's National Salvation, or *jiu guo*: "They [the Three Principles] will elevate China to an equal position among the nations...so that she can permanently exist in the world."[24]

The first of the Three Principles was nationalism, which Sun defined as the loyalty of the Chinese race or nation—and to Sun race and nation were virtually synonymous—to the Chinese state. China's history had been unique, Sun felt, in that all people of a particular race had been ruled by a single state. Throughout most of history the Chinese nation/race was far superior to all others. Indeed, in the 1920s it was still superior, Sun said, in terms of cultural level. Over the past few hundred years, however, the European nations had excelled in science and technology while China had gradually lost its sense of nationalism. Thus, while China ought to be advancing in line with the nations of Europe and America, Sun wrote, it faced instead the possibility of loss of its state and the eventual destruction of the Chinese race. Sun laid out a number of prerequisites for achieving national salvation, including popular solidarity with the state and the cultivation of virtue. "Coming to the crux of the matter," Sun wrote, "If we want to restore our race's standing, besides uniting all into a great national body, we must first recover our ancient morality—then and only then can we plan how to attain again the national position we once held."[25]

Mao Zedong was brought to political activity as a youth by an overriding concern with the possibility that the Chinese people might lose their state and become slaves without a country. Throughout his life, nationalism remained a key theme of his thought. But Mao was a revolutionary as well as a nationalist. This meant that he went much further than Sun Yat-sen in terms of the scope of social change necessary to accomplish China's national restoration. According to Mao, to emancipate itself from imperialist domination China had to destroy the social and political power of the classes and groups in Chinese society that were linked to and served the interests of foreign imperialism. Foremost among these were the landowners and the capitalists who cooperated with foreign interests. After the foreign and domestic exploiters of the Chinese people were swept away by revolution, the Chinese people, and especially the Han people, would once again manifest their genius to the world.[26]

Nationalism has been the lingua franca of successful politics in twentieth-century China. Those who would rule had to propound, and successfully implement, a program of national salvation that would save China from national extinction and then restore its lost national grandeur. A central aspect of the long contest between the Nationalists and the Communists from 1921 to 1949 was a struggle to win nationalist legitimacy. Both Chiang Kai-shek and Mao Zedong propounded nationalist programs to win popular support.

Chiang Kai-shek's program centered on national unification, moral rejuvenation, and the abolition of unequal treaties imposed on China in the nineteenth century. The practice of extraterritoriality was especially pernicious, in Chiang's view, and Chiang's government devoted a considerable amount of energy to renegotiating those treaties. Extraterritoriality was finally ended during World War II.[27] Chiang's nationalist program also included the recovery of China's "lost territories." At a minimum these included Hong Kong and Macao, Outer Mongolia, Xinjiang, Manchuria, and Taiwan. Maximally, they included the Ryukyu Islands, parts of Soviet Siberia, the Pamir Mountains region of Soviet Central Asia, and northern Myanmar.

Chiang's nationalist program seemed adequate and persuasive to most Chinese in the 1920s, and Chiang's Nationalist Party (the Kuomintang, or KMT) rode to national power on a wave of patriotism that swept across south and central China in the middle of that decade.

Once ensconced in Nanjing, the Nationalist government set out to unite China by subordinating various regional warlords and crushing the Communist insurgency; oust the Russians from Manchuria; negotiate an end to the special treaty privileges of the European powers; and develop a modern army and munitions industry, with German help. (Germany was the only major power then having no special rights in China, having lost them during World War I.) Nationalist implementation of this program was disrupted first by mounting Japanese pressure in the early 1930s and then by all-out Sino-Japanese war after 1937.

The Japanese invasion of China during the 1930s was, from the Chinese perspective, the bitter culmination of the century of National Humiliation. It began with the seizure of Manchuria by the Japanese army in September 1931. Early the next year, the Japanese set up a puppet government in Manchuria that declared Manchuria an independent nation, named Manchukuo and allied with Japan. Manchukuo was ostensibly the homeland of the Manchu people. (The Manchu were once a distinct people whose homeland was in fact in Manchuria. Massive migration of Han from north China into Manchuria during the early twentieth century had, however, rendered the Manchu a small minority of that region's population by the 1930s. Moreover, most of the Manchu were highly sinicized.)

After seizing Manchuria, Japan began expanding step by step into north China. Chiang Kai-shek's government, convinced that China was too weak to win a war against Japan and that defeat by Japan would only further embolden Japanese aggression and create opportunities for the Chinese Communist Party, initially retreated before the Japanese advance. By 1937, however, mounting nationalist sentiment within China, together with the success of the German-assisted military and industrial development program—and deepening Soviet, British, and American concern about Japan's advance in Asia—persuaded Chiang that China had to risk a war with Japan. The result was a Chinese refusal to back down after a clash between Chinese and Japanese patrols at the Marco Polo Bridge outside Beijing. The Sino-Japanese conflict rapidly turned into a large and open-ended conflict, with Japan steadily escalating the war in a quest for victory.

For the next eight years Japan expanded the war in an effort to force China into submission. Japanese armies advanced southward from Beijing into the Yangtze River valley and westward up that valley. Shanghai fell in November 1937, and Nanjing, then China's capital, in December. Wuhan in central China fell in October 1938, as did Canton. Japanese forces seized one coastal city after another in an attempt to stanch the flow of foreign war materials into China. But while Japan could defeat China's armies, it could not destroy Chinese resistance. China was simply too vast and Japan's military forces simply too limited. By 1940 Japan controlled the main cities and transportation lines of northern, eastern, and southeastern China, but the northwest and southwest still provided a base for continued powerful Chinese Nationalist resistance. In the huge rural areas behind Japanese lines, extensive guerrilla war developed against the occupying forces. Japan's forces were stretched so thin that they were always vulnerable at some places to resistance forces who could concentrate and disperse rapidly. Very often these guerrilla forces were organized and led by the Chinese Communist Party.[28]

Ultimately Japan's attack on the United States at Pearl Harbor precipitated the Sino-American alliance and laid the conditions for Japan's ultimate defeat and dislocation from the Asian continent. Had Tokyo and Washington been able to avert war, China's situation would have been desperate. At a minimum, its recovery of Manchuria and Xinjiang would have been extremely problematic. In the worst case, a partition of China between Russia and Japan could not be ruled out. Figure 1–3 depicts China's situation in 1941.

The Sino-Japanese war of 1937–1945 was a brutal, searing experience for China. Japanese occupation forces were imbued with a spirit of contempt for China and the Chinese, and they often acted barbarically. Calculated brutality was also sometimes a deliberate part of Japanese policy, used in an attempt to break the spirit of Chinese resistance. The murder of perhaps 200,000 civilians in Nanjing after the fall of that city in December 1937 was the most infamous instance of such barbarity, but many other smaller incidents occurred. In 1940 Japanese forces began trying systematically to depopulate areas affected by guerrilla activity. Chinese civilian and military casualties were heavy.[29]

The Japanese aggression from 1931 to 1945 had a deep impact on PRC foreign relations. Fears of Japan rooted in that experience contributed, for example, to China's 1949 decision to ally with the USSR and, again in the 1980s, to the decision to normalize relations with Moscow as Japan reemerged as a major military power. Memories of the period from 1937 to 1945 also colored China's reaction to the extensive Japanese economic relations with China that developed after 1978. Student demonstrators in 1985 and 1986, for example, condemned the flood of Japanese goods into China as a "second Japanese invasion." (The first invasion, of course, began in 1937.) China's experience of Japanese aggression also influenced Chinese perceptions of the United States, which was closely associated with Japan after 1945. For several decades Chinese propaganda proclaimed that Washington was trying to revive Japanese militarism to serve as an instrument of aggression against China. As we shall see in our subsequent discussion of China's national security, for many years China's security policy was oriented toward defeating a large-scale U.S. invasion of China. To some degree, this was a manifestation of the lesson learned during the period from

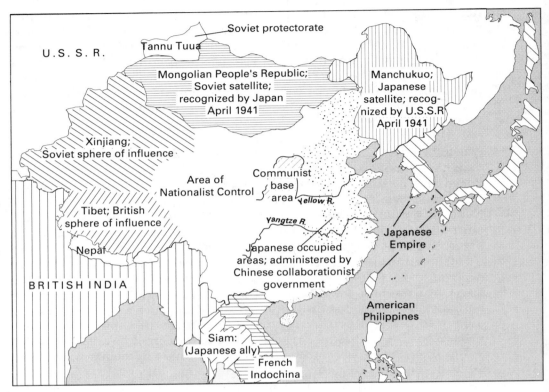

Figure 1–3   China in 1941

1931 to 1945. And in 1950, when U.S. forces approached China's borders with Korea, memories of the earlier Japanese invasion of China over this route contributed to China's decision to go to war to push back the United States.

The prominent international standing of the PRC is also rooted in China's contribution to the defeat of Japan during World War II. During that war Chiang Kai-shek was able to use China's role in tying down a million or so Japanese troops to win American, Soviet, and British support for his nationalist program. Manchuria and Taiwan were returned to China. China became one of the Allied Big Four and won a permanent seat on the Security Council of the newly created United Nations. Chiang secured (half-hearted) American support and Soviet acquiescence for his efforts to crush the CCP, thereby restoring—so Chiang hoped—national unity. Chiang also seized the opportunity presented by the Soviet-German war to oust the Soviets from Xinjiang and reintegrate that vast mineral-rich region into China. These were impressive achievements and Chiang hoped that they would win popular acclaim, if not active popular support, for his post-war regime.

One important factor that led to the failure of Chiang's expectations was the strongly negative, patriotic reaction to his acceptance of the

Soviet demands on China that flowed from the American-Soviet-British agreement at Yalta in February 1945. On the basis of the Yalta agreement, Moscow demanded that China formally recognize Outer Mongolian independence and grant the USSR extensive special rights in Manchuria. (This is discussed in greater detail in the next chapter.) In practical terms it is difficult to see how Chiang could have rejected joint U.S., Soviet, and British demands; the realities of international politics in 1945 left Chiang very little room to maneuver. But to Chinese nationalist sentiment, the agreements imposed on China in 1945 were akin to the "humiliating" unequal treaties of the last century. Nationalist passions had been fanned to a white heat by the searing experiences and sacrifices of China's eight-year war against Japan. Those absolutist passions found no room for compromise, and Chiang's pragmatism was condemned.[30] Chiang Kai-shek's experience stands as a warning to Chinese leaders who are tempted to compromise Chinese nationalism.

The Nationalists and the Communists tried to undermine each other's nationalist credentials. The Communists charged that the KMT was subservient to the interests of one or another imperialist power. The proof of this, they said, lay first in the Nationalist refusal to resist Japanese aggression prior to 1937 and then, once the Sino-Japanese war began, in the KMT's efforts to limit the CCP's expansion of its anti-Japanese guerrilla forces in the hinterlands of north and central China. This was a strategy admirably designed to combine the expansion of Communist-led revolutionary power with nationalist appeal. It worked marvelously. The KMT's efforts to curb the growth of Communist power were hamstrung by popular nationalist sentiment. To the extent that the KMT ignored this sentiment and tried to check the Communists, it undermined its own nationalist credentials. The Communists were effectively able to depict KMT moves against the CCP as traitorous attempts to weaken national resistance to Japan.

For their part, the Nationalists condemned the CCP as a Soviet puppet, a mechanism of Soviet aggression against China. The CCP's base area in China's northwest was, the KMT charged, the Soviet Union's equivalent of Japan's Manchukuo. To substantiate these charges, the Nationalists pointed to the CCP's long and apparently loyal obedience to the Communist International (the Comintern). They also pointed to the Comintern documents seized during a raid on the Soviet embassy in Beijing in 1927, which made clear the extent to which Moscow directed CCP policy in the mid-1920s. At that time there was little evidence suggesting that the CCP was other than what the KMT said it was—a loyal and pliant component of Moscow's Third International. Moreover, in retrospect, it seems clear that from the founding of the CCP in 1921 through 1935, Moscow did effectively dominate that party.[31]

It is also apparent that Mao Zedong's rise to power within the CCP was closely tied to a nationalist rebellion against Comintern control.

After pushing aside the Comintern's loyalists and seizing paramount power within the Party at the Zunyi Conference in January 1935, Mao reduced Soviet influence on the CCP. Then after the Nazi attack on the Soviet Union in June 1941, he eliminated that influence entirely. To emancipate the CCP from Moscow, Mao had to defeat the Soviet-dominated Internationalists within the CCP, a group led by Wang Ming. For a number of very practical reasons, Mao could not afford to break with the Soviet Union. He was convinced, however, that if the policies of the CCP were based on Soviet national interests rather than on the expansion of revolutionary power within China, the CCP would fail in its historic mission of "saving China." This was unacceptable to Mao, and he outmaneuvered both Stalin and Wang Ming to persist in the implementation of his independent, revolutionary line.

Mao's emancipation of the CCP and the Chinese revolution from Comintern domination was a major victory for Chinese nationalism. It helped in two ways to win power for Mao. First, Mao's independent, nationalist line increasingly made sense to the other leaders of the CCP. During the war against Japan they came to realize that Mao's combination of patriotic resistance to Japan and determined expansion of Communist power was the key to the eventual conquest of full state power in China. Conversely, they realized that adopting the policies urged by Wang Ming and Moscow would sacrifice the expansion of revolutionary power for the sake of enhancing Soviet national security as defined by Soviet diplomacy. Further, the sinicization of Marxist-Leninist doctrine, which was the theoretical underpinning of Mao's independence from Moscow, greatly enhanced the appeal of that doctrine to Chinese intellectuals. Marxism-Leninism appeared to educated and patriotic Chinese no longer as an alien, European doctrine, but as a Chinese philosophy based on Chinese history and incorporating a large part of Chinese culture. This made it much easier for them to accept. Thus, in several ways Mao's successful amalgamation of Communism and nationalism played a crucial role in his and the CCP's rise to power.[32]

Just as the KMT and the CCP represented different brands of Chinese nationalism before 1949, so too there have been different variants of Chinese nationalism within the PRC. Michel Oksenberg has built on his earlier concept of the Chinese political spectrum to develop a four-category topology of Chinese nationalism. Each variant posits different explanations of China's weakness, as well as solutions for overcoming those weaknesses. "Xenophobic nationalists" have believed that the subversion of indigenous Chinese virtues and strength was the root of China's weakness, and argued that the eradication of foreign influences was the route to revived national strength. "Emotional nationalists" have been deeply ambivalent about foreign contacts, feeling that China's ills are primarily due to foreign transgressions and that the sine qua non of national recovery is vigilance against foreign insults and pressure. "Assertive nationalists" also see foreign economic exploitation and cultural infiltration as a key reason for China's weakness, but recognize that interaction with the outside world, and especially the acquisition of advanced technology, is essential for China's advance. The favored solution of "assertive nationalists" is to limit interactions with the outside world to transactions clearly beneficial to China's economic development, while watching carefully for unwanted consequences. Finally, there are what Oksenberg calls "confident nationalists." Leaders of this type attribute China's weakness primarily to its low level of economic development, and prescribe extensive interactions with foreign countries to secure a wide range of inputs essential to the development process. "Confident nationalists" are no less determined than the others to establish China as a leading nation, but they are more confident than the others that China's distinctive culture is sufficiently resilient to survive extensive contact with the outside world.[33]

The four different nationalist perspectives have addressed essentially the same agenda. One item on that agenda is to maintain China's distinctive character while developing the economy so as to provide the basis for national wealth and power. This issue was addressed earlier in our discussion of the Chinese political spectrum. A second item on China's nationalist agenda has been the defense of current national boundaries and the recovery of lost territories. This too was discussed above and will be discussed further in the subsequent chapter on China's national security.

A third agenda item is securing international recognition as a great power. As with all other items on the nationalist agenda, the way in which that is to be done has been a subject of considerable experimentation and debate. China has used various forums to establish itself as a major international actor. At times it has claimed leadership of the Third World, of the Socialist Camp, or of the World Revolutionary Movement. China's decision to acquire nuclear weapons, its very expensive space program, and its vigorous participation in international athletic competitions all have national prestige as one objective. A desire for international status has also influenced the PRC's international alignments vis-à-vis the great powers. During the late 1950s, the desire for recognition as an independent great power, and, conversely, a sense of humiliation because China was regarded as Moscow's "little brother," probably contributed to Mao's decision to challenge Moscow's leadership of the socialist camp, even though that challenge was extremely costly in terms of China's economic development. In the early 1980s, China rejected close alignment with the United States, partly out of a fear that it was becoming a junior partner of the American superpower.

Concerns with security, development, and status are not unique to China. All nations seek security. Many poor nations are concerned with development. And many Third World nations that experienced European domination in the pasts are highly sensitive to perceived slights and infringements on sovereignty. But in China's case there is something more: a deep and abiding conviction that China ought, by historical right, to be one of the great powers of the world. Only a very few contemporary countries have developed and still widely believe in such a myth justifying their putative world role. China's aspiration to a global role and recognition places it among a very small set of contemporary nations.

The importance of nationalism in Chinese politics increased in the 1970s and 1980s as revolutionary fervor ebbed. The reasons for what the Chinese media dubbed a "crisis of faith" are extremely complex and need not concern us here. It will suffice to note that by the 1980s, more and more Chinese doubted the attainability of the utopian goals extolled by the CCP and used to justify the heavy demands placed on the people. As noted earlier, Mao had welded together Chinese Communism and nationalism during the 1930s. But the Communist component of that amalgam became less and less appealing during the 1980s, and the CCP turned to nationalism to fill the ideological void. Nationalist themes were increasingly used in lieu of Marxist-Leninist-Maoist appeals to rally popular support. Allen Whiting points to the use of confrontations with foreign governments to rouse emotional, nationalist reactions among Chinese; e.g., Beijing's bitter condemnation of the 1982 move by Japan's Ministry of Education to revise the school textbook interpretation of Japan's aggression in China in the 1930s. By tapping deep-rooted feelings of resentment at foreign efforts to belittle or humiliate China, Beijing hoped to rally the Chinese people around the government.[34]

Lucian Pye has also suggested that as ideological values recede, nationalist objectives, such as overtaking the most advanced countries, will become more salient—even though the policies extrapolated from those values might not make the most sense in terms of a narrower economic rationality. China may insist on acquiring the most sophisticated technology, for example, not because of a hard analysis of the economic costs and benefits of that technology, but because of a desire to catch up with more technologically advanced nations.[35]

NOTES

1. Regarding the events constituting the century of National Humiliation, see John K. Fairbank, Edwin O. Reishauer, and Albert M. Craig, *East Asia, the Modern Transformation,* Boston: Houghton Mifflin, 1965; Paul H. Clyde and Burton F. Beers, *The Far East: A History of Western Impacts and Eastern Responses, 1830–1975,* Englewood Cliffs, N.J.: Prentice Hall, 1975; *The Cambridge History of China,* John K. Fairbank and Kwang-ching Liu, eds., vol. 11 (1800–1911), New York: Cambridge University Press, 1988. An older but still extremely valuable work is Hosea B. Morse, *The International Relations of the Chinese Empire,* three volumes, London: Longmans, Green, and Co., 1910–1918. Regarding the Opium War, see Hsin-pao Chang, *Commissioner Lin and the Opium War,* Cambridge: Harvard University Press, 1964; Jack Beeching, *The Chinese Opium Wars,* New York: Harcourt Brace, 1975; Maurice Collis, *Foreign Mud: The Opium Imbroglio at Canton in the 1830s and the Anglo-Chinese War,* New York: W.W. Norton, 1946. Regarding the "carving of the melon" in the 1890s, see Philip Joseph, *Foreign Diplomacy in China, 1894–1900*, London: Allen and Unwin, 1928. An authoritative Chinese interpretation of events is Hu Sheng, *Imperialism and Chinese Politics*, Beijing: Foreign Languages Press, 1981.

2. Regarding the destruction of China's tributary relationship with Korea, see Key-Hiuk Kim, *The Last Phase of the East Asian World Order*, Berkeley: University of California Press, 1980; Hilary Conroy, *The Japanese Seizure of Korea, 1868–1910*, Philadelphia: University of Pennsylvania Press, 1960. Regarding the end of the Sino-Vietnam tributary relationship, see Lloyd E. Eastman, *Throne and Mandarins: China's Search for a Policy During the Sino-French Controversy, 1880–1885*, Cambridge: Harvard University Press, 1967. Regarding China's frontiers with Burma and India, see Dorothy Woodman, *Himalayan Frontiers: A Political Review of British, Chinese, Indian, and Russian Rivalries*, New York: Praeger, 1970.

3. "The Chinese People Have Stood Up," *Selected Works of Mao Tse-tung*, vol. 5, Beijing: Foreign Languages Press, 1977, 16–17.

4. Lucian W. Pye, *The Spirit of Chinese Politics: A Psychocultural Study of the Authority Crisis in Chinese Development*, Cambridge: MIT Press, 1968, 50–61.

5. C.P. Fitzgerald, *The Chinese View of Their Place in the World*, Cambridge: Harvard University Press, 1964, 1–26.

6. Regarding China's impact on Enlightenment Europe, see G.F. Hudson, *Europe and China: A Survey of Relations from the Earliest Times to 1800*, Boston: Beacon Press, 1931.

7. Pye, *Spirit of Chinese Politics*, 50.

8. Regarding the origin of distinction between Chinese "civilization" and non-Chinese "barbarism," see Benjamin J. Schwartz, *The World of Thought in Ancient China*, Cambridge: Harvard University Press, 1985, 16–55. Regarding the institutionalization of that concept in the area of foreign relations, see Wang Gungwu, "Early Ming Relations with Southeast Asia: A Background Essay," in John King Fairbank, ed., *The Chinese World Order: Traditional China's Foreign Relations*, Cambridge: Harvard University Press, 1968, 34–62. Also, John Cranmer-Byng, "The Chinese View of Their Place in the World: An Historical Perspective," *China Quarterly*, no. 53 (January–March 1973), 67–79.

9. Regarding China's assimilation of Indian Buddhism, see Kenneth Kuan-sheng Ch'en, *The Chinese Transformation of Buddhism*, Princeton, N.J.: Princeton University Press, 1973.

10. Regarding the workings of the tribute system, see the essays in Fairbank, ed., *The Chinese World Order*; John King Fairbank and S.Y. Teng, "The Traditional Role of Tribute," in *The Foreign Policy of China*, King C. Chen, ed., Roseland, N.J.: East-West Who?, 1972, 13–24; Morris Rossabi, ed., *China Among Equals*, Berkeley: University of California Press, 1983.

11. Mark Mancall, *China at the Center: 300 Years of Foreign Policy*, New York: Free Press, 1984; Mark Mancall, "The Persistence of Tradition in Chinese Foreign Policy," in *The Foreign Policy of China*, King C. Chen, ed., 25–44; Fitzgerald, *The Chinese View*.

12. "For Peace in Asia, the Pacific Region, and the World." *People's China* (Beijing), September 17, 1952.

13. Fitzgerald, *The Chinese View*, 71.

14. Benjamin I. Schwartz, "The Maoist Image of World Order," *Journal of International Affairs*, vol. 21, no. 1 (1967), 92–102; John King Fairbank, "The People's Middle Kingdom," *Foreign Affairs*, vol. 44, no. 4 (July 1966), 574–86; Albert Feuerwerker, "Relating to the International Community," in *China's Development Experience*, Michel Oksenberg, ed., New York: Praeger, 1972, 42–54.

15. Fred W. Drake, *China Charts the World: Hsu Chi-yu and His Geography of 1848*, Cambridge: Harvard University Press, 1975. Wei Yuan was another Chinese official who wrote unorthodoxly and objectively about the outside world in the 1840s. See Jane Kate Leonard, *Wei Yuan: China's Rediscovery of the Maritime World*, Cambridge: Harvard University Press, 1984. For a selection of writings by Chinese leaders about how to respond to the West, see Ssu-yu Teng and John King Fairbank, *China's Response to the West: A Documentary Survey, 1839–1923*, New York: Atheneum, 1963.

16. Michael H. Hunt, "Chinese Foreign Relations in Historical Perspective," in *China's Foreign Relations in the 1980s*, Harry Harding, ed., New Haven, Conn.: Yale University Press, 1984, 1–42.

17. Regarding the Self-Strengthening movement, see Jerome Chen, *China and the West:*

Society and Culture, 1815–1937, London: Hutchinson, 1979, 265–75, 426–52; Mary C. Wright, *The Last Stand of Chinese Conservatism: The T'ung-Chih Restoration, 1862–1874*, Stanford, Calif.: Stanford University Press, 1957.

18. Kwang-Ching Liu, "The Confucian as Patriot and Pragmatist: Li Hung-chang's Formative Years, 1823–1866," *Harvard Journal of Asiatic Studies*, vol. 30 (1970), 5–45; Immanuel C.Y. Hsu, "The Great Policy Debate in China, 1874: Maritime Defense vs. Frontier Defense," *Harvard Journal of Asiatic Studies*, vol. 25 (1964–1965), 212–28.

19. Regarding Kang Youwei and Liang Qichao's philosophy, see Joseph R. Levinson, *Confucian China and Its Modern Fate: A Trilogy*, Berkeley: University of California Press, 1968; Philip C. Huang, *Liang Ch'i-ch'ao and Modern Chinese Liberalism*, Seattle: University of Washington Press, 1972; Chester C. Tan, *Chinese Political Thought in the Twentieth Century*, Garden City, N.Y.: Doubleday, 1971.

20. Benjamin Schwartz, *In Search of Wealth and Power: Yen Fu and the West*, New York: Harper, 1964, 15–19.

21. Michel Oksenberg and Steven Goldstein, "The Chinese Political Spectrum," *Problems of Communism*, vol. 21, no. 2, (March–April 1972), 1–13.

22. See Deng Xiaoping, *Build Socialism with Chinese Characteristics*, Beijing: Foreign Languages Press, 1985. The Four Cardinal Principles are the leadership of the Communist Party, adherence to the socialist road, the dictatorship of the proletariat, and belief in Marxism-Leninism–Mao Zedong Thought.

23. Deng Xiaoping, *Fundamental Issues in Present-Day China*, Beijing: Foreign Languages Press, 1987, 122–23.

24. Sun Yat-sen, *San Min Chu I: The Three Principles of the People*, Taipei: China Publishing Co., n.d., 1, 5, 7, 37.

25. Ibid.

26. Stuart R. Schram, *Mao Zedong: A Preliminary Reassessment*, New York: St. Martin's Press, 1983, 3–7, 24–25.

27. See Wesley R. Fishel, *The End of Extraterritoriality in China*, Berkeley: University of California Press, 1974.

28. Regarding the Japanese invasion and the CCP's rise to power, see Chalmers A. Johnson, *Peasant Nationalism and Communist Power: The Emergence of Revolutionary China, 1937–1945*, Stanford, Calif.: Stanford University Press, 1962; Tetsuya Kataoka, *Resistance and Revolution in China: The Communists and the Second United Front*, Berkeley: University of California Press, 1974.

29. Regarding the 1937–1945 war, see Dick Wilson, *When Tigers Fight*, New York: Viking Press, 1982; Arthur N. Young, *China and the Helping Hand, 1937–1945*, Cambridge: Harvard University Press, 1963; F.F. Liu, *A Military History of Modern China, 1924–1949*, Princeton, N.J.: Princeton University Press, 1956, 103–242. Regarding the nature of the Japanese occupation of China, see Saburo Ienaga, *The Pacific War, 1931–1945: A Critical Perspective on Japan's Role in World War II*, New York: Pantheon Books, 1978.

30. See John W. Garver, *Chinese-Soviet Relations, 1937–1945: The Diplomacy of Chinese Nationalism*, New York: Oxford University Press, 1988.

31. Regarding Comintern-CCP relations, see Conrad Brandt, *Stalin's Failure in China, 1924–1927*, New York: Norton, 1966; Harold R. Isaacs, *The Tragedy of the Chinese Revolution*, Stanford, Calif.: Stanford University Press, 1978; Richard C. Thornton, *The Comintern and the Chinese Communists, 1928–1931*, Seattle: University of Washington Press, 1969; John E. Rue, *Mao Tse-tung in Opposition, 1927–1935*, Hoover Institution Press, 1966; Robert C. North, *Moscow and Chinese Communists*, Stanford, Calif.: Stanford University Press, 1965; Garver, *Chinese-Soviet Relations, 1937–1945*.

32. Raymond F. Wylie, *The Emergency of Maoism. Mao Tse-tung, Ch'en Po-ta and the Search for Chinese Theory*, Stanford, Calif.: Stanford University Press, 1980.

33. Michel Oksenberg, "China's Confident Nationalism," *Foreign Affairs*, vol. 65, no. 3 (1987), 501–23.

34. Allen S. Whiting, "Assertive Nationalism in Chinese Foreign Policy," *Asian Survey*, vol. 23, no. 8 (August 1983), 913–31.

35. Lucian W. Pye, "On Chinese Pragmatism in the 1980s," *China Quarterly* (June 1986), 207–234.

Part Two

China and the Superpowers

Chapter Two

Formation and Collapse of the Sino-Soviet Alliance

THE CONCEPT OF A STRATEGIC TRIANGLE

A central characteristic of the post–World War II international system with which China has had to deal has been the overwhelming preeminence of the United States and the USSR. The fact that the power of either of those two nations far exceeded that of any other nation, that each of those superpowers stood at the center of a broad alliance system, and the fact that those alliance systems were engaged in an intense and protracted global conflict created a bipolar international system with which China had to come to terms. Given this essential bipolarity, the CCP has had four options. At one time or another, it has tried each of the following approaches:

1. alliance with the USSR against the U.S.(1949–1963)
2. alignment with the U.S. against the USSR (1972–1982)
3. opposition to both the U.S. and the USSR (1945–1949 and 1963–1970)
4. cordial relations with both superpowers (1986–1992)

China has demonstrated remarkable agility in its alignments vis-à-vis the superpowers. Unless one counts Egypt's 1972 break with the Soviet Union, China is the only major power to have actually switched sides in the post-1945 East-West confrontation. Moreover, if one counts the regime change of 1949 and the shift in alignment that that change entailed, then China has changed sides not once, but *twice*. China is also the only major country to have engaged, in seriatim, in military conflict with both superpowers, and the only major country, again excluding Egypt, to have been militarily allied with both. Finally, China is the only major country to have simultaneously opposed both superpowers. Again, if one counts the period from 1945 to 1949 as well as the 1960s, China's Communist rulers have *twice* found themselves confronting both superpowers. This striking fluidity has made Moscow and Washington apprehensive about China's future alignments. This, in turn, has enhanced Beijing's diplomatic leverage with the superpowers.

Several basic factors have influenced Beijing's decisions regarding its triangular alignments. One has been perceptions of threat posed by each superpower and the level of hostility of each superpower to China's essential national goals. To a considerable degree, Beijing has responded to the perceived policies of the superpowers. These perceptions and responses are discussed in this chapter.

A second major influence has been Mao Zedong's *theory of contradiction*. According to this theory, while history is moving toward the final objective of communism, it advances by stages. Each stage has its own distinctive tasks, the completion of which will create the conditions for advance to the next stage. In each stage there is a primary contradiction embodying the struggle to accomplish the essential tasks of that particular stage. In political terms, this means that at each stage of history, there is a primary enemy blocking the progressive advance of history: the Japanese occupiers in the 1930s and 1940s, the Chinese Nationalists in the 1940s, the U.S. imperialists in the 1960s, the Soviet social imperialists in the 1970s. A correct revolutionary strategy requires the identification of the primary enemy at a particular stage, and the mobilization of all possible forces to defeat that primary enemy. The broadest possible united front should be engineered to confront the primary enemy. Less threatening secondary enemies—forces that are fundamentally reactionary but that nonetheless have some conflict with the primary enemy—should be drawn into the united front. All possible contradictions in the enemy camp should be exploited. All middle and even anti-revolutionary forces should be won over or neutralized, so that the most reactionary, primary enemy finally stands alone, confronted by the broadest possible coalition.[1] This dialectical framework leads to the possibility that the less threatening superpower be included in the united front against the other one.

A third fundamental factor influencing China's alignments vis-à-vis the superpowers has been its leaders' dissatisfaction with the international status quo on the one hand, and the great disparity between China's power and that of the superpowers on the other hand. China has persistently felt aggrieved by the international status quo and has sought to alter it. Beijing's desire to liberate Taiwan, to achieve international respect, or to foil American or Soviet efforts at encirclement have led it to challenge one or the other superpower. But because

China's power paled in comparison with that of the superpower that supported the status quo, the simple realities of power inclined Beijing to look toward the other superpower for help.

A fourth factor arose from the fact that if China aligned with one superpower it could expect that nation to be more supportive, while the other superpower would become more hostile. For Beijing, alignment with one superpower was a high-payoff, high-risk game. Alignment would secure generous support for China's economic and military development efforts, but at the cost of antagonizing the other superpower. Throughout the post-1945 period, both Moscow and Washington valued China as a major asset in their bipolar rivalry. Each superpower was extremely apprehensive about China's alignment with its rival. China's large population and aggregate economic resources, its central geographic location, and its military prowess (demonstrated during the war against Japan from 1937 to 1945 and again in Korea in 1950) meant that it could make a substantial contribution to a superpower's camp. Preventing, limiting, or undoing a hostile China-superpower alignment has, therefore, been one of the prime objectives of both superpowers.

A final factor influencing China's triangular diplomacy has been the possibility of joint Soviet-American combination against China. This is China's strategic worst case. China's ability to achieve its international objectives, its room for diplomatic maneuver, is at a minimum when it is confronted by coordinated opposition from the two superpowers. It is often difficult for Americans to understand, but such a superpower condominium is a situation that China's leaders have taken quite seriously; and as noted earlier, they believe they have already confronted it twice. The fear of a superpower combination against China runs like a red thread throughout the CCP's post-1945 diplomacy. Avoiding such a combination has been a prime objective.

YALTA AND THE ORIGIN OF THE SINO-SOVIET-AMERICAN TRIANGLE

Some analysts have maintained that the strategic triangle originated with the escalation of Sino-Soviet tension in the late 1960s.[2] Other analysts, including this author, have argued that the origins of the triangle must be traced back to the end of World War II. According to the latter view, the CCP's entry onto the stage of international high diplomacy coincided with the rise of the United States and the Soviet Union to superpower status in the period from 1944 to 1945. Moreover, the CCP's relations with the Soviet Union and the United States during this period created perceptions that had an important influence on post-1949 policy.[3]

By late 1944, events within China were increasingly favorable to the

CCP. Communist forces were expanding rapidly. The Communist movement was dynamic and increasingly seemed to represent the hope of the nation. The Nationalist Chinese regime, on the other hand, was confronted with mounting corruption, demoralization, inflation, and catastrophic military defeat before renewed Japanese offensives. So severe was the crisis of the Nationalist regime that the U.S. government feared that it might collapse before Japan's surrender. The anticipated surrender of Japan would bring additional benefits to the CCP. Communist forces were positioned to disarm many Japanese units, thereby substantially augmenting their own arsenals, and to seize cities and regions evacuated by Japanese forces. This situation presented great opportunities for the CCP.[4]

Over all, however, loomed the danger of U.S. intervention. American political and military power in Nationalist China was already great by 1944 and was certain to become even greater once Japan surrendered. There seemed to be good reason for CCP apprehension of U.S. intervention. The Nationalist regime was a close and valued ally of the United States. It had played an important role in World War II, for example, by making feasible the Europe First strategy by tying down large Japanese forces. Washington also viewed Nationalist China as a pillar of the post-war world order. According to Roosevelt's grand concept, China was to replace Japan as the great-power "policeman" of East Asia. Moreover, anti-communist sentiments were also strong among U.S. leaders. Meanwhile in Greece, British forces were engaged in military operations against a Communist-led liberation movement that had attempted to seize power as German forces withdrew.

Confronted with the distinct possibility of U.S. intervention on behalf of the Nationalists, the CCP endeavored to persuade the United States to disengage from the KMT. The CCP began its diplomatic groundwork to achieve this objective in July 1944, when a mission of U.S. military and diplomatic officers arrived at the Communist capital at Yan'an, in Shaanxi, to assess prospects for U.S.-CCP cooperation in fighting Japan. When the U.S. mission arrived, Mao was aware that many American representatives in China were thoroughly disillusioned with Chiang Kai-shek and his regime. Moreover, Mao knew that some top-ranking U.S. military officers (including General Joseph Stilwell, the top-ranking American military officer in China and adviser to Chiang Kai-shek) were impressed by the military capabilities of the CCP's guerrilla armies in north China and wanted to provide them with U.S. arms and training to further enhance their effectiveness against Japanese forces. At best, Mao hoped to persuade the American mission of the wisdom of military cooperation between CCP and U.S. military forces when the U.S. military forces landed on the north China coast. If the CCP were a valued military ally of the United States, Mao probably calculated, Washington was less likely to want to support the KMT.

As part of their effort to woo the Americans, CCP leaders offered the U.S. mission military cooperation against Japan and markets for American goods and capital in a Communist ruled post-war China. They downplayed their Marxist-Leninist ideology, and stressed reformist and nationalist themes. Most important for our purposes, they stressed the CCP's independence of the Soviet Union. During discussions with the U.S. observers' mission, CCP leaders hinted at political differences between the CCP and Moscow. They intimated that a Communist China would not align with the USSR, but was quite willing to maintain friendly relations with the United States. When Mao concluded that obstruction from the U.S. ambassador in China was preventing these proposals from being communicated fully to Washington, he proposed that he and Zhou Enlai travel to Washington for talks with Roosevelt.

One of the unknowns of history is the extent to which these offers of neutrality between the Soviet Union and the United States were genuine. Some analysts have argued that the CCP was quite sincere and that Washington's failure to respond amounted to a lost chance for preventing Chinese Communist alignment with the USSR.[5] The CCP's revolutionary ideology remained a potent force, but perhaps if the United States had disengaged from the Nationalist regime, this, combined with past and present Soviet encroachments on China, would have led Mao to reevaluate his views of the United States and the Soviet Union twenty years earlier than he did. This will never be known, for Roosevelt rejected the idea of cutting support for the Nationalists and attempting to reach some sort of understanding with the Chinese Communists.

As the firmly pro-Nationalist orientation of U.S. policy that followed from Roosevelt's decision became clear in the spring of 1945, the CCP moved back toward Moscow in a quest for Soviet support. The CCP now attempted to persuade Moscow to support a CCP drive to seize power in China. In line with this, CCP propaganda again stressed its ideological kinship with the Soviets and began condemning "U.S. imperialists" for the first time since the German attack on the Soviet Union in June 1941. CCP hopes were buoyed in April 1945 when Moscow announced its intention to cancel its 1941 neutrality agreement with Japan. This meant that the Soviet Red Army would soon invade Japanese-held Manchuria and that it would welcome cooperation with the CCP's armies in that effort.

Mao was again disappointed. Stalin refused to support the CCP and instead struck a deal with the United States to support the Nationalist regime. At the Yalta conference in February 1945, American and Soviet leaders worked out arrangements to minimize inter-Allied tension in the Far East. This arrangement provided for full Soviet support for the establishment of Nationalist China as a major Asian power. The Soviet

Union pledged to give no support to the CCP while providing full political support for the Nationalist government. In exchange, the Soviet Union received this: co-ownership of the railways across northern Manchuria and southward from Haerbin to the Liaodong peninsula; military transit rights across these lines in wartime; a commercial port at Dairen from which third powers were excluded; a naval base and a large defense zone at Port Arthur (today's Lushun) on Manchuria's Liaodong peninsula; a role in the exploitation of Manchurian and Xinjiang's mineral resources; and Chinese recognition of Outer Mongolian independence. These terms were embodied in a USSR-ROC treaty and ancillary agreements concluded in August 1945.

Stalin's major gain from the Yalta arrangements had to do with Soviet-American relations. Yalta helped prevent a Soviet-American confrontation over China, and it helped perpetuate the Soviet-American alliance into the post-war era. At the same time, the 1945 Sino-Soviet treaty provided that Nationalist China would not join any anti-Soviet bloc. In other words, Nationalist China was to be allied with neither superpower against the other, but friendly toward both. The triangular system set up in 1945 envisioned a friendly triumvirate of the United States, Nationalist China, and the Soviet Union that would maintain peace and stability in post-war Asia.[6]

Yalta was a major setback for the CCP. Upon learning of the terms of the USSR-ROC treaty, the CCP scrapped well-advanced plans to seize major cities once Japan surrendered, reopened negotiations with the KMT, and toned down its anti-KMT and anti-U.S. propaganda. It then moved to accommodate the wishes of the United States as represented by former Chief of Staff General George C. Marshall, who came to China in December 1945 to mediate the CCP-KMT dispute.

In the months following Japan's surrender, the United States tried to prevent a civil war in China, largely because it shared Moscow's fears that such a conflict would undermine Soviet-American cordiality. Yet as China slid into civil war, the United States sided with the Nationalists. Technically, U.S. policy toward the CCP-KMT dispute was impartial, but since Washington had decided that suspending aid to the Nationalists would indicate partiality toward the Communists, the United States continued to furnish large-scale support to the Nationalists throughout the civil war, albeit with increasing misgivings and recriminations.[7]

In spite of Moscow's Yalta pledges, the CCP did receive covert Soviet assistance in the form of large stockpiles of captured Japanese weapons, which Soviet military commanders in Manchuria allowed to fall into CCP hands.[8] But Stalin remained apprehensive that an all-out CCP drive to seize power would precipitate a strong American counteraction. Such a move would, he feared, be interpreted by Washington as a Soviet-supported overturning of the Yalta arrangement. This might lead to

United States intervention in China, or might lead the United States to challenge Soviet control over Eastern Europe, a control also legitimized by Yalta. In extremis, Stalin feared, World War III might result.[9]

To avoid such an outcome, Stalin urged the CCP to abandon plans for a nationwide seizure of power and reach an accommodation with Chiang Kai-shek. In early 1948, once the Chinese civil war was well underway, the Soviet ambassador to China proposed Soviet mediation of the conflict to Nationalist officials. This offer and the fact that Moscow still maintained quite cordial relations with the Nationalists implied support for some sort of compromise settlement between the CCP and the KMT. Then in May 1948, just as CCP armies were moving out of Manchuria for north China and the Yangtze basin, Soviet Deputy Prime Minister Anastas Mikoyan traveled clandestinely to north China for discussions with CCP leaders. Mikoyan advised the CCP to halt their offensive and forgo the liberation of south China. Several years later (in 1954), while briefing a new Chinese ambassador about to depart for the Soviet Union, Premier Zhou Enlai said that Soviet actions in 1948 implied a Korea-like division of China between a Communist north and a non-Communist south. Stalin's starting point, Zhou said, was a desire for a stable relation with the United States. To achieve this, Stalin felt that the CCP should accept China's indefinite partition.[10] The CCP ignored Soviet advice, crossed the Yangtze, and conquered all of mainland China. In doing this, it ran the risk of provoking U.S. intervention with little hope of Soviet support. The gamble paid off, and the CCP thwarted both Soviet and American designs for China.

From the CCP's perspective, the period from 1945 to 1949 represented the first instance of Soviet-U.S. collaboration against the Chinese revolution. For the sake of facilitating cooperation between themselves and in order to secure their respective special positions in China, the two superpowers agreed to support China's counterrevolutionary forces. This attempted superpower diktat compelled the CCP to modify its strategy, but ultimately the CCP relied on the strength of the revolutionary forces and foiled the designs of Washington and Moscow.

It is important to note, however, that one reason why the CCP was able to succeed in the face of Soviet-American collusion was that the United States did not go along with the Soviet proposal for the partition of China. When Foreign Minister V.M. Molotov proposed to Secretary of State George Marshall during the Moscow foreign ministers conference in April 1947 that their two governments discuss the China question, Marshall agreed only to an informal discussion, with the Chinese Nationalist government being kept fully informed. The matter was dropped there. Marshall apparently believed that Molotov wanted to use the withdrawal of Soviet troops from Manchuria as a quid pro quo to demand the withdrawal of U.S. troops from China. Not until a year later, after Tito's break with Stalin in April 1948 had enlightened Washington about Stalin's fears of nationalist communism, did U.S. leaders (Marshall included) begin to understand that Moscow might be aiming for territorial division of China. By that time, however, U.S. leaders had decided in favor of a policy designed to draw a united Communist China away from the USSR.[11]

It is by no means certain that the CCP would have failed even if Washington had accepted the Soviet proposal for a partition of China. It seems unlikely that by 1948 the KMT could have rallied and held south China without a very large direct U.S. military intervention, and such intervention was politically infeasible in the United States. In other words, even had the superpower condominium begun at Yalta been consummated by agreement to partition China, it is likely that the CCP would still have prevailed. Nonetheless, the United States' rejection of Moscow's bid did facilitate the CCP's victory. The CCP prevailed in part because it was able to keep the two superpowers divided.

THE ESTABLISHMENT OF THE SINO-SOVIET BLOC

The establishment of the People's Republic of China on September 21, 1949, (October 1 was designated as the PRC's National Day), had a great impact on the global balance of power. For the first time since 1915, all of China (except for Taiwan and Hong Kong) was united under a single authority that was able to mobilize the resources of the entire country to achieve national objectives. China was now ruled by a tightly organized elite committed to development regardless of costs. China was also the first major country to come under Communist rule since Russia in 1917, and it represented an addition to the socialist camp as significant as the Soviet conquest of Eastern Europe in 1944 and 1945. This depended, of course, on whether New China aligned with the Soviet bloc.

In June 1949, Mao Zedong announced that New China would "lean to one side" in the struggle between imperialism and socialism. In December 1949, Mao left China for the first time in his life to travel to Moscow to negotiate a treaty of alliance with the USSR. Stalin was reluctant to enter into an alliance with Communist China. He had long been skeptical of Mao's nationalism and disregard for Soviet instructions. He also feared the American response to an overturn of the Yalta Far Eastern arrangements. Stalin also wanted to retain the special rights in China won by the USSR in 1945. On the other hand, he did not want to alienate Mao Zedong. The result was two months of tough negotiation.

Stalin eventually agreed to relinquish Soviet special rights in the Manchurian region, although only after a delay of several years. Mao was forced to agree, however, to a ruble-renminbi exchange rate that he felt was unfair and to the establishment of joint Sino-Soviet stock companies to develop the petroleum and non-ferrous metal resources of Xinjiang. These companies deeply rankled Chinese sensibilities. Regarding Outer Mongolia, Mao was forced to accept unequivocal PRC recognition of that country's independence. Mao probably agreed to these concessions because he wanted Soviet military and economic backing. In 1958 Mao described his 1950 talks with Stalin:

> In 1950, I argued with Stalin in Moscow for two months. On the question of the treaty of mutual assistance, the Chinese Eastern Changchun Railway, the joint-stock companies, and the border [this is probably a reference to Outer Mongolia], we adopted two attitudes. One was to argue when the other side made proposals we did not agree with. The other was to accept their proposal if they absolutely insisted. This was out of consideration for the interests of socialism.[12]

A thirty-year treaty of friendship and alliance between the PRC and the USSR was signed on February 14. It was directed against Japan or any state aligned with Japan, a euphemism for the United States.

Exactly why the PRC allied with Moscow in 1950 has been a subject of considerable debate among American scholars. After Sino-American rapprochement in 1971, some scholars concluded that the United States had *pushed* the PRC into alignment with Moscow in 1950. The advocates of this "second lost chance" theory maintain that in early 1949, Zhou Enlai signaled his hopes for cordial relations with the United States by inviting U.S. Ambassador John L. Stuart to visit Beijing for talks with CCP leaders. Zhou's policy of maintaining a balance in relations with the United States and the Soviet Union was strongly opposed by other top CCP leaders who favored outright alliance with Moscow against the United States. The intra-CCP factional balance was tipped in favor of the pro-Soviet faction when Washington scotched the proposed trip by Stuart. Shortly afterwards the CCP began moving toward alignment with Moscow. Had Washington responded positively, analysts of the "second lost chance" school maintained, the CCP might not have embraced Moscow so decisively.[13]

Other scholars have rejected the proposition that there was a chance for U.S.-CCP amity in 1949. The Marxist-Leninist ideology shared by Mao and his comrades, and previous U.S. support for the KMT, inclined the CCP toward the Soviet Union regardless of what the United States did in 1949. This did not rule out all contact with the United States, however, and it is wrong to interpret contacts such as a willingness to talk with Stuart as enthusiasm for the United States. There were solid tactical reasons for the CCP's acceptance of Stuart's visit; e.g., preventing U.S. intervention just as the People's Liberation Army (PLA) was preparing to cross the Yangtze River, and demoralizing the KMT by creating the impression that Washington was about to strike a deal with the CCP and abandon the Nationalists. Nor was the Stuart mission that critical, the "anti–lost chance" analysts maintain. There were other contacts between the CCP and the United States during this period that went nowhere.[14]

The debate over China's motives for allying with Moscow in 1950 will not be definitely settled until China opens its diplomatic archives to scholars, but the evidence presented by recently published Chinese memoirs and interviews with Chinese close to Zhou Enlai in 1949 supports the thesis of voluntary rather than forced alignment. Huang Hua, the CCP representative in Nanjing who agreed to Stuart's visit, for example, explained the acceptance of Stuart's proposed trip to Beijing in terms of tactical considerations, such as demoralizing the Nationalists.[15]

While a strong logical case could have been made in 1949 and 1950 in favor of a more balanced PRC relation with the United States and the Soviet Union, several factors combined to rule out a more neutral PRC orientation toward the superpowers in 1949.[16] Ideology was one factor. Mao and other CCP leaders were dedicated Marxist-Leninists. Though critical of Stalin's "great-power chauvinism," they considered the USSR a progressive, socialist country and the United States a monopoly capitalist, imperialist country. As early as 1940, Mao had divided the world into imperialist and socialist camps, and argued that China and other revolutionary countries should align with the socialist camp. This approach fit with Mao's theory of a single major contradiction for any given historical period.

A close relationship with the Soviet Union would also help persuade Moscow to assist China's economic development. The CCP had little experience in running modern industries or in administering a planned economy. The CPSU, however, had thirty years' experience in "building socialism," experience that could be immensely valuable to the CCP. Stalin's suspicions of Mao's "nationalist deviations" and his apprehensions that Mao might rebel against Moscow, as Tito had already done, also argued in favor of unswerving Chinese loyalty to Moscow to assuage Stalin's fears and secure large-scale Soviet support for China's socialist development. Mao also had to consider the possibility that if he alienated Stalin by maintaining cordial relations with Washington, it might prove impossible to dislodge the Soviet Union from Manchuria and Xinjiang.

Expectations of U.S. hostility were the other half of the equation that induced the CCP to align with the Soviet Union in 1950. Whatever its rationalizations and misgivings, the United States had supplied large amounts of aid to the Nationalists throughout the civil war. In terms of U.S. policy toward the newly established PRC, Secretary of State Dean Acheson on October 12 had left open the door for possible U.S. recognition. At the same time, however, a de facto economic embargo of the PRC was already beginning. Moreover, in the United States anti-Communist passions in Congress were becoming extreme, and the strength of the pro–Nationalist China lobby was growing. In Japan, U.S. occupation policy had reversed course in 1948, shifting from reform of Japanese society in cooperation with Japan's left wing to reconstruction of Japanese society in cooperation with conservative forces. Given Chinese sensitivity to Japanese power, this was an ominous development.

Considerations having to do with the liberation of Taiwan also argued in favor of alliance with the Soviet Union. In March 1949, while still confined to north China, the CCP declared its intention of liberating Taiwan. Preparations for an invasion of Taiwan began during the winter of 1949–1950 with the concentration of troops and junks in the provinces along the Taiwan Strait.[17] In January 1950, President Harry Truman disclaimed any intention of using armed forces to interfere in the present situation in China, or of providing military aid or advice to Chinese forces on Taiwan.[18] But in spite of U.S. disclaimers regarding Taiwan, Beijing remained suspicious. Even if intervention on behalf of Nationalist Taiwan was not the U.S. objective in January 1950, it might become so under the combined impact of an invasion of Taiwan by the PLA and mounting anti-Communist passions in the U.S. Congress. It was wise, therefore, to take out insurance against possible U.S. intervention. Alliance with Moscow seemed to fit the bill. If the PRC were allied with the Soviet Union, Washington would be less likely to intervene, since to do otherwise might touch off a third world war.

If the thinking of China's new rulers ran along this line, they miscalculated. The conclusion of the Sino-Soviet alliance increased U.S. hostility to the PRC and made U.S. intervention in Taiwan more likely. Prior to Beijing's clear alignment with Moscow and, more especially, prior to the outbreak of the Korean War, U.S. policy aimed at disengaging from the Nationalists, letting the dust settle in China, and then trying to work out a modus vivendi with the new Communist government. This policy was based on the assumption that keeping China free of Soviet domination was the overriding U.S. interest in the region. Moreover, the Soviet threat to China, Communist or Nationalist, was greater than any conceivable U.S. threat. Therefore, unless the United States turned itself into an enemy of the PRC by egregious actions, within a fairly short period of time tensions between the PRC and the Soviet Union would mount and Beijing would look to the United States for support. In other words, United States policy should attempt to draw Communist China away from the USSR. U.S. actions were not entirely consistent with such a policy, but Washington did signal its willingness to reach an accommodation with the PRC.[19]

According to Wu Xiuquan, a member of the Chinese negotiating team in Moscow in February 1950, CCP leaders were aware of U.S.

willingness to strike a deal with the PRC but were suspicious of Washington's underlying purposes. Stalin was very suspicious of U.S. efforts to exploit Sino-Soviet tensions and of the possibilities of Chinese "Titoism." Against this background, Wu viewed the signing of the treaty as "tantamount to the complete failure of the imperialists headed by the United States to sow dissension between China and the Soviet Union."[20]

Stalin's suspicions regarding CCP nationalist tendencies were not eased until the Korean War began. The circumstances surrounding the outbreak and China's entry into the Korean War will be considered in Chapter Thirteen. It will suffice here to note that during the war the Sino-Soviet alliance proved its ability to deter U.S. attack on China. U.S. Far Eastern Commander Douglas MacArthur favored such an attack, arguing that only the use of overwhelming U.S. military power to carry the war to Chinese territory would win the war for the United States. President Truman rejected MacArthur's advice, then removed him when he refused to follow orders to refrain from public pronouncements on U.S. policy. A key reason why Truman rejected MacArthur's advice was fear of bringing in China's ally, the Soviet Union, thereby possibly precipitating World War III.

A new level of Sino-Soviet trust and cooperation emerged during the Korean War. Once the PRC dared to confront the United States in Korea, Stalin's fears of Mao's possible Titoism abated. Soviet leaders also gained a new appreciation of China's value as a military partner. Moscow provided substantial military assistance to China during the war; however, there were frictions within the alliance. Moscow provided less economic and military assistance than Beijing desired, and insisted that China pay for all the Soviet weapons it received. Beijing felt that its effort in Korea benefited the entire socialist camp and that Moscow should provide gratis the material wherewithal for that struggle. But these differences were contained within a context of comprehensive and cordial cooperation in other areas.[21]

Stalin's death in March 1953 further strengthened the Sino-Soviet bond. The new Soviet leaders agreed to abandon the USSR's special privileges in Manchuria and to increase Soviet economic assistance to China. The mid-1950s saw the apogee of the Sino-Soviet alliance.

CONTAINMENT AND PEACEFUL COEXISTENCE

The conclusion of the Sino-Soviet alliance and the eruption of the Korean War prompted the United States to extend containment to Asia. As noted earlier, the Soviet-U.S. agreements of 1945 were premised on China's neutrality vis-à-vis the two superpowers. The conclusion of the Sino-Soviet alliance effectively overturned that system and, as Stalin had feared, greatly antagonized the United States. When a North Korean attack on South Korea followed in June 1950, barely four months after the Sino-Soviet treaty, Washington became convinced of the need for a firm policy to halt the expansion of the new Sino-Soviet bloc.

U.S. policy toward China hardened rapidly after June 1950.[22] Economic sanctions against the PRC were strengthened, while hostile propaganda and diplomatic maneuvers designed to isolate "Red China" intensified. The U.S. began using its considerable diplomatic influence to dissuade countries from recognizing the PRC or voting for the admission of the PRC to the United Nations. Throughout the 1950s and 1960s, Nationalist China on Taiwan held China's seat in the United Nations General Assembly and Security Council. United Nations votes on the question of Chinese representation are illustrated by Table 2-1.

Once the Korean War began, U.S. naval forces began to protect Taiwan from invasion by the PLA. The U.S.-KMT military relationship, which had lapsed under the earlier U.S. policy of disengagement from the Nationalists, was renewed and the United States began reorganizing Nationalist forces on Taiwan. Washington also shelved its earlier aversion to French colonialism in Indochina and began assisting French efforts to repress the Communist-led, PRC-supported independence movement there. Finally, the United States accelerated its efforts to rebuild Japanese military and economic strength. In September 1951, Japan signed a peace treaty with forty-eight pro-Western countries, but not with the USSR or the PRC. Simultaneously, Japan and the United States concluded a mutual security treaty providing for the long-term deployment of U.S. military forces to Japan. From Washington's perspective, these were all responses to "Communist aggression."

From Beijing's perspective, what the United States condemned as Chinese aggression was not aggression at all. The Korean conflict had begun, according to Beijing, as a purely Korean affair involving the exercise of the Korean people's right to national liberation and self-determination. Regarding China's role, Chinese forces had intervened only after U.S. forces had advanced to China's borders and threatened China. Concerning Taiwan, that island was an integral part of the Chinese nation and its "liberation" too was entirely a domestic matter. In Vietnam, Ho Chi Minh's Vietminh were Vietnamese patriots struggling to liberate their nation from French colonialism. China's support for them was not "aggression," but "proletarian internationalism." It was U.S. support for France that was aggression against Vietnam, according to Beijing. Nonetheless, Beijing sought to avoid provoking the United States by keeping its support for the Vietminh clandestine.

U.S. pressure further intensified with the Republican accession to the White House in January 1953. The Republicans were critical of what they felt had been U.S. weakness in the Far East under Truman, and set about to build a position of strength. Republican strategists concluded that the Communist invasion of South Korea had demonstrated that any doubt about whether the United States would defend positions along the

Table 2–1 United Nations Votes on PRC Representation

The following table indicates the relative strength of the move for representation of the People's Republic of China (PRC) and the removal of the Republic of China (Nationalists) in the U.N. General Assembly during the years 1950–1971: The China question was on the provisional agenda for the 1964 session but did not come to a vote because of the U.N. stalemate over peacekeeping assessments.

The votes on the issue:

Year			For	Against	Abstentions
1950	(a) Indian resolution to seat PRC	Rejected	16	32	10
	(b) USSR resolution to unseat Nationalists	Rejected	10	38	8
1951	Moratorium (U.S. resolution not to consider any changes in Chinese representation)	Adopted	37	11	4
1952	Moratorium	Adopted	42	7	11
1953	Moratorium	Adopted	44	10	2
1954	Moratorium	Adopted	43	11	6
1955	Moratorium	Adopted	42	12	6
1956	Moratorium	Adopted	47	24	8
1957	Moratorium	Adopted	48	27	6
1958	Moratorium	Adopted	44	28	9
1959	Moratorium	Adopted	44	29	9
1960	Moratorium	Adopted	42	34	22
1961	(a) Five-power resolution (United States, Australia, Colombia, Italy, and Japan) making any proposal to change the representation of China an "important question" requiring a two-thirds majority for approval	Adopted	61	34	7
	(b) USSR resolution to oust Nationalists and seat the PRC	Rejected	37	48	19*
1962	USSR resolution to oust Nationalists and seat PRC	Rejected	42	56	12*
1963	Albanian resolution to oust Nationalists and seat PRC	Rejected	41	57	12
1965	(a) Eleven-power resolution (United States, Australia, Brazil, Colombia, Madagascar, Nicaragua, Gabon, Italy, Japan, Philippines, and Thailand) declaring 1961 vote on "important question" still in force	Approved	56	49	11
	(b) Twelve-power resolution (Albania, Algeria, Cambodia, Congo-Brazzaville, Cuba, Ghana, Guinea, Mali, Pakistan, Romania, Somalia, and Syria) to oust Nationalists and seat PRC	Rejected	47	47	20*
1966	(a) Fifteen-power resolution (United States, Australia, Belgium, Bolivia, Brazil, Colombia, Gabon, Italy, Japan, Malagasy Republic, New Zealand, Nicaragua, Philippines, Thailand, and Togo) declaring China entry motion an "important question"	Approved	66	48	7
	(b) Ten-power resolution (Albania, Algeria, Cambodia, Congo-Brazzaville, Cuba, Guinea, Mali, Pakistan, Romania, and Syria) to oust Nationalists and seat PRC	Rejected	46	57	17*

45

Table 2–1 continued

Year		For	Against	Abstentions
1966	(c) Italian proposal (with Belgium, Bolivia, Brazil, Chile, Trinidad and Tobago) to appoint special committee to investigate PRC's position vis-à-vis U.N. membership and report to Assembly by July 1967 Rejected	34	62	25*
1967	(a) Fifteen-power resolution (United States, Australia, Belgium, Bolivia, Brazil, Colombia, Gabon, Italy, Japan, Malagasy Republic, New Zealand, Nicaragua, Philippines, Thailand, and Togo) declaring China entry motion an "important question" Approved	69	48	4
	(b) Eleven-power resolution (Albania, Algeria, Cambodia, Congo-Brazzaville, Cuba, Guinea, Mali, Mauritania, Pakistan, Romania, Syria—Sudan later became the twelfth cosponsor) to seat PRC Rejected	45	58	17*
	(c) Italian proposal (with Belgium, Chile, Luxembourg, Netherlands) to appoint special committee to investigate PRC's position vis-à-vis U.N. membership and report to Assembly during 1968 session (also made an "important question" under Article 18) Rejected	32	57	30
1968	(a) Thirteen-power resolution (United States, Australia, Bolivia, Brazil, Colombia, Gabon, Japan, Malagasy Republic, New Zealand, Nicaragua, Philippines, Thailand, Togo—Italy later became fourteenth cosponsor) declaring China entry motion an "important question" Approved	73	47	5
	(b) Fifteen-power resolution to oust Nationalists and seat PRC Rejected	44	58	23*
	(c) Italian proposal (with Belgium, Chile, Iceland, Luxembourg) to appoint special committee to investigate PRC's position vis-à-vis U.N. membership and report to Assembly during next session (made an "important question") Rejected	30	67	27
1969	(a) Eighteen-power resolution declaring China entry motion an "important question" Approved	71	48	4
	(b) Seventeen-power resolution to oust Nationalists and seat PRC Rejected	48	56	21*
1970	(a) Eighteen-power resolution declaring China entry question an "important question" Approved	66	52	7
	(b) Eighteen-power resolution to oust Nationalists and seat PRC Rejected	51	49	25*
1971	(a) Nineteen-power resolution declaring China entry question an "important question" Rejected	55	59	15
	(b) Twenty-one-power resolution to oust Nationalists and seat PRC Approved	76	35	17

*Two-thirds majority required for adoption.

Source: China, U.S. Policy Since 1945, Washington, D.C.: Congressional Quarterly, 1980. Reprinted with permission of Congressional Quarterly, Inc.

periphery of the Sino-Soviet bloc had to be eliminated. This led to the conclusion of a series of bilateral and multilateral mutual security treaties between the United States and various Asian states: with South Korea in August 1953; with Taiwan in December 1954; and with the Philippines, Thailand, Pakistan, Australia, New Zealand, Britain, and France under the South East Asian Treaty Organization (SEATO) in September 1954. South Vietnam, Laos, and Cambodia were brought under the collective security provision of the SEATO treaty through a protocol. Washington also strongly supported the 1955 formation of the Central Treaty Organization (CENTO), including Iran, Iraq, Turkey, Pakistan, and Britain. Behind this system of collective security was a growing arsenal of U.S. atomic and nuclear weapons. Figure 2–1 illustrates the structure of U.S. containment in Asia in the 1950s.

The traditional interpretation of U.S. containment of China during the 1950s was that it was ideologically motivated. An insensitivity to nationalistic differences between Moscow and Beijing deriving from intense anti-Communist ideology was deemed to be the basis of containment. In line with this, Washington dropped the idea that it could exploit differences between the USSR and the PRC, and began treating the Sino-Soviet bloc as a monolith joined together in ideological hostility to the United States.[23]

The publication of State Department documents during the 1980s led to a revision of this interpretation. Based on an analysis of previously classified documents, these revisionist scholars concluded that the United States did not abandon its goal of splitting China and the Sino-Soviet bloc, but adopted a considerably more devious way of achieving that end under the conditions of Sino-Soviet alliance. The hard line of containment was intended, according to this analysis, to break apart the Sino-Soviet alliance by stepped-up pressure. By pressuring China and forcing it into greater dependence on Moscow, U.S. leaders hoped to induce Beijing to make demands on its Soviet partners that Moscow could not satisfy. Chinese pride and ambition would then combine with Soviet arrogance and caution to create fissures in the bloc. Gradually, Beijing would be drawn away from the Soviet Union. This strategy was camouflaged by a manichaean anti-Communist rhetoric that lumped all Communists together as equally evil. In fact this was one more way of stepping up the pressure on the Sino-Soviet bloc. As U.S. Secretary of State John Foster Dulles explained to President Dwight Eisenhower after the Geneva Conference of 1954, by threatening massive nuclear retaliation against *both* the Soviet Union and China if *China* misbehaved, the United States increased its chances of creating tensions within the alliance.[24]

Peaceful coexistence was Moscow and Beijing's counter to the U.S. policy of containment. Announced early in 1953, the strategy was

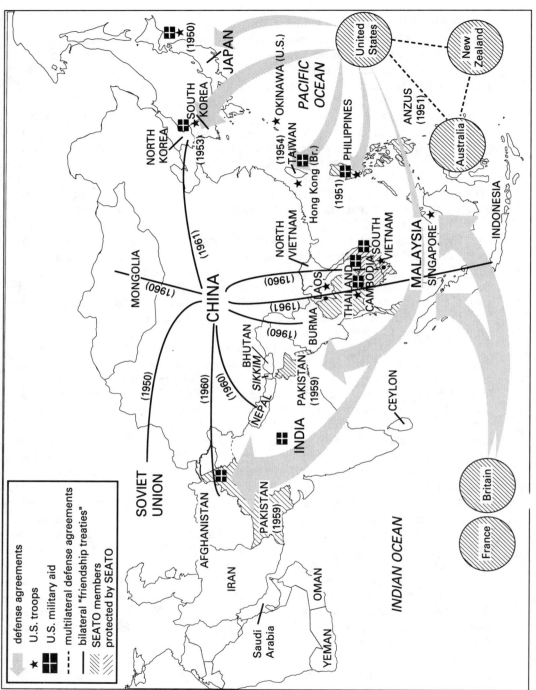

Figure 2–1 United States' Encirclement of China, 1950–1972 (*China, U.S. Policy Since 1945*, Washington, D.C.: Congressional Quarterly, 1980. Reprinted by permission of Congressional Quarterly, Inc.)

Map legend:
- defense agreements
- ★ U.S. troops
- ■ U.S. military aid
- ---- multilateral defense agreements
- —— bilateral "friendship treaties"
- SEATO members
- protected by SEATO

elaborated over the next several years. Under this approach, Moscow and Beijing moderated policies toward the United States in an attempt to reduce tensions, lessen the likelihood of war, and persuade Washington to relax its economic and diplomatic sanctions. Moscow and Beijing also moderated their policies toward other countries in order to persuade those countries not to go along with U.S. containment schemes.[25]

China put the policy of peaceful coexistence into practice at the first Afro-Asian conference at Bandung, Indonesia, in April 1955. The Bandung conference was a seminal event in the evolution of the post–World War II non-aligned and Afro-Asian movements, and China utilized this opportunity to expand its ties with those countries. China was represented by Zhou Enlai, who employed his considerable charm and diplomatic skills to appear moderate and conciliatory. So impressive was Zhou's performance that the term *Bandung* is often used to denote the entire moderate orientation of Chinese foreign policy between 1954 and 1957. With Indonesia, Zhou attempted to ease fears of a Chinese fifth column by signing a treaty providing that overseas Chinese with dual citizenship should opt for one nationality or the other. Toward the Philippines, a SEATO member and close U.S. ally, Zhou offered to sign a non-aggression treaty. Thailand's representatives were invited to inspect the Thai Autonomous Zone of Yunnan to assure themselves of the peaceful purposes of that zone. With Pakistani representatives, Zhou was understanding of their assurances that Pakistan's membership in SEATO was not directed against China. Zhou even made a bid toward the United States, offering to open negotiations with Washington regarding the status of Taiwan—a point discussed further below.

About the same time, Chinese propaganda became considerably less militant. Gestures of good will toward even pro-Western Afro-Asian countries proliferated. Beijing's objective was to reassure the moderate governments of the newly independent countries of the Third World, and dispel the then prevalent U.S.-encouraged image of China as a belligerent and aggressive nation. Moscow worked in tandem with Beijing in this effort. From the perspective of both Beijing and Moscow, if the Third World countries could be persuaded of the benign intentions of the socialist camp, those countries might be induced to dissociate themselves from U.S. containment efforts. Aside from helping to thwart U.S. containment, Beijing probably saw such a moderate approach as a way of expanding China's international contacts and enhancing China's stature. Success in courting the Third World would have given China an arena other than the socialist camp in which to play a role. This, in turn, would have lessened China's dependence on Moscow. Conflicts between Chinese and Soviet interests in the Third World remained largely latent, however, until 1959 when the Sino-Indian conflict erupted.

India played an especially important role in the Sino-Soviet opening to the Third World in the mid-1950s. India's size and population, its leadership in the struggle against colonialism, and the moralistic tone and global ambitions of its leaders gave India a high status among the newly independent and still-colonial nations. Moreover, India under Jahawarhal Nehru refused to join U.S. containment schemes, but stood ready to develop friendly ties with both the Soviet Union and China. Sino-Indian and Soviet-Indian ties became quite cordial. The link to India was extremely important to both Communist powers.[26]

THE LIBERATION OF TAIWAN AND NUCLEAR WEAPONS

Beijing's strategy of peaceful coexistence did not mean abandonment of the struggle to liberate Taiwan. Indeed, that was a high priority throughout the entire post-1949 period. Twice during the 1950s, from 1954 to 1955 and again in 1958, Beijing's desire to liberate Taiwan led it to confront the United States in the Taiwan Strait. These crises precipitated Sino-American crises which, in turn, catalyzed differences between Moscow and Beijing over policy toward the United States—differences that ultimately destroyed the Sino-Soviet bloc.

From Beijing's perspective, Taiwan was (and is) an inalienable part of China's national territory, stolen by Japanese imperialism in 1895 and rightfully returned to China via the Cairo Declaration of December 1943. The United States (along with Britain and China) was a party to the Cairo Declaration and was instrumental in transferring Taiwan to effective Chinese control during 1945 and 1946. Moreover, during the immediate post–World War II period the United States recognized that Taiwan was Chinese territory. During the revolt against KMT rule on Taiwan in February 1947, for example, the United States refused to intervene on the grounds that it was an internal Chinese affair. The American attitude changed, however, once the Chinese revolution was victorious—at least this was Beijing's perspective. Washington then began trying to split Taiwan from China. U.S. support for Chiang Kai-shek's Nationalist forces on Taiwan was imperialist aggression against China. The defeat of that aggression and the victorious liberation of Taiwan would represent a major step toward China's national liberation.

From Washington's perspective, once the outbreak of the Korean War demonstrated that Moscow and Beijing were determined to expand Communism in Asia by force of arms, Taiwan became a valuable link in the chain of containment around the periphery of the Sino-Soviet bloc. Washington legally defended its involvement with Taiwan on the grounds that the Cairo Declaration had merely expressed the *intent* of the World War II Allies. The actual implementation of that intention awaited a peace conference formally concluding the war. Pending such a conference, the status of Taiwan was indeterminate.

Beneath such legalistic arguments were cc
realpolitik. The existence and viability of the Nationalis.
was useful in the U.S. effort to isolate and pressure the PRc
propaganda, subversion, and paramilitary operations a&
mainland were a useful instrument for pressuring and harass.
Chinese Communist regime. In the event of a war between Comm.   .t
China and the United States, the Nationalist regime and its armies could
play an extremely useful political and military role. The island of Taiwan
itself provided a bastion that could be easily defended by U.S. air and
naval forces, and from which military and espionage operations could be
launched against the central China coast. The utility of Nationalist
Taiwan in containing China was, thus, considerable, and led to U.S.
determination to keep Taiwan out of Chinese Communist hands.

The Taiwan issue was further complicated by Nationalist
occupation of several islands just off the China coast, and, relatedly, by
disagreements between Chiang Kai-shek and U.S. leaders over policy
toward Communist China. As Nationalist forces fled mainland China in
1948 and 1949, they were able to hold several small islands a few miles
off the continental coast. The most important of these were Jinmen (also
known as Quemoy), situated a mere two miles from Xiamen, and the
smaller island of Mazu (Matzu), lying some ten miles off Fuzhou.

U.S. leaders felt that these islands were of marginal military value
and that the commitment of substantial forces to their defense did not
make sense. Chiang Kai-shek thought otherwise. To Chiang, the offshore
islands were useful jumping-off points for offensive operations against
the mainland—either small operations such as commando raids, or a
full-scale invasion to overthrow the Communist regime—operations that
Chiang strongly favored. Chiang also maintained that loss of the offshore
islands would be a severe, probably fatal, blow to Nationalist morale. The
loss of the mainland to the Communists had deeply demoralized
Nationalist forces, Chiang argued, and the loss of the offshore islands
would make Nationalist soldiers doubt their own ability to defend
Taiwan. Such a collapse of Nationalist morale would make Taiwan
vulnerable to Communist subversion or invasion. The defense of the
offshores thus became linked to the defense of Taiwan via the
mechanism of Nationalist morale. More fundamentally, Chiang
suspected Washington of conniving to make Taiwan an independent
country and saw retention of a close geographic link with the Chinese
mainland as a way of thwarting that ambition.

U.S. leaders felt strongly that Nationalist forces should be
evacuated from the offshore islands and that the defense perimeter of
the Free World should be drawn down the middle of the 100-mile-wide
Taiwan Strait, where U.S. naval and air superiority could be brought
fully into play. U.S. officials tried repeatedly to pressure Chiang to do
this. When Chiang refused, the United States backed down because U.S.

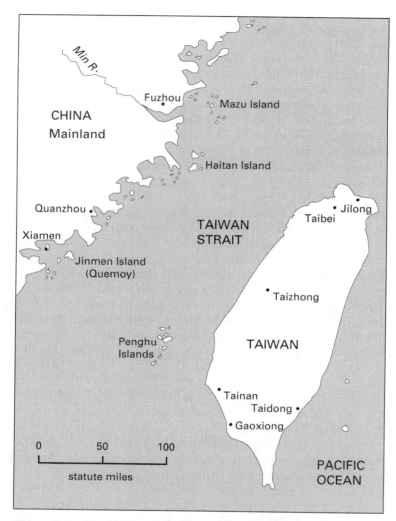

Figure 2–2 The Taiwan Strait and the Offshore Islands

leaders accepted Chiang's argument regarding the danger of the collapse of Nationalist morale. Since Chiang refused to draw down the large Nationalist garrison on Taiwan, the loss of that garrison could, Washington concluded, lead to Nationalist demoralization. Underlying the dispute over the offshores was a deeper disagreement between Washington and Taibei (Taiwan). U.S. policy was predicated on containment—rhetoric about "rolling back" Communist rule notwithstanding—while Chiang Kai-shek favored an all-out invasion of the mainland to liberate the Chinese people from Communist rule. The disagreements between Taibei and Washington probably figured prominently in Mao Zedong's calculations regarding the liberation of Taiwan during the 1950s.[27]

The various Taiwan Straits crises have been well researched. Scholars have long debated the motives and calculations underlying Beijing's decisions to bombard the offshore islands in 1954 and 1955 and again in 1958. The view held by most U.S. officials at the time took Beijing's professed intentions at face value: the moves were the first steps of a campaign to liberate Taiwan. According to this view, Beijing fully intended to force the Nationalist garrisons on the offshores to capitulate as a prelude to intensified action against Taiwan, and was prevented from accomplishing that only by forceful U.S. intervention. Later analysts tended to doubt whether Beijing ever actually intended to seize the offshores. Some, however, continue to stress the liberation of Taiwan as Beijing's goal. Thomas Stolper, for example, argued that Mao was apprised of the disagreements between Taibei and Washington over the wisdom of defending the offshores, and he struck at the locus of disagreement as a way of driving a wedge between Chiang Kai-shek and the United States. Washington was loath to risk war with China over territory that the U.S. public and U.S. allies in Europe would not deem worthwhile. Mao thus decided to force Washington to choose between risking a costly and unpopular war for inconsequential objectives, or breaking with the Nationalists and sacrificing the Nationalist garrisons on the offshores.[28]

Some scholars have argued that Beijing's desire to abort the U.S.-Taiwan treaty underlaid the bombardment of 1954 and 1955. Taibei presented a draft treaty to the United States in December 1953 and it was discussed in official circles in Washington over the following year. According to this perspective, Beijing saw such a treaty as a major step toward detaching Taiwan from China and wished to abort it, or at least to demonstrate to the United States and other countries that they could ignore PRC wishes regarding Taiwan only at substantial risk. Moreover, if China accepted the conclusion of the U.S.-Taiwan treaty without a strong reaction, Washington would interpret it as a sign of Chinese weakness—as a sign that Beijing was, in fact, willing to accept the status quo regarding Taiwan.[29]

Still other scholars have stressed the larger context of Sino-American relations. According to this interpretation, Beijing saw the United States as increasingly belligerent and arrogant. U.S. containment pressure on China was mounting. U.S.-supported Nationalist harassment of PRC and PRC-bound East European shipping was increasing. The proper way to deal with such a swaggering enemy was tit-for-tat struggle. Failure to do this would only further embolden the arrogant enemy; the way to deal with the tiger was to strike it firmly on the nose, not to attempt to appease or placate it. Thus, limited, controlled strikes at imperialist positions on the offshores might cause

Washington to come to its senses, and act more cautiously and realistically.[30]

The 1954 Straits crisis began building in July, when PRC media began proclaiming the imminent liberation of Taiwan. Heavy Chinese artillery bombardment of the offshores began on September 3. The United States responded forcefully. A large naval task force was deployed to the area. As the crisis escalated in February and March of 1955, U.S. forces made preparations to use tactical atomic weapons to defend the offshores. To warn Beijing that atomic weapons would be used and to prepare U.S. public opinion, top U.S. officials made public comments revealing U.S. intentions. When deliberating whether to use tactical nuclear weapons against China in 1954 and 1955, U.S. leaders minimized the likelihood of a forceful Soviet response to such an eventuality. In fact, Secretary of State Dulles tried to persuade Moscow to dissociate itself from Beijing's actions. To this end, Dulles mixed threats of nuclear war against China with warnings to Moscow about the costs of supporting Beijing's ambitions and hints of a reactivation of the "historic friendship" between Russia and America.[31]

Zhou Enlai took the initiative in defusing the first Taiwan Strait crisis in April 1955 when he announced at the Afro-Asian conference in Bandung that his government did not want war with the United States and was willing to negotiate with the United States to reduce tensions in the Taiwan area. Washington responded promptly and indicated that it was willing to open talks with the PRC. The shelling of the offshores soon tapered off.

Soviet pressure *may* have played a role in Beijing's decision to defuse the crisis. The United States received intelligence reports to this effect at the time.[32] Khrushchev made his first visit to China in September and October of 1954, in the midst of the crisis, and discussed the Taiwan issue with Mao. Some scholars have detected subtle differences between Moscow and Beijing at this juncture over such critical issues as the role of the Sino-Soviet alliance in maintaining world peace.[33] Most analysts agree, however, that if differences arose between Moscow and Beijing during the 1954–1955 crisis they were minor and well contained—very different from the disputes that rocked the alliance during the 1958 crisis.

U.S. nuclear threats during the 1954–1955 crisis reinforced a belief among the Chinese leadership that the PRC had to acquire nuclear weapons. In January 1955 the CCP Politburo made a decision to this effect.[34] The complex reasoning that underlay this momentous decision will be discussed in Chapter Eleven. It will suffice here to note that Washington regarded its nuclear arsenal as its ace in confrontations with China. U.S. leaders felt that they could risk support for the Nationalist garrisons on the offshores, for example, because if it came to war, U.S. nuclear superiority would allow it to prevail with acceptable levels of American casualties. If Washington's nuclear ace could be neutralized, if its nuclear monopoly could be broken, then it would be forced to deal more cautiously and respectfully with the PRC.

When the CCP Politburo decided in January 1955 to launch a crash program to develop nuclear weapons, it opted for a two-track effort. China would solicit Soviet support, while simultaneously pursuing an independent development program. In line with this decision, in June 1955 Defense Minister Peng Dehuai conveyed to Khrushchev China's request for assistance. Khrushchev agreed to consider China's request, but stressed his desire to reduce international tension. He also queried Peng about China's approach to the liberation of Taiwan. Peng agreed with Khrushchev's general views on the international situation, but stressed that China must still liberate Taiwan.[35]

In the year following Peng's visit the Soviet Union provided some assistance to China's embryonic nuclear weapons program. It was only in 1957, however, that large-scale Soviet assistance began. Marshal Nie Rongzhen, then the head of China's nuclear program, attributed Moscow's willingness to increase its assistance to the Soviet need for Chinese support in the face of difficulties in Eastern Europe.[36] PRC ambassador to the Soviet Union Liu Xiao attributed it to Khrushchev's desire for Chinese support in the showdown with the CPSU's Stalinist faction that was then looming.[37] In any case, in October 1957 Moscow and Beijing signed a New Defense Technical Accord under which the Soviet Union agreed to supply China a prototype atomic bomb and related technical data. Moscow also agreed to assist in the construction and operation of a gaseous diffusion plant at Lanzhou to produce enriched uranium-235. Under the terms of the 1957 agreement, Soviet assistance to China's nuclear effort deepened considerably. Ironically, it was just at this juncture that basic differences began to emerge between Moscow and Beijing over policy toward the United States.

THE 1958 TAIWAN STRAIT CRISIS AND THE SINO-SOVIET SCHISM

Zhou Enlai's offer of negotiations with the United States at the Bandung conference in April 1955 led to the beginning of ambassadorial-level talks between the United States and the PRC at Geneva in August 1955. Beijing's primary objective at the talks was to persuade the United States to ease its military and economic pressure against China. To achieve this Beijing adopted a conciliatory attitude on the critical issue of Taiwan, indicating its intention to resolve that question by peaceful means and its willingness to reach agreement on a mutual U.S.-PRC renunciation of use of force in the Taiwan area. This implied that China would renounce the use of force to liberate Taiwan, which was as close as Beijing would ever come to consenting to Taiwan's de facto separation from the PRC. This latter proposal was contingent, however, on the initiation of direct U.S.-PRC talks at the foreign ministerial level; in other words, on de facto U.S. recognition of the People's Republic of China. This was unacceptable to Washington. U.S. objectives were limited to securing the release of American airmen held prisoner by China, while avoiding moves that would enhance China's international status.

The only agreement reached at the Geneva talks regarded the release of U.S. citizens held by China and of Chinese nationals detained in the United States. The two sides disagreed, however, even on the implementation of this agreement. China insisted that Americans convicted of crimes in China could be released only after appropriate action by Chinese courts, while Washington insisted on immediate release of all Americans. From Beijing's perspective, the U.S. demand was reminiscent of earlier imperialist claims for special immunities and privileges for their citizens in China. Washington, however, seized on the incident to generate additional hostile propaganda against China.

When it was apparent by mid-1956 that China's earlier proposals had gone nowhere, Beijing proposed a series of cultural exchanges. When the United States rejected this, Beijing unilaterally invited U.S. journalists to China. This was blocked by Washington. Finally, in December 1957, the U.S. ambassador to Geneva, U. Alexis Johnson, was assigned elsewhere. Washington did not promptly assign a replacement, thereby effectively suspending the talks unless, as Beijing pointed out, the United States expected the Chinese ambassador to hold talks with a U.S. First Secretary. When no new U.S. ambassador was appointed by June 1958, in spite of repeated Chinese calls for a renewal of talks, Beijing issued an ultimatum that the talks must resume within two weeks. The United States deliberately waited until after that deadline passed before responding. By then Beijing had concluded that an armed strike against Quemoy was necessary to deflate U.S. arrogance and force Washington to adopt a more reasonable attitude at the talks.[38] Beijing saw carefully limited use of armed force as complementary to the process of diplomatic negotiation. Mao referred to this strategy as one of "talk, talk, fight, fight."

Most analysts, Chinese and foreign, have attributed U.S. intransigence during the Geneva talks to the impact of anti-Communist ideology.[39] Recent research suggests, however, that U.S. policy was not as ideologically motivated as previously thought. It now seems that hard-line U.S. policy was intended to keep pressure on China until it broke with the Soviet Union. A soft, conciliatory approach would not, U.S. leaders felt, undermine the Sino-Soviet alliance, but merely confirm to the two Communist powers the utility of that relation. Until China began moving away from the USSR, pressure would not be eased.[40]

Underlying Beijing's decision to return to a more militant approach toward the United States was dissatisfaction with the results of the moderate approach of the Bandung era. That moderate approach did reap some rewards in the Third World, but not enough to fundamentally undermine the U.S. containment system or to achieve the PRC's goal of winning admission to the United Nations. Nor had the moderate approach induced Washington to adopt a more lenient policy toward China. Indeed, U.S. pressure continued to increase and the integration of Taiwan into the American sphere continued unabated.

Mao apparently concluded that the conciliatory policies of China and the socialist camp were being taken by Washington as evidence of weakness, further emboldening the United States. Washington's strategy, Mao concluded, was to increase pressure on China until it was willing to capitulate on the Taiwan issue. Thus, China should adopt a firmer attitude to force the United States to realize that its hope of pressuring China into giving up Taiwan was futile, and persuade Washington to reconsider its whole China policy. The appropriate way to deal with an aggressive and arrogant opponent was by resolute struggle. The bombardment of Jinmen and Mazu commenced on August 23, 1958.[41]

Mao apparently did not tell Khrushchev about the imminent bombardment of the offshores during the Soviet leader's visit to Beijing in July 1958. Mao probably feared that Khrushchev would disapprove of the planned military action against the offshores, but calculated that when confronted by a fait accompli, Moscow would support its Chinese ally, however reluctantly.[42] Mao may also have hoped that a renewed crisis in the Taiwan Strait would force Khrushchev to reconsider his policies toward the United States. Since late 1957, Mao had become increasingly skeptical of the socialist camp's strategy of peaceful coexistence with the United States. If the United States did not react strongly, as Mao apparently expected would be the case, this would substantiate Mao's thesis that the socialist camp could adopt a more activist, offensive policy without running a high risk of U.S. retaliation. If, on the other hand, the United States did react forcefully, the Soviet Union would be forced, as China's ally, to support China. A crisis between the PRC and the United States would thus force Moscow to choose between its alliance with China and its desire for better relations with America. Although we can only guess on this issue, it seems likely that Mao expected Moscow to choose in favor of its alliance with China.[43]

Available documentation suggests that Mao underestimated the U.S. response to China's artillery blockade of the offshores. There had been no U.S. response to China's intense media campaign about the imminent "liberation of Taiwan" during June and July—a campaign intended, in part, to test U.S. intentions. Moreover, the United States was just then involved in a crisis in the Middle East. That, Mao expected, would force the United States to disperse its forces, inclining it toward caution in the Far East in order to avoid simultaneous crises in the Eastern Mediterranean and the Western Pacific. Mao's calculations were wrong; the U.S. reaction was much more forceful than he had anticipated. Six U.S. aircraft carriers carrying atomic bombs steamed toward Taiwan and atomic-capable eight-inch howitzers were deployed to the offshore islands. U.S. warships escorted Nationalist resupply ships up to the three-mile limit, and Chinese artillery did not bombard the U.S. warships or their Nationalist charges beyond that limit. When Nationalist air supremacy was challenged, the United States supplied advanced air-to-air Sidewinder missiles to Nationalist forces, enabling them to maintain superiority over the battlefield. This was adequate to break the Communist blockade and resupply the besieged Nationalist garrisons. Had those means not been adequate, the United States was prepared to use stronger means. President Eisenhower and Secretary Dulles publicly warned during the crisis that in extremis the United States was prepared to use tactical nuclear weapons. Mao later admitted in a secret speech in September 1958 that the U.S. response was much more forceful than he had anticipated: "I simply did not calculate that the world would become disturbed and turbulent....Who would have thought when we fired a few shots at Quemoy and Matzu that it would stir up such an earth-shattering storm?"[44]

Mao was correct, however, in his calculation that Moscow could not afford to dissociate itself from its Chinese ally. During the crisis Moscow issued several warnings to the United States not to attack China. Western analysts have disagreed about whether Beijing was satisfied with the level of Soviet support. Some have argued that Soviet support was adequate to meet Chinese needs and expectations, and that the Chinese did not emerge from the crisis with major doubts about their ally's reliability. Other scholars believe that the Chinese felt that Soviet support came only after the crisis had peaked and was on its way to being resolved.[45] Liu Xiao, China's ambassador to the Soviet Union at that time, supports the latter view. According to Liu, China's leaders felt that Soviet statements were weak and were issued only after it was clear that they involved little risk of a confrontation with the United States.[46]

To Soviet leaders, Beijing's decision to precipitate a military confrontation in the Taiwan Straits was extremely reckless. Once the crisis erupted, Soviet Foreign Minister Andrei Gromyko and sinologist M.S. Kapitsa made a secret trip to Beijing to discuss the situation. The Soviet leaders returned home feeling that Mao and his comrades had gravely underestimated the danger of war.[47] Early in September, as the crisis was still escalating, Soviet leaders summoned Ambassador Liu Xiao to the Crimea to discuss the Straits crisis. Khrushchev told Liu Xiao that the United States and its policy of nuclear "brinkmanship" was "extremely dangerous." Under certain conditions the United States might even resort to aggression against the socialist countries. In line with this, further escalation of tension in the Taiwan Strait must be prevented. Khrushchev also hinted at the limits of Soviet support for China by suggesting to Liu Xiao that the PRC could itself deal with any developments that might arise in the Straits.[48]

Underlying Soviet apprehensions over Mao's moves in the Taiwan Strait was a belief that Mao simply did not understand the awesome destructive power of thermonuclear weapons. In his memoir Khrushchev recounts a speech by Mao to a November 1957 conference of Communist parties commemorating the fortieth anniversary of the Bolshevik revolution:

> Mao gave a speech, the gist of which was as follows. "We shouldn't fear war. We shouldn't be afraid of atomic bombs and missiles. No matter what kind of war breaks out—conventional or thermonuclear—we'll win. As for China, if the imperialists unleash war on us, we may lose more than three hundred million people. So what? War is war. The years will pass, and we'll get to work producing more babies than ever before."...The content of [Mao's] speech was deeply disturbing. Except for...one outburst [of laughter]...the audience was dead silent. No one was prepared for such a speech.[49]

During his visit to Beijing just before the beginning of China's bombardment of the offshores, Khrushchev again discussed nuclear war with Mao. Lying in the shade beside a swimming pool, Mao expressed the view that because of its superior manpower, the socialist camp could defeat the imperialists in an all-out war waged with nuclear weapons. Khrushchev replied:

> Comrade Mao...you are making a fundamental error in your calculations....Battles are no longer won by bayonets, or bullets either, for that matter....Now, in the age of missiles and nuclear bombs, the number of divisions on one side or the other has practically no effect on the outcome of the battle. A hydrogen bomb can turn whole divisions into so much cooked meat. One bomb has an enormous radius of destruction....[Mao] was the leader of such a great country as China, but he expressed opinions...that were hopelessly outdated. Later, when I informed our leadership about my conversation with Mao, everyone was perplexed; no one supported Mao's point of view. We couldn't understand how our ally...could have such a childish outlook on the problem of war. Mao had given us a lot of food for thought.[50]

Khrushchev firmly believed that the interests of mankind and the Soviet Union required the avoidance of nuclear war. The development of thermonuclear weapons meant, Khrushchev believed, that another world war would be too costly be to undertaken rationally. Moreover, the new American strategy of massive retaliation and brinkmanship were extremely dangerous and meant that the United States might unleash its nuclear arsenal at the Soviet Union. To prevent this, peaceful coexistence between the Soviet Union and the United States, between East and West, should be developed and actions contrary to this end should be avoided.

Khrushchev had also used his 1958 visit to pressure Mao to agree to Soviet proposals for Soviet submarine bases and naval radio stations in China. These proposals had been discussed during a November 1957 visit by Defense Minister Peng Dehuai to Moscow. From Moscow's perspective such proposals made sense. Since 1955, Chinese leaders had been pushing for increased Soviet support for China against the United States. Soviet leaders had agreed in principle, but explained that this would entail greater Chinese cooperation with Soviet air and naval forces in the Far East since it was these forces that would have to counter the U.S. maritime threat to China.[51]

From the Chinese point of view, Moscow's demands for military bases were reminiscent of those imposed on China by imperialist powers during its century of National Humiliation. The implicit linkage between Soviet support for China against U.S. threats generated by the Taiwan Straits crisis and Chinese acceptance of Soviet requests for bases was also unacceptable. A direct Soviet military presence in China could also limit China's ability to initiate independently military operations. Probably for such reasons, in October 1958 Ambassador Liu Xiao received instructions from Mao Zedong to "graciously reject" Moscow's requests for naval facilities in China.[52]

The Taiwan Straits crisis of 1958 was a turning point in Sino-Soviet relations. Mao emerged from the crisis convinced that Khrushchev grossly overestimated the probability of U.S. attack on the socialist countries, at least as long as those countries stood together. Because of this miscalculation, Khrushchev was unwilling to challenge the United States. In the first instance, this meant that Khrushchev was not willing to use the power of the Soviet Union and the Warsaw Pact to backstop China's efforts to liberate Taiwan. From Mao's perspective, this was tantamount to a "two China policy," not much different from that of the United States. Phrased differently, Mao concluded that the Soviet Union was not willing to support its ally, China, on a matter vital to China's national interest. Khrushchev, on the other hand, emerged from the 1958 crisis convinced that Mao did not understand how dangerous the international situation was, how great the risk of nuclear war was, and how devastating such a war would be. Mao and his comrades were prone to reckless actions that threatened to drag the Soviet Union into a war with the United States, Khrushchev concluded.

Following the 1958 crisis Moscow suspended its assistance to China's nuclear program. In June 1959 the CCP Central Committee received a letter from the Central Committee of the CPSU informing it that the Soviet Union would not be able to supply a prototype atomic bomb, blueprints, or other technical data regarding the manufacture of atomic weapons as provided for by the October 1957 agreement. The reason given was Soviet-U.S. negotiations underway in Geneva regarding a treaty banning nuclear tests. (These talks began in November 1958.) Marshal Nie Rongzhen later quoted the Soviet letter as saying: "If the Western countries learn that the Soviet Union is supplying China with sophisticated technological aid, it is possible that the socialist community's efforts for peace and relaxation will be seriously sabotaged."[53]

During 1959, Chinese and Soviet policy toward the United States steadily diverged. China's international policies became increasingly militant, intended to catalyze a revolutionary united front against U.S. imperialism—a development discussed in Chapter Six. The Soviet Union, on the other hand, continued the policy of peaceful coexistence. Indeed, that policy moved into high gear in August 1959, when Khrushchev made the first-ever visit to the United States by a top Soviet leader. While Khrushchev was in the United States, the CCP's theoretical journal *Red Flag* issued a bitter condemnation of people who harbored illusions about imperialism. Among the illusions specified by the article were the beliefs that imperialism was no longer vicious, that it should be appeased rather than struggled against, and that it could not be defeated.

Adam Ulam suggests that during 1959 Khrushchev was seeking a broad understanding with the United States, giving Soviet guarantees regarding China in exchange for U.S. guarantees regarding Germany. According to this grand design, the Soviet Union would undertake to prevent, or at least delay, China's acquisition of atomic weapons in exchange for U.S. agreement to keep atomic weapons out of West German hands and accept the legitimacy of the East German state. Ulam cites as evidence the well-known Soviet desire to keep West Germany non-nuclear, Moscow's proposal of an atomic-free zone in the Far East in January 1959, the cancellation of the atomic cooperation treaty with China in June, Khrushchev's probing of Eisenhower regarding the Chinese question during their September 1959 discussions at Camp David (a matter discussed below), and a Soviet attempt to secure U.S. acceptance of a peace treaty involving both East and West Germany in May 1959.

According to Andrei Gromyko, the Soviet foreign minister at the time, U.S. Secretary of Defense Neil McElroy had dropped broad hints of Soviet-U.S. cooperation against China during their meeting en route to John Foster Dulles' funeral in May of 1959. According to Gromyko:

> McElroy came over to me and asked: "May I join you, Mr. Gromyko? There are one or two things I'd like to talk over with you." "Be my guest," I replied. I knew perfectly well that no Secretary of Defense was going to say anything on his own initiative to the Soviet Foreign Minister, especially with the

Secretary of State [Christian Herter] sitting in the same plane. McElroy began talking about what he called the "yellow peril"; that is, China. "The yellow peril," he said, "is now so great that it just cannot be dismissed. And it's not just a matter of taking it into consideration—it has to be dealt with." Although I could guess where he was going, I said nothing and let him carry on. "We ought to combine against China." He stopped to see what effect this had on me....In reply I said: "You and I—that is to say, the United States and the USSR—have the much more important job of finding a solution to the difficulties in Europe and trying to improve Soviet-U.S. relations." "But, still," he insisted, "there's a big problem here. We both have to think about it." That was the end of the conversation.[54]

Khrushchev raised the China issue during his August 1959 talks with Eisenhower. According to Ulam, Eisenhower completely failed to understand Soviet concerns regarding China. According to Eisenhower's own memoir, he (Eisenhower) refused to discuss the topic, apparently because he believed that the Soviet leader intended to argue for the PRC's admission to the United Nations.[55] Confronted with Eisenhower's disinterest, Khrushchev dropped the issue. Khrushchev's dilemma, according to Ulam, was that until he had some indication that the United States would cooperate with Moscow on the China problem, he had to cover up the evidence of disputes between Beijing and Moscow. To do otherwise would reveal to the United States Moscow's new vulnerability and invite stepped-up U.S. pressure on Moscow or U.S. moves to exploit the new Sino-Soviet tensions.[56]

Chinese leaders, unlike the American ones, were quick to see anti-Chinese impulses behind Khrushchev's moves in 1959. According to Beijing, Khrushchev's cancellation of the 1957 nuclear technology agreement shortly before his visit to the United States was a "present" to Eisenhower.[57] An anti-China purpose lay behind the agreement reached by Eisenhower and Khrushchev at Camp David regarding the desirability of an agreement banning nuclear tests in the earth's atmosphere, Beijing declared. Since China did not possess the sophisticated technology necessary for subterranean nuclear tests, such an agreement would put the two superpowers on record as opposing Chinese nuclear tests. Moreover, if the two superpowers agreed to restrict their own development of nuclear weapons, they might also decide to put similar restrictions on other nations. Thus, CCP alternate Politburo member Kang Sheng let Moscow know that China would not go along with such an arrangement during a secret speech to the Warsaw Treaty Organization conference in February 1960: "If China is not a signatory to any agreement, no matter what agreement Khrushchev and Eisenhower sign it will have no binding effect on China."[58]

Divergent policies toward India also figured prominently in the emerging Sino-Soviet rupture in 1959. The deterioration of Sino-Indian relations in 1959 will be discussed in Chapter Twelve. Here we may merely recall that in the mid-1950s India played an important role in

Moscow's counter-containment diplomacy, and note that once the Sino-Indian border dispute erupted in 1959, Soviet leaders believed that China should do whatever was necessary to avoid alienating India—even to the extent of accepting India's territorial claims. Beijing's refusal to do this was, according to Khrushchev, part of Mao's "systematic campaign to torpedo and subvert our efforts at promoting peaceful coexistence."[59] In line with this perception, Moscow adopted a neutral position on the Sino-Indian dispute. From Beijing's perspective, Moscow's failure to support China, which was not only the Soviet Union's ally but also a socialist country, was an unprincipled betrayal.

Khrushchev was aware of Chinese displeasure over Soviet neutrality in the escalating Sino-Indian dispute, and in October 1959, just after his return from the United States, he flew to Beijing to explain Soviet Indian policy to China's leaders. The first acrimonious face-to-face confrontation between the leaders of the two countries ensued. Khrushchev tried to persuade his Chinese opposites of the importance of cordial relations with India. Speaking for the Chinese side, Foreign Minister Chen Yi and Premier Zhou Enlai reiterated China's demand for full Soviet support in the confrontation with India. Khrushchev failed to see the logic of China's position and took Beijing's forceful approach toward India as further evidence of Chinese recklessness. In his view, "Mao created the Sino-Indian conflict precisely in order to draw the Soviet Union into it. He wanted to put us in the position of having no choice but to support him."[60]

By 1960 Mao saw a pattern emerging in Soviet policy toward China. Moscow, Mao believed, refused to give China firm support against the United States and wanted Beijing to forgo indefinitely the recovery of Taiwan. It wanted China not to acquire nuclear weapons. It refused to support China against India. In sum, Soviet policies seemed to indicate that Moscow did not genuinely support China's emergence as a great power. Moscow also seemed to be inching toward an agreement with the United States to keep China weak. The United States, for its part, seemed to be ready to apply the doctrine of peaceful coexistence to relations with the Soviet Union, but not with China, and Moscow was apparently willing to go along with this arrangement. From Mao's perspective, China was left to face American pressure without Soviet support. That was tantamount to Soviet abandonment of its alliance with China and entailed a refusal to place China's interests on a par with those of the Soviet Union.

FROM POLEMIC TO CONFRONTATION

From 1959 until mid-1963, Beijing tried to force Moscow to abandon its policy of peaceful coexistence with the United States. It did so by polemicizing against that policy within the world Communist and revolutionary movements. Until April 1960, China avoided direct criticisms of Soviet policy, relying instead on elliptical attacks via criticisms of Yugoslavia or by limiting its more direct criticism of Soviet policy to closed meetings of the international Communist movement. This allowed Moscow to conceal from American eyes the Soviet estrangement of its major ally. This ended in April 1960 when, on the occasion of the 100th anniversary of Lenin's birth, China issued a strong public denunciation of "modern revisionism." These "modern revisionists" were not named, but it was clear that this was a euphemism for the Soviet leadership. By publicly airing Sino-Soviet differences, Mao stepped up the pressure on Moscow. Now Moscow would have to either move quickly to repair its relations with Beijing or invite U.S. exploitation of the Sino-Soviet schism. By making public his dispute with Khrushchev, Mao was, in effect, threatening the public termination of the Sino-Soviet alliance, thereby exposing the isolation of the Soviet Union to American eyes.[61]

We still do not know the precise nature of Mao's calculations in early 1960 when he launched the open polemical struggle against Khrushchev. He probably did not expect a complete break with Moscow. The costs of such a break for Moscow were so great, Mao probably calculated, that the rational solution for Moscow would be to return to its alliance with China. The creation of the Sino-Soviet alliance had greatly strengthened Moscow's position vis-à-vis the United States, and Mao probably believed that Moscow would not wish to go down a road leading to Sino-Soviet rupture. If this speculation is correct, Mao again miscalculated. Instead of prompting a Soviet return to solidarity with China, Beijing's polemics produced intensified Soviet pressure. In the summer of 1960, Moscow abruptly suspended its economic assistance to China and recalled its thousands of advisers and technicians from China in a fashion calculated to inflict maximum damage on China's development efforts. Soviet polemics matched the Chinese blow for blow, and the ideological debate intensified.

In 1963 Mao seized on Khrushchev's inadvertent resurrection of long dormant territorial disputes between China and the Soviet Union to intensify psychological-political pressure on Moscow. Responding to Chinese charges of capitulation to the United States during the Cuban missile crisis, Khrushchev had noted that for all Beijing's anti-imperialist militancy, it had not seen fit to take Hong Kong from the British imperialists. Mao responded that as long as Khrushchev had raised the issue of imperialist aggression against China in the nineteenth century, that question should be discussed, and once this was done, it was apparent that the various "unequal treaties" imposed on China by czarist Russia were without any validity. The existing USSR-PRC boundaries were based on these "unequal treaties." Mao then began dropping broad hints that large tracts of land ceded by China under those treaties should be returned to China. (China's implicit territorial claims against the USSR were depicted by Figure 1–2 in Chapter One.[62]) Moscow responded by fortifying the Sino-Soviet border. Soon an escalating spiral of measures and countermeasures set in along the border. Tensions mounted and increasingly assumed a military character.

NOTES

1. See Mao Zedong, "On Contradiction," *Selected Works of Mao Tse-tung*, vol. I, Beijing: Foreign Languages Press, 1967, 311–46.

2. See Thomas M. Gottlieb, *Chinese Foreign Policy: Factionalism and the Origins of the Strategic Triangle*, R-1902-NA, Santa Monica, Calif.: Rand, November 1977; William G. Hyland, "The Sino-Soviet Conflict: A Search for New Security Strategies," in *Asian Security in the 1980s: Problems and Policies for a Time of Transition*, Richard H. Solomon, ed., R-2492-ISA, Santa Monica, Calif.: Rand, November 1979, 39–53; William G. Hyland, "The Sino-Soviet Conflict: Dilemmas of the Strategic Triangle," *The China Factor: Sino-American Relations and the Global Scene*, Richard Solomon, ed., Englewood Cliffs, N.J.: Prentice Hall, 1981, 137–58.

3. Regarding the CCP's diplomacy toward Moscow and Washington during World War II, see James Reardon-Anderson, *Yenan and the Great Powers*, New York: Columbia University Press, 1980; Michael Schaller, *The U.S. Crusade in China, 1938–1945*, New York: Columbia University Press, 1979; John W. Garver, *Chinese-Soviet Relations, 1937–1945: The Diplomacy of Chinese Nationalism*, New York: Oxford University Press, 1988.

4. Regarding the decline of the Nationalist regime, see Lloyd E. Eastman, *Seeds of Destruction: Nationalist China in War and Revolution, 1937–1949*, Stanford, Calif.: Stanford University Press, 1984; Barbara Tuchman, *Stilwell and the American Experience in China, 1911–1945*, New York: Bantam, 1972. The Nationalist view of the Chiang-Stilwell conflict is presented in Liang Chin-tung, *General Stilwell in China, 1942–1944: The Full Story*, New York: St. John's University Press, 1972.

5. Proponents of the 1944–1945 "lost chance" include Barbara Tuchman, "If Mao Had Come to Washington: An Essay in Alternatives," *Foreign Affairs*, vol. 51, no., 1 (October 1972), 44–64; Joseph W. Esherick, *Lost Chance in China: The World War II Despatches of John S. Service*, New York: Random House, 1974.

6. Regarding the 1945 Sino-Soviet treaty, see Chin-jung Liang, "The Sino-Soviet Treaty of Friendship and Alliance of 1945: The Inside Story," *Nationalist China During the Sino-Japanese War, 1937–1945*, Paul K. Sih, ed., Hicksville, N.Y.: Exposition Press, 1977; John W. Garver and Ralph N. Clough, "The Nationalist-U.S. Alliances, 1941–1978," in *Patterns of Cooperation in the Foreign Relations of Modern China*, Harry Harding, ed., forthcoming; Garver, *Chinese-Soviet Relations, 1937–1945*. Regarding Yalta, see Akira Iriye, *The Cold War in Asia: A Historical Introduction*, Englewood Cliffs, N.J.: Prentice Hall, 1974; Diane S. Clements, *Yalta*, New York: Oxford University Press, 1970; Forest C. Pogue, "The Big Three and the United Nations," *The Meaning of Yalta*, John C. Snell, ed., Baton Rouge: Louisiana State University Press, 1956.

7. Regarding U.S. policy during the early post-war period, see Herbert Feis, *The China Tangle*, Princeton, N.J.: Princeton University Press, 1953; Paul A. Varg, *The Closing of the Door*, Ann Arbor: Michigan State University Press, 1973; John Robinson Beal, *Marshall in China*, Garden City, N.Y.: Doubleday, 1970; Tang Tsou, *America's Failure in China, 1941–1950*, 2 volumes, Chicago: University of Chicago Press, 1963; Kenneth S. Chern, *Dilemma in China: America's Policy Debate, 1945*, Hamden, Conn.: The Shoe String Press, 1980; Kenneth E. Shewmaker, *Americans and Chinese Communists, 1927–1945: A Persuading Encounter*, Ithica, N.Y.: Cornell University Press, 1971. Extensive primary documentation is available in the White Paper published in 1949, U.S. Department of

State, *United States Relations with China, with Special Reference to the Period 1944–1949*, Washington, D.C.: Department of State, 1949.

8 According to the Chinese ambassador to the Soviet Union in the 1950s, Moscow's modus operandi was to abandon warehouses of captured Japanese weapons after notifying local CCP representatives. Liu Xiao, *Chushi Sulian Banian* (Eight Years as Ambassador to the Soviet Union), Beijing: CCP Party History Materials Publishing House, 1986, 4–5. Regarding Soviet-CCP relations in Manchuria at this juncture, see Steven I. Levine, *Anvil of Victory: The Communist Revolution in Manchuria, 1945–1948*, New York: Columbia University Press, 1987.

9. Regarding Stalin's calculations, see Vladimir Dedijer, *The Battle Stalin Lost: Memoirs of Yugoslavia, 1948–1953*, New York: Viking Press, 1971, 68; Vladimir Dedijer, *Tito Speaks: His Self-Portrait and Struggle with Stalin*, London: Weidenfeld and Nicolson, 1953, 331; Milovan Djilas, *Conversations with Stalin*, New York: Harcourt, Brace, and World, 1963, 182. Regarding Mao's views of Stalin's policy, see Stuart Schram, ed., *Chairman Mao Talks to the People: Talks and Letters, 1956–1971*, New York: Pantheon, 1974, 191.

10. Liu Xiao, *Eight Years as Ambassador*, 4–5. Regarding the Soviet mediation bid, *Foreign Relations of the United States*, (hereafter cited see *FRUS*), 1948, vol. 7, 133–35.

11. Memoir of the April 1947 Molotov-Marshall discussion and also Ambassador Stuart to Secretary of State, March 8, 1948, in *FRUS*, 1947, vol. 7, 609–25, 133–36.

12. Cited in John Gittings, "New Light on Mao: His view of the World," *China Quarterly*, no. 60 (October–December 1974), 759. The text of the 1950 treaty and agreement regarding the Manchurian railways and ports is in Aitchen K. Wu, *China and the Soviet Union*, London: Methuen, 1950. Studies analyzing those agreements include Harry Schwartz, *Tsars, Mandarins, and Commissars: A History of Chinese-Russian Relations*, New York: Anchor, 1973; O. Edmund Clubb, *China and Russia: The "Great Game"*, New York: Columbia University Press, 1971.

13. Proponents of the 1949–1950 "lost chance" thesis include Robert M. Blum, *Drawing the Line: The Origins of the American Containment Policy in East Asia*, New York: W.W. Norton, 1982; Nancy B. Tucker, *Patterns in the Dust: Chinese-American Relations and the Recognition Controversy, 1949–1950*, New York: Columbia University Press, 1983; N.B. Tucker, "An Unlikely Peace: American Missionaries and the Chinese Communists, 1948–1950," *Pacific Historical Review*, vol. 45, no. 1, 1976, 104; Michael H. Hunt, "Mao Tse-tung and the Issue of Accommodation with the United States, 1948–1950," in *Uncertain Years: Chinese-American Relations, 1947–1950*, Dorothy Borg and Waldo Heinrichs, eds., New York: Columbia University Press, 1980, 185–233; John Gittings, *The World and China, 1922–1972*, New York: Harper and Row, 1974, 163–69; Bernard Gwertzman, "The Hostage Crisis—Three Decades Ago," *The New York Times Magazine*, May 4, 1980, 41–43, 101–4.

14. Opponents of the "lost chance" hypothesis include Steven M. Goldstein, "Chinese Communist Policy Toward the United States: Opportunities and Constraints, 1944–1950," and Steven I. Levine, "Notes on Soviet Policy and Chinese Communist Perceptions, 1945–1950," in *Uncertain Years*, 35–278, 293–303; Steven I. Levine, "If My Grandmother Had Wheels She'd Be a Trolley, or Reflections on the 'Lost Chance in China'," in *Contemporary China*, vol. 1, no. 3 (December 1976), 31–32; Okabe Tatsumi, "The Cold War and China," in *The Origins of the Cold War In Asia*, Yonosuke Nagai and Akira Iriye, eds., New York: Columbia University Press, 1977, 224–51; Yu-ming Shaw, "John Leighton Stuart and U.S.-Chinese Communist Rapprochement in 1949: Was There Another 'Lost Chance in China'?" *The China Quarterly*, no. 89 (March 1982), 74–96; Clubb, *China and Russia*, 373–86; A. Doak Barnett, *China and the Major Powers in East Asia*, Washington, D.C.: Brookings, 1977, 25–26.

15. Cited in Zhigong Ho, "'Lost Chance' or 'Inevitable Hostility?' Two Contending Interpretations of the Late 1940s Chinese-American Relations," *Chinese Historians*, vol. 2, no. 1 (December 1988), 39; Warren I. Cohen, "Conversations with Chinese Friends: Zhou Enlai's Associates Reflect on Chinese-American Relations in the 1940s and the Korean War," *Diplomatic History*, vol. 11 (Summer 1987), 283–89; Gordon H. Chang, *Friends and Enemies: The United States, China, and the Soviet Union, 1948–1972*, Stanford, Calif.: Stanford University Press, 1990.

16. See Barnett, *China and the Major Powers*, 24–27; Harold Hinton, *China's Turbulent Quest*, Bloomington: Indiana University Press, 1973, 35–40; Nineo Nakajima, "Foreign Relations: From the Korean War to the Bundung Line," *The Cambridge History of China*, vol. 14 (The People's republic of China, Part I: The Emergence of Revolutionary China, 1949–1965), Roderick MacFarquhar and J.K. Fairbank, eds., New York: Cambridge University Press, 1987, 259–70.

17. Regarding the 1949–1950 campaign to liberate Taiwan, see Allen S. Whiting, *China Crosses the Yalu: The Decision to Enter the Korean War*, Stanford, Calif.: Stanford University Press, 1960, 20–22; John W. Hueber, "The Abortive Liberation of Taiwan," *China Quarterly*, no. 110 (June 1987), 256–75.

18. *The New York Times*, January 6, 1950. For additional indications of U.S. disengagement from the Nationalist regime and the abandonment of Taiwan, see John W. Spanier, *The Truman-MacArthur Controversy and the Korean War*, Cambridge: Harvard University Press, 1959, 51–57.

19. See Lewis McCarroll Purifoy, *Harry Truman's China Policy: McCarthyism and the Diplomacy of Hysteria, 1947–1951*, New York: New Viewpoints, 1976; June Grasso, *Truman's Two-China Policy*, New York: M.E. Sharpe, 1987.

20. Wu Xiuquan, *Eight Years in the Ministry of Foreign Affairs, January 1950–October 1958: Memoirs of a Diplomat*, Beijing: New World Press, 1985, 16.

21. See Barnett, *China and the Major Powers*, 27, footnote 20. Robert Simmons argues that intra-alliance strains during the Korean War were much greater. Robert R. Simmons, *The Strained Alliance: Peking, P'yongyang, Moscow and the Politics of the Korean Civil War*, Boston: Free Press, 1975.

22. The standard studies of PRC-U.S. relations during the 1950s and 1960s are Roderick MacFarquhar, *Sino-American Relations, 1949–1971*, New York: Praeger, 1972; Foster Rhea Dulles, *American Policy Toward Communist China, 1949–1969*, New York: Crowell, 1972; John K. Fairbank, *The United States and China,* Cambridge: Harvard University Press, 1971; A more up-to-date revisionist work is Chang, *Friends and Enemies*.

23. This interpretation is advanced by Robert G. Sutter, *China Watch: Toward Sino-American Reconciliation*, Baltimore and London: Johns Hopkins University Press, 1978, 31–34; Michael Schaller, *The United States and Chines in the Twentieth Century*, New York: Oxford University Press, 1979, 114–45; Arnold Xiangze Jiang, *The United States and China*, Chicago and London: University of Chicago Press, 1988, 134–53; Purifoy, *Harry Truman's China Policy*, 298–306.

24. David Allen Mayers, *Cracking the Monolith: U.S. Policy Against the Sino-Soviet Alliance, 1949–1955*, Baton Rouge: Louisiana State University Press, 1986. Also review of Mayers' book by John W. Garver, in *Journal of Asian Studies*, vol. 47, no. 4 (November 1988), 863–65; Chang, *Friends and Enemies*, 80–118.

25. Regarding the general Sino-Soviet strategy of peaceful coexistence, see Adam B. Ulam, *Expansion and Coexistence: The History of Soviet Foreign Policy, 1917–1967*, New York: Praeger, 1968, 539–71; Donald F. Lach and Edmund S. Wehrle, *International Politics in East Asia Since World War II*, New York: Praeger, 1975, 165–76; Nakajima, "Foreign Relations: From the Korean War to the Bandung Line"; Hinton, *China's Turbulent Quest*, 57–77.

26. Regarding Indian relations with Moscow and Beijing in the 1950s, see Bhabani Sen Gupta, *The Fulcrum of Asia: Relations Among China, India, Pakistan, and the USSR*, New York: Pegasus, 1970, 41–92; William J. Barnds, *India, Pakistan, and the Great Powers*, New York: Praeger, 1972, 113–25, 135–41; John Rowland, *A History of Sino-Indian Relations: Hostile Coexistence*, Princeton, N.J.: Van Nostrand, 1967.

27. Regarding U.S.-Nationalist disagreements over the offshores, see John W. Garver and Ralph N. Clough, "The Nationalist-U.S. Alliances, 1941–78" in *Patterns of Cooperation*; Tang Tsou, "The Quemoy Imbroglio: Chiang Kai-shek and the United States," *Western Political Quarterly*, vol. 12 (1959), 1075. Regarding the dispute over containment vs. rollback, see Franz Schurmann, *The Logic of World Power*, New York: Pantheon, 1974, 161–83.

28. Thomas E. Stolper, *China, Taiwan, and the Offshore Islands*, New York: M.E. Sharpe, 1985.

29. Sutter, *China-Watch*, 37.

30. See Gittings, *China and the World*, 196–200; Jan H. Kalecki, *The Pattern of Sino-U.S. Crises: Political-Military Interactions in the 1950s*, London and New York: Cambridge University Press, 1975, 120–55. John W. Lewis and Xue Litai, *China Builds the Bomb*, Stanford, Calif.: Stanford University Press, 1988, 25–34.

31. Gordon H. Chang, "To the Nuclear Brink: Eisenhower, Dulles, and the Quemoy-Matsu Crisis," *International Security*, vol. 12, no. 4 (Spring 1988), 96–123. H.W. Brands, in "Testing Massive Retaliation, Credibility and Crisis Management in the Taiwan Strait," in the same issue of *International Security*, argues that U.S. leaders took seriously the possibility of Soviet intervention in a *general* Sino-American war, 128–29.

32. Chang, "To the Nuclear Brink," 117.

33. Sutter, *China-Watch*, 38–40.

34. Lewis and Xue, *China Builds the Bomb*, 35–39.

35. Liu Xiao, *Eight Years as Ambassador*, 9–10.

36. Nie Rongzhen, *Nie Rongzhen Huiyilu* (Memoir of Nie Rongzhen), Beijing: Jiefangjun Chubanshe, 1984, 803.

37. Liu Xiao, *Eight Years as Ambassador*, 45–46.

38. Ibid, 65.

39. Jiang, *The United States and China*, 148–49; Schaller, *The United States and China*, 140–44; Sutter, *China-Watch*, 47–62; Kenneth T. Young, *Negotiating with the Chinese Communists: The United States Experience, 1953–1967*, New York: McGraw-Hill, 1968, 116–34. Young's is the standard work on the Sino-U.S. talks.

40. See the sources cited in note 24.

41. Regarding Chinese calculations at this juncture, see Liu Xiao, *Eight Years as Ambassador*, 65; Allen S. Whiting, "New Light on Mao: 3. Quemoy 1958: Mao's Miscalculations," *China Quarterly*, no. 62 (June 1975), 263–70.

42. Barnett, *China and the Major Powers*, 345, footnote 40; Whiting, "New Light on Mao," 269. According to Liu Xiao, the staff office of China's ministry of national defense informed the Soviet ministry of defense of impending action toward the offshores. This notification apparently did not come to the attention of the top Soviet leadership prior to the outbreak of the crisis. Liu Xiao, *Eight Years as Ambassador*, 72.

43. Some analysts have argued that Beijing's 1958 bombardment of Quemoy and Matsu was motivated by a fear that the United States might be about to authorize a Nationalist invasion of China, backing up that invasion with a nuclear strike against Chinese military installations. As evidence for this proposition, those analysts point to stepped-up Nationalists raids against China at this juncture and to Chinese statements that the U.S. was about to attack China. Melvin Gurtov and Byong-Moo Hwang, *China Under Threat: the Politics of Strategy and Diplomacy*, Baltimore and London: Johns Hopkins University Press, 1980, 63–98. There is, however, substantial evidence indicating that China's leaders did not take seriously their own propaganda about the "American threat" at this juncture. At the Moscow Conference of Communist Parties in December 1957, for example, Mao argued that as long as the socialist camp was united and stable there was little danger that the American imperialists would dare to attack the socialist countries. In a speech just after the 1958 Taiwan Straits crisis, Mao reiterated his belief that the United States was in an essentially defensive position: "All the evidence proves that imperialism has adopted a defensive position, and that it no longer has an ounce of offensiveness [toward the socialist camp]. How to handle this in our propaganda is another matter, and we must go on saying that it is on the offensive." Cited in John Gittings, "New Light on Mao: 1. His View of the World," *China Quarterly*, no. 60 (October–December 1974), 754–55. In his talks with Khrushchev during the 1958 Straits crisis, Ambassador Liu Xiao also stressed that in spite of the tense situation in the Strait, the United States would not dare to attack China. The Soviets were, Liu said, overestimating U.S. resolve. Liu Xiao, *Eight Years as Ambassador*, 63, 72. Chinese propaganda about the danger of U.S. attack was very probably not reflective of how China's top leaders actually viewed the world, but was a convenient way of justifying Chinese actions and dividing opinion in the Western governments and countries.

44. Cited in Whiting, "New Light on Mao," 265, 267.

45. Among those analysts arguing that no major differences between Moscow and Beijing emerged during the crisis are Barnett, *China and the Major Powers*, 34–37, 344–46, footnote 40; Morton H. Halperin and Tang Tsou, "The 1958 Quemoy Crisis," in *Sino-Soviet Relations and Arms Control*, Cambridge: Harvard University Press, 1967, 265–303; Morton H. Halperin, *China and the Bomb*, New York: Praeger, 1965, 55. Those maintaining that Chinese leaders were dissatisfied with the level of Soviet support during the crisis include Donald S. Zagoria, *The Sino-Soviet Conflict, 1956–1961*, New York: Atheneum, 1964, 200–221; John R. Thomas, "The Quemoy Crisis of 1958," in *Sino-Soviet Military Relations*, Raymond L. Garthoff, ed., New York: Praeger, 1966, 114–49.

46. Liu Xiao, *Eight Years as Ambassador*, 64–65.

47. Barnett, *China and the Major Powers*, 36, and footnote 4, 344–45.

48. Liu Xiao, *Eight Years as Ambassador*, 62–63.

49. Khrushchev, *Khrushchev Remembers*, 255.

50. Ibid., p. 261.

51. Liu Xiao, *Eight Years as Ambassador*, 9–11.

52. Ibid., p. 65.

53. Nie Rongzhen, *Memoir*, 803–4.

54. Andrei Gromyko, *Memories*, London, Sydney, Auckland: Hutchinson, 1989, 174.

55. Dwight D. Eisenhower, *The White House Years, Waging Peace: 1956–1961*, Garden City, N.J.: Doubleday, 1965, 445.

56. Ulam, *Expansion and Coexistence*, 621–33; Adam B. Ulam, *Dangerous Relations: The Soviet Union in World Politics, 1970–1982*, New York: Oxford University Press, 1983, 28–30.

57. Raymond L. Garthoff, "Sino-Soviet Military Relations, 1945–1966," *Sino-Soviet Military Relations*, Garthoff, ed. 90; "Statement by the Spokesman of the Chinese Government," in *Peking Review*, August 16, 1963, 7–15.

58. Liu Xiao, *Eight Years as Ambassador*, 87–88. The circumstances of the Warsaw Pact conference in which Kang's statement was made conform to Ulam's hypothesis regarding Khrushchev's hope for a Soviet-U.S. deal linking Germany and China. The conference dealt mainly with bloc strategy toward Germany and disarmament. Khrushchev wanted the bloc to push for the United States to agree to making Berlin a free city and sign a peace treaty involving West and East Germany. Were Washington to do this, it would break with Bonn over important issues. Regarding disarmament, Khrushchev hoped for progress in the ten-nation (of which China was not one) East-West disarmament talks scheduled to begin in March 1960 in Geneva. Wu Xiuquan was also a CCP delegate to the Warsaw Pact conference. Unfortunately, Wu's published memoir concludes in 1958. The U.S.–West German position at this juncture was to uphold the prospect of eventual German reunification.

59. Khrushchev, *Khrushchev Remembers*, 265. Regarding Sino-Soviet differences over policy toward India, see "The Truth About How the Leaders of the C.P.S.U. Have Allied Themselves with India Against China," *Peking Review*, no. 45 (November 8, 1963), 18–27; Richard L Siegel, "Chinese Efforts to Influence Soviet Policy to India," *India Quarterly*, vol. xxiv, no. 3 (July–September 1968), 223–35.

60. Khrushchev, *Khrushchev Remembers*, 306–11. For the Chinese side, See Liu Xiao, *Eight Years as Ambassador*, 74–77.

61. *Long Live Leninism* is in *Peking Review*, April 26, 1960. Compendium of documents from the Sino-Soviet polemical debates are listed in note 9 of Chapter Six. Regarding the evolution of the Sino-Soviet split, see Allen S. Whiting, "The Sino-Soviet Split," *The Cambridge History of China*, Denis Twitchett and John King Fairbank, eds., vol. 14 (The People's Republic, Part I: The Emergence of Revolutionary China, 1949–1965), Cambridge: Cambridge University Press, 1987, 478–538; Donald S. Zagoria, *The Sino-Soviet Conflict, 1956–1961*,Princeton, N.J.: Princeton University Press, 1962; Clubb, *Great Game*, 426–50; Barnett, *China and the Major Powers*, 21–87; Hinton, *Turbulent Quest*, 96–126.

62. Regarding the territorial conflict, see Dennis J. Doolin, *Territorial Claims in the Sino-Soviet Conflict: Documents and Analysis*, Stanford, Calif.: Hoover Institution, 1965; Tai Sung An, *The Sino-Soviet Territorial Dispute*, Philadelphia: Westminster, 1973.

Chapter Three

The Period
of Sino-American Cooperation
against the Soviet Union

SOVIET-AMERICAN COLLUSION AGAINST CHINA

The road to Sino-American anti-Soviet cooperation led through Soviet-American "collusion," as China's leaders termed it, against the PRC. By 1963 at the latest, U.S. leaders were aware of the reality of the Sino-Soviet split and began considering its implications for U.S. policy. American leaders tended to perceive the Sino-Soviet schism through the lens of "convergence theory" then popular in the United States. According to this theory, the complexities of industrial society were incompatible with ideological dogmatism. While a relatively simple, agrarian society might find adequate ideological solutions to its problems, this would not be the case with a complex industrial society. Thus, as a society industrialized, it would become less ideological. China, being a poor, pre-industrial society, was still in the ideological stage of development. Moreover, China was still in the utopian messianic stage of its revolution, and it would take some time before the expansionist militancy characteristic of that stage burned itself out. The Soviet Union, on the other hand, was already well along the road to industrialization. Soviet leaders were, therefore, beginning to understand the inadequacy of ideology and were becoming increasingly pragmatic. This translated into a businesslike approach to interactions with the United States. The relative wealth of the Soviet Union also meant that it was comparatively satisfied and had more to lose in the event of war. The poverty of China, on the other hand, meant that it was more dissatisfied and had less to lose in the event of war. In sum, the PRC was judged to be a militant and ideologically driven state, while Soviet Communism was presumed to be "mellowing." It followed that China still had to be contained, while the Soviet Union could be worked with.

A key area in which Washington hoped to work with the Soviet Union had to do with preventing the proliferation of nuclear weapons. As was noted earlier, agreement to discuss a ban on nuclear tests was reached during Khrushchev's 1959 visit to the United States. By early 1963, those talks were approaching agreement and in August a treaty was signed banning nuclear tests in the earth's atmosphere.

The conclusion of the partial test ban treaty was an important juncture for triangular relations. It was the first superpower action to jointly regulate their nuclear competition. As such it set the superpowers on the path that led to the Strategic Arms Limitations Talks (SALT) agreements of the 1970s. From China's perspective, however, the 1963 test ban agreement represented a definitive Soviet reiteration of its commitment to peaceful coexistence and rejection of China's calls for a more militant approach to the United States. It also touched directly on China's own nuclear ambitions. If China could not test nuclear weapons, it could not develop them; or at least, it could not be confident that its designs would work. More generally, the test ban agreement implied that Moscow and Washington would work together to prevent the proliferation of nuclear weapons; that is, to prevent other countries from developing such weapons. In Beijing's words, Moscow had "joined imperialists to consolidate their nuclear monopoly and bind the hands of all peace-loving countries subjected to the nuclear threat." The test ban treaty's central purpose, according to Beijing, was to "prevent all threatened peace-loving countries, including China, from increasing their defense capacity."[1]

Beijing sent a series of memoranda to Moscow warning that China "would not tolerate" steps aimed at limiting its nuclear options and explicitly asking Moscow not to sign the test ban agreement. One Chinese memorandum of September 1962 said: "It was a matter for the Soviet government whether it committed itself to refrain from transferring nuclear weapons and technical information concerning their manufacture to China; but...the Chinese government hoped the Soviet government would not infringe on China's sovereign rights and act for China in assuming an obligation to refrain from manufacturing nuclear weapons."[2]

Moscow ignored Beijing's protests. To Beijing this was final proof that Moscow set higher value on cooperation with the United States than on maintaining its putative alliance with the PRC. After the test ban treaty, plans for new discussions between the CCP and the CPSU collapsed, polemics became more explicit and bitter, and China began rejecting the idea of cooperation with the Soviet Union against the

United States. After 1963, Beijing treated the Soviet Union not as a revolutionary, but a counterrevolutionary country. This was a crucial stage, probably essential in psychological terms, that opened the door to eventual Sino-American rapprochement.

From 1963 until 1970, Beijing bitterly condemned Soviet-American "collusion" against China. The two superpowers were working hand in glove against China, Beijing charged. They wished to keep China vulnerable to their "nuclear blackmail," and otherwise weaken and oppose it. From the perspective of China's Communist leaders, this was the second time they faced a joint superpower condominium antithetical to the interests of their revolution.

American and Soviet policies toward China were, in fact, increasingly similar during the 1960s. The basic premise of U.S. Asian policy remained unchanged: the containment of China. Events in Indochina (or more precisely, U.S. perceptions of those events) gave additional emphasis to this objective. The Soviet Union too thought increasingly in terms of political-military arrangements that would constrain China. This convergence of Soviet and American goals sometimes translated into parallel policies. In South Asia, for example, both Moscow and Washington encouraged Pakistan and India to settle the differences between themselves and to direct their energies toward containing China. When those efforts failed and war erupted between India and Pakistan in September 1965, Washington supported a Soviet mediation effort to end that war. Throughout the 1960s, both superpowers worked to strengthen India against China. More generally, as hundreds of thousands of American soldiers were committed to South Vietnam, largely in order to contain China (or so U.S. leaders thought), more and more Soviet troops were deployed to China's northern and western borders. From Beijing's perspective, the USSR and the United States were cooperating to threaten revolutionary China.[3]

Beijing also saw anti-China purposes in various Soviet-U.S. strategic arms agreements. In fact, Beijing maintained, these agreements amounted to a superpower anti-China "nuclear alliance." In June 1967, President Lyndon Johnson and Soviet Premier Alexi Kosygin met at Glassboro, New Jersey, for the first superpower summit since the aborted meeting between John Kennedy and Khrushchev at Geneva in 1961. During the Glassboro meeting, Johnson and Kosygin agreed to conclude a non-proliferation treaty (NPT) committing their nations, and other countries that could be persuaded to sign the treaty, not to support the development of atomic and nuclear weapons by currently non-nuclear powers. Press reports at the time of the Glassboro meeting (as well as Johnson's own subsequent memoirs) indicated that a desire to hobble China's rapidly advancing nuclear weapons program was a key factor underlying the agreement.[4] Foreign ministerial and sub-cabinet level talks followed the Glassboro summit. Progress was rapid. The NPT was made public in August 1967 and signed in July 1968.

Beijing denounced the Glassboro talks as an important development in the superpower anti-China alliance. According to *Peking Review*, "The Soviet revisionists are out to conclude a worldwide package deal with the U.S. imperialists...directed primarily at socialist China."[5] Regarding the NPT, it was a joint superpower move to keep China weak and vulnerable to superpower nuclear threats. Moscow and Washington "had to come up with the [NPT] in the hope of using it as a means of agitation against China and to contain socialist China's influence abroad." The superpowers hoped to "have a free hand to vigorously carry out their nuclear blackmail and nuclear threats to control and bully other countries."[6]

Another step in the superpower anti-China nuclear alliance came with Soviet and American decisions to develop anti-China anti-ballistic missile (ABM) systems. Moscow announced development of an effective anti-missile missile in 1963, and in November 1966 announced the deployment of an ABM system to protect Moscow. Soviet shock at China's seemingly cavalier attitude toward nuclear war had apparently combined with the escalation of the Sino-Soviet conflict and China's rapid progress toward the acquisition of nuclear weapons to persuade Soviet leaders of the wisdom of a defense against Chinese nuclear rockets.

But while the Soviet ABM program was directed at a perceived Chinese threat, it also had important implications for the Soviet-U.S. nuclear balance. If either superpower developed an ABM system adequate to provide a credible defense against the incoming ICBMs of the other, a so-called "thick" ABM system, it might seriously erode the second-strike capability (the assured retaliatory capability) of the other superpower. Since a stable deterrent balance between the superpowers rested on their mutual assured destruction—on each side's vulnerability to the certain retaliatory strike that would follow any first strike—"thick" ABM systems might lead to a destabilization of the superpower deterrent balance. If, on the other hand, the superpowers agreed to forgo "thick" ABM systems, they would be agreeing to remain vulnerable to each other's retaliatory forces, thereby implicitly ruling out the use of nuclear weapons against one another. Further, if they agreed that they would both develop only "thin" ABM systems that would be effective against a strike by a secondary nuclear power such as China, they would be agreeing that they would both maintain a first-strike capability against China while ruling out the use of nuclear weapons against one another.

U.S. leaders were very concerned about the potentially destabilizing consequences of Moscow's ABM decision and pushed during the Glassboro summit for an agreement to mutually limit ABM systems to "thin" systems. Kosygin was willing to begin discussions on a mutual Soviet-U.S. limitation of ABM systems, but insisted that these talks be linked to talks on limitations on offensive land- and sea-based missile forces. Those talks did not begin until 1969. In the meantime, the United States decided to deploy a "thin" ABM system of its own. In announcing that decision in September 1967, U.S. Secretary of Defense Robert McNamara explained that the system was intended to guard against a nuclear threat from China over the next decade or so. To maintain the credibility of the U.S. "nuclear umbrella" over the non-Communist countries of Asia, McNamara explained in his memoir, the United States had to convince those countries and China that the United States was prepared to use nuclear weapons to protect China's neighbors against Chinese nuclear threats. To do this, the United States had to retain the capability to use nuclear weapons against China without fear of Chinese retaliation-in-kind.[7]

From Beijing's perspective, U.S. and Soviet decisions to deploy light ABM systems constituted a major step forward in the superpower "nuclear alliance" against China. As a commentary in *People's Daily* said in response to the U.S. decision to deploy a light anti-China ABM system:

> The Johnson Administration recently yelled about constructing a so-called "anti-ballistic missile system" in an all-out agitation against China....It is clear that China's possession of nuclear weapons and missiles has sent a chill down the spine of the U.S. imperialists....A French newspaper pointed out recently that the U.S. undertaking to build a thin anti-ballistic network was the result of a "tacit understanding reached by Lyndon Johnson and Alexi Kosygin at their Glassboro talks." The Johnson Administration informed the Soviet revisionist ruling clique of its decision before announcing it....All this reveals the insidious scheme of the U.S. imperialists and the Soviet revisionists to step up their military collaboration against China....Khrushchev and his successors, Brezhnev and Kosygin, threw off all disguises and openly concluded one dirty nuclear deal after another with U.S. imperialism. Washington not only feels perfectly at ease with nuclear weapons in the hands of the Soviet revisionist clique, but also plots with the Kremlin to oppose socialist China.[8]

Such strident condemnations of Soviet-U.S. collusion continued until 1970. They did little to reverse the trend toward superpower cooperation. They may, in fact, have been counterproductive, since they confirmed American and Soviet images of an irrational and bellicose China.

SOVIET-AMERICAN CONTENTION AND THE DECISION FOR RAPPROCHEMENT WITH THE UNITED STATES

By the fall of 1968, major differences of opinion began to emerge within China's elite over China's alignments vis-à-vis the superpowers. One group of leaders, led by Zhou Enlai, argued against continuing a simultaneous confrontation with both superpowers and in favor of a tilt toward the United States. A second group, led by Defense Minister Lin Biao, advocated continued opposition to the United States, probably in loose alignment with the Soviet Union.

The debate between Lin and Zhou was conducted in terms of an analysis of U.S. imperialism and the threat it posed to China. Lin and Zhou agreed that U.S. imperialism was in a state of severe crisis. It was bogged down in an unwinnable war in Vietnam, the human, fiscal, and political costs of which were mounting. Internally, the United States was racked by the turmoil associated with the civil rights movement and riots in black ghettos of many U.S. cities. Inflation was also mounting, and the United States was moving rapidly toward a deficit in its merchandise trade accounts.

While agreeing that the United States was in a crisis, Lin and Zhou drew very different conclusions. Lin argued that the United States still posed the greatest threat to China and to all the peoples of Asia. U.S. imperialism continued to occupy Taiwan and prevent its liberation. It still waged war to suppress the Vietnamese people's national liberation movement. It still attacked China's ally, North Vietnam. It still occupied South Korea, the Philippines, Thailand, Japan, and many other places in Asia, and oppressed and exploited their peoples. And it still encouraged the revival of Japanese militarism.

Lin agreed that the United States was reeling from defeat. Yet this was precisely the moment to push the revolutionary struggle against U.S. imperialism to a new stage. Mao Zedong's writings on warfare taught that the time to attack the enemy was precisely when his forces were in disarray and retreat. Now was the time, Lin argued, for an offensive by the revolutionary peoples of Asia against U.S. imperialism. The vanguard of this offensive would be the armed national liberation movements of the people of Asia: South Vietnam, Laos, Japan, Thailand, Burma, Indonesia, Malaysia, India, the Philippines. Behind this front line would stand the Asian socialist countries—North Vietnam, North Korea, and China—who would give solid support and encouragement. The objective of this revolutionary offensive was nothing less than toppling the whole system of U.S. power in Asia and driving the U.S. imperialists out of the entire region. Prospects for the victory of such a revolutionary united front against U.S. imperialism were, Lin believed, excellent.

The deepening crisis of U.S. imperialism made it more dangerous than ever, Lin argued. As U.S. imperialism went down in defeat it could lash out in its death throes, attacking China or the other Asian socialist countries. To deal with such an eventuality, China should substantially increase defense spending and maintain vigilance against possible U.S. attack. To adopt a conciliatory attitude toward the United States at this juncture, Lin argued, would only make it more arrogant and reckless.

Lin's policy prescriptions regarding the Soviet Union are less clear than those regarding the United States. Some analysts have argued that Lin favored a continuation of the dual adversary approach, relying on increased defense expenditures and military preparations to deal with joint superpower hostility. Others have argued that while Lin may have initially favored such an approach, by 1970 he had decided that it was untenable and favored a tilt toward the Soviet Union.[9] Scholars are unanimous, however, in concluding that Lin adamantly opposed improved relations with the United States.

Zhou Enlai reached quite different conclusions from the apparent crisis of U.S. imperialism. Because the United States was increasingly enfeebled, Zhou maintained, it was unlikely to attack China. U.S. rulers increasingly realized the limitations of their power and were looking for ways to retrench their commitments. In such circumstances, Washington might be willing to relax its policy of containment of China. Washington was already searching for a way out of Vietnam, and sooner or later the United States would withdraw its military forces from that country. The Soviet Union, on the other hand, was a rising imperialist power that was increasingly aggressive—a fact demonstrated by the Soviet occupation of Czechoslovakia in August 1968. It followed that China should rebuild its international ties to place more constraints on the Soviet Union.

A major factor in the Lin-Zhou debate, and in China's decision for rapprochement with the United States, was a spiraling military confrontation between the USSR and China following a clash on the Ussuri River in March 1969. This is discussed in Chapter Fourteen. Here we may note that as the 1969 crisis escalated, Chinese fears of Soviet attack mounted and Chinese leaders concluded that China's isolation heightened the dangers of such an attack.

Zhou Enlai argued, and Mao Zedong eventually accepted Zhou's argument, that the superpowers were contending with one another as well as colluding against China, and that China should seek to exploit this contention via diplomatic maneuver. The intensity of the contradiction between U.S. imperialism and "Soviet social imperialism" was so intense, Zhou argued, that it was possible for China to use U.S. power to help check Soviet aggression. Through deft diplomacy China could divide the superpowers by improving relations with the United States, then use the strength of the United States to offset that of the Soviet Union. In ancient Chinese statecraft such a strategy was known as "using barbarians to control barbarians."[10] Internal PLA documents issued in 1973 explained Sino-American rapprochement in the following terms:

> Chairman Mao invited Nixon to visit China in order to exploit contradictions. He teaches us: "It is necessary to pool together all struggles and grasp all contradictions which exist in the enemy camp and use them

as a weapon of primary importance against the existing enemy." Our invitation to Nixon to visit China proceeded precisely from Chairman Mao's tactical thinking: "exploiting contradictions, winning over the majority, opposing the minority, and destroying them one by one."[11]

The debate between Zhou Enlai and Lin Biao occurred against a backdrop of rapidly developing Soviet-American detente that increased the danger that, unless China acted quickly, the two superpowers might step up their cooperation against China. In his inaugural address in January 1969, President Richard Nixon announced his desire for basic improvements in American-Soviet relations. Moscow responded with alacrity and Soviet-American negotiations were soon underway over strategic arms limitations, trade, cultural exchanges, and other issues. There were also signs that cooperation against China might be one element of the new American-Soviet detente. In accepting Nixon's bid for talks on the limitation of strategic missile forces, Moscow proposed that the stalled talks on the ABM issue be revived as well. Nixon accepted. He also announced a decision to continue with development of a thin ABM system, saying that it was directed against China and not the Soviet Union, and noting that the Soviet Union had an interest similar to that of the United States in countering China's nuclear threat.[12]

As the Sino-Soviet border confrontation escalated during 1969, Moscow pushed for an understanding with the United States that would allow Moscow to launch a preemptive strike against China's nuclear facilities. During discussions with National Security Adviser Henry Kissinger in April 1969, Soviet Ambassador Anatoli Dobrynin insisted that China "was everyone's problem" and suggested joint Soviet-U.S. action to deal with that problem before it was too late. Dobrynin hinted that Soviet support for an independent Taiwan might be part of such a superpower understanding regarding Beijing.[13] As the border crisis escalated during the summer and fall, Soviet proposals became more blunt. Soviet efforts took the most explicit form during the first round of SALT talks at Vienna in July 1970 when the Soviet delegate tabled a draft Soviet-American agreement regarding nuclear "provocations" by third powers. According to the agreement, if such provocations were being prepared, the Soviet Union and the United States would inform one another. If "provocative actions" actually took place, each superpower was to take retaliatory action against the offending party. As Henry Kissinger saw this proposal, the United States was "being asked to give the USSR a free hand against China; it was a blatant embodiment of condominium."[14]

From the Soviet perspective, time was running out for preemptive action against China. China's drive to build a viable nuclear force was proceeding rapidly. China tested its first atomic bomb in 1964 and its first hydrogen bomb in 1967. In October 1966 a rocket carried an atomic warhead to a test target some 800 kilometers distant.[15] By early 1969 Western intelligence agencies estimated that the PRC would soon test a rocket with a 6,000-mile range.[16] Unless Moscow acted promptly to destroy China's nuclear arms facilities, it would soon be able to exercise that option only at the risk of Chinese nuclear retaliation. Moscow was seriously considering such a preemptive strike against China, but wanted an assurance that the United States would not seek to exploit ensuing Sino-Soviet difficulties.

Joint superpower action to preempt China's nuclear threat would have been a logical development of certain trends in Soviet-American cooperation. With the NPT the superpowers had agreed to cooperate to prevent the spread of nuclear weapons. By 1969 both superpowers were deploying thin ABM systems to counter a nuclear threat from China. Both superpowers were at loggerheads with China. Why not cooperate to preempt China's burgeoning nuclear program?

China's leaders were extremely apprehensive that the United States might accept Soviet offers. They watched carefully for signs that the superpowers were moving toward greater collusion. Xinhua was very suspicious, for example, when Soviet Marshal Vasily Chuikov went to Washington in April 1969 to attend the funeral of Dwight Eisenhower and took the occasion to hold talks at the Pentagon with top U.S. military leaders. When Soviet-U.S. preliminary SALT talks began in Helsinki in November 1969, Beijing saw this as a "further development of the U.S.-Soviet nuclear military alliance against China."[17]

In Washington, Nixon and his National Security Adviser Henry Kissinger were well aware of the opportunities and dangers that the Sino-Soviet conflict presented the United States. Moscow's desire for U.S. support against China, or alternately, Moscow's desire to prevent a U.S.-Chinese alignment against the Soviet Union, created important incentives for Moscow to cooperate with the United States. As Nixon explained, "I understood the pressure placed on Moscow by the rivalry with Peking....The greatest incentive for Soviet cooperation on Vietnam was our new relationship with the Chinese."[18] Regarding China, Beijing's desire to dissuade Washington from endorsing Soviet actions against China might induce it to improve relations with the United States and to lessen its opposition to the United States' Vietnam policy. Most fundamentally, Nixon believed that U.S. interests would not be served by a Chinese military defeat by the Soviet Union. If China were "smashed" or humiliated in a Sino-Soviet war, Moscow would be able to shift its entire military weight to oppose the Western alliance. Moreover, a demonstration of such Soviet ruthlessness might intimidate other countries along the periphery of the Soviet Union, further enhancing Soviet influence. Since the Soviet Union constituted a greater threat to the United States than did China, Nixon concluded that the United States should support China against Soviet pressure.[19]

During 1969 and 1970 United States actions toward the Sino-Soviet conflict generally confirmed Zhou Enlai's predictions about China's ability to maneuver Washington against Moscow. During a tour of Asian countries in mid-1969, Nixon informed Asian leaders that the United States would not support Soviet proposals for collective security in Asia. "A [Soviet-American] condominium is out of the question," he told Thailand's prime minister.[20] To Pakistan's leader, Nixon said that the United States would not join with the Soviet Union to isolate China but hoped, instead, for better Sino-American relations. When Sino-Soviet border confrontation peaked during the fall of 1969, Under Secretary of State Elliot Richardson announced that, while the United States would not side with either Communist power against the other, it would nonetheless be "deeply concerned...with an escalation of [the Sino-Soviet quarrel] into a massive breach of international peace and security."[21] In effect, Washington used its influence to deter a Soviet attack on China. During the first meeting of the renewed ambassadorial-level talks in Warsaw in January 1970, the U.S. side informed China that the United States would not participate in a condominium with the Soviet Union in Asia or elsewhere. That July, Washington indirectly informed Beijing of Moscow's Helsinki proposal, and the U.S. rejection, of a joint superpower response to provocative actions by nuclear third powers. All these moves substantiated Zhou Enlai's assertion regarding the possibility of using U.S. influence to offset Soviet pressure.

China's response to U.S. overtures during 1969 and 1970 was strongly influenced by the struggle between Zhou Enlai and Lin Biao. As a result of that conflict, Chinese policy was erratic, with initiatives toward one superpower, initiated by one faction, being negated and superseded by moves toward the other superpower initiated by the other faction. In November 1968 China agreed to reopen the ambassadorial talks with the United States at Warsaw in February 1969, only to cancel those talks the day before they were scheduled to begin. The Warsaw talks were finally resumed in January 1970, only to be suspended again when U.S. and South Vietnamese forces invaded Cambodia in April 1970. Chinese policy then moved in a sharply anti–United States direction, before finally moving back toward an anti-Soviet orientation in October.

The turning point in the struggle between Lin and Zhou came at a plenary session of the Central Committee in September 1970, at which a strong elite coalition coalesced around Zhou. At that plenum, key military leaders broke with Lin, and Mao Zedong came down unequivocally on Zhou's side. Shortly after the plenum, Zhou sent a message to Nixon via Pakistan's president (Pakistan was Mao and Zhou's preferred channel of communication with Washington during this period) saying that Nixon's special envoy would be welcome in Beijing to discuss outstanding issues. Mao also sent his own signal by inviting American writer Edgar Snow, an old friend of his, to stand beside him atop Tiananmen gate during the National Day celebrations on October 1, 1970. This latter signal was too oblique, however, to be understood by the Americans.

China's decision for rapprochement with the United States was also tied to shifts in Washington's Indochina policies. In March 1968, President Johnson rejected the U.S. military's request for 206,000 more U.S. troops for Vietnam, halted the U.S. bombing of North Vietnam, indicated a willingness to begin peace talks with Hanoi, and withdrew from the 1968 presidential race. Zhou Enlai apparently concluded from these dramatic moves that the United States had changed directions in Vietnam and would eventually withdraw from that country. At a minimum, this would ease U.S. military pressure on China's southern flank. The U.S.–South Vietnamese invasion of Cambodia in April 1970 led to a temporary suspension of moves toward the United States, but progress in that direction resumed in late 1970. The first public bid to the United States—an invitation to a U.S. table tennis team competing in Japan to visit China—came only in April 1971, after the United States did not reescalate the Indochina war in response to the February 1971 defeat of a South Vietnamese invasion of southern Laos.

The terms of Sino-American rapprochement were worked out during a secret trip to China by Henry Kissinger in July 1971 and during a well-publicized visit by President Nixon in February of 1972. The new Sino-American relation was multidimensional, but at its core was an understanding regarding the relations of both powers with the Soviet Union. This understanding was embodied in an article of the joint communiqué providing that "neither should seek hegemony in the Asia-Pacific region and each is opposed to efforts by any other country or group of countries to establish such hegemony."[22] In effect, this was a promise by China not to support Soviet policies against the United States in East Asia and a promise by the United States to use its influence to prevent a Soviet attack on China. In exchange for China's pledge of independence from Moscow, the United States agreed to stop trying to block Chinese efforts to expand its own contacts and influence. That is, the United States agreed to abandon the containment of China.

One result of China's rapprochement with the United States was the rapid expansion of Beijing's diplomatic relations with U.S. friends. The expansion of diplomatic ties with other countries in fact became a key component of the PRC's new foreign policy line. The restoration of diplomatic links severed during the Cultural Revolution had begun in May 1969 under the impetus of the mounting military confrontation with the Soviet Union. Beijing's renewed diplomatic activism soon developed, however, into more than a mere restoration of old ties. Beijing's immediate objective was admission to the United Nations. To this end, Beijing began showing a high degree of flexibility in an effort to establish diplomatic ties with former enemies. Between October 1970 and October 1971, diplomatic links were established with an additional fourteen countries, while relations with an additional two countries were upgraded to ambassadorial level. Table 3–1 illustrates the expansion of China's diplomatic relations.

Beijing also worked to "thicken" ties with various countries. Sending and receiving official and unofficial delegations of all sorts was one way of doing that. In 1971 alone 290 delegations from eighty foreign countries were sent or received. During their visits in China these delegations were fêted, a practice that the foreign media dubbed "banquet diplomacy." In 1970 Beijing also resumed the practice of giving development assistance, pledging the huge amount of $700 million in that year alone. To facilitate the expansion of interstate ties, the volume and stridency of Chinese revolutionary propaganda substantially diminished.[23]

Beijing's campaign to assume China's seat in the United Nations was greatly facilitated by the easing of U.S. hostility. But while Washington had dropped its policy of isolating the PRC, it remained committed to the continued de facto independence of Taiwan. In August 1971 the United States submitted resolutions to the United Nations calling for admission of the PRC to the U.N. Security Council while allowing Nationalist China on Taiwan to retain its seat in the General Assembly. Japan co-sponsored the resolution. The U.S.-Japan resolution was sidetracked in October when the General Assembly rejected 59 to 55 (with 15 abstentions) a U.S. resolution declaring the expulsion of Taiwan and admission of the PRC to be an "important question" requiring a two-thirds majority. This opened the way for approval of an Albanian resolution expelling Taiwan and admitting the PRC by a simple majority. The vote was 76 to 35, with 17 abstentions. Before the Albanian resolution came to a vote, however, Taiwan's representatives withdrew from the United Nations to avoid expulsion. The U.S. resolution on dual representation was thus mute and never came to a vote.

The hope of driving a wedge between Washington and Taibei may have been one factor entering into Beijing's decision for rapprochement with the United States. At least, this was later used to justify rapprochement with the United States. The internal PLA educational documents referred to earlier explained that improvement of relations with the United States was a way of exploiting contradictions between U.S. imperialism and its "lackeys," especially Chiang Kai-shek's "gang."[24] It is entirely possible, however, that it was intended to rebut critics of the opening to Washington. More likely yet, it was a manifestation of the common psychological tendency of people's belief structures to tend toward consistency. That is, if several important

Table 3–1 Countries Recognizing the PRC

1949	Union of Soviet Socialist Republics	1963	Kenya	1974	Guinea Bissau
	Bulgaria		Burundi		Gabon
	Romania	1964	Tunisia		Malaysia
	Hungary		France		Trinidad and Tobago
	Czechoslovakia		Congo (Brazzaville)		Venezuela
	Democratic People's Republic of Korea (North Korea)		Central African Republic		Niger
			Zambia		Brazil
			Dahomey		Gambia
	Poland	1965	Mauritania	1975	Botswana
	Yugoslavia	1968	South Yemen		Philippines
	Mongolia	1970	Canada		Mozambique
	German Democratic Republic (East Germany)		Equatorial Guinea		Bangladesh
			Italy		Thailand
			Ethiopia		Sao Tome
	Albania		Chile		Fiji
	Burma	1971	Nigeria		Western Samoa
	India		Kuwait		Comoros
1950	Pakistan		Cameroon	1976	Cape Verde
	United Kingdom		Austria		Surinam
	Ceylon		Sierra Leone		Seychelles
	Norway		Turkey		Papua New Guinea
	Denmark		Iran	1977	Liberia
	Israel		Belgium		Barbados
	Afghanistan		Peru		Jordan
	Finland		Lebanon	1978	Oman
	Sweden		Rwanda		Libya
	Democratic Republic of Vietnam (North Vietnam)		Senegal	1979	United States
			Iceland		Djibouti
	Switzerland		Cyprus		Portugal
	Netherlands	1972	Argentina		Ireland
	Indonesia		Mexico	1980	Colombia
1955	Nepal		Malta		Ecuador
1956	United Arab Republic (Egypt)		Mauritius		Kiribati
			Greece	1982	Vanuatu
	Syria		Guyana		Angola
	Yemen		Togo	1983	Antigua and Baruda
1958	Cambodia		Japan		Ivory Coast
	Iraq		German Federal Republic (West Germany)		Lesotho
	Morocco			1984	United Arab Emirates
1959	Sudan		Maldives	1985	Bolivia
1960	Ghana		Malagasy		Grenada
	Cuba		Luxembourg		Nicaragua
	Mali		Zaire	1987	Belize
	Somalia		Chad		Uruguay
1961	Senegal		Australia	1988	Qatar
	Tanzania		New Zealand		Palestinian state
1962	Laos	1973	Spain	1989	Bahrain
	Algeria		Upper Volta	1990	Marshall Islands
	Uganda				

Sources: For the 1949–1964 period, adapted from A.M. Halpern, *Policies Toward China: Views from Six Continents*, New York: McGraw-Hill, 1965, 496–97. For years 1965–1979, *China: U.S. Policy Since 1945*, Washington, D.C.: Congressional Quarterly, 1980, 202. Data for years 1980–1990 are from *China Quarterly* and *Beijing Review*.

aspects of something are judged to be "good," there will be a strong tendency for other aspects to be judged "good" as well. Since Sino-American rapprochement made sense from the standpoint of security against the Soviet Union and the easing of U.S. containment, there was thus a psychological tendency to conclude that it made sense from the standpoint of the recovery of Taiwan as well.

CHINA AND SOVIET-AMERICAN DETENTE

From 1972 until 1978, Sino-American rapprochement and Soviet-American detente unfolded more or less in tandem. The Sino-American summit in early 1972 was followed by a Soviet-U.S. summit in May and the conclusion of the first SALT agreement and a comprehensive trade agreement at that meeting. Soviet-American detente continued with Brezhnev's visit to the United States in June 1973, a second Nixon visit to Moscow in June 1974, and summit agreements regarding preventing accidental nuclear war and creating a standing Soviet-American consultation committee.

Chinese leaders had grave doubts about Soviet-U.S. detente because it worked against the Chinese strategy of using the United States to offset Soviet pressure. To the extent that Washington was set on a course of cooperation with Moscow, it would be unwilling to antagonize Moscow by working against Soviet moves—including, perhaps, those directed against China. Beijing was also suspicious that Washington's real purpose was to use improved Sino-U.S. relations to gain leverage with the Soviet Union, after which Washington would strike a deal with Moscow at China's expense, rather as Khrushchev had attempted to do (or so China believed) with the United States in 1959. Superpower detente was too close to collusion for Beijing's comfort.

Because of such misgivings, Beijing downplayed the significance of superpower detente. The first SALT agreement, for instance, was dismissed by a joint editorial of *People's Daily*, *Red Flag*, and *Liberation Army Daily* as "a superficial compromise and easing off [which will] only serve to prepare for a new fight."[25] The agreement did not represent any real reduction of Soviet-U.S. tension or limitation of the superpower arms race. Nor did other detente agreements mean a lessening of the superpower contest for world hegemony. In China's annual address to the U.N. General Assembly in 1973, for example, Foreign Minister Qiao Guanhua condemned the Soviet-U.S. agreement on the prevention of nuclear war in the following terms:

> What they have done is simply to wrap up this contest [for world hegemony] in the form of an agreement. In fact, this agreement is a mere scrap of paper....The desperate struggle for nuclear superiority and world

hegemony still goes on. The contention between the Soviet Union and the United States now extends all over the world.[26]

Soviet leaders were as apprehensive about the new Sino-American relations as Beijing was about Soviet-U.S. detente. Moscow feared that the Sino-American tie would develop into a military alliance. It attempted to prevent this in two ways. First, it issued warnings to both Washington and Beijing about the dire consequences of such a development. Second, it pursued detente with the United States.[27] From the Soviet perspective, detente with the United States, and with the West generally, served two China-related purposes. First, it reduced the Western threat to the Soviet Union, thereby allowing Moscow to concentrate on China. Second, improved relations with the United States created additional incentives for Washington to abstain from military cooperation with China, for to do otherwise would risk a deterioration of cordial Soviet-U.S. relations. To the extent that the United States valued cooperative ties with the Soviet Union, and to the extent that it feared that overly close ties with China would alienate the Soviet Union, Washington would limit its military relations with China.

Moscow largely achieved this objective until late 1978. The Nixon and Ford administrations rejected the idea that Soviet apprehensions should limit U.S. relations with China, but during those years there was little Chinese interest in direct military ties with the United States. The steady expansion of Soviet power during the latter half of the 1970s, and the defeat of China's radicals by more pragmatic leaders in 1976 and 1977, led to increased Chinese interest in security links to the United States. But now U.S. policy had changed. Under President Jimmy Carter and Secretary of State Cyrus Vance, Washington sought to avoid moves toward China that would antagonize Moscow, and until late 1978, U.S. leaders declined Chinese bids out of fear of alienating the USSR. Carter's policy was to maintain a balanced relation with both Communist powers, avoiding military links with China in order to avoid endangering detente with the Soviet Union. It was only after the Vietnamese invasion of Cambodia in December 1978 and, more especially, after the Soviet invasion of Afghanistan in December 1979, that Carter became disillusioned about detente, and began heeding the advice of his more anti-detente National Security Adviser Zbigniew Brzezinski.[28]

Ironically, the U.S. refusal to join with Moscow against China may have been one factor inducing Moscow to adopt the more aggressive policies that ultimately precipitated Sino-American cooperation against the Soviet Union. Adam Ulam suggests that during the May 1972 summit, Leonid Brezhnev indicated willingness to cut aid to North Vietnam in exchange for U.S. cooperation with Soviet efforts to deal with the Chinese problem. Again during discussions at the June 1973 Nixon-Brezhnev summit, the Soviets made clear their fear of China's growing nuclear power and pushed for a Soviet-American understanding, this time in the form of an agreement on the non-use of nuclear weapons which would have put obstacles in the way of U.S. deterrent support for China. Nixon and Kissinger dodged Soviet hints, not wishing to entirely squelch Soviet hopes of eventual American assistance in this regard, which they saw as serving U.S. purposes, nor wishing to give Beijing reason to fear that the United States was using its ties with China as a way of gaining leverage with Moscow. By late 1974 it was clear to Moscow, according to Ulam, that Washington was not interested in trading U.S. support for Moscow against China for Soviet support for Washington against Vietnam. Moscow's interest in detente with the United States faded and it adopted increasingly aggressive moves in the Third World to counter the incipient Sino-American bloc.[29]

THE UNITED FRONT AGAINST HEGEMONY

During the early 1970s, Beijing agreed to certain improvements in Sino-Soviet relations as a way of lessening extreme tensions. Beijing continued the bilateral talks with Moscow that had begun in October 1969, largely as a way of keeping alive Soviet hopes for improvement in Sino-Soviet relations and dissuading Moscow from resorting to force against China. No progress was made at these talks, however, in part because China's Maoist radicals believed that any improvement in Sino-Soviet relations would only embolden Moscow to further aggression.[30]

By 1973 Mao Zedong and Zhou Enlai were increasingly troubled by what they took to be U.S. irresolution in the face of increasingly active Soviet expansionism, and concerned that the global balance of power might shift in favor of the Soviet Union. Consequently, they urged U.S. leaders to maintain vigorous containment of the Soviet Union.[31] Chinese concerns deepened in 1975. The inability of the United States to intervene in support of its client governments in Cambodia and South Vietnam as they collapsed during March and April boded ill for the ability of the United States to act as a check on Soviet ambitions. Shortly thereafter, Washington closed down U.S. bases in Thailand and withdrew the 23,000 U.S. troops from that country. In February of the next year SEATO was formally dissolved. Meanwhile, discussion mounted in the United States about abandoning the U.S. military bases in the Philippines in favor of bases in the Marianas Islands, a thousand miles further east.[32]

These events made Chinese leaders increasingly fearful that the United States was so traumatized by its Vietnam experience and befuddled by detente with the Soviet Union that it was retreating into isolationism and appeasement. Beijing also feared that Moscow had concluded from the historic defeat of the United States in Indochina that the global correlation of forces increasingly favored the Soviet Union, and that Moscow would seize on the collapse of U.S. power to expand the Soviet global position. These apprehensions were dramatically demonstrated on April 29, 1975, the day that Saigon fell to North Vietnamese forces. Xinhua's lead foreign story on that day dealt not with the historic events in Vietnam, but with a worldwide Soviet naval maneuver then underway. After noting Soviet naval activities in various oceans, the article called for increased vigilance against the danger of social imperialist aggression and expansion.[33]

Beijing responded to the collapse of the U.S. position in Indochina by stepping up its efforts to stabilize the East Asian balance. Within five weeks of Hanoi's victory over Saigon, Beijing established diplomatic relations with the Philippines and Thailand on the basis of a communiqué containing "anti-hegemony" provisions. Beijing thereby attempted to reassure these two pro-American governments, preventing them from reaching some sort of hasty accommodation with the Soviet Union. Beijing also launched a major propaganda campaign, warning Asian countries against allowing the Soviet social imperialist "tiger" in the back door while driving the U.S. imperialist "wolf" out the front door. Beijing also became increasingly explicit in its endorsement of the U.S. military presence in Asia. Most significantly, Chinese sources became increasingly supportive of the Japanese-U.S. alliance.[34]

Soviet activities in Africa added to Chinese concerns. 1975 and 1976 saw large-scale Soviet-supported Cuban interventions in Angola and Ethiopia. In neither case was the United States able to block Soviet advances. Both African countries swung into alignment with the Soviet Union. The Soviet position in South Yemen and Somalia also grew. Beijing believed that Moscow intended to use these footholds in the Third World to control the sea lanes over which flowed petroleum and raw materials vital to the Western nations.

Still another trend that disturbed Beijing was the rapid growth of Soviet military power combined with stagnating or declining Western defense budgets. Chinese analysts noted the rapid growth of Soviet arsenals of intercontinental ballistic missiles and observed that, unless these trends were reversed, the Soviet Union would soon enjoy nuclear superiority. Since 1971 the Chinese had been very skeptical of the U.S. doctrine of "essential equivalency" of Soviet and American strategic forces, fearing that this doctrine lulled the United States into acquiescing to a Soviet drive for strategic superiority.[35]

Beijing was also troubled by the steady advance of East-West detente in Europe. From Beijing's perspective, Moscow's "intention is to relax the situation in Europe and to stabilize the Western front so that it may spare both hands for fully opposing China."[36] Beijing was especially apprehensive of West Germany's Ostpolitik, the policy of normalizing relations with the Communist states of Eastern Europe initiated under

Chancellor Willy Brandt in October 1969 and continued under Helmut Schmidt after May 1974. Beijing feared that Bonn's Ostpolitik would undermine NATO and weaken West German military preparedness. Should this happen, Moscow would be able to concentrate its forces in the Far East. Beijing restrained its criticism of Bonn's Ostpolitik, however, because it was aware that too strident condemnation might induce Bonn to distance itself from China. When Bonn's Ostpolitik and Soviet-American detente culminated in the European Security Conference at Helsinki in August 1975, Beijing's apprehension deepened. "Instead of helping promote security and cooperation in Europe," *Beijing Review* said of the Helsinki conference, "[it] will only bring a false sense of security to the West European people." Moscow's objective was to split Western Europe and NATO, lull the people of Europe, and achieve domination in Europe under the smokescreen of detente.[37]

Chinese leaders also noted the steadily increasing strength of the Soviet divisions deployed along China's northern borders. These forces were increasingly supplied with Moscow's most up-to-date weapons: T-72 tanks, SS-20 intermediate range missiles, Backfire bombers, and chemical weapons. Meanwhile the Soviet Pacific fleet was being rapidly augmented.[38]

Taken together, international developments after 1974 were very ominous from Beijing's point of view. Because of detente in Europe, Moscow was able to concentrate its forces in the East against China. Soviet influence around the periphery of China was expanding. China was increasingly encircled by Soviet power. This situation is illustrated by Figure 3–1. Beijing feared that if existing trends continued unchecked, the Soviet Union might become dominant in East Asia and, perhaps, in the world. If this occurred, China's position would be extremely tenuous, as it would be virtually encircled by Soviet military positions while Moscow's Western rivals would be weak and disunited. China would then be compelled to either substantially step up its defense expenditures or accept Moscow's terms.

Mao, Zhou, and other Chinese leaders expressed their fears to U.S. leaders during various consultations, but probably felt that their warnings were less well understood by the Carter Administration than by the Republican practitioners of Realpolitik of the pre-1977 period. In early 1977, the Carter Administration announced its decision (later reversed) to withdraw U.S. ground forces from South Korea. And throughout the second half of the 1970s, the strength of U.S. military forces in East Asia and the Western Pacific steadily declined.[39] In a confidential report on the world situation in July 1977, Foreign Minister Huang Hua conveyed his concern over the direction of U.S. policy:

> Isolationism is rising in the United States while [U.S.] alienation of friendly nations is increasingly growing....With American power shrinking and

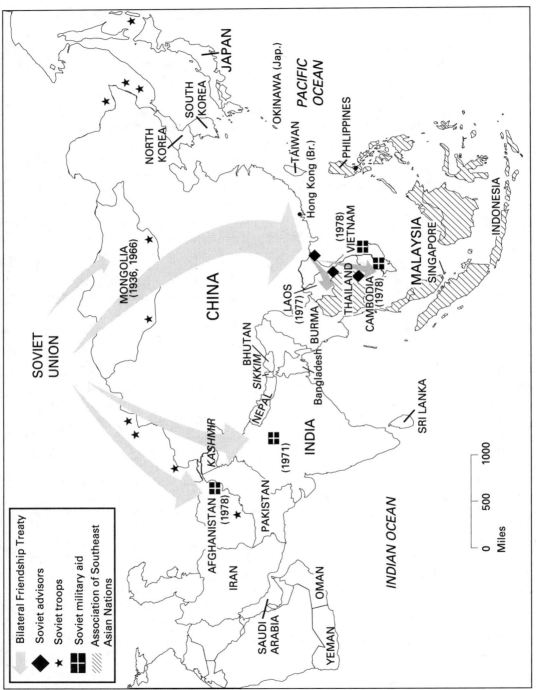

Figure 3–1 Soviet Encirclement of China, 1972–1982 (*China,' U.S. Policy Since 1945*, Washington, D.C.:: Congressional Quarterly, 1980. Reprinted with permission of Congressional Quarterly, Inc.)

Legend:

- Bilateral Friendship Treaty
- ◆ Soviet advisors
- ★ Soviet troops
- ⊞ Soviet military aid
- ░ Association of Southeast Asian Nations

SOVIET UNION

MONGOLIA (1936, 1966)

CHINA

NORTH KOREA

SOUTH KOREA

JAPAN

OKINAWA (Jap.)

PACIFIC OCEAN

TAIWAN

Hong Kong (Br.)

PHILIPPINES

LAOS (1977)

VIETNAM (1978)

THAILAND

CAMBODIA (1978)

BURMA

MALAYSIA

SINGAPORE

INDONESIA

BHUTAN

SIKKIM

NEPAL

Bangladesh

INDIA

SRI LANKA

KASHMIR

PAKISTAN (1971)

AFGHANISTAN (1978)

IRAN

SAUDI ARABIA

YEMAN

OMAN

INDIAN OCEAN

Miles

0   500   1000

isolationism surging, the revisionist Soviet social-imperialists are filling the vacuum left by the United States and are taking advantage of U.S. weakness to make expansionist and infiltrative moves. The retreat of U.S. influence, and the policy of appeasement and conciliation fueled by Western countries, will...help increase the haughtiness of the revisionist Soviet social-imperialists, and confront other countries...with a more dangerous and horrendous enemy. It is the business of the whole world to prevent the spread of revisionist Soviet social-imperialism's rampant aggressive forces....We must unite with the Third World, win over the Second World, and take advantage of the splits between the two superpowers to divide them and to undermine their collusive scheme to divide the world behind the scenes. By winning the United States over to our side, we can concentrate all our forces to deal with the arch-enemy—revisionist Soviet social-imperialism.[40]

Beijing responded to those alarming developments by calling for a global united front against Soviet hegemonism. Public Chinese statements carefully hedged the issue of Sino-American strategic cooperation, speaking instead in general terms of the unity of all possible forces to oppose Soviet expansionism. The implication was clear, however: a Sino-American united front to contain the Soviet Union. According to Beijing, the Soviet Union was too powerful to be dealt with by any one country. Moscow's drive for world hegemony could be frustrated by the broadest possible coalition of forces. All countries threatened by Soviet expansionism should increase their guard and actively counter Soviet thrusts. They should seek to disrupt Moscow's strategic preparations, supporting one another in their efforts. China's foreign propaganda became more strident, exhorting peoples and governments of the world to beware of Soviet duplicity. Detente was, Beijing increasingly warned, a sham to cover a more aggressive Soviet expansionism.[41]

Europe figured prominently in Beijing's putative global united front. Beijing did everything possible to raise Western European anti-Soviet vigilance. Chinese spokesmen and propaganda maintained that Moscow's global strategy remained focused on the domination of Europe, and that the danger of war in Europe was still very great. The Western European countries should not, Beijing warned, repeat the mistake of the 1930s by appeasing Soviet expansionism under the cover of detente. Such a course would only further embolden the Soviet Union and enhance the danger of war. Beijing was increasingly explicit in demanding higher Western European defense spending, a continuation of the U.S. military's role in Europe, and greater Western European unity.[42] Privately, the Chinese reminded Western leaders that Stalin had dealt with Hitler in 1939 only after Franco-British appeasement of Hitler at Munich had convinced him of the unreliability of the Western democracies as a counterweight to Nazi Germany.[43] Chinese leaders also let it be known that they thought that conservative European politicians had a more realistic view of the international situation than did more left-liberal leaders. They also indicated that they felt the entry of anti-NATO Euro-Communists into Western European governments would not be a good thing.

There were remarkable similarities between the united front against Soviet hegemony of the late 1970s and the united front against U.S. imperialism of the late 1950s. In both cases, all possible forces, including the less threatening superpower and all intermediate countries, were to be united to wage a tit-for-tat struggle against the more threatening imperialist superpower. But there were also important differences. The anti–United States united front was intended as a vehicle of revolutionary transformation of its member countries and ultimately of the world. The anti-hegemony united front had little if any revolutionary content. Maintenance of a favorable global balance of power was its objective.

The new doctrine of anti-hegemony united front led to a return to the more activist methods of the late 1950s. China's top leaders once again began traveling abroad to disseminate the united front doctrine. In August 1978, Prime Minister and CCP Chairman Hua Guofeng visited Romania, Yugoslavia, and Iran. The stop in Tehran marked the first visit by a top-ranking PRC leader to a non-Communist country and the first multination visit by a top Chinese leader since a visit by Liu Xiaoqi to Burma and Pakistan in April 1966. Hua Guofeng also made the first visit by a ranking PRC leader to Western Europe, visiting France, Italy, West Germany, and Britain in October and November of 1979. Deng Xiaoping made the first-ever visit of a top-ranking PRC leader to Japan in September 1978 and to the United States in January 1979. Deng returned to Japan in February 1979, while Hua Guofeng visited Japan in May and again in July of 1980. On all of these trips, PRC leaders worked to strengthen anti-Soviet unity.

The normalization of relations and the development of strategic cooperation with the United States were both central components of Beijing's anti-hegemony united front. Normal Sino-American diplomatic relations and strategic cooperation were two very different things, but they developed in close relationship in 1978. Beijing's early 1978 decision for war with Vietnam (discussed later in Chapter Fourteen) made closer alignment with the United States imperative. American support would be instrumental in deterring Soviet intervention on Vietnam's behalf. This led to rapid normalization of diplomatic relations with the United States on the basis of the anti-hegemony principles established in the 1972 communiqué. Sino-American normalization would have happened in any case; it was only a matter of time. That it happened when it did, on January 1, 1979, was a function of Beijing's decision for military action against Vietnam to disrupt Soviet strategic preparations. The vice president of the Chinese Academy of Social Sciences explained Beijing's view of the strategic basis of the new Sino-U.S. relation in an article in *Foreign Affairs*:

> Sino-American relations have now entered a new stage....A historic task facing both China and the United States is to consolidate and expand their relations so as to play a more effective role in defense of world peace and security against the threat of war....China and the United States were brought together again [in the 1970s] by the growing Soviet menace to world peace and security, which they both have to face. These common strategic interests constitute a very important basis underlying Sino-American relations which, it is hoped, will continue to grow on this basis.[44]

In order to clear the way to normalization in 1978, Washington acceded to "three conditions" that Beijing had demanded since 1975. They were: (1) withdrawal of all U.S. military forces from Taiwan, (2) severance of diplomatic relations between the U.S. and Taiwan, and (3) termination of the U.S.-Taiwan mutual security treaty of 1954. Beijing made several important concessions on the Taiwan issue. It agreed to establish normal U.S.-PRC relations one year prior to the actual cancellation of the 1954 U.S.-ROC treaty. It agreed to normalize relations, even though Washington said it would continue supplying weapons to Taiwan. It agreed not to contradict publicly a unilateral U.S. statement of concern about the peaceful future of the people of Taiwan. Beijing also agreed to make a unilateral statement regarding its intention of using peaceful means to settle the Taiwan question. At the same time, however, it insisted that "as for the way of bringing Taiwan back to the embrace of the motherland and reunifying the country, it is entirely China's internal affair."[45]

Precise language and calculated ambiguity were used to regulate the status of Taiwan in the normalization agreements. In the joint communiqué the United States "acknowledged" Beijing's claim that Taiwan was a part of the People's Republic of China. By avoiding the term "recognition," Washington maintained a thin legal basis for continued relations with Taiwan without Beijing's consent. "Recognition" would have implied acceptance of Beijing's sovereignty over Taiwan and, by extension, of its right to regulate relations between foreign countries and Taiwan. By merely "acknowledging" rather than "recognizing" Beijing's claim to Taiwan, Washington denied Beijing a veto over U.S. relations with Taiwan. In its *unilateral* statement China asserted that "as is known to all, the Government of the People's Republic of China is the sole legal Government of China and Taiwan is a part of China."[46]

To Beijing, these concessions on Taiwan were bitter. Washington's expressed determination to continue selling weapons to Taiwan was especially galling. Beijing agreed to those terms because it believed that strengthened Sino-American ties were essential to prevent a further shift of the global balance of power in Moscow's favor.

On the American side, during 1978 President Carter decided to uncouple advances in U.S.-Chinese relations from progress in U.S.-Soviet detente and to move forward with closer relations with China, even though this might upset Moscow. Carter also began moving toward the idea of an informal U.S.-PRC alliance directed toward containing the Soviet Union.[47] One aspect of this was the establishment of military cooperation between China and the United States. Thus, in May 1978 Washington announced that it would no longer oppose sales of military equipment by the Western European countries to China. Shortly afterwards China opened negotiations with Britain for the purchase of Harrier jets and with France for the purchase of anti-tank missiles. The defense establishments of China and the United States also began establishing contacts. U.S. Secretary of Defense Harold Brown and Defense Minister Geng Biao visited each other's country in January and May 1980 respectively. The United States also authorized the sale of dual use (military and civilian) technology to China, and then the sale of non-lethal military equipment. Then in June 1981, the United States agreed to sell arms to China. Sino-American military relations slowly increased throughout the remainder of the 1980s.[48]

Beijing and Washington also began concrete measures of security cooperation. At the time of normalization Beijing agreed to allow the United States to establish electronic listening stations in Xinjiang province to monitor Soviet rocket firings in Central Asia (replacing the U.S. listening posts in Iran shut down by the revolution in that country).[49]

Sino-American strategic cooperation also took the form of parallel efforts to counter the Soviet-supported Vietnamese invasion of Cambodia in December 1978 and the Soviet invasion of Afghanistan in December 1979. Cambodia and the Sino-Vietnamese war associated with it will be discussed in Chapter Fourteen. Regarding Afghanistan, Sino-American cooperation involved parallel efforts to support the anti-Soviet Afghan resistance groups (the Mujahadeen), and to support Pakistan, which provided sanctuary on its territory for the Mujahadeen. China and Washington discussed the Afghan situation intensively early in 1980. Beijing worked to improve U.S.-Pakistan relations, which had soured after Washington suspended military assistance to Pakistan in April 1979 because of Pakistan's nuclear weapons program and after the U.S. embassy in Islamabad was burned by a mob. Beijing and Washington both stepped up their deliveries of military and economic assistance to Pakistan and issued statements promising assistance for Pakistan in the event of Soviet or Soviet-backed Afghan attacks on it. China and the United States also began supplying and training the Mujahadeen resistance fighters. The contours of those covert efforts are still unclear, but it is apparent that they continued throughout the Soviet occupation of Afghanistan. China suspended its support for the Mujahadeen only after Soviet forces were withdrawn in March 1989.[50]

Joint support for Thailand against Vietnamese pressure was another component of the new Sino-American strategic relation. Like Pakistan in the Afghan conflict, Thailand decided to allow its territory to be used as sanctuary by resistance forces from the neighboring country. Beijing and Washington felt that the Vietnamese-Soviet thrust into Cambodia had to be countered, and they promised Bangkok support if it granted sanctuary to Cambodian resistance forces. These guarantees enabled Bangkok to run the risk of antagonizing Hanoi and deterred Vietnamese attack on the Cambodian resistance base areas on Thai territory.

Japan was another important member of Beijing's anti-hegemony united front. Sino-Japanese negotiations on a peace treaty formally ending World War II began in 1975. Little progress was made, however, because Beijing insisted that the treaty contain an anti-hegemony clause. This Tokyo refused because it would have meant abandoning Japan's policy of equidistance vis-à-vis the USSR and the PRC. By the spring of 1978, however, a number of factors came together to induce Japan to accept Beijing's demand for an anti-hegemony clause: the hopes of Japanese companies for a bigger share of the rapidly opening China market, increased Chinese flexibility on the precise wording of the anti-hegemony clause, and U.S. urging. In August 1978, a Sino-Japanese treaty of peace and friendship was signed. Article II of that treaty declared that neither party would "seek hegemony in the Asia-Pacific region or in any other region and that each is opposed to efforts by any other country or group of countries to establish such hegemony." Moscow was outraged by Tokyo's acceptance of an anti-hegemony clause. It responded by strengthening its military forces stationed on the islands off Hokkaido and stepping up its air and naval patrols around Japan. From Beijing's perspective, the Soviet Union was thus forced to further disperse its forces and Japan's substantial weight was added to the anti-Soviet camp. As *Red Flag* pointed out in its January 1, 1979, issue: "The normalization of relations between China and the United States and the conclusion of a treaty of peace and friendship between China and Japan will help hold any war plotter in check, delay the outbreak of a world war, and maintain peace and stability in the Asia-Pacific region and the whole world."[51]

The greatest success for the global anti-Soviet front, the election of President Ronald Reagan in November 1980, was related only indirectly, if at all, to China's anti-Soviet efforts. Although the question has not been researched, it is possible that Chinese anti-Soviet exhortations in the late 1970s helped to create a climate of anti-detente opinion and to catalyze the conservative movement in the United States—developments instrumental in Reagan's election. If such a link existed, it was subtle and weak. Nonetheless, Chinese propaganda and activities may well have contributed to the sea change in U.S. public opinion about relations with the Soviet Union in the late 1970s. In any case, Reagan's election brought a revitalization of U.S. containment policies, a deliberate suspension of detente with the Soviet Union, and the largest peacetime military buildup in U.S. history.

NOTES

1. "Statement of the Chinese Government Advocating the Complete, Thorough, Total and Resolute Prohibition and Destruction of Nuclear Weapons and Proposing a Conference of the Government Heads of All Countries in the World" (July 31, 1963), *People of the World, Unite, for the Complete, Thorough, Total and Resolute Prohibition and Destruction of Nuclear Weapons!*, Beijing, 1963.

2. "Statement by the spokesman of the Chinese Government," in *Peking Review*, August 15, 1963, 7. Analyses of Beijing's appraisal of the 1963 treaty include Walter Clements, *The Arms Race and Sino-Soviet Relations*, Stanford, Calif.: Hoover Institution Press, 1968; Morton H. Halperin, *China and the Bomb*, London: Pall Mall Press, 1968, 62–70; Morton H. Halperin and Dwight H. Perkins, *Communist China and Arms Control*, East Asian Research Center, Center for International Affairs, Harvard University, 1965; Alice Langley Hsien, "The Sino-Soviet Nuclear Dialogue: 1963," *Sino-Soviet Military Relations*, Raymond L. Garthoff, ed., New York: Praeger, 1966, 150–70.

3. Regarding Beijing's view of Soviet-American collaboration, see John Gittings, *The World and China, 1922–1972*, New York: Harper and Row, 1974, 255–59; John W. Garver, *China's Decision for Rapprochement with the United States, 1968–1971*, Boulder, Colo.: Westview, 1982, 32–50.

4. *U.S. News and World Report*, July 3, 1967, 29–31; *Newsweek*, July 10, 1967, 94–96; Lyndon Baines Johnson, *The Vantage Point: Perspectives on the Presidency, 1963–1969*, New York: Popular Library, 1971, 469, 476.

5. "Soviet Revisionism Steps Up Collaboration with U.S. Imperialism," *Peking Review*, December 25, 1967, no. 52, 40–43.

6. "Nuclear Hoax Cannot Save U.S. Imperialism and Soviet Revisionism," *Peking Review*, September 8, 1967, no. 37, 34.

7. Robert S. McNamara, *The Essence of Security: Reflections in Office*, New York: Harper and Row, 1968, 141–66; Also, A. Doak Barnett, "China and U.S. Policy: A Time of Transition," *Current Science*, vol. 8, no. 10, (May 5, 1970), 2.

8. "The Pitiful Struggle of U.S. 'Nuclear Overlord,'" *Peking Review*, October 27, 1967, no. 44, 37.

9. For the former view, see Greg O'Leary, "Chinese Foreign Policy—from "Anti-Imperialism to 'Anti-Hegemony,'" Bill Brugger, ed., *China: The Impact of the Cultural Revolution*, New York: Barnes and Noble, 1978, 203–48. For the latter view, see John W. Garver, "Sino-Soviet Relations in 1970: The Tilt Toward the Soviet Union," *China Quarterly*, no. 82 (June 1980), 214–49; Thomas M. Gottlieb, *Chinese Foreign Policy Factionalism and the Origins of the Strategic Triangle*, R-1902-NA, Santa Monica, Calif.: Rand, November 1977; Michael Y.M. Kau, *The Lin Piao Affair: Power Politics and Military Coup*, New York: International Arts and Sciences Press, 1975, xxv-xxxvii. One author went so far as to assert that Lin Biao planned to touch off a war with the Soviet Union, use this war to assassinate Mao Zedong and Zhou Enlai, and then make peace with the Soviet Union and restore the Sino-Soviet alliance. Yao Ming-le, *Conspiracy and Murder of Mao's Heir*, New York: Knopf, 1983. For a critical analysis of this farfetched view, see Robert Delfs, "Marshal's Mystery," *Far Eastern Economic Review* (hereafter *FEER*), May 10, 1990, 14–15.

10. Regarding this rationale for better relations with the United States, see W.A.C. Adie,

"'One World' Restored? Sino-American Relations on a New Footing," *Asian Survey*, vol. 12, no. 5 (May 1973), 365–85; Thomas W. Robinson, "The View from Peking: China's Policies Toward the United States, the Soviet Union, and Japan," *Pacific Affairs*, vol. 45, no. 3 (Fall 1972), 333–55; Harold Hinton, *The Bear at the Gate: Chinese Policymaking Under Soviet Pressure*, Washington, D.C. American Enterprise Institute for Public Policy Research, 1972; Albert Feuerwerker, "Chinese History and the Foreign Relations of Contemporary China," *The Annals of the American Academy of Political and Social Sciences*, vol. 402 (July 1972), 1–11; Robert Scalapino, "China and the Balance of Power" *Foreign Affairs*, vol. 52, no. 2 (January 1974), 349–85; Franz Michael, "The New United States China Policy," *Current History*, vol. 63, no. 373 (September 1972), 126–29, 133.

11. Reference Material Concerning Education on Situation, Number 43, Issued by the Kunming Military Region, April 4, 1973, in *Chinese Communist Internal Politics and Foreign Policy*, Taipei: Institute of International Relations, 1974, 135–37.

12. *The New York Times*, March 15, 1969. Regarding the development of Sino-U.S. rapprochement, see Richard M. Nixon, *Memoirs of Richard Nixon*, vol. 2, New York: Warner Books, 1978, 7–56; Henry A. Kissinger, *White House Years*, Boston: Little, Brown, 1979, 163–94, 684–787. Scholarly treatments include Allen S. Whiting, "The Sino-American Detente: Genesis and Prospects," *China and the World Community*, Ian Wilson, ed., Sydney: Australian Institute of International Affairs, 1973, 70–89; Gene T. Hsiao, *Sino-American Detente and Its Policy Implications*, New York: Praeger, 1974; Akira Iriye, "The United States in Chinese Foreign Policy," *China and America: The Search for a New Relationship*, William Barnds, ed., New York: New York University Press, 1977; Linda D. Dillon, Bruce Burton and Walter C. Soderlund, "Who Was the Principal Enemy? Shifts in Official Chinese Perceptions of the Two Superpowers, 1968–1969," *Asian Survey*, May 1977, vol. XVII, no. 5, 456–73; Robert G. Sutter, *China-Watch, toward Sino-American Reconciliation*, Baltimore: Johns Hopkins university Press, 1978.. A chronology of PRC-U.S. interactions is available in *China: U.S. Policy Since 1945*, Washington, D.C.: Congressional Quarterly, 178–208.

13. Kissinger, *White House Years*, 172–73.

14. Kissinger, *White House Years*, 554. Also, John Newhouse, *Cold Dawn: The Story of SALT*, New York: Holt, Rinehart, and Winston, 1973, 189.

15. John W. Lewis, Xue Litai, *China Builds the Bomb*, Stanford, CA: Stanford Press, 1988, 202.

16. *The New York Times*, February 3, 1969, 11.

17. *Survey of China Mainland Press*, U.S. Consulate, Hong Kong,, November 5, 1969, A1.

18. Nixon, *Memoirs*, vol. I, 511. The notion of a U.S. opening to China had percolated throughout the 1960s. See, for example, Robert P. Newman, *Recognition of Communist China? A Study in Argument*, New York: Macmillan, 1961; *U.S. Policy with Respect to Mainland China*, hearings before the Committee on Foreign Relations of the United States Senate, 86th Congress, 2nd Session, March 1966. A contemporary and influential thinking-through of some of the problems involved in U.S. China policy during the first Nixon Administration was Richard Moorsteen and Morton Abramowitz, *Remaking China Policy: U.S.-China Relations and Government Decision Making*. Cambridge: Harvard University Press, 1971.

19. Nixon, *Memoirs*, vol. I, 502–11. Kissinger, *White House Years*, 177, 764.

20. Kissinger, *White House Years*, 180–81.

21. *China: U.S. Policy Since 1945*, 18. Also, Kissinger, *White House Years*, 171–91.

22. *China: U.S. Policy Since 1945*, 22.

23. Regarding the diplomatic offensive of 1970–1971, see Joseph Camilleri, *Chinese Foreign Policy: The Maoist Era and Its Aftermath*, Seattle: University of Washington Press, 1980, 111–17; Samuel S. Kim, *China, the United Nations, and the World Order*, Princeton, N.J.: Princeton University Press, 1979, 102–3.

24. "Reference Material, No. 43," 135–37.

25. Cited in Michael Pillsbury, *SALT on the Dragon: Chinese Views of Soviet-American Strategic Balance*, P-5457, Santa Monica, Calif.: Rand Corporation, April 1975, 33.

26. "Chairman of Chinese Delegation Chiao Kuan-hua's Speech," *Peking Review*, no. 40, October 5, 1973, 10–17.

27. Nixon, *Memoirs*, vol. I, 501, vol. II, 424–28; Kissinger, *White House Years*, 1142, 1146, 688; Adam B. Ulam, *Dangerous Relations: The Soviet Union in World Politics, 1970–1982*, New York: Oxford University Press, 1983, 39–82. In Nixon's opinion, a major reason for Moscow's interest in an agreement between the Soviet Union and the United States regarding the non-use of nuclear weapons was that it would check movement toward a Sino-U.S. military alliance and bind U.S. hands in the event of a Sino-Soviet war.

28. Regarding the debate between Vance and Brzezinski, see Cyrus Vance, *Hard Choices*, New York: Simon and Schuster, 1983, 76–83, 110–22; Zbigniew Brzezinski, *Power and Principle—Memoirs of the National Security Advisor, 1977–1981*, New York: Farrar, Straus & Giroux, 1983, in passim. Nayan Chanda provides a good summary of this conflict in *Brother Enemy: The War After the War*, New York: Macmillan, 1986, 269–92. Regarding the shifting role of China in U.S. foreign policy, see Banning Garrett and Bonnie Glaser, "From Nixon to Reagan: China's Changing Role in American Strategy," *Eagle Resurgent? The Reagan Era in American Foreign Policy*, Kenneth A. Oye, Robert J. Lieber, and Donald Rothchild, eds., Boston: Little, Brown, 1986, 255–95.

29. Ulam, *Dangerous Relations*, 75–76. Some analysts have argued that by forgoing such an agreement with Moscow, Nixon passed up his best chance for securing genuine Soviet assistance in forcing Hanoi to suspend its war against South Vietnam. For example, William G. Hyland, "The Sino-Soviet Conflict: A Search for New Security Strategies," *Asian Security in the 1980s: Problems and Policies for a Time of Transition*, Richard H. Solomon, ed., R-2492-ISA, Santa Monica, Calif.: Rand, 1979, 139.

30. Regarding Sino-Soviet relations in the 1970s, see Harry Gelman, "The Sino-Soviet Dispute in the 1970s: An Overview," in Herbert Elliot, ed., *The Sino-Soviet Conflict: A Global Perspective*, Seattle: University of Washington Press, 1982, 355–72; Gerald Segal, "China and the Great Power Triangle," *China Quarterly*, no. 83 (September 1980), 490–509; Harvey W. Nelsen, *Power and Insecurity: Beijing, Moscow and Washington, 1949–1988*, Boulder, Colo.: Lynne Rienner, 1989.

31. Henry A. Kissinger, *Years of Upheaval*, Boston: Little, Brown, 1982, 678–99.

32. John W. Garver, "The Reagan Administration's Southeast Asian Policy," *U.S.-Asian Relations: The National Security Paradox*, James C. Hsiung, ed., New York: Praeger, 1983, 95.

33. Cited in Chandra, *Brother Enemy*, 22.

34. *China and Asia—An Analysis of China's Recent Policy Toward Neighboring States*, Report by the Foreign Affairs and National Defense Division, Congressional Research Service, Library of Congress, Washington, D.C.: Government Printing Office, 1979, 23–24.

35. Pillsbury, *SALT on the Dragon*, v–vi.

36. "Reference Materials, No. 42" (April 2, 1973), *Chinese Communist Internal Documents*, 131.

37. "European Press on European Security Conference" *Beijing Review*, vol. 18, no. 33 (August 15, 1975) 22–23. Also, "European Security Conference: An Analysis of Its Final Act," *Beijing Review*, vol. 18, no. 32 (August 8, 1975), 5–6.

38. Regarding the Soviet military buildup in Asia, see Donald S. Zagoria, "The Strategic Environment in East Asia," and Paul F. Langer, "Soviet Military Power in Asia," in *Soviet Policy in East Asia*, New Haven, Conn.: Yale University Press, 1982, 1–28, 266–80; Richard H. Solomon and Masataka Sosaka, eds., *The Soviet Far East Military Buildup: Nuclear Dilemmas and Asian Security*, Westport, Conn.: Auburn House, 1986; Donald S. Zagoria, "The USSR and Asia in 1984," *Asian Survey*, January 1985, 21–32; Steven J. Solarz, "The Soviet Challenge in Asia," *Asian-Pacific Community* (Summer 1984), 1–27.

39. Garver, "The Reagan Administration's Southeast Asian Policy," 96.

40. "Huang Hua's Report on the World Situation," Part III, in *Issues and Studies*, vol. xiv, no. 1 (January 1978), 110–11.

41. Regarding the strategy of a united front against hegemonism, see William R. Heaton, Jr., *A United Front Against Hegemonism: Chinese Foreign Policy into the 1980s*, National Defense University, National Security Affairs Monograph Series 80-3, March 1980; Jonathan Pollack, *The Lessons of Coalition Politics: Sino-American Security Relations*, Santa Monica, Calif.: Rand Corporation, February 1984.

42. Regarding Europe's putative role, see Philip Brick, "The Politics of Bonn-Beijing Normalization, 1972–84," *Asian Survey*, vol. 25, no. 7, (July 1985), 773–91; Dick Wilson, "China and the European Community," *China Quarterly*, no. 56 (October–December 1973), 647–66; William E. Griffith, "China and Europe, 'Weak and Far Away,'" *The China Factor: Sino-American Relations and the Global Scene*, Richard H. Solomon, ed., Englewood Cliffs, N.J.: Prentice Hall, 1981, 159–77.

43. Michael Pillsbury, "Strategic Acupuncture," *Foreign Policy*, no. 41 (Winter 1980–1981), 62–81.

44. Huan Xiang, "On Sino-U.S. Relations," *Foreign Affairs*, vol. 60, no. 1 (Fall 1981), 36–7.

45. "People's Republic of China Statement," in *China: U.S. Policy Since 1945*, 342.

46. Ibid. Regarding the Taiwan issue and Sino-American normalization, see "China Debate," *Congressional Quarterly Weekly Report*, vol. 37, no. 9 (March 3, 1979), 351–65; Robert G. Sutter, *China-U.S. Relations*, Issue Brief Number 76053, Congressional Research Service, May 21, 1981; *Taiwan*, Hearings Before the Committee of Foreign Relations, United States Senate, 96th Congress, 1st Session, February 5–8, 21–22, 1979, Washington, D.C.: U.S. Government Printing Office, 1979.

47. Regarding Carter's China policy, see Michel Oksenberg, "China Policy for the 1980s," *Foreign Affairs*, vol. 59, no. 2 (Winter 1980–1981), 318; Michel Oksenberg, "A Decade of Sino-American Relations," *Foreign Affairs*, vol. 61 (Fall 1982), 176–95. Oksenberg was Carter's top China expert.

48. Regarding Sino-U.S. military relations, see Robert G. Sutter, *U.S.-China Strategic Relations*, Washington, D.C.: Congressional Research Service, 1980; Leslie H. Gelb, "U.S. Defense Policy, Technology, Transfer, and Asian Security," in *Asian Security in the 1980s*, Richard H. Solomon, ed., 258–75; Allen S. Whiting, "Sino-American Military Relations," in *The United States and the People's Republic of China: Issues for the 1980's*, Hearings Before the Subcommittee on Asian and Pacific Affairs, 96th Congress, 2nd Session, 1980, 44–58; Henry B. Gass, *Sino-American Security Relations: Expectations and Realities*, National Security essay series 84-2, Fort Lesley J. McNair, Washington, D.C.: National Defense University Press, 1984; William T. Tow, "The U.S., Mainland China and Japan: Military Technology Transfer Policies and Strategic Collaboration," *Issues and Studies*, vol. 23, no. 10 (October 1987), 110—28; Kerry B. Dumbaugh and Richard F. Grimmett, *U.S. Arms Sales to China*, Congressional Research Service Report 85-138F, July 8, 1985. For a critical view of U.S. arms sales to China, see James A. Gregor, *Arming the Dragon: U.S. Security Ties with the People's Republic of China*, Washington, D.C.: Ethics and Public Policy Center, 1987.

49. Regarding the Xinjiang listening posts, see Jeffrey T. Richelson, *Foreign Intelligence Organizations*, Cambridge: Ballinger, 1988, 291–92.

50. Regarding China's reaction to the Soviet invasion of Afghanistan, see Gerald Segal, "China and Afghanistan," *Asian Survey*, vol. 21, no. 11 (November 1981), 1158–74; Yaacov Vertzberger, "Afghanistan in China's Policy," *Problems of Communism*, vol. 31, no. 3 (May–June 1982), 1–23; John W. Garver, "The Indian Factor in Recent Sino-Soviet Relations," *China Quarterly*, no. 125 (June 1991), 55–85.

51. FBIS, DRC, January 29, 1979. Regarding the Sino-Japanese treaty, see Avigdor Haselkorn, "Impact of Sino-Japanese Treaty on the Soviet Security Strategy," *Asian Survey*, vol. xix, no. 6 (June 1979), 558–73; Hiroshi Kimura, "The Conclusion of the Sino-Japanese Peace Treaty (1978): Soviet Coercive Strategy and Its Limit," *Studies in Comparative Communism*, vol. xviii, no. 2 & 3 (Summer–Autumn 1985), 151–80; Robert E. Bedeski, *The Fragile Entente: The 1978 Japan-China Peace Treaty in a Global Context*, Boulder, Colo.: Westview, 1983; Daniel Tretiak, "The Sino-Japanese Treaty of 1978: The Senkaku Incident Prelude," *Asian Survey*, vol. 18, no. 12 (December 1978), 1235–49. The text of the treaty is in *China: U.S. Policy Since 1945*, 340–41.

Reagan → build-up

Chapter Four

Toward Triangular Disengagement

CHINA'S "INDEPENDENT FOREIGN POLICY"

In 1982 Beijing moved away from a united front with the United States and toward a policy of peaceful coexistence with both superpowers. Talk of a united front against Soviet hegemony disappeared and the notion of military alliance or strategic cooperation with the United States was explicitly rejected. Military contacts and strategic cooperation with the United States were not suspended, but were handled in a more low-key fashion. Beijing began trying to balance criticism of Soviet moves with criticism of American moves, while distancing itself from Soviet-American rivalry. Perhaps most important, Beijing also began a slow but steady improvement in relations with the Soviet Union. This approach is usually known as China's "independent foreign policy."[1]

In many regards the 1982 shift was a watershed. Prior to that point Beijing's approach to the superpowers was essentially confrontational. After 1982, however, it began seeking peaceful, non-confrontational, cooperative relations with both superpowers. The factors underlying this transition are examined in Parts Three and Four: a decline of revolutionary zeal and an overriding emphasis on economic development.

Several considerations underlay the 1982 shift. In the first instance, Ronald Reagan's election as president of the United States in November 1980, and the rapid restoration of American military strength over which he presided, meant that there was less need for China to rally the world's anti-Soviet forces. The Americans had apparently awakened from their slumber and the Soviets were increasingly on the defensive. Ironically, perhaps, the very success of the anti-hegemony strategy made its continuation risky. From Moscow's point of view, the collapse of Soviet-Western detente; increased Western European, Japanese, and American defense spending; China's support for NATO; the conclusion of the Sino-Japanese "anti-hegemony treaty"; and burgeoning Sino-American security cooperation were an extremely ominous combination. To Moscow, the developments of the late 1970s were a realization of its worst nightmare—a two-front threat. China, the United States, Japan, and Western Europe seemed to be drawing together into an anti-Soviet military bloc. These developments strengthened arguments of Soviet hawks that the USSR should strike against China "before it was too late." Confronted by the apparent growing integration of China into an anti-Soviet military bloc and the rekindling of the Cold War, time seemed to be running out for the Soviet Union, at least from the perspective of Soviet hawks. There was thus a greater temptation in Moscow to cripple China before the seemingly inevitable confrontation with the United States or before Sino-American ties solidified into a full alliance. Ominous threats indicated that Soviet leaders seriously considered such hawkish arguments. In January 1980, for example, Leonid Brezhnev warned that the Soviet Union "would not tolerate" certain actions by the West, including Western assistance to China's nuclear weapons program. If the Americans went too far they would have "only minutes to decide their options" in response to a Soviet preemptive nuclear strike against China. "Believe me," Brezhnev said, "after the destruction of Chinese nuclear sites by our missiles, there won't be much time for the Americans to choose between the defense of their Chinese allies and peaceful coexistence with us."[2] In such circumstances China could reduce the risk of a Soviet attack by distancing itself from the United States and improving relations with Moscow.

Shifting resources from defense to economic development was another objective served by China's reduction of tension with Moscow. By the early 1980s, a new leadership consensus had emerged in support of an ambitious program of economic modernization.

Nor was a close relationship with the United States necessarily the best way for China to counter Soviet advances in the Third World. Many Third World countries did not wish to become involved in the East-West conflict, especially one that had escalated to the highest levels of tension since the 1950s. As China moved toward quasi-alliance with the United States, many Third World countries became increasingly wary of expanding ties with it. India was especially important in this regard. India was Moscow's most important friend in the Third World and the pivotal power in South Asia. Since the basis of Indo-Soviet friendship was Moscow's guarantee of India against Chinese attack, improvements in Sino-Indian relations would help weaken Soviet influence over India. Yet China's anti-Sovietism was a key factor leading successive Indian governments to reject Beijing's overtures for better relations. A reduction of Sino-Soviet hostility might, therefore, open the door to improved Sino-Indian relations and, ultimately, to a lessening of Soviet influence in South Asia.[3]

Finally, China's position as junior partner of the United States had made the Americans less sensitive to Chinese concerns, especially regarding Taiwan. The passage of the Taiwan Relations Act (TRA) by the U.S. Congress in April 1979 had greatly angered Chinese leaders. They felt that the TRA involved unilateral alteration of a delicate compromise negotiated bilaterally. Washington then sold $292 million in military equipment to Taiwan in 1980. When press reports indicated in 1981 that Washington was considering the sale of advanced fighter aircraft to Taiwan, Beijing was further outraged. It concluded that U.S. disregard for PRC sensitivities on Taiwan was related to China's seeming strategic dependence on the United States. If China positioned itself somewhat more independently of the United States, thereby threatening to defect from the anti-Soviet camp, Washington would be more sensitive to Chinese wishes on the Taiwan issue.[4] A long article in *Beijing Review* in July 1982 expressed Beijing's anger over U.S. policy toward Taiwan and hinted at the dire consequences for Washington if its policy toward Taiwan did not change:

> Frankly speaking, the fact that there still remains a "Taiwan issue" in the relations between China and the United States is the consequence of imperialistic expansionist policy on the part of the United States. To China, it is the aftermath of the century-old history of being subject to foreign aggression and partition. It is inconceivable that the Chinese people...would tolerate for long the continuation of such a state. But it is conceivable what a difficult situation the United States will find itself in [sic] if it clings to its policy which was already discredited in its heyday. How Sino-U.S. relations will develop in the future depends on whether U.S. policy-makers will awaken to the irresistible law from historical experience, throw off their heavy burden and catch up with the tide of the times.[5]

The most important component of Beijing's "independent foreign policy" was gradual improvement of relations with the Soviet Union. The process of Sino-Soviet rapprochement began in October 1982 when vice-ministerial level consultations on outstanding issues, suspended in early 1980 after the Soviet invasion of Afghanistan, were resumed. In November 1982 Foreign Minister Huang Hua visited Moscow for Leonid Brezhnev's funeral. While in Moscow, Huang met with the Soviet foreign minister—the first such meeting in twenty years. Bilateral contacts slowly expanded in the months that followed. Initially, little progress was made in resolving fundamental disputes. China demanded that Moscow remove "three obstacles" before there could be "normal" Sino-Soviet relations. These three "obstacles" were: (1) Moscow must pressure Vietnam to withdraw its military forces from Cambodia; (2) Soviet forces must withdraw from Afghanistan; and (3) Moscow must withdraw militarily from Mongolia and substantially reduce its forces along the Sino-Soviet border. During 1980 and 1981, Beijing insisted that Moscow meet those demands before there could be major improvements in bilateral relations. After 1982, Beijing held that while resolution of the three obstacles was necessary for a "normalization" of Sino-Soviet relations, it was no longer a precondition for expanded relations. Consequently, Sino-Soviet trade increased rapidly. By the end of 1984, the Soviet Union had agreed to help refurbish some of the industrial enterprises it had helped construct in the 1950s. Cross-border trade was resumed. Student exchanges were resumed in 1983, with five students going each way; by 1989, China was sending 450 students per year to the Soviet Union. Cultural exchanges were resumed in 1985, and by 1989 over 100 items were included in the cultural exchange program.

By the time Mikhail Gorbachev came to power in March 1985, Sino-Soviet relations were already the most cordial they had been since the late 1950s. The pace of Sino-Soviet rapprochement accelerated under Gorbachev because the latter proved willing to address Beijing's "three obstacles." Gorbachev gave early signs of wishing major improvements in relations with China. Deng Xiaoping responded in October 1985 by sending a letter to Gorbachev via Romanian President Nicolai Ceausescu saying that he was willing to meet with Gorbachev if the Soviet Union urged Vietnam to withdraw from Cambodia. Chinese leaders found several opportunities to reiterate this during the next two years. Gorbachev welcomed Deng's proposal of a Sino-Soviet summit, but pressed for an early meeting without preconditions. Beijing refused; solution of the three obstacles was a necessary prerequisite, it insisted.[6]

Chinese firmness paid off. Gorbachev proceeded to satisfy Chinese demands regarding the "three obstacles." In April 1988, a Soviet-American agreement was reached at Geneva providing for the withdrawal of Soviet troops from Afghanistan. By March 1989 those troops had been withdrawn. A desire to open the door to cordial relations with China was a major consideration underlying this move.[7] In December 1988 Gorbachev announced a 500,000-man reduction in the Soviet army. Forty percent of this cut was to be in the Soviet military regions east of the Urals. By mid-1991 Soviet Asian forces had been reduced by 120,000. All Soviet forces had also been withdrawn from Mongolia. Soviet training was also reoriented from nearly exclusive preparation for offensive operations to emphasis on defensive operations. Soviet Far Eastern forces were also configured to confront Japan, and U.S. forces in Japan, rather than China. In terms of sheer military capability, however, it was difficult to conclude that the smaller Soviet Asian military force was less capable, since it was armed with more modern weapons withdrawn from Eastern Europe.[8]

The Cambodian issue was the most difficult for Gorbachev to resolve. Nonetheless, during talks between Foreign Minister Qian Qichen and Soviet leaders in Moscow in December 1988, agreements were reached regarding Cambodia. The next month, Hanoi announced that it would withdraw all its forces from Cambodia that September. This was adequate to clear the way for a meeting between Deng and Gorbachev. When that summit took place in May 1989, it was hailed by both sides as marking the restoration of normal state-to-state relations and party-to-party ties.[9]

The normalization of Sino-Soviet relations did not entail the suspension of Sino-American security relations. While Beijing downplayed its strategic links with the United States after 1982, those links continued throughout the 1980s. Before the Tiananmen massacre of June 1989, they included:

1. U.S. support for PRC military modernization. This took many forms, ranging from collaboration in research in high-energy physics to sales of sophisticated computers and military avionics.
2. A proliferation of personnel exchanges between the PLA and U.S. armed forces.
3. Cooperation in monitoring Soviet rocket and nuclear tests in Central Asia and Siberia, most importantly via the two electronic listening posts in Xinjiang.
4. The exchange of intelligence regarding Soviet military capabilities and deployments.
5. Joint support for Thailand and Pakistan.
6. Joint covert operations supporting the Afghan Mujahadeen.
7. Quiet Chinese diplomatic support for a continued U.S. military presence in the Philippines, for the U.S.-Japan alliance, and for the maintenance of peace in Korea.
8. Occasional port calls by naval units: e.g., November 1986 and May 1989 visits by U.S. squadrons to Qingdao and Shanghai, and a June 1989 visit by a PLA squadron to Pearl Harbor.
9. Occasional joint maneuvers: e.g., a joint naval signaling exercise in the South China Sea in January 1986.

Moscow remained highly sensitive to Sino-American security links. When the U.S. squadron called at Qingdao in November 1986, for example, the Soviets responded by simulating bombing attacks on the Alaskan and Chinese coasts.[10]

One key advantage for China of continuing security links with the United States while "normalizing" Sino-Soviet relations was that such links helped prevent Sino-American relations from deteriorating as Sino-Soviet relations improved. Beijing was very concerned that its relations with the superpowers would prove to be a zero-sum game; that improved

Sino-Soviet relations would antagonize the U.S., leading to a deterioration of Sino-American relations. This would endanger U.S. support for the Four Modernizations. A central element of Sino-American cooperation since 1971 had been anti-hegemonism. U.S. support for the Four Modernizations was rooted initially in the Sino-American quasi-alliance of the late 1970s. Moreover, American strategic planners had assumed that they derived substantial advantages from Sino-Soviet tension. How would they respond if faced with a loss of that leverage? In short, Beijing now faced the task of ensuring the continuation of U.S. support for the Four Modernizations under radically different triangular circumstances. Continued security links with the United States was one way of doing this, by giving substance to Beijing's repeated assertions that improvements in Sino-Soviet relations would injure U.S. interests and would not develop into a 1950s-style military alliance against America. It helped keep Sino-American relations "one step ahead" of Sino-Soviet relations.

SINO-AMERICAN RELATIONS AND THE UPHEAVAL OF 1989

Beijing's triangular balancing act was thrown off balance by the 1989 upheaval in China. The use of armed force to repress the pro-democracy movement in June led to a sharp deterioration of Sino-American relations. In response to the repression in China, President George Bush suspended military sales to China, banned high-level diplomatic and military exchanges, and froze $1.3 billion in loans for China pending before various international lending agencies. Following more executions of democratic activists in July, Congress voted further sanctions.

There were significant differences between Bush and Congress over how far sanctions should go. Bush believed that China's crackdown, while regrettable, was outweighed by the value of cordial Sino-American relations to the United States. Bush therefore dispatched his National Security Adviser Brent Scowcroft to Beijing in July and again in December 1989 to maintain contact with China's leaders. He also blocked various sanctions proposed by Congress, vetoing a congressional bill to allow all Chinese students to stay in the United States after their visas expired and recommending a continuation of Most-Favored-Nation (MFN) status for China against strong Congressional opposition. In spite of Bush's determination to continue a workable relation with China, the repression of 1989 had cost Beijing heavily: The remarkable intra-U.S. consensus that had characterized U.S. China policy throughout the 1980s was no more. After June 1989, China policy was once again a subject of much debate in the United States, with many leaders opposed to friendly relations with the brutally repressive regime in Beijing.

Beijing's response to American sanctions was not entirely

consistent. On the one hand it blamed the United States for the upheaval in China. Chinese propaganda charged that the United States was pursuing a systematic strategy of subverting socialism and encouraging the peaceful evolution of capitalism in China and around the world. In July 1989, *People's Daily* discussed the doctrine of "peaceful evolution" at length:

> The anticommunists within the international capitalist class have always alternately resorted to force and subversive activities on the one hand and the "peaceful evolution" strategy on the other in an attempt to nip the newly-born socialist system in the bud....In the eyes of anticommunists...the 1980s provides a golden opportunity for them to bring about "peaceful evolution."...The socialist cause has run into some new difficulties and problems in spite of the great success achieved....Therefore,...China and some other socialist countries have successively initiated comprehensive socialist structural reforms....[However,] in the eyes of anticommunists...in the West, the reforms in socialist countries precisely provide a golden opportunity for them to engineer "peaceful evolution" in these countries.[11]

But while damning putative U.S. interference in Chinese internal affairs, China's leaders tried to staunch the deterioration of Sino-American relations. When he met with Scowcroft in December 1989, for example, Deng Xiaoping called for improvements in Sino-American relations for the sake of maintaining world peace. Beijing also made some modest moves in response to U.S. human rights concerns. In early 1990, as the U.S. Congress was considering revocation of China's MFN status, martial law was lifted in Beijing, several hundred people arrested for opposition activity were released, and dissident scientist Fang Lizhi was allowed to leave the U.S. embassy in Beijing for Britain. One of Beijing's main tactics for trying to block further U.S. sanctions was to threaten that such moves would force China into closer alignment with the Soviet Union. The effectiveness of this tactic was limited, however, by declining U.S. fear of the Soviet Union.

CHINA, THE STRATEGIC TRIANGLE, AND THE COLLAPSE OF THE USSR

The years 1989 through 1991 saw a fundamental change in the international order. The East-West confrontation that had dominated global politics since the mid-1940s ended. The Soviet Union acquiesced to the nationalist revolutions of Eastern Europe and then committed itself to military withdrawal from that region. During 1990 Moscow also accepted German unification within the framework of continued German participation in NATO. America's major European ally, Germany, emerged from these changes deeply committed to a cooperative relation with the Soviet Union. At the core of the old "Western threat" to the

Soviet Union was Germany. By permitting the reunification of Germany, Gorbachev opened the way to a new Russo-German relation. Since 1989 Germany has provided 60% (as of early 1992) of all Western economic assistance to the former Soviet republics, and assisted Russia with a range of problems from the depoliticalization of the ex-Soviet army, to the drafting of legal codes, to the privatization of state enterprises. Simultaneously, the withdrawal of Soviet forces from Eastern Europe eliminated (or at least very greatly reduced) the Russian military threat to united Germany, while German pledges regarding the non placement of NATO forces in eastern Germany and recognition of existing Germany-Polish boundaries mitigated against the reemergence of Russian fears of Germany. By 1992 Russo-German hostility had been replaced by Russo-German amity. Russia no longer faced a western threat.

The transformation of Russian-German relations occurred within the framework of a broader rapprochement with the United States. Soviet-American cooperation was strengthened in 1991 when those two countries cooperated to undo Iraq's annexation of Kuwait. The end of the same year saw the collapse of Communist rule in Russia and then the disappearance of the USSR itself. Taken together, these changes meant the end of the cold war. The question to be asked here is: Did this historic change also mean the end of the strategic triangle?

The answer to this question seems to be "no." The redefinition of Russian-American relations with the end of the cold war has not ended the triangular interactions between those two countries and China. It has, however, produced very considerable modifications in the way the Russian-American-Chinese triangle operates. While Russia and American are no longer entangled in hostile confrontation, the relations between them continue to have considerable impact on China.

Perhaps the most important change in the Beijing-Washington-Moscow triangle is that Russia no longer faces a major two-front threat as the USSR did from 1931 to 1945 and again from 1963 to about 1985. As discussed in earlier chapters, with the deterioration of Sino-Soviet relations in the 1960s Moscow had to grapple with the fact that it might confront simultaneous large scale conflicts with NATO in Europe and with China in the east. This fact imposed significant constraints on Moscow. Beijing was cognizant of this fact and attempted to manipulate Moscow's two-front threat. During the 1970s, to cite but one case reviewed in earlier chapters, Beijing saw a united, military strong, U.S.-linked, and anti-Soviet Western Europe as a major guarantee of China's own security. As long as the Soviet Union was forced to divide its resources between European and Far Eastern theaters, its ability to act forcefully in either theater was lessened. The end of Moscow's two-front threat eliminates this leverage.

What are the implications for China of the substantial alleviation of the Western threat to Russia? Most generally, Beijing will no longer be able to count on Moscow's desire to uncouple China from Moscow's Western adversaries. Conversely, Moscow may be better able to concentrate forces in the east in the event of some future confrontation with China. Nor will Beijing be able to gain leverage with Washington by stressing the utility of China's military strength and geographic position in terms of constraining Moscow.

From Beijing's point of view, the end of the Cold War may well mean the intensification of trends toward Russian-American cooperation against China, toward joint Russian-American pursuit of aims antithetical to China.

Developments in Eastern Europe in 1989 and 1990 provide a good example of this. The collapse of socialism in that region was a severe setback for China. It deepened the legitimacy crisis faced by the incumbent Chinese regime and encouraged U.S. anti-communists to step up their "peaceful evolution" conspiracy against China. (At least this was Beijing's perception of matters.) From the standpoint of the CCP, the pivotal developments in Eastern Europe were largely a function of Gorbachev's desire for cooperation with the United States. In China's view, Gorbachev was a traitor to the international proletariat who sacrificed the socialist regimes of Eastern Europe for the sake of better relations with the United States. According to the semi-official journal *Shijie zhishi* (World Knowledge), for example, Gorbachev's overriding objective was "economic integration with the West."[12] Presidents Reagan and Bush were skeptical about this, however, and on several occasions during mid-1989, top U.S. officials told Moscow that a fundamental change in Soviet policy toward Eastern Europe was an essential precondition for substantially improved economic relations. According to the article, "The United States stressed [to Moscow] that the Eastern European issue still constituted the principal stumbling block which must be removed before the United States and the Soviet Union could establish mutually beneficial relations. The demolition of the Berlin Wall has finally freed the United States of all misgivings." Gorbachev's shift in Eastern European policy opened the way to broad Soviet-American understandings during the Malta summit of December 1989. The United States "put an end to its economic cold war against the Soviet Union and showed greater enthusiasm than ever before in helping the Soviet Union join the international community." The article also noted that the new Soviet-American relation set the stage for cooperation in settling various regional problems.

Soviet-American cooperation in reversing Iraqi aggression against Kuwait provides another example of Soviet-American cooperation in ways antithetical to Chinese interests. Beijing quickly condemned Iraq's invasion of Kuwait in August 1990, and called for an immediate end to Iraqi military actions and for peaceful settlement of Iraqi-Kuwaiti disputes. In the United Nations Security Council, China voted for eleven resolutions directed against Iraq—including Resolution 661, providing for mandatory economic sanctions. In spite of Iraqi lobbying, China did not once use its veto power to block Security Council actions against Iraq, or join Cuba and Yemen in voting against several resolutions. When Iraqi officials visited Beijing seeking support, China declined and reiterated its opposition to Iraq's occupation of Kuwait. On Resolution 678, setting a January 15 deadline for Iraqi withdrawal and authorizing the use of force after that date, China abstained.

But China was also highly critical of the military buildup by "big powers" such as the United States in the Gulf region. It criticized the Western naval blockade of Iraq and condemned the U.S.-U.N. use of force against Iraq. According to China's permanent representative to the United Nations, Li Daoyu, further resort to military action would only aggravate the situation, escalate the conflict with unpredictable consequences, and fail to help resolve problems. The proper course of action, according to Li, lay with earnest implementation of measures already adopted (i.e., economic sanctions) rather than resort to military force. China supported a political solution of the crisis by peaceful means, Li said.

Fear of increased American power was one factor shaping Chinese policy during the Gulf War. A number of Chinese commentaries asserted that Washington wanted to use war against Iraq to bring the entire Middle East region under U.S. domination. Washington's planners wanted to seize the opportunity presented by the decline of countervailing Soviet power to expand U.S. hegemony in the Middle East. American success in this endeavor would embolden Washington even more in its anti-China policies. For example, according to a paper on "The Gulf War and China" drafted by one of Premier Li Peng's key foreign policy advisers and circulated among the senior cadre after the Gulf War, the U.S. goal is world domination. Following its recent series of victories in Eastern Europe and the Gulf, "yankee imperialism" would now turn to deal with China, the major remaining obstacle to the U.S. goal of world unification. "The U.S. has decided it must thoroughly destroy the existing order of China," the paper asserted. To achieve this, Washington planned to isolate China, blockade it, and disintegrate it via internal disorder, eventually rendering China innocuous by democratizing it.[13] Although Chinese commentary was not explicitly critical of Moscow for working with the United States to reverse Iraqi aggression, the implication was clear enough.

It is not difficult to imagine scenarios of future Russian-American "collusion" against China. They might involve, for example, Korea, Taiwan, or the South China Sea. In Korea, Russo-American collusion might take the form of Russian assistance in removal of the Kim Il-sung dynasty and the initiation of a process of opening and liberalization in the North, and ultimately the reunification of Korea along German lines.

This would clearly run counter to Chinese policy, which has sought to bolster the Communist regime in North Korean since 1989.

Regarding Taiwan, Russo-American collusion would most probably take the form of joint moves to secure Taiwanese entry into international organizations over PRC opposition, to deter PRC military moves against Taiwan, or, in extremis, to recognize Taiwanese independence. Beijing has perennially been concerned about the establishment of some sort of link between the Soviet Union and Taiwan. In 1989 it became especially concerned with developments in Moscow's Taiwan policy under Gorbachev's New Thinking. When Gorbachev arrived in Beijing in May 1989 for his summit with Deng Xiaoping, the first Soviet delegation to visit Taiwan openly since 1949 arrived in Taibei. Made up of academicians from the Institute of World Economy and International Relations, the Soviet delegation was hosted by quasi-private organizations, and stressed Russia's hope for economic cooperation with Taiwan.

Beijing was dismayed by the shift in Soviet policy, and feared that Moscow might go further in developing relations with Taiwan. According to some reports, some Chinese leaders even feared that Moscow might go so far as to recognize Taiwan. Early in 1990 while a proposed visit by Premier Li Peng to Moscow was being debated within the CCP, veteran hard-line leader Wang Zhen, along with others, reportedly opposed such a visit on the grounds that China did not need to reward Gorbachev for its obnoxious new policies on Taiwan. This approach was overruled, in part on the grounds that by going to Moscow Li would be able to deliver a warning about what Beijing would and would not accept over Taiwan. When CCP Secretary General Jiang Zemin visited Beijing in May 1991 Soviet spokesmen made clear that the USSR recognized Taiwan as a province of the PRC over which Beijing exercised sovereignty. With the demise of the USSR, this position has not been explicitly reiterated by Russia.

In the South China Sea, Russo-American collusion might take the form of joint support for a solution of the dispute over the Spratly Islands on terms favorable to the Philippines, Malaysia, and Vietnam and less favorable to the PRC. In February 1992 issue a professor at the Institute of World Economy and International Relations in Moscow suggested that Washington and Moscow might work together to settle the dispute over the Spratly Islands and, in conjunction with Indonesia, help organize the multilateral exploitation of mineral resources beneath the surrounding seabed.[14] In other words, the United States and Russia should jointly pressure China to relinquish part of its claims to the entire South China Sea, or if that failed, jointly protect exploitation of the resources of that region in the face of Chinese protests.

If a cordial, cooperative relation continues to develop between the United States and Russia, Beijing will be extremely sensitive of any form of Russo-American cooperation in ways it deems antithetical to China's interests. To deal with such threats, Beijing will have to resort to deft triangular diplomacy. Of course, Japan's steadily increasing power introduces a new and important variable into the equation. Yet it will probably make sense for some time to think in terms of a Russian-American-Chinese triangle.

CHINA'S SUPERPOWER DIPLOMACY

China's leaders demonstrated great flexibility in maneuvering between the American and Soviet superpowers to obtain their goals. China's alignments with one or the other of the superpowers were brief. The Sino-Soviet alliance of the 1950s lasted about eight years, from 1950 to 1958. The Sino-American united front of 1978 through 1981 lasted less than half that long. Figure 4–1 depicts the variability of China's triangular relations.

One structural factor helping to account for the transient nature of China's superpower alignments was the great reluctance of the superpowers to challenge and confront one another. Because of this reluctance, China frequently was disappointed by the level of support provided by its superpower ally. Beijing found Soviet support during the 1958 Taiwan Straits crisis, for example, tardy and weak. Again during the 1979 Sino-Vietnamese war, Beijing judged American support to be lukewarm. (The 1979 war is discussed in Chapter Fourteen.) In both cases, China's ally wanted to stand by it, but feared that overly bold actions would lead to confrontation with the other superpower. In both instances, this caution disappointed Chinese leaders.

China's deep sense of pride also helps explain its remarkable reluctance to attach itself to either of the superpowers. When it entered into a partnership with one of the superpowers, China's lesser economic, diplomatic, and military resources inevitably made it the junior partner. This inferior status was extremely galling to the Chinese, with their recollection of their nation's ancient grandeur and recent humiliation. China's sense of self-confidence also inclined it toward independence. Its size, large population and, most important, its endurance as a nation over several thousand years gave China a strong sense that it could go it alone. When one considers, for example, China's very real weaknesses of the 1960s—the economic collapse following the Great Leap Forward and then the disruption and deep divisions of the Cultural Revolution—it is amazing that during this period China's leaders dared to confront the United States and the USSR simultaneously. The confrontation with the United States over Indochina was kept carefully within bounds. Nonetheless, the fact that China dared to confront both superpowers at once during its period of maximum weakness demonstrated great self-confidence.

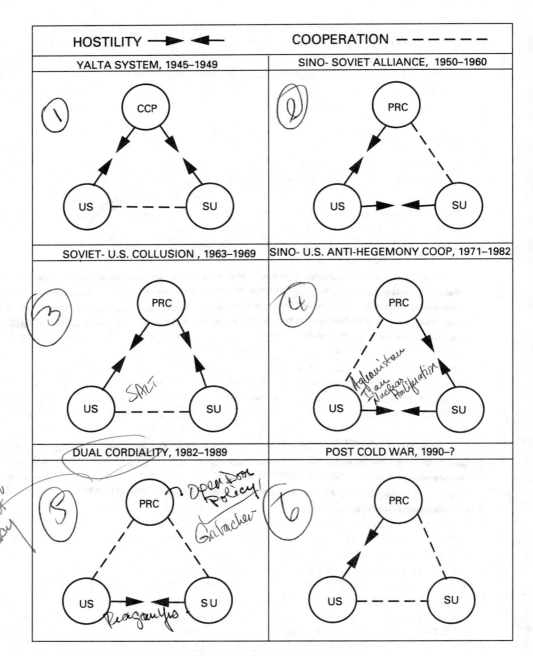

Figure 4–1   Evolution of the Triangular System

Yet another psychological factor that helps explain China's triangular independence is its deep sense of uniqueness. China viewed its society and its values as fundamentally different from those of either the Soviet Union or the United States. China's leaders may genuinely have believed in Marxist-Leninist philosophy, but they took great pride in the fact that they have sinicized that philosophy and were "building socialism with Chinese characteristics." Conversely, they recognized the advanced state of Western science, industry, and technology, but found Western values and forms of social organization profoundly repugnant. Most of China's leaders felt no real kinship with either superpower and, therefore, felt free to align or disalign with either according to China's momentary needs.

Two other structural factors also influenced China's triangular interactions. First, a primary Chinese objective was to prevent an American-Soviet diktat against China. From China's viewpoint, Soviet-American collusion against China has occurred twice: in the periods from 1945 to 1948 and 1963 to 1971. In neither case was superpower collusion fully consummated. The superpowers did not agree to partition China in 1948 nor to jointly preempt its nuclear program in the 1960s. Yet in both cases, China's leaders saw a trend in that direction, feared the possible consummation, and worked to abort it. The second structural factor was a belief that China's interests are best served when the two superpowers are hostile to one another. In such a situation both superpowers will seek China's support or at least seek to minimize its support for the rival superpower, giving China more room for maneuver. Thus, China opposed Khrushchev's policy of peaceful coexistence in the 1950s and Soviet-American detente in the 1970s. This is not to say that Beijing desired a war between the superpowers. It almost certainly did not, although Khrushchev suspected that it did. Rather, what Beijing desired was a high but manageable level of superpower hostility that would give China leverage with both. From this perspective the new post-Cold War world order based on Russian-Western amity rather than hostility may be especially dangerous to Beijing.

NOTES

1. Regarding the 1982 shift, see Donald Zagoria, "Soviet Policy and Prospects in East Asia," *International Security*, vol. 5, no. 2 (Fall 1980), 66–78; Carol Lee Hamrin, "China Reassesses the Superpowers," *Pacific Affairs*, vol. 56, no. 2 (Summer 1983), 209–31; Donald Zagoria, "The Moscow-Beijing Detente," *Foreign Affairs*, vol. 6, no. 4 (Spring 1983), 853–73; Su Chi, "U.S.-China Relations: Soviet Views and Policies," *Asian Survey*, vol. 23, no. 5 (May 1983), 555–79; William E. Griffith, "Sino-Soviet Rapprochement?" *Problems of Communism*, vol. 32, no. 2 (March–April 1983), 20–29; Samuel S. Kim, "China and the Third World: In Search of a Neorealist World Policy," *China and the World: China Foreign Policy in the Post-Mao Era*, Samuel Kim, ed., Boulder, Colo.: Westview, 1984, 200–207; Jonathan Pollack, *The Lessons of Coalition Politics: Sino-American Security Relations*, Santa Monica, Calif.: Rand Corporation, February 1984.

2. *The New York Times*, January 30, 1980, A15. During 1980, NATO analysts felt that a Soviet attack on China was highly likely before too long. *The New York Times*, May 21, 1980.

3. Regarding the application of this logic to the case of India and South Asia, see John W. Garver, "The Indian Factor in Recent Sino-Soviet Relations," *China Quarterly*, no. 125 (June 1991), 55–85. Regarding Soviet efforts to prevent Sino-Indian rapprochement, see Robert C. Horn, "The Soviet Union and Sino-Indian Relations," *Orbis*, vol. 26, no. 4 (Winter 1983), 900–901.

4. Regarding the Taiwan issue and the 1982 adjustment of PRC triangular policy, see John W. Garver, "Arms Sales, the Taiwan Question, and Sino-U.S. Relations," *Orbis*, vol. 26, no. 4 (Winter 1983), 999–1104; Thomas W. Robinson, "Choice and Consequences in Sino-American Relations," *Orbis*, vol. 25, no. 1 (Spring 1981), 29–51; James C. Hsiung, "Reagan's China Policy and the Sino-Soviet Detente," *Asian Affairs*, vol. 11, no. 2 (Summer 1984), 1–11; A. Doak Barnett, *The FX Decision: "Another Crucial Moment" in U.S.-China-Taiwan Relations*, Washington, D.C.: Brookings Institute, 1981. Regarding U.S. congressional-executive conflicts over the Taiwan issue, see Robert L. Downen, *The Taiwan Pawn in the China Game: Congress to the Rescue*, Washington, D.C.: Georgetown University, The Center for Strategic and International Studies, 1979; Michael S. Frost, *Taiwan's Security and United States Policy: Executive and Congressional Strategies in 1978–1979*, Baltimore: University of Maryland, School of Law, 1982, no. 4, Occasional Papers/Reprints Series in Contemporary Asian Studies. Regarding the Taiwan issue more generally, see Hungdah Chiu, ed., *China and the Taiwan Issue*, New York: Praeger, 1979; Ralph N. Clough, *Island China*, Cambridge: Harvard University Press, 1978.

5. Zi Zhongyun, "U.S. Policy toward Taiwan (1948–50)," Part II, *Beijing Review*, vol. 25, no. 28 (July 12, 1982), 25. Part I of this article is in *Beijing Review*, vol. 25, no. 7 (July 5, 1982), 14–20.

6. Sources on Sino-Soviet relations in the Gorbachev era include Steven I. Levine, "The End of Sino-Soviet Estrangement," *Current History*, vol. 85, no. 512 (September 1986), 245–48, 279; William DeB. Mills, "Baiting the Chinese Dragon: Sino-Soviet Relations After Vladivostok," *Journal of Northeast Asian Studies*, vol. 6, no. 3 (Fall 1987), 3–30; William DeB. Mills, "Gorbachev and the Future of Sino-Soviet Relations," *Political Science Quarterly*, vol. 101, no. 4 (Centennial year 1986), 535–57; Chun-tu Hsueh, "Sino-Soviet Relations as Viewed from Moscow: An Account of a Meeting with Soviet Deputy Foreign Minister Kapitsa," *International Studies Notes*, vol. 12, no. 3 (Fall 1986), 64–66; Gerald Segal, "The USSR and Asia in 1987: Signs of a Major Effort," *Asian Survey*, vol. 28, no. 1 (January 1988), 1–9; Robert G. Sutter, *Sino-Soviet Relations: Recent Improvements and Implications for the United States*, Congressional Research Service, Issue Brief 86138, January 6, 1988; Guo-cang Huan, *Sino-Soviet Relations to the Year 2000*, The Atlantic Council of the United States, Occasional Papers, 1986; Gary Klintworth, "Gorbachev's China Diplomacy," *The Soviet Union as an Asian Pacific Power*, Ramesh Thakur and Carlyle A. Thayer, eds., Boulder, Colo.: Westview, 1987, 39–57. A useful chronology of Sino-Soviet relations is in *FBIS, DRC*, February 17, 1989, 8–9.

7. Regarding the Chinese role in the Soviet withdrawal from Afghanistan, see Leslie Holmes, "Afghanistan and Sino-Soviet Relations," in *The Soviet Withdrawal from Afghanistan*, Amin Saikal and William Maley, eds., New York: Cambridge University Press, 1989, 122–41; *Strategic Survey, 1987–88*, London: International Institute for Strategic Studies, 1988.

8. Tai Ming Cheung, "Holding the Line," *FEER*, June 27, 1991, 23–30.

9. Regarding the Deng-Gorbachev summit, see John W. Garver, "The 'New Type' of Sino-Soviet Relations," *Asian Survey*, vol. 29, no. 12 (December 1989), 1136–52.

10. "Soviets Simulating Attacks on Alaska, China, Says U.S. Admiral on Port Call," *Atlanta Journal and Constitution*, November 6, 1986, 28.

11. Wu Ge, "Voice of America's Performance and 'Peaceful Evolution' Strategy," *Renmin Ribao*, July 9, 1989, 4, in *FBIS, DRC*, July 11, 1989, 4–8.

12. *FBIS, DRC*, November 28, 1990, 6–8.

13. *FBIS, DRC*, February 27, 1991, 5–6.

14. Eduard Grebenschshikov, "Place in the Sun," *Far Eastern Economic Review*, February 13, 1992, 24.

Part Three

China as a Revolutionary Power

Chapter Five

Revolutionary China in the Socialist Camp

THE DYNAMICS OF REVOLUTION

Revolutions and states born of revolutions share certain common characteristics. One is inspiration by a vision of a fundamentally good and just society, a vision of utopia. This vision explains the "necessity" of drastic social reorganization and "justifies" the violence and human suffering associated with that reorganization.[1] The content of the utopian vision varies. In the case of the American and French revolutions it was derived from theories of natural right and social compact propounded respectively by John Locke and Jean-Jacques Rousseau. The American revolutionaries believed that establishing a system of government based upon the consent of the governed would ensure the exercise of natural rights free from tyranny. They could imagine no more perfect earthly state. For twentieth-century revolutions, while there have been important non-Marxist variants of utopian vision—the Ayatollah Khomeini's Islamic fundamentalist vision, for example—most have been inspired by the utopian vision of Karl Marx and Vladimir Ilyich Lenin.

Marx and Lenin believed that the seizure of power through armed insurrection by the proletariat would usher in a new era in human existence. All of history, they believed, had been a chronicle of the exploitation of the laboring classes by the property-owning classes. On such class exploitation was built a civilization of war, oppression, and human degradation, and the juxtaposition of poverty and misery with wealth and leisure. Once the proletariat seized power, however, it would eliminate the exploitation of man by man. Private ownership of the means of production would become a thing of the past. After a transitional period of revolutionary dictatorship, a classless society would emerge. Everyone would now enjoy a similar standard of living. Because they now collectively controlled their own labor, people would work diligently, creatively, and joyfully. War would become a thing of the past. Indeed, the armed, repressive apparatus that had dominated class-divided societies—the state—would become unnecessary and disappear.[2]

In China, Mao Zedong believed deeply in the utopian vision of Marx and Lenin. Some of Mao's comrades were ready by the 1960s to shelve the pursuit of communist utopia, concentrating instead on more mundane problems of economic development. Mao, however, remained committed to the realization of the vision. This profoundly influenced China's foreign relations under Mao.

A second characteristic of revolution is a messianic urge, an impulse to carry the message of the revolution to other peoples and other lands. This messianic urge is probably rooted in the general tendency to judge strange things by that which is known, to judge foreign lands by one's own standards. With revolutionary states, this tendency is exacerbated by intense ideological belief. Revolutionaries must believe fervently in their ideology, otherwise they would be unwilling to sacrifice themselves and others to achieve victory. Without this willingness to sacrifice, the revolutionary movement would fail. The claim to universality made by most modern revolutionary ideologies also contributes to the messianic urge. The creators of modern revolutionary ideologies invariably claim that their systems of thought are applicable to all people of all ages. This claim to universality combined with the intensity of revolutionary conviction makes revolutionary leaders believe that it is their duty to carry their message to other lands.

The amalgamation of revolutionary ideology and national interest also fuels the revolutionary messianic impulse. Modern revolutions have been carried out on a national basis; that is, by the peoples constituting various large ethnic communities—the French, Russians, Chinese, Vietnamese, Persians, and so on. After the revolutionaries seize power they reorganize national institutions. A new national state is created by the revolution to protect the revolution. The interests of the revolution and the nation are thereby meshed. Once the nation becomes a revolutionary nation, defense of the nation becomes defense of the revolution and expansion of national power furthers the revolutionary mission. The combination of nationalism and revolution has proved extremely potent. Citizens of most modern nations have found satisfaction in identifying with "their" nation. When they become convinced that the destiny of their nation is to carry a particular utopian vision to other lands, an expansionist dynamic is easily set in motion.

Of the many examples of revolutionary messianism, perhaps the one most familiar to U.S. students is the American revolution. From the earliest beginnings of English settlement on the Atlantic seaboard, the colonists had a strong sense that they had been chosen by God to serve as a model and inspiration for the rest of mankind. God had given them this vast and rich land, they believed, so that they might create a new society based on true religion free from the corruption of the "old world." This new society would stand as "a city on a hill," lighting the way for the rest of humanity. These notions of a unique American mission were strengthened by the revolt against English rule. The leaders of the revolution, and indeed many ordinary Americans, felt that it was part of the historic, divinely ordained mission of America to provide an example of liberal law, representative government, and true religion. This sense of mission was, however, combined with a strong belief that America should not become entangled in the affairs of the corrupt old world. Thus, while early revolutionary America had great sympathy for foreign revolutionary movements (for example, those of France, Eastern Europe, and Latin America), this sympathy was not translated into active support. America was to fulfill its revolutionary mission by serving as a beacon to mankind; that is, by a passive rather than an active role.

There was an expansionist zeal in revolutionary America, but it was directed westward rather than toward Europe or Latin America. The conquest of the lands between the Appalachian Mountains and the Pacific Ocean was seen by many of the Americans involved in that process as the expansion of representative government, freedom, and liberty to the lands set aside by God for those institutions. It was the Manifest Destiny of America to spread its enlightened values and institutions across the North American continent. The creation of a free, liberal republic of continental scope was seen, in turn, as greatly strengthening the American beacon of hope to the benighted masses of the world.

CHINA AS A GREAT AND REVOLUTIONARY POWER

As with other modern revolutions, the attainment of China's revolutionary objectives was inextricably tied to achievement of national goals. The radical reorganization of Chinese society would, the CCP believed, strengthen China. The stronger China became, the sooner it would be able to complete China's national liberation; for example, by liberating Taiwan. It would also be more able to assist the national liberation struggles of other peoples. More generally, China's new leaders believed that the existing international system was profoundly unjust. To them, the established international order was a system set up and run by robbers, and nothing less than a complete change in the world system would ensure China's genuine independence or the liberation of other oppressed nations. PRC leaders were vague about what the new international system would look like—other than it would *not* be imperialistic and would be based on strict national equality.[3]

Achievement of China's revolutionary and nationalist objectives required, PRC leaders believed, the overthrow of the U.S.-dominated international order. Across Asia, Washington was playing a counterrevolutionary role. In Japan, U.S. occupation authorities had "reversed course" in 1948 and 1949, switching from radical reform to anti-leftist policies. From Beijing's point of view, Washington was attempting to crush Japan's "progressive forces," prevent revolution, and restore to power the industrial and military circles that had ruled pre-war Japan. In 1950 the United States intervened to prevent the liberation of South Korea by the forces led by Kim Il-sung's Korean Workers Party. In the Philippines and French Indochina, the United States was playing a major role in the suppression of powerful Communist-led insurgencies. In Malaya, America's close associate Great Britain was playing a similar role. The United States still threatened and pressured China and was increasingly involved in Taiwan. Revolutionary ideology and national interests seemed to mesh. The overthrow of U.S. power in East Asia would give a tremendous boost to Communist-led revolutionary movements throughout that region. At the same time, it would reduce the U.S. threat to revolutionary China and permit China to complete its own national liberation struggle.

During its first two years, the PRC proclaimed sweeping support for revolution in all non-socialist countries of Asia. During the first months of the PRC's existence, the CCP also claimed that China's own revolutionary experience—protracted guerrilla war in the rural areas led by a "proletariat party"—was a model applicable for the colonial and "semi-colonial" countries of the Third World, especially those of Asia. These claims of broad applicability of the Chinese revolutionary model ceased early in 1950, probably as a result of Soviet pressure. They reappeared in the late 1950s and remained prominent until the mid-1970s.[4]

Beijing's material support for foreign revolutionary struggles during the PRC's early years was limited to Korea and North Vietnam. In those cases, Chinese support was large and decisive. Regarding Chinese intervention in Korea in 1950, concern for PRC security was the CCP's major consideration. But considerations of ideological solidarity with the North Korean Communist regime also played a role. (China's entry into the Korean War is discussed in Chapter Thirteen.) As for Vietnam, PRC support for Vietnam's Communist-led national liberation struggle began in December 1949 (prior to the outbreak of the Korean War) when the People's Liberation Army (PLA) reached the Sino-Vietnamese border. Beijing saw the Vietnamese struggle against French colonial rule as the critical wedge of the socialist camp in Southeast Asia and began providing large-scale support for the Vietminh. (The Vietminh was a united front led by Ho Chi Minh and his Vietnam Workers Party (VWP), Vietnam's communist party.) Chinese military assistance to the Vietminh was substantial and quickly transformed it into an efficient force capable of capturing major French fortifications. Large amounts of U.S.-made arms—including heavy mortars, 105 mm howitzers, and recoilless rifles—taken from defeated KMT forces were given to the Vietminh. By the summer of 1950, about half of Vietminh forces were equipped with U.S. weapons obtained from China. The PLA set up three camps in Yunnan and Guangxi to train Vietminh recruits. By August 1950, over 20,000 Vietminh had passed through these camps. Roads and rail lines were pushed close to Vietnam's borders, and large numbers of Chinese personnel were involved in the logistics effort to supply the Vietminh. China's support was critical to the Vietminh defeat of France in 1954.[5]

When the Democratic Republic of Vietnam (DRV) was formed in December 1950, the PRC immediately established relations with it on a "comradely" basis. PRC-DRV relations were simplified by the fact that both were socialist states led by Marxist-Leninist parties. The PRC's relations with most of the governments of the newly independent countries of Asia and Africa were more complex. Following World War II, the vast European colonial empires rapidly evolved into dozens of independent countries. The governments of most of these ex-colonies were non-socialist, linked to indigenous property-owning elites, and oriented culturally and economically toward the West. As such, they were not "progressive" from a Marxist point of view. Yet to a degree their interests clashed with those of the Western powers, and to this degree, they were "progressive." In Marxist-Leninist parlance, these governments were bourgeois nationalist regimes with a dual progressive and reactionary nature. They had led their countries to formal independence, but they remained tied to feudalism, capitalism, and imperialism.

Chinese and Soviet revolutionary strategy toward these so-called bourgeois nationalist regimes went through several stages. From 1949 to 1953, Beijing and Moscow divided the world into two camps—an imperialist camp led by the United States and a socialist camp led by the Soviet Union. There was nothing in between. The bourgeois regimes of the newly independent countries were lackeys of imperialism and oppressors of their own peoples. As such, they were to be swept into the dustbin of history by popular revolutionary forces.

The CCP's acceptance of this simple dualistic perspective may have reflected Mao's deference to Stalin. The two-camp theory predated the formation of the PRC; it was first announced in an international conference of Communist parties held in Calcutta, India, in 1947. As we saw in Chapter Two, Stalin was very suspicious of Mao's nationalist tendencies. Wanting to assure Stalin of his loyalty and consolidate the Sino-Soviet alliance, Mao may have accepted this two-camp theory, even though it did not fit with his own ideas about the importance of united fronts.

In any case, the two-camp perspective was drawn into question during the Korean War when it became apparent that some of the newly independent countries (most particularly India) were skeptical of U.S. policy and willing to support certain Sino-Soviet diplomatic objectives. Moscow and Beijing concluded that a more flexible approach toward the bourgeois nationalist regimes might be an effective way to counter U.S. containment efforts. Both Communist powers thus moderated their propaganda and began courting Third World bourgeois nationalist governments under the rubric of "peaceful coexistence." It was Stalin himself who raised the possibility of "peaceful coexistence" among countries with different social systems in a speech at the nineteenth congress of the Communist Party of the Soviet Union (CPSU) in October 1952. After Stalin's death in March 1953, his successors, first Gregori Malenkov and then Nikita Khrushchev, embraced and developed this new line. Beijing, too, welcomed the new, moderate orientation.

There were two main reasons for Beijing's decision. First, "socialist construction" within China was still in its early stages and the nation was still weak. China had just completed nationwide land reform and was still in the midst of reorganizing and modernizing its military, establishing a planned economy, and setting up a system of CCP hegemony over the political system. Losses in the Korean War had also been heavy. Several years of international relaxation would give China time to accomplish these tasks, thereby strengthening itself. Second, there was a possibility that by reducing international tension and improving China's relations with its neighbors, Washington might be persuaded to ease its containment policies. Failing this, Beijing's new friendly approach might dissuade various countries from participating in Washington's containment schemes.

The PRC's moderate diplomacy of the period from 1954 to 1957 was an attempt to divide the enemy camp, drawing various countries away from U.S. imperialism. To a degree this can be construed as an international united front, the first of several broad international coalitions that Beijing tried to catalyze over the years. According to J.D. Armstrong, however, the moderate approach of the 1950s should not be deemed a true united front, since it lacked the drive to revolutionize the constituent members of the united front that is essential to Mao Zedong's version of the united front.[6] According to Armstrong, China did not develop a true united front until 1958.

China's moderate foreign policy brought it into conflict with the Vietnamese revolution at the Geneva Conference on Indochina in April 1954. China was represented at Geneva by Zhou Enlai, whose principal objective was to end the fighting in Indochina (thereby denying the United States a pretext for intervening and threatening China's southern borders). Secondary objectives were to demonstrate Chinese moderation and, perhaps, to keep Cambodia and Laos out of Vietnamese control. These goals were very different from those of DRV representative Pham Van Dong. Dong sought Vietnamese unification under VWP rule, and a special role for the Laotian and Cambodian liberation movements linked to the VWP. Dong felt that the military situation in Vietnam justified these claims; the day before the Geneva conference began, the French fort at Dien Bien Phu surrendered.

Zhou worked with great skill to pressure Dong to accept a compromise settlement. In the middle of the conference, Zhou flew to South China to tell Ho Chi Minh that unless Hanoi adopted a more flexible position at Geneva it would receive no more Chinese aid. Eventually Zhou, along with the Soviet foreign minister, British prime minister, and French premier, forced Dong to accept the partition of Vietnam. Moreover, the partition line was placed at the seventeenth parallel, not at the thirteenth parallel as Dong had demanded once he was pressured into accepting partition. To add insult to injury, elections for an all-Vietnam government were not to be held for two years, thereby allowing anti-Communist forces in South Vietnam time to consolidate. Finally, the pro-Hanoi Cambodian and Laotian liberation movements were to play no role in Cambodia and were merely given two provinces as a regroupment zone in Laos. Pham Van Dong was furious with Zhou's role at Geneva and reportedly walked away from the last round of bargaining muttering to an aide: "He has double-crossed us."[7]

This was the first of two instances where China's national interests led to policies contradictory to those pursued by Vietnam's revolutionary leaders. (The second, in 1972, will be discussed later.) Because of geography, China's support for Vietnam's revolutionary struggle was often especially important. By the same token, when China's broader interests led it to seek better relations with the United States, the contradictions between the dictates of that policy and those of the Vietnamese revolution became most acute.

CHINA IN THE SOCIALIST CAMP

During the period of moderate diplomacy in the mid-1950s, Beijing's revolutionary energies were directed toward reorganizing relations within the socialist camp. Since the emergence of the international Communist movement in 1919, that movement had been dominated by the CPSU. In theory, all parties were equal, but since only the CPSU had at its disposal the assets of a powerful nation—the USSR—that party dominated the movement. With the creation of an additional eleven

Eastern European and Asian socialist states between 1945 and 1950, however, the old basis for Moscow's leading role no longer held: The USSR was no longer the only socialist state, nor even the most populous one. Stalin's death in 1953 further diminished the Soviet claim to preeminence, since none of his successors in the CPSU enjoyed his exalted status.[8]

Mao's blueprint for reorganization of the socialist camp called for the equality and unity of all socialist countries and the Communist parties ruling those countries. Unity of the socialist camp was a matter of paramount importance for the world revolution, Mao believed. Unity was essential to protect the individual socialist countries from imperialist attack and to facilitate revolutionary advances around the world. Unity could not be achieved, however, if the Soviet Union continued to dominate other socialist countries. Soviet domination of other socialist countries would generate anti-Soviet sentiments, and direct nationalist feelings against the local Communist governments that had agreed to Moscow's onerous terms. This would weaken and divide the socialist camp. Genuine unity within the socialist camp could be achieved, Mao believed, only if the "national chauvinist errors" of Stalin's era were overcome.

When anti-Soviet ferment erupted in Eastern Europe in 1956, Mao saw Moscow's unequal treatment of those countries as one important cause of this turmoil. From Mao's Marxist-Leninist perspective, there was no underlying social or economic reason for Soviet efforts to dominate other countries—what Mao termed "great-power chauvinism." Rather, this resulted merely from Stalin's ideological mistakes, from misinterpretations of revolutionary theory. In the words of a major Chinese statement following the Eastern European upheavals of 1956:

> On the whole, in relations with brother countries and parties Stalin took an internationalist stand and helped the struggle of other peoples and the growth of the socialist camp; but in tackling certain concrete questions, he showed a tendency toward great-nation chauvinism and himself lacked a spirit of equality....Sometimes he even intervened mistakenly, with many grave consequences, in the internal affairs of certain brother countries and parties. Stalin's mistakes did not originate in the socialist system; it therefore follows that it is not necessary to "correct...the socialist system" in order to correct these mistakes.[9]

Mao believed that Stalin's "errors" should be rectified. There should be complete equality between all fraternal Communist parties and socialist countries. One aspect of this equality was that the general line of the socialist camp and the world Communist movement should no longer be set by Moscow alone, but through consultations among the fraternal parties and countries. The Soviet Union was to remain, however, the leader. The international revolutionary movement required a leader, and that leader could only be the USSR. But the line implemented under Soviet leadership should be determined collectively. In effect, Mao was trying to balance equality with central leadership. Quoting again from the Chinese statement of 1956:

> During the past thirty-nine years the Soviet Union has been the center of the international Communist movement, owing to the fact that it is the first country where socialism triumphed, while after the appearance of the camp of socialism—[it was] the most powerful country in the camp, having the richest experience and capable of rendering the greatest assistance to other socialist countries and to the peoples of various countries in the capitalist world. This is not the result of anyone's arbitrary decision, but the natural outcome of historical conditions. In the interests of the common cause of the proletariat of different countries, of joint resistance to the attack on the socialist cause by the imperialist camp headed by the United States, and of the economic and cultural upsurge common to all socialist countries, we must continue to strengthen international proletarian solidarity with the Soviet Union as its center.[10]

According to Mao, relations among all socialist countries should be founded on the basis of the Five Principles of Peaceful Coexistence. These principles were: (1) mutual respect for territorial integrity and sovereignty, (2) mutual non-aggression, (3) mutual non-interference in internal affairs, (4) equality and mutual benefit, and (5) peaceful coexistence. A PRC government statement of November 1956 on relations among socialist states, after listing the principles, said:

> The socialist countries are all independent, sovereign states. At the same time they are united to the common ideal of socialism and the spirit of proletarian internationalism. Consequently, mutual relations between socialist countries all the more so should be established on the basis of these five principles. Only in this way are the socialist countries able to achieve genuine fraternal friendship and solidarity and, through mutual assistance and cooperation, their desire for a mutual economic upsurge.[11]

The Five Principles of Peaceful Coexistence were worked out by Chinese and Indian leaders in April 1954. Initially Beijing applied them only to Sino-Indian relations. At the Bandung Conference in April 1955, Beijing extended them to China's relations with all non-socialist Third World countries. Later the principles were expanded further, until by the 1970s they applied to relations among all countries of the world. From Beijing's perspective, these principles embodied a code of international behavior radically different from imperialism and hegemonism. As such, the Five Principles were to be the basis of the post-imperialist international order. Table 5–1 illustrates the evolution of the Five Principles.

There were two major problems regarding the application of the Five Principles: first, whether they, or the more intimate principles of proletarian internationalism, should govern relations among socialist states. Although the 1956 declaration applied peaceful coexistence to intra-socialist camp relations, at other times, proletarian internationalism was upheld as the proper principle governing these relations. Proletarian internationalism implied a higher degree of mutual support than did peaceful coexistence. The second problem was whether peaceful coexistence applied to an aggressive superpower. During periods when Beijing tried to mobilize united fronts to struggle against one of the superpowers, it typically concluded that the Five Principles were inapplicable—although this conclusion was never made explicit. In 1960, when he was challenging Khrushchev's application of peaceful coexistence to relations with the United States, Mao Zedong elaborated in private writings his views about the limits of the doctrine:

> It is inconceivable that war can be abolished completely when the capitalist system still exists in the world. Can it be said that there has now emerged the possibility of abolishing war forever and utilizing all the world's...resources in the service of the whole of mankind? In this kind of interpretation there is no Marxism, no class analysis....Only through war can we eliminate classes and only through eliminating classes can we abolish war forever. We do not believe that classes can be eliminated without carrying out a revolutionary war. It is just not possible to destroy the weapons of war without eliminating classes.[12]

From a Leninist perspective, Mao's drive to reorganize the socialist camp and the world Communist movement involved organization of the vanguard of the world revolutionary process. At the core of Lenin's doctrine is the idea that only the proletariat, acting through its most class-conscious elements organized into the Communist party, can provide ideologically correct leadership for the revolutionary process. It followed that the Communist party was the vanguard, the leader of the revolutionary process. In global terms, the vanguard of the world revolution was made up of the collection of proletarian states and parties.

While Stalin was alive there was little Mao could do to reorganize the socialist camp. After Stalin's death, however, Mao began pushing for change. During an October 1954 visit to Beijing by CPSU First Secretary Nikita Khrushchev, relations among the socialist countries were the main topic of discussion. The new Soviet leader was willing to concede many points to Mao, since according to Khrushchev's memoirs, he agreed with many of Mao's criticisms of Stalin's heavy-handed policies. Accordingly, Khrushchev and his comrades agreed to relinquish the USSR's special rights in China. This established the precedent for the liquidation of similar special privileges in the Eastern European socialist countries several years later.[13]

Significant differences between Mao and Khrushchev over questions

Table 5–1 Application of Five Principles of Peaceful Coexistence

April 29, 1954	Indian-Chinese agreement enumerates Five Principles and proclaims them basis of bilateral relations.
April 19, 1955	Zhou Enlai at Bandung conference proclaims Principles as basis for "normal relations with all the Asian and African countries, and with all the countries in the world, and first of all, with our neighboring countries."
November 1, 1956	PRC government statement applies Principles to "relations among the nations of the world" and especially among socialist nations since "only in this way are [they] able to achieve genuine fraternal friendship and solidarity."
December 12, 1963	Anti-Soviet polemic proclaims, "It is possible for the socialist countries to compel one imperialist country or another to establish some sort of peaceful coexistence with them by relying on their own growing strength, the expansion of the revolutionary forces of the people, the unity with the nationalist countries, the struggle of the peace-loving people, and by utilizing the internal contradictions of imperialism. . . . We [must] actively support the national liberation movements of Asia, Africa, and Latin America."
April 14, 1969	Lin Biao's report to 9th Congress, in context of discussion of Sino-Soviet relations, says that Principles apply to relations among "countries having different social systems." Relations among socialist countries to be based on proletarian internationalism.
February 27, 1972	Sino-U.S. communiqué says, "The two sides agree that countries, regardless of their social systems, should conduct their relations on the principles of respect for the sovereignty and territorial integrity of all states, non-aggression . . . , non-interference in internal affairs . . . , equality and mutual benefit, and peaceful cooperation."
August 18, 1977	Hua Guofeng's report to 11th Congress says, "We will . . . continue to wage a tit-for-tat struggle against [Soviet] hegemonism. At the same time, we have always held that China and the Soviet Union should maintain normal state relations on the basis of the Five Principles."
September 1, 1982	Hu Yaobang's report to 12th Congress says, "The Five Principles . . . are applicable to our relations with all countries, including socialist countries."

of bloc policy first emerged in 1956, over destalinization. Khrushchev's program of destalinization raised questions of bloc organization and line. While Mao was critical of Stalin's domineering attitude toward other socialist countries, he endorsed Stalin's emphasis on development of heavy industry and defense. There were nationalist and ideological reasons for this. From an ideological standpoint, Mao, like Stalin, saw heavy industry as the foundation of industrialization, which was, in turn, the basis for Communism. A shift away from heavy industry meant that mankind's achievement of Communism would be delayed. Downgrading heavy industry also implied a reduction in defense spending, which implied, in turn, reduced struggle against imperialism.[14]

During the 1953–1955 power struggle within the CPSU for

succession to Stalin, Mao supported Khrushchev, who then favored traditional Stalinist industrial priorities. After Khrushchev defeated his key opponents within the CPSU, however, he proceeded to adopt their economic program. With this about-face, Mao began to doubt the direction in which Khrushchev was leading the socialist camp. These doubts deepened when Khrushchev denounced Stalin at a closed session of the twentieth CPSU Congress in February 1956. Mao objected to the attack on Stalin because, first of all, Khrushchev had not consulted beforehand with other fraternal parties, but had presumed to declare unilaterally a line that would have major ramifications for the entire socialist camp and the world Communist movement. This was a gross violation of the principle of intra-camp equality that Mao was attempting to establish. In response, Mao wrote a polemical critique of Khrushchev's attack on Stalin as a way, among other things, of asserting the right of other camp members to have a say in deciding such fundamental questions of line.

Mao also feared that Khrushchev's criticism of Stalin's dictatorship implied a retreat from the revolutionary transformation of society. Abolition of dictatorship meant that progress toward Communist utopia and industrialization would be slowed. One of the functions of Stalinist control was to hold in check popular demands for more consumer goods and motivate people by non-economic methods, thereby making possible high levels of investment in basic industry. Mao also feared that Khrushchev's attack on Stalin would destabilize the newly established socialist regimes in Eastern Europe. Since those regimes had been created by Stalin, how could they defend their legitimacy once Stalin was denounced? Moreover, what would be the consequences of relaxing tight police control?

The question of destalinization became intertwined with relations between the socialist countries because of the anti-Soviet nationalist forces unleashed by destalinization in Eastern Europe. In the spring of 1956, first the Polish and then the Hungarian Communist parties began liberalizing their regimes—releasing political prisoners, allowing greater public discussion and autonomous political activity, and rehabilitating previously purged leaders. The most prominent rehabilitated Polish leader was Wladislav Gomulka. The most prominent Hungarian was Imre Nagy. Both had been purged for nationalism. Throughout the summer of 1956, there was mounting anti-Soviet nationalism in Poland and Hungary. When it became apparent in mid-October that the Central Committee of the Polish Communist Party intended to elect Gomulka First Secretary, a very high-powered CPSU delegation, including virtually the entire top CPSU leadership and eleven Soviet generals in full dress uniform, traveled to Warsaw to veto Gomulka's election. The Polish leadership held firm. Regarding the question of national independence, Gomulka told the outraged Soviet delegation: "It is up to our Central

Committee and to it alone to determine the membership of our Politburo....The composition of the leadership of a Communist party cannot, in my opinion, be discussed with a fraternal party."[15] In the end the Soviets backed down because of solid Polish unity behind Gomulka—and because of Chinese opposition to Soviet military intervention in Poland.

Beijing strongly supported the Polish Communist claim to independence from Moscow. In September 1956, when Polish First Secretary Gomulka's confidant, Edward Ochab, was in Beijing to attend a CCP Congress, Mao Zedong showed sympathy for Gomulka and his nationalist faction, an attitude that encouraged Ochab to speak out about Poland's troubles with Moscow. On one occasion, Mao and Ochab were discussing recent riots in Poland with Soviet leader Anastas Mikoyan, who was also in Beijing for the CCP Congress, when Mikoyan took objection to Ochab's description of events in Poland. Ochab retorted that the Poles knew more about what was happening in Poland than did the Soviets, adding that "Our people will no longer tolerate taking orders from abroad."[16] At that point Mikoyan exploded in anger. Ochab rose, silently shook hands with Mao, and left the room. Mao followed Ochab out, ignoring Mikoyan. Such Chinese support strengthened Polish resolve to stand fast before Soviet pressure. Several weeks later, when Moscow was considering using military force to reassert its authority in Poland, Mao Zedong advised against such a course.

Events in Hungary during 1956 were similar to those in Poland, with the crucial difference that the Hungarian Communists lost control over events and were swept along by the tide of popular nationalism—ultimately going so far as to scrap the Communist system. Nagy, who had been purged in 1954 for opposing the hyper-industrialization imposed on Hungary by Stalin, was sworn in as prime minister on October 24, 1956. Nagy's regime proved unable to contain the rapidly burgeoning mass movement that was increasingly taking outright anti-Communist forms. During the last days of October, Nagy saw that the Hungarian people would not accept continued Communist dictatorship and began moving toward a free political system. He also proclaimed Hungary's withdrawal from the Warsaw Pact. These developments were crushed by Soviet forces in November 1956.

In the case of Hungary, Mao Zedong urged Soviet military intervention. Mao concluded that military force had to be used to maintain the "unity of the socialist camp," and he urged Moscow to act quickly. Beijing's hard-line stance at this juncture won it considerable respect among the hard-pressed Stalinist regimes of Eastern Europe.[17]

Two factors explain Beijing's contrasting approaches to Poland and Hungary. One is ideological: Mao and his comrades were Marxist-Leninists who were convinced of the superiority of the socialist system and also believed that that system had to be founded and maintained by force. In Poland the socialist system was not threatened; in Hungary it was. The second explanation has to do with China's security and economic interests. Mao believed that the overthrow of Eastern European Communist regimes would weaken China's own security by weakening the Warsaw Pact. This would be the case especially if other Eastern European countries followed Hungary in withdrawing from the Warsaw Pact. Soviet acquiescence in the demise of socialism in Hungary would also be extremely troubling, implying, in the words of a major Chinese statement in December 1956 on events in Hungary, that "countries in the camp of socialism will...be picked off one by one by the forces of Western imperialism."[18] The demise of socialism in Eastern European countries would also have reduced China's claim on those relatively industrialized countries for development assistance.

Through its intra-bloc diplomacy in 1956, Beijing made substantial gains in achieving its objective of socialist unity through sovereign equality. On October 30, 1956, in the midst of the upheaval in Hungary and with strong Chinese urging, Moscow issued a declaration formally recognizing that relations among socialist states were governed by the principles of full equality, national independence, sovereignty, and non-intervention in internal affairs, as long as indigenous Communist government did not permit "foreign and international reactionary forces to shake the foundation of the People's Democratic regimes."[19]

In line with its desire to balance national equality with Soviet central authority, Beijing moved quickly to bolster Soviet leadership in the aftermath of the Polish and Hungarian revolts of 1956. In January 1957, Zhou Enlai visited Poland, East Germany, and Hungary. In discussions with leaders of those countries, Zhou stressed the importance of intra-bloc equality *and* Soviet leadership within the bloc. The socialist camp, Zhou said, must form a solid, united front to counter imperialist pressure, and Moscow had to be at the center of that united front. Moscow was very grateful for Chinese support in Eastern Europe at this juncture, and Beijing's leverage in Moscow correspondingly increased. As Richard Lowenthal noted, Beijing's efforts to influence bloc policy in 1957 were probably influenced by a belief that Moscow now needed Chinese support to legitimize its leadership of Eastern Europe.[20]

MAO'S CHALLENGE AT THE MOSCOW CONFERENCE

During the debates of 1956, Mao had established the principle that the line of the socialist camp should be set through consultations among the fraternal parties. On the basis of this, in November 1957, at a conference of Communist parties in Moscow commemorating the fortieth anniversary of the Bolshevik revolution, Mao attempted to commit the socialist camp, led by the Soviet Union, to militant struggle against U.S.

imperialism. Leaving China for the second and last time in his life, Mao led the CCP delegation to the Moscow conference, where he took the lead in formulating China's position. The CCP delegation played a high-profile role. According to a later account, the CCP delegation "had full consultations with the leaders of the CPSU, and where necessary and appropriate, would struggle against them, in order to help them correct their errors; on the other hand, it held repeated exchanges...with the leaders of other fraternal parties...."[21]

The issues raised at the Moscow conference foreshadowed many of the disputes that would split the world revolutionary camp over the next several years, destroying the Sino-Soviet alliance in the process. The major explicit dispute at the Moscow conference had to do with the nature of the transition between capitalism and socialism.[22] Was it possible for Communist parties in some countries to carry out a revolutionary transformation of society via peaceful, parliamentary means? Or did revolution require the armed seizure of power and violent destruction of the old state apparatus? Soviet representatives argued that the steady growth in strength of the socialist camp and world revolutionary forces made peaceful transition a real and important possibility in many countries. CCP representatives agreed to the abstract theoretical possibility that conditions might permit a peaceful transition to socialism in some countries. Moreover, they agreed that there were certain tactical advantages in a general endorsement of the possibility of peaceful transition: "It enables the Communist parties in the capitalist countries to sidestep attacks on them on this issue and it is politically advantageous...for winning the masses and...for depriving the bourgeois of its pretexts for attacks." But the CCP discounted the practical likelihood of a peaceful transition, saying, "To the best of our knowledge, there is still not a single country where this possibility is of any practical significance." Moreover, stressing such a remote possibility would lead to dangerous mistakes for the revolutionary movement. "The bourgeoisie will not step down from the stage of history voluntarily....In no way should the proletariat and the Communist party slacken their preparations for the revolution in any way." Too much stress on the possibility of peaceful transition "is liable to weaken the revolutionary will of the proletariat."[23] Eventually the Moscow conference agreed on a compromise formulation. But dispute over this point was not over.

The question of the possibility of a peaceful transition to socialism was closely linked to the question of relations between the socialist camp and the imperialist countries. If, as the CCP maintained, revolutionary transitions required war, the socialist camp should stand ready to support those revolutionary wars politically and materially. While this would probably create tension and confrontations between the imperialist and socialist countries, such risks had to be accepted. Refusal to render such support because of fear of confronting imperialist powers was tantamount to abandoning the quest for socialist revolution. If, on the other hand, peaceful transitions to socialism were a viable possibility, as the CPSU maintained, then confrontations between the socialist and imperialist countries might be avoided and tensions reduced. Disagreements over these points remained latent at the 1957 Moscow conference. A compromise formulation regarding the possibility of peaceful coexistence that was acceptable to everyone—which could be interpreted differently by both sides—was written into the official declaration of the conference, to wit: "At the present time the forces of peace have grown to such an extent that there is a real possibility of averting wars....The Leninist principle of peaceful coexistence of the two systems...is the sound basis of the foreign policy of socialist countries and the dependable pillar of peace."[24]

Underlying the CCP-CPSU debate over peaceful coexistence were differing appraisals of the consequences of a shift in the "global correlation of forces," a term referring to a broad balance of power encompassing economic, political, psychological, and military factors. By 1957 both Mao and Khrushchev agreed that there had been a fundamental shift in the global correlation of forces in favor of the socialist camp and against the imperialist camp. They pointed to a number of developments: the creation of eleven new socialist countries in Eastern Europe and Asia since 1945; the victory of the Chinese revolution and the formation of the Sino-Soviet alliance; the accelerating collapse of European colonialism; the outcome of the Korean War; the economic advances of the USSR and the PRC; and the USSR's acquisition of nuclear weapons and intercontinental rockets. The latter point was especially significant. The month before the Moscow conference the Soviet Union had launched humanity's first artificial earth satellite, Sputnik. This graphically demonstrated the prowess of Soviet rockets, showing the world that the USSR now had the ability to deliver hydrogen bombs against cities in the continental United States. No longer could the United States contemplate war with the USSR with fair assurance of the invulnerability of its home territory against attack. Instead, nuclear retaliation against the United States was now virtually certain.

Khrushchev and Mao reached very different conclusions regarding "peaceful coexistence" from this shift in the global correlation of forces. Khrushchev concluded that because of this shift the danger of imperialist attack on the socialist countries had been greatly reduced and a new era of cooperative relations between the socialist and capitalist countries was possible. Moreover, the growing strength of the socialist camp meant that the imperialist countries would hesitate to conduct counterrevolutionary interventions in other countries. This, in turn, made peaceful transitions to socialism more likely. The development of thermonuclear weapons also meant, according to

Khrushchev, that war had to be avoided. A nuclear war between the United States and the Soviet Union would be so immensely destructive that in no way could it be considered progressive.

To Mao the favorable shift in the global correlation of forces meant that the socialist camp could assume greater risks and support foreign revolutionary movements without the imperialists daring to attack the socialist countries. Moreover, even if the imperialist countries did attack, even if they did launch a nuclear war against the socialist countries, the revolutionary forces would win, capitalism and imperialism would be swept away around the world, and humanity would proceed to build a Communist world many times more brilliant than the old capitalist civilization. Even if one-third to one-half of the world's population was annihilated in a nuclear war, Mao told the Moscow conference, the ultimate result would still be progressive, since imperialism would be destroyed entirely and there would be only socialism in all the world.

One reason for the differing appraisals of the impact of nuclear war was that Mao thought in terms of the Third World as the leading edge of the global revolutionary process. Whereas the industrialized and highly urbanized countries of North America and Europe (including the Soviet Union) would certainly be devastated by a nuclear war, this was less of a danger to the agricultural and rural countries constituting the Third World. In the worst case, according to Mao, once the capitalist countries were devastated by nuclear war, the surviving revolutionary masses of the Third World could easily overwhelm the capitalist countries. In the best case, nuclear war would be avoided and the rising Third World revolutionary wave, supported by the socialist camp, would, in any case, overwhelm the imperialist countries. Mao elucidated this Third World vision of the global revolutionary process in a speech to Chinese students in Moscow during his November 1957 visit:

> Who is stronger, the underdeveloped or advanced countries? Who is stronger, India or Britain, Indonesia or Holland, Algeria or France? To my mind all the imperialist countries are in a position which is like the position of the sun at 6 P.M., but ours is like the position of the sun at 6 A.M. Thus the tide has turned. And this means that the Western countries have been left behind, that we have outdistanced them considerably. Undoubtedly, it is not the Western wind that prevails over the Eastern wind, for the wind from the West is so weak. Undoubtedly, the Eastern wind prevails over the Western wind, for we are strong.[25]

While formulated in ideological terms, the debates at the Moscow conference were about more than revolutionary theory. They were about national power, too. What was involved was where ultimate authority lay within the world revolutionary movement and the socialist camp. Did that authority reside with Moscow? In effect, Mao was saying that it did not, and he was claiming the right to himself define the politically correct line. He did not, however, make this explicit at Moscow in 1957. Indeed, explicitly he upheld Moscow's claim to a leadership role. To Chinese students in Moscow Mao said: "The socialist camp must have a leader and this leader is the Soviet Union. All the socialist countries must unite unanimously around the leadership of the Soviet Union."[26] Mao and other CCP leaders also attempted to convince Yugoslavia to accept Soviet leadership. Khrushchev was skeptical of Mao's affirmation of Soviet leadership: "As we listened to Mao pay recognition to the Soviet Union...we couldn't help suspecting that his thoughts were probably very different from his words. We had the unsettling feeling that sooner or later, friction was bound to develop between our countries and our parties."[27] Khrushchev suspected that Mao wanted to maneuver the USSR into a nuclear war with the United States, which would, Mao hoped, open the way to world revolution while incidentally, perhaps, destroying the Soviet Union.

NOTES

1. Regarding the characteristics of revolution, see Hannah Arendt, *On Revolution*, New York: Viking Press, 1963; Crane Brinton, *The Anatomy of Revolution*, New York: Vintage Press, 1965; Richard Lowenthal, "Development vs. Utopia in Communist Policy," *Revolutionary Change*, Chalmers Johnson, ed., Boston: Little, Brown, 1966, 33–116. Regarding the psychological profile of revolutionary leaders, see Bruce Mazlish, *The Revolutionary Ascetic: Evolution of a Political Type*, New York: Basic Books, 1976.

2. The classic presentations of this vision are Karl Marx, *The Communist Manifesto*, Arlington Heights, Ill.: Harlan Davidson, 1955; V.I. Lenin, "The State and Revolution," in *Essential Works of Lenin*, New York: Bantam Books, 1966.

3. Regarding the CCP's views of the international system and possible alternatives, see Edward Friedman, "On Maoist Conceptualizations of the Capitalist World Systems," *China Quarterly*, no. 80 (December 1979), 806–37; Tang Tsou and Morton H. Halperin, "Mao Tse-tung's Revolutionary Strategy and Peking's International Behavior," *American Political Science Review*, vol. 59, no. 1 (March 1965), 80–99.

4. A.M. Halperin, "The Foreign Policy Uses of the Chinese Revolutionary Model," *The Foreign Policy of China*, King Chen, ed., Roseland, N.J.: East-West Who?, 1972, 117–19.

5. Regarding Chinese support for the VWP, see Jay Taylor, *China and Southeast Asia: Peking's Relations with Revolutionary Movements*, New York: Praeger, 1974, 1–16; J.S. Zasloff, *The Role of Sanctuary in Insurgency: Communist China's Support for the Viet Minh, 1946–1954*, Rm-4618TR, Santa Monica, Calif.: Rand Corporation, 1967; Bernard B. Fall, *Street Without Joy*, New York: Schocken Books, 1972, 32–33; Harold Hinton, *China's Relations with Burma and Vietnam*, New York: Institute for Pacific Relations, 1958; King C. Chen, *Vietnam and China, 1938–1954*, Princeton, N.J.: Princeton University Press, 1969, 260–78; Anne Gilks and Gerald Segal, *China and the Arms Trade*, New York: St. Martin's Press, 1985, 33–36.

6. J.D. Armstrong, *Revolutionary Diplomacy: Chinese Foreign Policy and the United Front Doctrine*, Berkeley: University of California Press, 1977, 70–73. Armstrong traces the emergence of the PRC's moderate orientation to late 1950.

7. Stanley Karnow, *Vietnam: A History*, New York: Penguin, 1984, 204; Melvin Gurtov, *The First Vietnam Crisis: Chinese Communist Strategy and United States Involvement, 1953–1954*, New York: Columbia University Press, 1967, 116–30; Chen, *Vietnam and China*, 312–21.

8. Franz Michael, "Communist China and the Non-Committed Countries: Motives and Purposes of Communist China's Foreign Policy," *New Nations in a Divided World*, Kurt

London, ed., New York: Praeger, 1963, 236–55. Technically, the Soviet Union was not the only socialist state prior to 1945. The Mongolian People's Republic, a small and docile Soviet satellite, was created in 1921.

9. "More on the Historical Experience of the Dictatorship of the Proletariat," *The Historical Experience of the Dictatorship of the Proletariat*, Beijing: Foreign Languages Press, 1961, 33–34.

10. Ibid., 55–56.

11. *National Communism and Popular Revolt in Eastern Europe*, Paul E. Zinner, ed., New York: Columbia University Press, 1956, 493.

12. "Reading Notes on the Soviet Union's 'Political Economics,'" *Miscellany of Mao Tse-tung Thought (1949–1968)*, Part II, Arlington, Va.: Joint Publications Research Service, 1974, 264–65.

13. Nikita Khrushchev, *Khrushchev Remembers: The Last Testament*, Boston: Little, Brown, 1974, 240–41. Other sources on this redefinition of intra-camp relations include A. Doak Barnett, *China and the Major Powers in East Asia*, Washington, D.C.: Brookings Institute, 1977, 31; Harold Hinton, *China's Turbulent Quest: An Analysis of China's Foreign Relations Since 1949*, Bloomington: Indiana University Press, 1973, 62.

14. Regarding the debates over destalinization, see Francois Fejto, *A History of the People's Democracies: Eastern Europe Since Stalin*, Middlesex, England: Penguin, 1974, 52–53; Robert Conquest, *Power and Policy in the U.S.S.R.: The Struggle for Stalin's Succession*, New York: Harper, 1961, 249–51.

15. Fejto, *People's Democracies*, 106.

16. Flora Lewis, *A Case History of Hope*, New York: Doubleday, 1958, 182–85.

17. Fejto, *People's Democracies*, 100–120.

18. *Renmin Ribao*, November 3, 1956, cited in Donald Zagoria, *The Sino-Soviet Conflict 1956-61*, New York: Antheneum, 1969, 63.

19. Fejto, *People's Democracies*, 105, 133–34. Also, Adam B. Ulam, *Expansion and Coexistence: The History of Soviet Foreign Policy, 1917–1967*, New York: Praeger, 1968, 599.

20. Richard Lowenthal, "Factors of the Unity and Factors of Conflict," *The Foreign Policy of China*, King Chen, ed., Roseland, N.J.: East-West Who?, 1972, 295.

21. "The Origin and Development of the Differences Between the Leadership of the CPSU and Ourselves," September 6, 1963, in *The Polemic on the General Line of the International Communist Movement*, Beijing: Foreign Languages Press, 1965, 71.

22. Liu Xiao, *Chushi sulian banian* (Eight Years as Ambassador to the Soviet Union), Beijing: Zhonggong dangshi ziliao chubanshe, 1986, 58–60.

23. "Outline of Views on Questions of Peaceful Transition," November 10, 1957, in *The Polemic on the General Line of the International Communist movement*, Beijing: Foreign Languages Press, 1965, 105–8.

24. Cited in O. Edmund Clubb, *China and Russia: The Great Game*, New York: Columbia University Press, 1971, 422.

25. Cited in ibid., 421.

26. Liu Xiao, *Eight Years as Ambassador*, 57.

27. Khrushchev, *Khrushchev Remembers*, 254.

Chapter Six

China as the Epicenter
of the World Revolution

MAO'S STRUGGLE AGAINST REVISIONISM

After the Moscow conference, it quickly became apparent to Mao that there was a substantial discrepancy between his own assessment of the world situation and that of Khrushchev. The interpretation Mao put on this situation was that the CPSU under Khrushchev had committed ideological errors by "revising" the fundamental principles of Marxism-Leninism. From about mid-1958 until mid-1963, Mao waged a complex struggle to persuade Khrushchev and the CPSU to reject their "revisionist" orientation and return to correct principles of revolutionary struggle against imperialism. The main instrument used by Mao in this anti-revisionist struggle was polemics argued within the framework of Marxism-Leninism and directed at adherents of that philosophy in Communist parties around the world. The main forums for this polemical struggle were various multi–Communist party conferences.

Again ideology commingled with considerations of national power. While Mao framed his critique of Soviet policy in ideological terms, implicitly minimizing the role of national interest in determining Soviet policy, his challenge struck directly at Soviet national power. Moscow's control over the international Communist movement had been a major instrument of Soviet power since the formation of the Communist International in 1919. Even in the late 1950s, Moscow's ability to guide the actions of Communist parties still gave it a voice, sometimes a significant one, in many countries. Coordinated with Soviet diplomacy, propaganda, and economic and military power, the loyal support of more than 100 fraternal parties was very useful in the pursuit of Soviet interests. One key mechanism through which Moscow maintained control over these diverse parties was its power to elaborate ideology. Mao's ideological challenge threatened precisely that power.

An odd coalition of radical forces supported the CCP's challenge to the CPSU during the period from 1958 to 1963.[1] Ironically, one group that supported the CCP were Western European Communist parties seeking power via parliamentary means and beginning to embrace the liberal, parliamentary, democratic traditions and institutions of their countries. These parties, later dubbed "Eurocommunists," were increasingly critical of the harsh, illiberal brand of socialism practiced in Eastern Europe and the Soviet Union. In this regard, they were quite different from Mao. What led them to support Mao's challenge to Khrushchev was their opposition to Moscow's efforts to impose its will on other parties and socialist countries.

The most outspoken and influential of these Eurocommunist parties in the late 1950s was the Italian Communist Party (ICP), led by Palmiro Togliatti. Togliatti rejected many of the key precepts of Mao's Marxism. He advocated a peaceful transition to socialism, rejected the concept of a dictatorship of the proletariat, and upheld individual liberties and parliamentary institutions as a central element of socialism. He also favored a reduction of East-West tension rather than militant struggle against imperialism, and he rejected Mao's propositions that the Soviet Union was the leader of the socialist camp. Yet on one key point Togliatti agreed with Mao: The CPSU had no right to dictate policy to any other fraternal party or to the world Communist movement as a whole. Each party and each socialist country had an absolute right to define policy for itself, a situation that Togliatti termed "polycentrism." The fact that Beijing was challenging Moscow's authority also made it easier for Togliatti to challenge Soviet authority from a different ideological direction. This translated into ICP opposition to Soviet efforts to condemn the CCP or to expel it from the world Communist movement.[2]

The second group that partly supported Mao's challenge to Khrushchev were Eastern European Stalinists. They accepted much more of Mao's philosophy than did the Western European Eurocommunists. The Eastern European regimes were still largely modeled after Stalinist Soviet socialism and their leaders were very apprehensive of the internal consequences of destalinization. The Eastern European crisis of 1956 and Mao's rebuttal to Khrushchev's criticism of Stalin had forced Khrushchev to retreat temporarily from destalinization. His victory over the Stalinist "anti-Party clique" in the CPSU in June 1957, however, reinvigorated his drive to liberalize Soviet socialism. The Eastern European regimes were soon under pressure to follow suit, even though they were not confident of their ability to retain power if social controls were relaxed. Consequently, they sought ways of resisting Khrushchev's pressure. Mao's opposition to destalinization proved most convenient. By arguing that the CPSU could not dictate policy to any other fraternal party (at least as long as that party did not lose control of the situation to the forces of "counterrevolution"), Mao upheld the right of the Eastern European Stalinists to resist Khrushchev's pressures to liberalize.

The Eastern European regimes also gained leverage with Moscow as a result of Beijing's challenge. Moscow now had to solicit Eastern European support against China, and the Eastern European regimes used this to secure more advantageous terms in their relations with the Soviet Union. This too led the Eastern European parties to resist Soviet efforts to expel the CCP from the international revolutionary movement. Had Moscow been successful, the Eastern European regimes would have lost an important instrument of leverage with Moscow.

Several Eastern European regimes also feared that Khrushchev's quest for detente with the West might lead Moscow to sacrifice their interests. The regimes in Tiriana, Warsaw, and East Berlin were especially apprehensive about such a possibility. Tiriana faced standing Yugoslav claims on Albanian territory and feared that Khrushchev's quest for rapprochement with Yugoslavia (a process that began in 1955) might lead him to give a green light to Belgrade's expansionist aspirations. In Poland, Warsaw was fearful of Moscow's desire for better relations with the Federal Republic of Germany, as long as that country maintained a formal claim to Poland's western provinces. Might not Moscow's desire for better relations with West Germany, Warsaw feared, lead to a weakening of Soviet support for Poland against West Germany's revanchist demands? Regarding East Germany, in 1953 Stalin had proposed German reunification and the withdrawal of Soviet forces from East Germany in exchange for the neutralization of all Germany. The East German government feared that such a solution would lead to its disappearance and, consequently, opposed too much stress on the search for East-West detente. Again, Mao's opposition to Soviet efforts to reach a modus vivendi with Western imperialism coincided with the interests of Tiriana, Warsaw, and East Berlin.

Because of the coincidence of Chinese and Eastern European interests, most Eastern European Stalinists gave the CCP at least some support during the late 1950s. As CPSU-CCP tensions escalated, however, dependence on Soviet trade, economic assistance, and military support, combined with a fear that Mao's policies would lead to war, caused all the Eastern European countries except Albania and Romania to revert to full support for Moscow. Ultimately only Tirana and Bucharest broke with Moscow and followed China down the path of national Communism. This polarization was a gradual process, however, and not complete until 1963 and 1964.

Initially both the CCP and the CPSU were careful to keep criticism of each other secret or, if public, indirect. This left the door open for compromise and concealed the dispute behind a public facade of bloc unity. Beijing criticized Yugoslavia, which had broken with the Soviet Union and come to an understanding with the West in 1948 and which followed a relatively moderate type of socialism. Moscow directed its criticism first against unnamed "dogmatists." Gradually, however, the true nature of the conflict emerged into public view. Beijing charged that Moscow's September 1959 declaration of neutrality in the Chinese-Indian border dispute first revealed the dispute to the outside world. This led Beijing to publish its first open anti-revisionist polemic, entitled "Long Live Leninism," in April 1960, the 100th anniversary of Lenin's birth. The polemic named only "modern revisionists," but it was clear to the world that this was a euphemism for the Soviet leadership. Beijing's polemic prompted the CPSU to launch counter-polemics at a Congress of the Romanian Worker's Party in June 1960. China waged a "tit-for-tat" struggle at the Bucharest meeting. Moscow responded the next month by suspending Soviet economic aid to China. Then at the 22nd Congress of the CPSU in October 1961, the Soviets publicly attacked by name Albania, China's main supporter in the polemical battles. By January 1963, Moscow and Beijing were publishing open, direct, and explicit criticisms of one another.[3]

THE ANTI-IMPERIALIST UNITED FRONT

While struggling against Khrushchev's "revisionist" ideology, Mao began to apply "correct ideology" to the construction of a global united front against U.S. imperialism. Mao believed, with Lenin, that true doctrine can change the course of history, and that the truth of doctrine is demonstrated by its successful application. By applying his revolutionary, united front doctrine and successfully mobilizing powerful forces against the United States, Mao would demonstrate the correctness of his theory. Eventually the falsehood of Khrushchev's mistaken hypotheses would become apparent, and the socialist camp and the world Communist movement would recognize and embrace Mao's "correct" doctrine.

Mao's concept of a united front was rooted in Lenin's concept of revolution by stages and Mao's own notion of contradiction. According to these doctrines, in countries such as Russia and China, the initial or "national democratic" stage of the revolution would aim at the accomplishment of anti-imperialist, anti-feudal objectives. After these were accomplished, the revolution could move into its higher, socialist stage. Within this context, the united front had dual objectives: first, to mobilize all possible forces against the immediate enemy (imperialism) in the anti-imperialist, "national democratic" stage of the revolution; second, to lay the base for transition to the second, socialist stage of the revolution. To win broad support during the national democratic stage, socialist objectives should be shelved and broad unity achieved on the basis of "national democratic" objectives, such as land reform, national independence, democracy, and so on. Local Communists might or might not lead the struggle in the first stage. But regardless, they should conduct ideological struggle *within* the united front to raise the level of ideological consciousness while organizing the more advanced forces. The process of struggle against imperialism would itself help raise the people's political consciousness. The sharper and more acute the anti-imperialist struggle became, the more progressive leaders and ideology would come to the fore. Protracted political struggle both *within* the united front and between the united front and the imperialist enemy would create political conditions necessary to move the revolution to the socialist stage once the anti-imperialist tasks of the revolution were accomplished.

Mao's united front against U.S. imperialism can be thought of as a series of concentric circles. The core of the united front was to be a strong, stable, and united socialist camp. About this proletarian core would be grouped armed wars of national liberation. Then came militantly anti-imperialist bourgeois nationalist regimes. Next came the worker, progressive, and peace movements within the imperialist, colonial, and neo-colonial countries. Near the outer fringes were imperialist regimes whose conflicts with the United States might lead them to support the anti-United States struggle to some degree. France was a prime example of a country in this category. By exploiting every contradiction in the imperialist camp in this fashion, all possible forces might be united against the primary enemy, U.S. imperialism. Figure 6–1 illustrates Mao's vision of the anti-United States united front.

Mao's attempt to build a global anti-United States united front was audacious. It was, as J.D. Armstrong noted, an attempt to orchestrate the development of the global correlation of forces on the basis of a long-term analysis of the forces at work in the world. Via protracted struggle, the United States would be isolated, and conditions made ready for eventual socialist revolution in much of the world.[4] Chalmers Johnson suggests that Mao hoped for minimal and maximal objectives from this revolutionary offensive. At a minimum, he hoped to pressure the United States to cease supporting the KMT, blocking China's entry into the United Nations, and economically isolating China. Maximally, if several foreign revolutions actually succeeded, China might emerge as the leader of a revitalized world revolutionary movement and the structure of U.S. power in Asia would either collapse or be rolled back.[5]

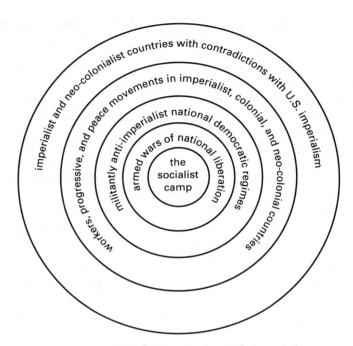

Figure 6–1   The United Front against U.S. Imperialism

The united front strategy was also an attempt to channel along revolutionary lines the profound political ferment that emerged in much of the Third World in the aftermath of decolonization. Throughout the colonial and ex-colonial areas of Africa and Asia, popular political consciousness was increasing rapidly. The bourgeois-dominated political systems established by the colonial powers as they exited these countries were often weak and vulnerable to revolution. In other cases, newly independent states were dominated or influenced by progressive bourgeois nationalist forces who, with encouragement, might be able to substantially liberate their nations from imperialist domination. Thus, Mao argued, prospects were excellent for revolutionary advance in the vast "intermediate zone" of developing countries lying between the socialist and the imperialist camps. Africa, especially, seemed to offer good revolutionary prospects. Internal CCP documents issued in 1961 indicated that "The center of the battle between East and West for the intermediate zone is in Africa; hence Africa has become the focus of contemporary world problems."[6]

The cutting edge of the global anti-United States struggle was to be armed wars of national liberation in the intermediate zone. During the late 1950s and early 1960s, the most important of these was the Algerian national liberation war led by the National Liberation Front of

Algeria (abbreviated FLN, in French). The FLN had been waging armed struggle for independence from France since 1954. In September 1958, the FLN declared a provisional government of the Republic of Algeria. Less than three months later, the PRC recognized that government. Then in 1959, the provisional Algerian government became the first foreign government to receive Chinese arms since the end of the Korean and Indochinese wars when China gave it $10 million to buy weapons and agreed to supply large quantities of U.S. weapons captured in Korea.[7] In May and September of 1960, top officials of the provisional Algerian government visited Beijing and were warmly fêted. Chinese support for the FLN continued through its victory and Algerian independence in 1962.

The radical nationalist regimes that emerged in several countries in the wake of decolonization played an important role in Beijing's revolutionary scheme. Egypt under Gamal Abdel Nasser was one such regime. After leading a military coup in 1952 that abolished Egypt's monarchy, Nasser scrapped Egypt's Western-style political institutions in favor of a highly centralized regime that he dubbed "Arab socialism." Nasser's socialism included a large public sector, but did not call for the nationalization of all means of production; embraced Islam; and rejected the concept of proletarian dictatorship. In terms of foreign relations, Nasser was a leading figure in the Afro-Asian and non-aligned movements, and gave a strongly anti-Western cast to those doctrines. He was also a proponent of pan-Arabism and sought to reduce Western influence in Egypt by nationalizing the Anglo-French–owned Suez Canal and expelling the citizens of those countries in 1956. Egypt's confrontation with Britain and France led it to establish diplomatic relations with China in May 1956. Egypt thus became the first African or Middle Eastern country to make such a move—a major breakthrough for China. Beijing's mission in Cairo soon made Beijing aware of the ferment then sweeping the Arab world and black Africa.

Beijing also saw the West African states of Ghana, Guinea, and Mali as militant national democratic constituents of the anti-imperialist united front. Kwame Nkrumah led Ghana to independence from Britain in 1957 and proceeded to set up a highly centralized state designed to transform Ghana into a socialist society. Three years later, Ghana proclaimed itself a republic, thereby severing its residual link to the British crown. Nkrumah scrapped Ghana's Western-style political institutions and was proclaimed president for life. His political party became the only legal party. Guinea gained full independence from France in 1958 and under Sekou Toure moved toward the creation of a Leninist-style state. Toure's party was given a legal monopoly on power and began creating a centralized, state-owned economy. Mali, led by Modibo Kita, initially opted for limited independence within the French community. But it also adopted leftist development policies, including state control and ownership of the economy along with mobilization of the populace for construction projects. In 1960 Mali also claimed full independence.

In each of these West African states there was a major confrontation between indigenous radical and moderate forces, with the latter favoring more capitalist modes of development and non-confrontational relations with the Western ex-colonial powers. Each also adopted hostile policies toward the ex-colonial power. The revolutionary states also supported the overthrow of colonial and moderate regimes in neighboring states, allowing their territory to be used as sanctuary by foreign insurgent groups. More broadly, Nkrumah, Toure, and Kita viewed Western influence in Africa as neo-colonialism and favored the expulsion of all such influence. To expel Western influence they experimented with various federation schemes (all short-lived) as the first step toward pan-African unification. Finally, they were willing to support China's diplomatic initiatives.

Militant national democratic states such as Guinea, Ghana, and Mali became favored recipients of a Chinese aid program initiated in 1958. While small by U.S. or Soviet standards, this aid program represented a substantial commitment of China's scarce resources. There were also frequent exchanges between Chinese leaders and those of Ghana, Guinea, Mali, and Egypt. Toure visited China in September 1960 to receive an interest-free loan of 100 million rubles. Nkrumah visited in August 1961, receiving an interest-free loan worth 7 million Ghanian pounds. China also lent selective support to efforts by several of these states to overthrow pro-Western governments in neighboring countries.

In line with the dual purpose of the united front, the CCP worked assiduously to strengthen the front's more radical forces. Chinese diplomats and trade and advisory officials abroad paid considerable attention to ideological work with the local people. Large amounts of revolutionary propaganda in foreign languages were churned out and distributed abroad at very low prices. Organizational and financial support was given to "progressive" organizations such as the Afro-Asian People's Solidarity Organization, the Chinese-African People's Friendship Association, the Afro-Asian People's Solidarity Council, and the Afro-Asian Journalists Association.[8]

The CCP's drive for world revolution met many difficulties. The CPSU and the parties and countries controlled by it rejected Beijing's radicalism. Beijing's revolutionary program flatly contradicted Khrushchev's program of peaceful coexistence with the United States and his desire to reduce East-West tension. To Mao, Khrushchev's obstinate refusal to recognize the correctness of the CCP's position, along with Soviet efforts to pressure the CCP to shelve its own program of revolutionary advance, indicated that Khrushchev had abandoned all revolutionary principles. By mid-1963, Mao had concluded that the CPSU could no longer be considered a revolutionary party, but must be treated as a counterrevolutionary group that had infiltrated the revolutionary ranks. To cooperate with the CPSU, to include it within the revolutionary united front, even to deem it a progressive group, would merely give the Soviet revisionists the opportunity to confuse the revolutionary forces and to cooperate with U.S. imperialism to abort the revolutionary struggle. The CCP itself, Mao concluded, would have to lead the world revolution.

CHINA AT THE CENTER

It is tempting to view the CCP's post-1957 attempt to rectify the world revolutionary movement and its post-1963 attempt to place itself at the head of that movement as a renewal of the ancient notion of China as the moral center of human society. It is indeed very likely that many Chinese took pride in the idea that China was leading the oppressed peoples of the world to enlightenment and emancipation. Modern nationalist pride probably overlaid traditional notions. But the most appropriate historical analogy is not China's traditional foreign relations, but Lenin's splits in the Russian and international revolutionary movements in the early twentieth century.

Lenin's starting point was the all-importance of correct ideology. If a movement had true doctrine, it would ultimately prevail against all odds. With incorrect doctrine, it was doomed to ultimate failure in spite of whatever momentary victories it might achieve. True doctrine was the key to history. It followed that upholding correct principles was far more important than mere numerical superiority of size of the organization. Thus, Lenin broke with the Menshevik faction of the Russian Social Democratic Labor Party once it abandoned the concept of seizure of power by insurrection. Later he broke with the Social Democratic parties of the Second International over the question of nationalism. Mao's understanding of his break with the CPSU and the Moscow-oriented international Communist movement was probably very similar to Lenin's regarding his break with the Mensheviks and Social Democrats. Both Lenin and Mao thought that they were upholding true doctrine that provided the ultimate key to revolutionary success.

Having broken with the CPSU, the CCP proceeded to build an ideologically correct world revolutionary movement. One component of this effort was the expulsion of the CPSU from the united front. To this end, Beijing ceased to participate in Moscow-sponsored Communist conferences and further escalated its polemical struggle against Moscow. Polemics against the CPSU became explicit, explaining the counterrevolutionary nature of the CPSU and exposing details of the secret conflict of the previous several years.[9]

The most dramatic demonstration of Beijing's expulsion of the CPSU from the united front came over the issue of "united action" by the PRC and the USSR in support of North Vietnam. As the confrontation between North Vietnam and the United States loomed in late 1964, Moscow proposed Sino-Soviet cooperation in support of North Vietnam, or "united action." Hanoi favored such a course. Beijing, however, rejected Moscow's proposal on the grounds that the CPSU had abandoned true revolutionary principles and capitulated to U.S. imperialism. In Beijing's own words:

> Between the Marxist-Leninists and the Khrushchev revisionists there is a difference of fundamental line....In the circumstances, how can there be "common ideology" and a "common purpose"...? There are things that divide us and nothing that unites us....The reactionary nature of Khrushchev revisionism is expressed in concentrated form in the line of Soviet-U.S. collaboration for domination of the world....The U.S. imperialists urgently need to extinguish the roaring flames of the Vietnamese people's revolution. And so do the Khrushchev revisionists because they want to carry out their line of Soviet-U.S. collaboration for world domination....At bottom, the new leaders of the CPSU are clamoring for "united action"...in order to worm their way into the anti-U.S. front and carry out their policy of involvement in the service of U.S. imperialism.[10]

Rejection of Moscow's proposal for united action in support of Hanoi was a costly decision for Mao. Hanoi's war against the United States was rapidly becoming a cause célèbre among leftist circles around the world. The CPSU leadership seized on Beijing's rejection of united action to attack Chinese "ultra-leftism" and regained much of the ground it had lost in "progressive" circles over the previous several years.

Another component of Beijing's effort to build a correct world revolutionary movement was sponsorship of Maoist, or "genuine Marxist-Leninist," parties in countries around the world. Conflict between pro-Chinese and pro-Soviet factions began first in the Indian Communist Party in 1959, when the divergent positions of Beijing and Moscow toward the Sino-Indian border conflict forced Indian Communists to rethink their loyalties.[11] As the polemic between the CPSU and the CCP escalated in the early 1960s, pro-Chinese factions developed in a number of Communist parties. In 1963 Beijing began encouraging these factions to seize control of their parties, or failing that, to secede and set up a new party on the basis of genuine Marxism-Leninism. Factionalism had long been endemic to the world Communist movement. The Sino-Soviet conflict exacerbated that problem by making it possible for disruptive groups within various parties to appeal to the authority of the world's largest party, the CCP, which presented itself as the guardian of doctrinal purity and which had the substantial resources of a vast country at its disposal.[12]

The first secessionist Maoist parties were established in Brazil in early 1963 and in Belgium at the end of that year. Over the next several years, Maoist parties and groups proliferated in Asia, Europe, Latin America, and North America. Maoist newspapers and journals also multiplied, usually linked to some group and intended to serve as the organizing tool for a full-blooded Marxist-Leninist party. By the fall of 1964, some twenty-seven such publications had appeared in fifteen countries. By the late 1960s, more than forty pro-Chinese Communist parties were functioning. Beijing did what it could to encourage this process. Foreign Maoist leaders were fêted in Beijing at China's expense. The volume of multilingual pamphlets and periodicals published by Beijing and distributed abroad at very cheap prices became a torrent. Chinese diplomats, journalists, and trade representatives maintained contact with foreign Maoists and sometimes distributed funds to support their activities. In all, the eruption of Maoist activity represented the most serious factionalism within the world Communist movement since the clash between Trotsky and Stalin in the 1920s and 1930s.

Still another component of the CCP effort to midwife a global anti-imperialist united front was radicalization of the Afro-Asian movement. This represented a continuation of the line in place since 1958, but Beijing's break with Moscow led it to put greater stress on the Third World while seeking to exclude the Soviet Union from various Afro-Asian forums. A central focus of CCP efforts in this regard was the convocation of a second Afro-Asian conference. As noted in Chapter Two, the first Afro-Asian conference had been held at Bandung, Indonesia, in 1955. It was a great success for China's efforts to break out of U.S.-imposed containment. Late in 1963, Beijing began pushing for a "second Bandung conference," which was to be more radical than the first. In December 1963 and January 1964, Premier Zhou Enlai led a Chinese delegation to Egypt, Algeria, Morocco, Tunisia, Ghana, Mali, Guinea, the Sudan, Ethiopia, Somalia, Burma, Pakistan, and Ceylon to lobby for a second Afro-Asian conference. This and other activities laid the ground for a preparatory meeting held in Djakarta, Indonesia, in April 1964 with representatives from twenty-two countries attending. Three months later the newly created Organization of African Unity agreed to sponsor the conference and designated Algeria as the host.[13]

Unfortunately for Beijing, conflicts plagued the Afro-Asian movement. Moderate governments were alienated by radical Algeria's refusal to invite South Korea and South Vietnam to the conference, even though the Djakarta preparatory meeting had agreed to invite those two pro-United States countries. Egypt and Algeria vied for leadership of the conference and of the Arab bloc. Then, early in 1965, ten moderate African states announced that they would boycott the conference because of the subversive activities directed against them by the radical African states organizing it. Perhaps most destructive of all was the deep mistrust between India and China. Since India was one of the sponsors of the 1955 Bandung conference, it would have been difficult for China not to invite India. This was done and India accepted. But New Delhi saw Beijing's efforts at Afro-Asian radicalization as directed against it. As Sino-Indian relations had deteriorated in the early 1960s, Indo-American relations had improved, and by 1964 India was receiving substantial U.S. military assistance. An anti-United States emphasis would, therefore, tar India. So too would China's anti-Western thrust. India's leaders placed priority on economic development and at that point still welcomed economic cooperation with the industrialized capitalist countries to achieve this.

In order to counter Chinese efforts at radicalization, India insisted that Malaysia and the Soviet Union be invited to the second Afro-Asian conference. Malaysia was a divisive issue because Indonesia, a radical state cooperating closely with China, was very hostile toward Kuala Lumpur. Malaysia also had close ties, including military links, with Great Britain, and shared India's development-oriented view of the world. Invitation of the Soviet Union was even more divisive. India's justification for this invitation was simple geography: A large part of the USSR was situated in Asia. But New Delhi probably had more subtle objectives. It clearly preferred a non-aligned movement led by India and excluding both of India's enemies—China, still technically allied with the USSR under the 1950 treaty, and Pakistan, allied with the United States. The first conference of non-aligned countries had met in Belgrade in 1961. To a considerable extent, Beijing's Afro-Asian movement and New Delhi's non-aligned movement represented rival movements with very different political orientations. When the effort to convene the second Afro-Asian conference collapsed, New Delhi was not unhappy.[14]

By June 1965 it was clear that a second Afro-Asian conference would be a display of disunity rather than unity. When Algerian leader Ahmed Ben Bella was overthrown on June 19, most of the conference participants seized on this event to indefinitely postpone the conference. In the words of Charles Neuhauser, "it is impossible to overestimate the damage to Chinese prestige" caused by cancellation of the Second Afro-Asian conference.[15]

Another component of the CCP's strategy for global revolution was stepped-up support for wars of national liberation. Beijing's emphasis on armed struggle increased after 1964, when it became almost the sole recognized form of anti-imperialist struggle. By 1965, Beijing endorsed wars of national liberation in twenty-three countries. Many of these revolutionary movements received financial support, arms, or training from Beijing.[16]

There were several reasons for the stress on armed struggle. One had to do with enhancing China's national security by counterencircling U.S. forces arrayed against China. This aspect is discussed in Chapter

Thirteen. Other reasons of relevance to us here had to do with the revolutionizing effects of armed struggle. According to Mao's analysis, violent struggle had a powerful psychological and political transformative effect on the country involved. Sustained armed struggle would polarize the political situation and raise the level of political consciousness in a country. As this happened, the revolutionary forces would gradually understand the violent nature of social change, understand the need for centralized revolutionary leadership, and embrace Marxist-Leninist ideology. This transformation would make it more likely that the anti-imperialist stage of the revolution would be pushed through to the end and that optimal conditions would exist for the transition of the revolution to its second, socialist stage.[17]

Armed struggle also increased the probability of provoking armed U.S. counterrevolutionary intervention, which would further polarize the political situation, discredit the local government that had invited U.S. intervention, and raise the anti-imperialist consciousness of the people. It would also expose the true imperialistic nature of the United States. With each episode of intervention, the U.S. government would lose support domestically and internationally, until finally it would be isolated.

While China endorsed wars of national liberation in principle, whether it in fact supported particular insurgencies depended on whether such support would strengthen or weaken the overall anti-United States united front. This depended, in turn, on the willingness of the government threatened by the insurgency to challenge the dictates of U.S. imperialism. If the established government was willing to go against Washington's wishes on key issues, Chinese support for insurgency against that government might push that government closer to the United States, weakening the overall anti-imperialist forces. The issues of greatest concern to Beijing were those having to do with U.S. containment. In practice, this meant that governments targeted for overthrow were ones that maintained diplomatic relations with Nationalist China, voted against admission of the PRC to the United Nations, and were signatory to a defense pact with the United States. Conversely, insurgencies were not supported by China if the threatened governments had diplomatic relations with China, voted in favor of the PRC entry into the United Nations, and carried on substantial trade with China. While foreign observers might be tempted to conclude that Beijing was simply using support for insurgencies to pressure governments to alter policies unfavorable to China, Beijing viewed the situation differently. From Beijing's perspective, this was not unprincipled pragmatism, but involved calculations about how to mobilize the maximum global forces against U.S. imperialism.

China's support for foreign revolutionary movements in the 1960s should not be overstated. Even when Beijing endorsed foreign revolutions, its material support was usually limited. Aggregate figures are not available, but it is apparent that, with a few exceptions (primarily Vietnam), Chinese material assistance was very limited. China supplied mainly small arms, and many of these were old. The Soviet Union was the principal supplier of heavy weapons, especially after Krushchev's overthrow in 1964. Training camps for rebel soldiers were set up in China and in several African countries, including Congo (Brazzaville), Tanzania, and Ghana. Radio broadcasts and printed propaganda were directed at the peoples of countries targeted for revolution, and expense-paid visits by insurgent leaders to China were used to encourage and support selected insurgencies. In a few cases, Chinese personnel *may* have assisted foreign revolutionary movements in-country. Evidence of this is strongest in the cases of South Vietnam and Burma.[18]

The broader point to be made is that China never employed its own military forces abroad as an instrument of revolution. This was in marked contrast to Soviet practice, where there is a long record of just such actions. According to Peter Van Ness, there were two reasons for this low-profile approach.[19] First, given the great disparity in United States and Chinese military power, Beijing did not want to risk war with the United States. Second, China's own revolutionary experience had convinced it that a revolution could be made only by the masses and could not be imposed from above or by a foreign country. The revolutionary movements of various countries had to be self-reliant. As Lin Biao put it in his September 1965 essay "Long Live the Victory of People's War": "Revolution, or people's war, in any country is the business of the masses of that country and should be carried out primarily by their own efforts. There is no other way."[20]

Lin Biao's 1965 essay placed people's war at the center of a global revolutionary strategy. According to Lin's essay, peasant-based protracted guerrilla wars led by local Communist parties were to proliferate throughout the rural areas of the Third World. Insurgencies would erupt in country after country, with each eruption sapping imperialist strength and thereby facilitating the emergence of more revolutionary uprisings. As the global revolutionary wave gained momentum, imperialist forces would become steadily weaker and revolutionary forces steadily stronger. Drawing lessons from the CCP's own struggles against the KMT and Japan, Lin argued that insurgent forces would expand through the rural areas, eventually surrounding and isolating the cities where imperialist strength was strongest. Eventually virtually the entire Third World, the world's countryside, would be controlled by revolutionary forces. The industrially developed capitalist countries, the world's "cities," would be isolated, surrounded by a hostile, revolutionary Third World. Ultimately, imperialism would collapse around the world.

Beijing's revolutionary drive in the early 1960s had a profound impact on U.S. policy in Asia. From Washington's perspective, Beijing's revolutionary militancy seemed proof that China was an expansionist power. Washington followed closely the debate between the CCP and the CPSU over support for wars of national liberation. Moreover, it placed China's support for Vietnamese revolutionary forces in this context. From Washington's point of view, China was using Vietnam as a "test case" of a war of national liberation that, if successful, would validate Beijing's militant stance as opposed to Moscow's more cautious orientation. This, in turn, might lead to further Communist-bloc support for other wars of national liberation. To prevent this, Washington concluded that Beijing's efforts in Vietnam had to be thwarted. Washington's estimate of the nature of the link between Beijing and Hanoi, and between both of those capitals and the insurgency in South Vietnam, was fundamentally flawed. Hanoi was not a proxy for China, and the insurgency in South Vietnam was not a case of Chinese expansionism. Yet, Washington was correct in its assessment of the link between Beijing's support for Hanoi and China's rejection of Moscow's policy of peaceful coexistence. It was also correct in its estimate that Beijing saw Vietnam as a test case that, if successful, would give a tremendous boost to national liberation struggles around the world.

THE BEIJING-HANOI-DJAKARTA AXIS

Geographic proximity made Southeast Asia the focus of China's revolutionary drive 1963 through 1965. Vietnam and Indonesia made up two flanks of the Chinese-supported revolutionary advance. There was a high degree of convergence between Beijing's objectives and those of Hanoi and Djakarta at this juncture, and the PRC joined enthusiastically with those two countries to achieve common purposes.

Hanoi's fixed objective was the unification of all of Vietnam under VWP rule. For several years after the Geneva Convention, Hanoi's energies were directed toward consolidating the socialist system within North Vietnam. By 1958, domestic and international conditions seemed propitious for a resumption of armed struggle in the south, with the socialist north serving as a base of support. Most important for our purposes, China's foreign policy was increasingly militant. Thus, in late 1958 and early 1959 the VWP made a series of decisions leading to the resumption of armed struggle in the South.[21]

We still know very little about the CCP's role in these critical VWP decisions. The CCP may or may not have assured the VWP of assistance to an armed struggle to liberate South Vietnam, but it is probable that the VWP was emboldened by China's increasing militancy. Offsetting this was the adverse consequences for Hanoi of deteriorating Sino-Soviet relations. The VWP was dismayed by Chinese-Soviet tensions. It would have much preferred united Sino-Soviet support for its efforts. At the same time, however, there were positive aspects to Sino-Soviet tensions—Hanoi could play on these tensions to achieve its objectives. Khrushchev was reluctant to cede Vietnam to Chinese influence and was increasingly sensitive to the impact that Beijing's charges of insufficient revolutionary ardor were having on Soviet standing within the international Communist movement. Khrushchev was willing, therefore, to give some degree of support to the VWP struggle—at least in the late 1950s. Ho Chi Minh was in Beijing in October 1959 for the PRC's tenth National Day celebrations. So was Khrushchev. It is likely that Ho returned to Hanoi with a degree of Chinese and Soviet sanction for the armed struggle in the South.

As the schism widened between Beijing and Moscow in the early 1960s, the VWP tended to favor Beijing's militant approach because it feared that Khrushchev's policy of peaceful coexistence with the United States would make Moscow reluctant to support insurgency in South Vietnam. But Hanoi also wanted to avoid having to choose between Soviet and Chinese support and feared that the deterioration of Sino-Soviet relations would force exactly such a choice. To avoid this, Hanoi proposed to Moscow and Beijing in January 1962 the cessation of polemics as a preliminary to bilateral CCP-CPSU conversations. When these efforts proved unsuccessful, Hanoi leaned toward Beijing, siding with it on such issues as the border dispute with India and the nuclear test ban treaty.[22]

Beijing had several reasons for supporting Hanoi's drive to liberate South Vietnam. Since 1955 South Vietnam had been an "associated state" of the Southeast Asia Treaty Organization (SEATO) and an integral part of the U.S. system of containment. The liberation of South Vietnam would therefore enhance China's security by expelling the United States from South Vietnam. A revolutionary offensive in South Vietnam would also force Moscow to choose between supporting that revolution, thereby shelving its quest for better relations with the United States, or not supporting it, thereby exposing Khrushchev's counterrevolutionary nature. A successful revolutionary offensive in South Vietnam would also give a boost to anti-imperialist forces around the world. Finally, victory of Vietnam's war of national liberation would prove the correctness of Beijing's line in its polemic with Moscow, greatly facilitating the rectification of the line of the world Communist movement along the more militant lines favored by Beijing.

In early 1964, revolutionary prospects in South Vietnam looked good. The overthrow and assassination of South Vietnam's leader Ngo Dinh Diem in October 1963 had thrown the counterrevolutionary forces into disarray. On the battlefield, National Liberation Front (NLF) forces held the initiative. (The NLF was the South Vietnamese united front through which Hanoi acted in the South.) At this critical juncture,

Beijing and Hanoi decided on a coordinated political-military strategy to win victory. Militarily, the infiltration from North Vietnam of native southerners and northern cadre to serve with the NLF was stepped up. Units of the DRV's regular army were also ordered south to fight with the NLF. The NLF was reorganized into larger units and provided with heavier crew-served weapons, many of which were operated by DRV regulars dressed as southern guerrillas. Politically, an effort was launched to reconvene the Geneva conference as a way of preventing U.S. intervention on behalf of Saigon. Here the idea was that apparent movement toward a diplomatic solution would create public pressure on Washington to forgo military moves that might torpedo a possible peaceful solution. To deter U.S. attacks against North Vietnam in response to stepped-up infiltration into the South, Beijing began warning the United States against intervention and underlined the message with military moves. The Sino-American confrontation that resulted will be discussed in Chapter Thirteen.

Indonesia was the southern flank of Beijing's revolutionary drive in Southeast Asia. Beijing's links with Indonesia operated at two levels: through Indonesian President Sukarno, and through the Indonesian Communist Party (usually known by its initials in Dutch, PKI). Sukarno was a radical nationalist par excellence. His objective was to establish his nation as the paramount power in Southeast Asia, a position to which he felt its large size and population, and Java's ancient cultural achievements, entitled it. He saw alignment with China as a way of achieving this objective.

Indonesia and the PRC began moving toward entente after the 1961 Belgrade non-aligned conference, where Sukarno's estimate of the world situation closely approximated that of Beijing and contrasted sharply with that of India. The Sino-Indonesian entente was strengthened by PRC President Liu Shaoqi's April 1963 visit to Indonesia, and again by Sukarno's September 1963 proclamation of "confrontation" with the Federation of Malaysia.[23]

The Indonesian-Malaysian "confrontation" had a great impact on the region. Sukarno's immediate objective was to prevent Malaysia's incorporation of Sarawak and Sabah, territories in north Borneo that Sukarno claimed for Indonesia. (Malaya gained independence from Britain in 1957. In 1963 it joined with Sarawak, Sabah, and Singapore to form Malaysia. Singapore left the federation two years later.) Sukarno's broader objective was to drive British influence out of the region. He could not believe that a genuinely independent government in Kuala Lumpur would want to retain a British presence, and he concluded that the Kuala Lumpur regime must be a neo-colony that had been created by the Anglo-American imperialists to block Indonesia's emergence as a great power. As the confrontation got under way, Indonesian military forces concentrated along the Sarawak and Sabah borders. By August 1964, Indonesian paratroops were raiding peninsular Malaysia.

Beijing enthusiastically endorsed Sukarno's confrontation with Malaysia because it mobilized Indonesia against the Anglo-American imperialists and made Sukarno more desirous of Chinese support. By early 1965, Beijing was publicly hinting of possible Chinese military assistance to Indonesia in the event of conflict with Great Britain or the United States. Beijing's and Sukarno's global objectives were also parallel. Sukarno sought to organize a coalition of anti-Western forces, which he dubbed the "New Emerging Forces," or NEFO, to constitute a new center of world power. This coincided with Beijing's conception of an anti-United States united front, and by 1963 the two countries were cooperating to create such a new bloc. Joint efforts to convene the second Afro-Asian conference (discussed earlier) were one aspect of this cooperation. Beijing also joined with Djakarta to sponsor the athletic Games of the New Emerging Forces (GANEFO) in November 1963. Conceived as an alternative to the United States–dominated International Olympic Committee, some fifty-one mostly Afro-Asian countries participated in GANEFO. Beijing also welcomed Indonesia's withdrawal from the United Nations at the end of 1964 (when Malaysia became a temporary member of the Security Council over Indonesia's strenuous protests) and supported its effort to organize a "new United Nations." As Mao Zedong told U.S. journalist Edgar Snow, the development of a permanent assembly of "have-not" nations existing independently of the United States–dominated United Nations was a natural outgrowth of the Afro-Asian movement.

As Indonesia's confrontation with Malaysia and Britain escalated ar.d as Indonesia grew increasingly isolated among the international community, Sukarno moved to strengthen relations with China, North Vietnam, and North Korea. He increasingly stressed the potential of a Pyongyang-Beijing-Hanoi-Djakarta axis for overturning the Western-dominated international order in Asia. Beijing lauded Sukarno's correct course.

The second component of Beijing's revolutionary front with Indonesia was its ties to the PKI. By the early 1960s, the PKI was the world's largest non-ruling Communist party. It had strong organizations in Indonesian villages and was a major force in Indonesian politics. In terms of its orientation in the CCP-CPSU dispute, the PKI was something of a paradox. Its strategy for effecting revolution approximated the model of transition propounded by Moscow: gradual, peaceful transition to socialism in alliance with progressive bourgeois elements—the latter being represented by Sukarno. On international issues, however, the PKI saw the world very much as the CCP did. As the split between the CCP and the CPSU widened, the PKI followed Beijing; by 1965, its split with the CPSU was complete.[24]

Sukarno played an important role in CCP and PKI strategy. Both believed that Sukarno would eventually convert to Communism and lead the Indonesian revolution into its second, socialist stage. Throughout 1964 and into 1965, Sukarno conformed to this expectation and steadily facilitated the expansion of PKI power. By 1965, open anti-Communism was virtually a crime in Indonesia. Anti-Communist, Islamic, and private business organizations had been suppressed. The Indonesian army was the sole remaining organized opposition to the PKI. To eliminate this last counterrevolutionary obstacle, the PKI was agitating for a restructuring of the army along leftist lines. As a showdown between revolutionary and anti-revolutionary forces loomed in 1965, the PKI pushed for the creation of an armed workers' and peasants' militia under PKI control. Under pressure from the army, Sukarno rejected this proposal. Then, under pressure from the PKI and China, he reversed himself.

Beijing assisted the PKI in its efforts to consolidate revolutionary gains. In January 1965, Zhou Enlai offered Indonesian Foreign Minister Subandrio (a close confidant of Sukarno's) 100,000 "pieces of light arms." During the following months, Chinese arms were shipped clandestinely to Indonesia. They arrived in crates marked "construction materials," avoided customs inspections by direct order of Sukarno, and were stored in air force bases in and around Djakarta for use in the upcoming showdown. Air force Minister Dani (another of Sukarno's confidants) flew secretly to Beijing in mid-September to expedite the shipment of Chinese arms through discussions with Zhou Enlai and CCP Secretary General Deng Xiaoping.[25]

On September 30, radical military officers attempted a coup against the top-level, anti-Communist leadership of the army. Several army leaders were assassinated, but others escaped and organized a counterstrike against their radical opponents. During the following days, the Chinese-supplied arms stored around Djakarta were distributed by the radical air force to a hastily organized militia. An anti-Communist reign of terror developed, fed by popular Islamic and anti-Chinese sentiments. The PKI's close identification with China and its earlier anti-religious efforts now worked against it. Tens of thousands of PKI members and sympathizers were killed. PKI organizations were broken up. Its leaders were killed or forced into exile. By early 1966, the PKI had been crushed and Indonesia was moving rapidly to repair its ties with the West.

The destruction of the PKI was one of the most catastrophic setbacks ever to befall the international Communist movement. Following this setback the CCP condemned the PKI's failure to launch a rural-based protracted guerrilla war as called for by Maoist theory. These were post hoc rationalizations. In the months preceding the September 1965 showdown there was no evidence that the CCP was troubled by the PKI's strategy, probably because it thought that chances for success were good. Moreover, the PKI and the CCP did not think of the September coup as an attempt to seize power, but merely as an effort to purge the top army leadership. The level of Chinese knowledge of and involvement in the attempted September 30 coup is still unclear. A Central Intelligence Agency report concluded that while Beijing probably had general knowledge of the coup plan and was certainly very much in sympathy with it, there is no evidence that it was directly involved in inciting or planning the coup.[26]

SOCIALISM IN ONE COUNTRY

In 1964, global revolutionary prospects as seen from Beijing were bright, a situation illustrated by Figure 6–2. The year 1965, however, was a year of unparalleled setbacks. In Africa, Beijing's support for revolution generated substantial hostility among established governments, and by 1965 the chickens started coming home to roost. In January 1965, China suffered its first public reverse in Africa when Burundi severed diplomatic relations with the PRC and expelled Chinese personnel. A year later, Dahomey and the Central African Republic followed suit. In June, China's efforts to convene a second Afro-Asian conference collapsed. In February 1966, Beijing lost another key radical nationalist supporter when Nkrumah was overthrown in Ghana.

Beijing's standing in the Third World also suffered because of the extremism of Chinese positions. Its insistence on the progressive nature of war and the necessity of violent revolution, for instance, alienated many moderate African and Asian governments. Nor was China's rejection of disarmament popular. In contrast to Chinese radicalism, Soviet and Indian positions often seemed reasonable. Chinese (and Soviet) insistence on injecting the Sino-Soviet dispute into Afro-Asian forums also alienated non-Communist neutralists who felt that these ideological issues were not related to the needs of the Third World. China's attacks on India and Yugoslavia, two leaders of the non-aligned movement, also alienated members of that movement. China's criticism of the United Nations alienated small countries who saw the UN as an important forum.

In September 1965, the same month the PKI went down in defeat, war broke out between China's friend Pakistan and India. China had given substantial military assistance to Pakistan and had made strong statements supporting Pakistan in the months preceding the outbreak of full-scale war. Once the war began, China mobilized its forces on the Sino-Indian border, picked a fight on that border, and issued an ultimatum to India–moves designed to force New Delhi to divert forces away from the India-Pakistan front. In spite of these moves, Pakistan was defeated by India. Moreover, Pakistan then accepted, over

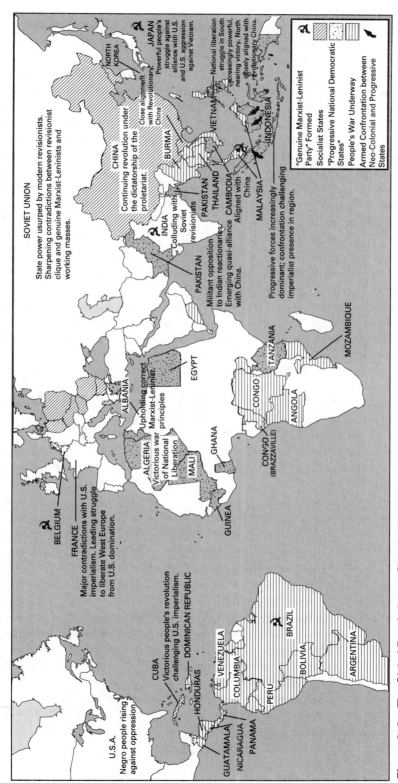

Figure 6–2 The Global Revolutionary Situation in 1964

153

strenuous Chinese opposition, Soviet mediation of the Indian-Pakistani dispute.[27]

Overshadowing all was U.S. intervention in Vietnam. Chapter Thirteen will discuss China's attempts to deter U.S. attacks on North Vietnam. For now we may simply note that those efforts failed. By mid-1965, U.S. warplanes were bombing North Vietnam and many tens of thousands of U.S. troops were pouring into South Vietnam. China had seen Vietnam's war of national liberation as the cutting edge of the global anti-U.S. struggle and had invested heavily in support of it. U.S. intervention made the prospects for VWP success much more problematic. U.S. bombing of North Vietnam also confirmed Khrushchev's contention that military support for wars of national liberation risked imperialist attack against the socialist countries and refuted Mao's proposition to the contrary.

It is interesting to speculate about the impact that the setbacks of 1965 had on China's turning inward in the mid-1960s. Here an analogy with the early Bolshevik experience may be useful. During the early years of the Soviet state, the Bolshevik leaders believed that revolution was imminent in Europe. The social upheavals at the end of World War I and the collapse of many of the old regimes of Europe was evidence of this, they believed. By 1923, however, it was apparent that this was not to be; aside from Russia, capitalist rule had been stabilized across Europe. This precipitated a major debate within Bolshevik ranks. Leon Trotsky, the leader of the Red Army and the No. 2 Bolshevik leader, argued that unless the revolution could be spread to other lands it was doomed. Consequently, he prescribed vigorous efforts to support foreign revolutionary movements. Joseph Stalin took a more cautious approach, arguing that it was possible to build socialism in one country and that Bolshevik energies should be aimed in this direction. In line with this, Stalin prescribed intensive socialist construction within the Soviet Union, together with preparation to withstand imperialist invasion. Stalin defeated Trotsky, expelling him from the Soviet Union in 1929. The reasons for Stalin's victory were extremely complex, but most historians agree that one factor had to do with an inward-looking-ness that prevailed within the Bolshevik party once the dreams of European revolution dissipated. Having lost their dream of imminent European revolution, many Bolsheviks directed their revolutionary aspirations inward and concluded that it was possible, after all, to construct a socialist utopia at home. A similar psychological dynamic may have been at work in China as the Cultural Revolution unfolded in 1965 and 1966.

By 1965, China's leaders were deeply divided over domestic and foreign policy. Following the collapse of the Great Leap Forward in 1961, Mao had retired from active direction of domestic policy while retaining control over foreign policy. (The Great Leap Forward was Mao's first attempt to create an egalitarian model of socialism during the period from 1958 to 1960.) Under the guidance of such men as Liu Shaoqi and Deng Xiaoping, domestic policy was increasingly oriented toward economic growth. Such an approach was anathema to Mao. He feared that such policies would take China away from the egalitarian, collectivist goals for which the revolution was made. Concerned with the direction of the revolution, Mao had begun challenging the pragmatic direction of policy as early as September 1962. By late 1965, the conflict between Mao and his pragmatic opponents was coming to a head.

In the view of his pragmatic opponents, Mao's utopianism was of little use in running a complex society or industrializing China. They felt that Mao's utopian vision might have been appropriate to an earlier era but had now become an obstacle to China's development. The pragmatists may also have questioned Mao's militant foreign policies.[28]

As Mao was struggling to reverse the unrevolutionary policies of the pragmatists, he was also trying to make sense of the USSR's imperialist-like international behavior from the standpoint of Marxist-Leninist doctrine. As long as the Sino-Soviet conflict remained at the level of a party-to-party polemic, it posed no theoretical problem for Marxism-Leninism. Up to that point it could be explained away as not involving *state* behavior. The escalation of that conflict to the state level, however, posed grave theoretical problems. From the standpoint of Marxism-Leninism, a country's foreign policy is a function of its domestic social structure and class relations. Imperialism supposedly arose out of the exploitative class relations of capitalist society. It followed then that elimination of exploitative class relations through the nationalization of private ownership of the means of production would eliminate the very possibility of imperialism. The socialist transformation of society should produce, according to Marxist-Leninist theory, a non-aggressive state and mutual solidarity between socialist states for the common advance of humankind.

By 1964, it was clear to Mao that these propositions did not provide an adequate explanation for the international behavior of the Soviet Union. Not only had the Soviet government refused to support the revolutionary struggle against U.S. imperialism, but, as we saw in Part Two, it had tried to keep China weak by blocking its acquisition of nuclear weapons, preventing the liberation of Taiwan, supporting India against it, and withdrawing economic assistance in its moment of greatest need. How was this possible according to Marxism-Leninism?

The theory of cognitive dissonance is useful in understanding Mao's efforts to come to grips with this dilemma. According to this theory, an individual's world view is laden with values, linked to many different elements of the personality, and rooted in subconscious needs. People have a need to make perceived "facts" fit with their world view, and when there is a contradiction, the individual experiences psychological discomfort that he or she will try to resolve. This may be done by altering or discarding the world view that does not fit with the perceived facts. But such a solution entails basic changes in personality, something that is extremely difficult and painful. It is psychologically easier to reinterpret the facts in such a way as to make them accord with one's underlying world view. It was in this latter fashion that Mao reconciled his Marxist-Leninist world view with the imperialistic behavior of the Soviet Union. The syllogism Mao constructed was this: If, according to Marxism-Leninism, a socialist state cannot be imperialist, and if it was apparent that the USSR acted in an imperialist way, then it followed that the USSR was not a socialist state. This was the genesis of Mao's theory of the restoration of capitalism in the USSR. According to this theory, "new bourgeois elements" had emerged "on a large scale" in Soviet society because of a failure to continue class struggle and abandonment of the dictatorship of the proletariat. According to a seminal polemic of 1964, one very probably authored by Mao: "Leading functionaries of some state-owned factories...abuse their positions and amass large fortunes by using the equipment and materials of factories to set up 'underground workshops' for private products, selling the products illicitly and dividing the spoils."[29] Such enterprise managers worked with "functionaries in the state departments in charge of supplies and in the commercial and other departments" to carry out their nefarious schemes. "Even high-ranking officials in the state organs support and shield them."[30] The factories operated in this fashion "are socialist...only in name." In fact:

> [They are] capitalist enterprises by which these persons enrich themselves. The relationship of such persons to the workers has turned into one between exploiters and exploited, between oppressors and oppressed. Are not such degenerates who possess and make use of means of production to exploit the labor of others out-and-out bourgeois elements?...Obviously all these people belong to a class that is antagonistic to the proletariat—they belong to the bourgeoisie.[31]

While such "new bourgeois elements" had existed under Stalin, after Khrushchev came to power their status "fundamentally changed" and their activities were no longer restricted and subject to attack. Rather, "the new bourgeois elements have gradually risen to the ruling position in the Party and government...and form a privileged stratum in Soviet society. This privileged stratum is the principal component of the bourgeoisie in the Soviet Union today and the main social base of the revisionist Khrushchevist clique."[32] Having usurped top leadership, the privileged stratum was "step by step...turning socialist ownership...into ownership by the privileged stratum."[33]

Mao's theory of the restoration of capitalism in the Soviet Union had a great impact on China's foreign relations. It contributed to the deterioration of Sino-Soviet relations. Eventually it provided the theoretical justification for Sino-American rapprochement. Since the USSR and the United States were both capitalist, imperialist powers, it became a matter of expedience, rather than principle, whether China tilted toward one rather than the other. The theory of capitalist restoration also affected Mao's struggle against his intra-CCP opponents. As Mao concluded that the policies advocated by his pragmatic opponents would lead China down the road of capitalist restoration already taken by the Soviet Union, his struggles against domestic and foreign revisionism became increasingly intertwined. Mao's linking of his domestic opponents to the "capitalist" Soviet Union undermined popular support for the CCP's pragmatists and their "capitalist road" policies. Increased popular hatred of the Soviet Union translated into decreased dislike of Chinese leaders putatively linked to the USSR. This was probably one factor in Mao's resurrection of the territorial issue with the Soviet Union in 1963 and his subsequent approval of escalation of tension along the border.

FOREIGN RELATIONS DURING THE CULTURAL REVOLUTION

The Cultural Revolution of 1966 through 1969 was an attempt to rekindle the utopian drive of the Chinese revolution. It also involved an intra-elite power struggle and policy debate between Mao's utopian vision of socialism and the development-oriented brand of socialism advocated by other senior CCP leaders. There were aspects of religious revivalism involved in Mao's efforts. Mao saw the ethos of the revolution being eroded by pragmatic policies and was determined to rekindle the fires of the true faith. The Cultural Revolution also involved a mass upheaval against established elites and bureaucracies. The instrument Mao chose to defeat his factional opponents was organizations of radical youth known as Red Guards. Loosely guided by top-level Maoists in the Cultural Revolutionary Small Group in Beijing, and supported by the Maoist-controlled police and army, the Red Guards became a genuine mass movement that acquired a momentum of its own. Inspired by Mao's vision of utopia commingled with their own desires for power and status, the Red Guard mounted sharp attacks on the established party and government structures of power.

The key focus of Chinese foreign policy from 1966 to 1969 became replication of the Maoist revolutionary model. The flexible approach toward governments and insurgent movements that had characterized Beijing's earlier efforts to maximize the aggregate strength of the anti-United States united front was abandoned. Instead, Beijing drew sharp ideological lines and excluded from the united front anyone who did not embrace Maoist ideology.

By 1967, China's media supported and encouraged only "genuine

Marxist-Leninist" parties that toed the Maoist ideological line. By Beijing's count, there were fifty such parties. Although they were usually quite small, their proclamations were nonetheless publicized and their leaders fêted during visits to China as though they were heads of powerful organizations. Beijing apparently hoped that these Maoist Communist parties would become the centers of the New Left movements that emerged in Western Europe, North America, and Japan in the 1960s. After the student-worker rebellion in France in May 1968, Beijing began paying considerable attention to the New Left, lauding it (for a period) as part of the rising global tide of world revolution inspired by Mao Zedong.[34] Among countries, only Albania measured up to Beijing's new, strict standards, although Pakistan was exempt from criticism because of the important role it played in China's efforts to counter India—and because of explicit instructions from Zhou Enlai. China's relations with virtually all other countries soured.[35]

China also stressed the foreign propagation of "Mao Zedong Thought" (the formal name for Maoist ideology) during the Cultural Revolution. China's foreign diplomatic missions often became involved in organizing local Maoist activities. Occasionally, Chinese diplomats aided such revolutionary activity as inciting overseas Chinese to disregard local laws. The communities of overseas Chinese in Southeast Asia figured prominently in Cultural Revolutionary diplomacy. They were encouraged to embrace Maoist ideology and emulate the Cultural Revolution in their own countries. In Hong Kong and Macao in late 1966 and early 1967, mobs of Maoist youths battled police, demanding the immediate British and Portuguese evacuation of those areas. Beijing issued statements lauding the Hong Kong rioters and condemning the Hong Kong police.

Burma was the most important example of Beijing's efforts to propagate Maoism among overseas Chinese to the detriment of cordial governmental relations. Burma had been the first non-Communist country to recognize the PRC, and until 1967 relations between the two countries were quite cordial. That cordiality was aborted in two weeks in June 1967, when a confrontation began over the right of overseas Chinese students in Rangoon to wear badges showing Chairman Mao. When Burmese authorities prohibited the badges, the students, supported by personnel from the Chinese embassy in Rangoon, ignored the prohibitions. Confrontations developed, escalating into full-scale anti-Chinese riots in which more than 100 overseas Chinese were killed. Beijing responded by condemning the Burmese government, calling for its overthrow, organizing massive demonstrations against the Burmese embassy in Beijing, and endorsing the insurgent Burma Communist Party.[36]

Analysts generally agree that the ideological fervor that characterized Chinese foreign relations during the Cultural Revolution was linked to domestic factional conflicts. They differ as regards the exact nature of that linkage. Peter Van Ness concluded that the emphasis on Maoist orthodoxy flowed from Mao's preoccupation with preventing a "restoration of capitalism" in China.[37] To legitimize their seizure of power and discredit their revisionist opponents, the Maoists sought to orchestrate a chorus of seeming universal acclaim, according to Van Ness. Statements by foreigners lauding Mao and condemning revisionism, or seeming to replicate the Maoist revolutionary model, strengthened the Maoist claim to power within China by demonstrating that Mao Zedong Thought was successful around the world. The setbacks that Chinese policy suffered in 1965 probably heightened the need of the Maoists for such seeming foreign acclaim.

Melvin Gurtov provided a different explanation.[38] China's leaders, Gurtov argues, were preoccupied with domestic events and paid little attention to developments in China's foreign missions during the Cultural Revolution. But the recall of China's ambassadors in late 1966 and early 1967 (to undergo ideological reeducation), combined with the mounting influence of radical elements within the Ministry of Foreign Affairs (MFA) in Beijing, opened the way for mid-level Maoist militants in foreign missions. As the Cultural Revolution developed in China, enterprising Maoists posted abroad were inspired to make revolution. They were able to do this because the recall of ambassadors had weakened the controls that ordinarily inhibited such activity.

Still another factor was efforts by Red Guard groups to prove themselves more revolutionary than their rivals. Within China and in China's overseas missions, as Red Guard groups vied with one another for power, they sought to demonstrate their revolutionary commitment by struggling against whatever foreign revisionist and reactionary targets were available. As each group sought to prove itself more revolutionary than the other, the militancy of struggle against available foreign targets escalated. A similar process may have been at work with China's diplomats, who may have felt a strong need to prove their political reliability; that is, their Maoism. The lifestyle enjoyed by Chinese diplomats overseas, while far from luxurious by Western standards, was considerably above the spartan level prevalent at home. Moreover, diplomats often had politically questionable backgrounds, either having themselves undergone foreign training or coming from the families of intellectuals. These diplomats knew that their colleagues back in China, including even Foreign Minister Chen Yi, were being criticized for various rightist errors. The ambassador heading their own mission had been recalled for ideological reeducation. Thus, diplomats abroad felt strong pressures to prove their revolutionary ardor. If this activity brought the diplomats into conflict with the local police, so much the better. What better way to prove that one "dared to struggle," as one Maoist slogan of that era phrased it, than by challenging the police power of a reactionary state? Through such means, according to Gurtov, the export of the Cultural Revolution was an unintended byproduct of the internal factional conflict.

In a study of policy toward the overseas Chinese communities, Stephen Fitzgerald reached conclusions similar to Gurtov's.[39] The Cultural Revolution marked a sharp break with Beijing's earlier policy of not using the overseas Chinese communities in Southeast Asia as agents of revolution. By 1967, it seemed that Beijing was attempting to mobilize those communities for a revolutionary offensive. This new orientation was not due to a top-level decision, Fitzgerald maintained, but to spontaneous emulation of the Cultural Revolution by disaffected, unassimilated, and "patriotic" overseas Chinese supported by militant Chinese diplomats acting on their own initiative. Beijing's statements supporting such activities were responses, not causes, Fitzgerald argued, and in most cases, they were not backed up by action. Moreover, as soon as the Red Guards were purged from the MFA in late 1967 (a matter discussed later), Beijing's comments on incidents involving the overseas Chinese became increasingly restrained and perfunctory. As Beijing reined in Red Guard radicalism, it reasserted its traditional policy toward the overseas Chinese.

There is little question that the Cultural Revolution upheaval greatly affected the organizational apparatus that normally regulated China's foreign policies. Red Guard groups began criticizing Chen Yi during the second half of 1966. Chen Yi was forced to make concessions to the Red Guards, but was generally able to keep radicalism within the MFA and its affiliated institutions under check. Early in 1967, radical influence intensified as the Cultural Revolution Small Group authorized a Red Guard seizure of power in party and government organs. In January, a Red Guard group was organized in the MFA. From June through August, Red Guard influence within the MFA was great.

Radicals in the MFA differed from previous power holders on the issue of China's relations with overseas Chinese communities. They seized on Chen Yi's efforts to limit the foreign spillover of the Cultural Revolution as evidence of his counterrevolutionary stance, and charged that over the years he and Liao Chengzhi, head of the Overseas Chinese Affairs Commission, had consistently failed to protect overseas Chinese communities in Southeast Asia against persecution. The late April 1967 return to China of Yao Dengshan, who had served as chargé d'affaires in Indonesia since 1965, added fuel to the radical assault on Chen Yi and Liao Chengzhi. Yao was a firebrand radical and provided a leader for the radicals in the MFA. He had also witnessed firsthand the anti-Chinese pogroms in Indonesia following the abortive September 30 coup and could draw on his experiences in Indonesia to prove the supposed crimes of Liao and Chen.

Radical influence on Chinese foreign relations reached its apex for two weeks in August 1967, when Red Guards seized the MFA building and sent cables to overseas missions without clearance from Zhou Enlai. On August 22, Red Guards seized and burned the British mission in Beijing, beating the British chargé d'affaires and several of his staff as they ran from the burning building. The Cultural Revolution Small Group *may* have authorized the demonstrations against the British mission as retaliation for London's firm handling of Red Guard rioters in Hong Kong, but they probably had not countenanced its destruction. This act seriously injured China's international standing, and following it, Mao and Zhou intervened to rein in radical influence over foreign relations. Yao Dengshan and his supporter in the Cultural Revolution Small Group, Wang Li, were purged. Red Guard organizations were directed not to violate the immunity of foreign diplomatic missions or personnel. Orders were sent to embassies abroad, directing them not to carry the Cultural Revolution into foreign countries. Measures were also gradually implemented to begin repairing relations with China's estranged neighbors. These moves were implemented in a way that avoided appearances of a humiliating retreat.[40]

Given the anti-revisionist thrust of the Cultural Revolution, it is not surprising that the Soviet Union bore the brunt of much of the zealotry during this period. Huge demonstrations were mobilized against the Soviet embassy in Beijing which, along with the Mongolian embassy, was kept under siege during January and February of 1967. Later in 1967, Red Guards invaded the Soviet embassy's consular section and burned its files. When Moscow withdrew its diplomats' dependents in February 1967, some were beaten or forced to crawl under pictures of Mao Zedong on their way to waiting planes. In August 1967, a Soviet freighter docked in Dalian was seized by Red Guards after a Soviet sailor made disparaging remarks about the Mao badge worn by a Chinese stevedore. Along the border, Chinese Red Guards taunted Soviet border guards.[41]

In many ways the Cultural Revolution was an era of isolation and xenophobia. By the spring of 1967, all but one of China's ambassadors had been recalled; only Huang Hua in Cairo was still at his post. The number of Chinese delegations going abroad and foreign delegations coming to China dwindled to a few dozen per year. Chinese students were recalled from abroad, and most foreign students studying in China were expelled. Chinese scholars, officials, and athletes ceased to participate in various international activities. Foreigners and all things foreign became highly suspect. Red Guards ransacked homes, looking for foreign books, records, or other articles. Mere contact with foreigners was grounds for suspicion and questioning by the Red Guards or police. The teaching of foreign languages and the translation of foreign journals and books into Chinese was suspended. Chinese who had studied abroad, who read foreign books, or who spoke foreign languages came under suspicion and criticism. Wearing foreign clothing became a counterrevolutionary act. The Red Guard's disgrace of Liu Shaoqi's wife Wang Guangmei, for example, was capped by forcing her to parade in her Western-style dresses.

Xenophobia has always run deep in Chinese popular culture. Ordinarily, chauvinistic sentiments are held in check by a more urbane and sophisticated elite whose members have read about or travelled in foreign countries, and who know the strengths as well as the shortcomings of other societies. It was precisely these worldly people who were those pushed aside by the Red Guards. The Red Guards, on the other hand, typically had minimal knowledge of the outside world and tended to think in very simplistic Maoist terms. Even if members of the more urbane elite remained in office, they were influenced by the climate of terror generated by the struggle against "bourgeois" and "revisionist" influences.[42]

As the Cultural Revolution escalated, governments around the world were deeply troubled by China's seemingly irrational extremism. Popular media abroad frequently explained China's international behavior in terms of psychosis. By 1968, China was generally perceived abroad as an embittered country that had withdrawn into its own shell, and it was regarded as dangerously irrational.

There is a curious fit between China's international orientation during the Cultural Revolution and its traditional world view. As we have seen, China traditionally saw itself as the center of civilization and the highest embodiment of human virtue. Foreigners were, to varying degrees, benighted barbarians who became civilized to the extent that they came into contact with and partook of Chinese culture. Similarly, during the Cultural Revolution, only China, or its close follower Albania, were truly virtuous (revolutionary) societies. China stood as the "red beacon" of all mankind, showing the oppressed peoples of the world the way to liberation and justice. Mao Zedong was the "great teacher" of the peoples of the world. If only they would study Mao's doctrine, those peoples would find their way to a glorious Communist future. Perhaps at some deep psychological level the ultra-revolutionism of this era appealed to the Red Guards and their Maoist mentors within the CCP leadership because it resonated with traditional notions about China's proper place in the world.

The isolationism of the Cultural Revolution cannot, however, be attributed entirely to lingering traditional influences. To a considerable extent, isolationism was a deliberate policy choice of the top Maoist leaders. Jiang Qing, (Mao's wife), her chief lieutenant Yao Wenyuan, and to a considerable extent Mao Zedong himself viewed the isolation of China as essential to the ideological transformation of the Chinese people, which was, in turn, necessary to create the "human material" appropriate for the creation of a genuine Communist society. Just as capitalism demanded and had created one type of human nature, the

Maoists believed, so Communism demanded and had to create another type of human nature. With China's populace isolated from corrupting foreign influences and subjected to constant indoctrination, sustained criticism–self-criticism, and repeated ideological "struggle," a new type of altruistic, collectivist, Communist person would eventually come into being. This new "human material" would then provide the basis for genuine Communism. This totalitarian notion remained the bedrock of China's foreign relations until after the death of Mao. Only in 1978 would China again open its doors to foreign influences and abandon the notion that society was a huge laboratory in which a new type of "human material" was to be created.

NOTES

1. Regarding some of the factors influencing the pro-Soviet or pro-Chinese alignment of various Communist parties, see William E. Griffith, "Communist Polycentrism and the Underdeveloped Areas," in Kurt London, ed., *New Nations in a Divided World*, New York: Praeger, 1963, 274–86.

2. William E. Griffith, "The Diplomacy of Eurocommunism," in *Eurocommunism and Detente*, Rudolf L. Tokes, ed., New York: New York University Press, 1978, 385–416.

3. For an example of China's early polemics, see *In Refutation of Modern Revisionism*, Beijing: Foreign Languages Press, 1958. Regarding Moscow's targeting of Albania, see Donald S. Zagoria, "Khrushchev's Attack on Albania and Sino-Soviet Relations," *China Quarterly*, no. 8 (October–December 1961), 1–19; Daniel Tretiak, "The Founding of the Sino-Albanian Entente," *China Quarterly*, no. 10 (April–June 1962), 123–43; William E. Griffith, *Albania and the Sino-Soviet Rift*, Cambridge: MIT Press, 1963. Regarding the evolution of the confrontation through various multi-party conferences, see David Floyd, *Mao Against Khrushchev*, New York: Praeger, 1963, 261–363; William E. Griffith, "The November 1960 Moscow Meeting: A Preliminary Reconstruction," *China Quarterly*, no. 11 (July–September 1962), 38–57.

4. J.D. Armstrong, *Revolutionary Diplomacy: Chinese Foreign Policy and the United Front Doctrine*, Berkeley: University of California Press, 1977, 74–90.

5. Chalmers Johnson, *Autopsy on People's War*, Berkeley: University of California Press, 1973, 33–37.

6. "Gongzuo tongxun" (Bulletin of Activities), April 1961, in *The Politics of the Chinese Red Army: A Translation of the Bulletin of Activities of the People's Liberation Army*, J. Chester Cheng, ed., Stanford, Calif.: The Hoover Institution, 1966, 484. CCP pronouncements on the African situation are available in *The Chinese People Resolutely Support the Just Struggle of the African People*. Beijing: Foreign Languages Press, 1961.

7. Anne Gilks and Gerald Segal, *China and the Arms Trade*, New York: St. Martin's Press, 1975, 37.

8. Regarding Beijing's relation to these Afro-Asian organizations, see Charles Neuhauser, *Third World Politics: China and the Afro-Asian People's Solidarity Organization, 1957–1967*, Cambridge: Harvard University Press, 1968.

9. The editorial departments of *People's Daily* and *Red Flag* produced a series of nine articles comprehensively outlining CCP differences with the CPSU. The series began on September 6, 1963, and ended on July 14, 1964. They are available in *Peking Review*, September 13, 20, 27, October 25, November 22, December 20, 1963, and February 7, April 3, and July 17, 1964. The single most comprehensive Chinese statement is *The Polemic on the General Line of the International Communist Movement*, Beijing: Foreign Languages Press, 1965. Western anthologies include William E. Griffith, *Sino-Soviet Relations, 1964–65*, Cambridge: MIT Press, 1967; William E. Griffith, *The Sino-Soviet Rift*, Cambridge: MIT Press, 1964; John Gittings, *The Sino-Soviet Dispute, 1956–63*, London: Oxford University Press, 1964; John Gittings, *Survey of the Sino-Soviet Dispute: A*

Commentary and Extracts from the Recent Polemics, 1963–1967, New York: Oxford University Press, 1968.

10. "Refutation of the New Leaders of the CPSU on 'United Action'," *Peking Review*, vol. 8, no. 46 (November 12, 1965), 10–21. Regarding Soviet-Chinese rivalry in Hanoi, see Donald S. Zagoria, *Vietnam Triangle: Moscow, Peking, Hanoi*, New York: Pegasus, 1967.

11. Sathi, "The Strategic Triangle: India," *Survey*, no. 54 (January 1965), 105–12; Savak Katrak, "India's Communist Party Split," *China Quarterly*, no. 7 (July–September 1961), 138–47.

12. See Kevin Devlin, "Schism and Secession," *Survey*, no. 54 (January 1965), 29–30; Parris H. Chang, "Chinese Perceptions and Relations with Eurocommunism," in *Eurocommunism Between East and West*, Vernon A. Aspaturian, et al., ed., Bloomington: Indiana University Press, 1980, 296–325; Hsia Chung-mao, "Maoist-Oriented Communist Parties and Their Splinter Organizations: An Instrument of World Revolution," *Issues and Studies*, vol. xiii, no. 4 (April 1977), 57–65.

13. Guy J. Pauker, "The Rise and Fall of Afro-Asian Solidarity," *Asian Survey*, vol. 5, no. 9 (September 1965), 425–32. Regarding China's diplomatic preparations for the conference, see *Afro-Asian Solidarity Against Imperialism: A Collection of Documents, Speeches, and Press Interviews from the Visits of Chinese Leaders to Thirteen African and Asian Countries*, Beijing: Foreign Languages Press, 1964.

14. Regarding rivalry between the Afro-Asian and non-aligned movements, see B.D. Arora, *Indian-Indonesian Relations (1961–1980)*, New Delhi: Asian Educational Series, 1981; Gopal Chandhuri, *China and Nonalignment*, New Delhi: ABC Publishing House, 1986.

15. Neuhauser, *Third World Politics*, 60.

16. Peter Van Ness, *Revolution and Chinese Foreign Policy: Peking's Support for Wars of National Liberation*, Berkeley: University of California Press, 1971, 78, 90, 114; Franz Michael, "Communist China and the Non-Committed Countries, Motives and Purposes of Communist China's Foreign Policy," *New Nations in a Divided World*, Kurt London, ed., New York: Praeger, 1963, 251; Johnson, *Autopsy*, 32–34.

17. Van Ness, *Revolution*, 157–84.

18. Sources on PRC material assistance to foreign revolutionary movements include Van Ness, *Revolution and Chinese Foreign Policy*, 82, 90, 115–21; Gilks and Segal, *China and the Arms Trade*, 39–43; Stockholm International Peace Research Institute, "The People's Republic of China," *The Arms Trade with the Third World*, New York: Holmes and Meier, 1975, 141–45. Regarding CCP activities in Africa, see Bruce E. Larkin, *China and Africa, 1949–1970*, Berkeley: University of California Press, 1971; Philip Snow, *The Star Raft: China's Encounter with Africa*, London: Weidenfeld and Nicolson, 1988. For an African perspective on China's infatuation with Africa, see Emmanuel John Hevi, *An African Student in China*, New York: Praeger, 1963. Regarding the CCP's links with the Latin American insurgencies, see Ernst Halperin, "Peking and the Latin American Communists," *China Quarterly*, no. 29 (January–March 1967), 111–54; Cecil Johnson, *Communist China and Latin America, 1959–1967*, New York: Columbia University Press, 1970.

19. Peter Van Ness, "Is China Expansionist? Mao Tse-tung and Revolutionary Self-Reliance," *Problems of Communism*, vol. 20, no. 1–2 (January–April 1971), 68–74.

20. Lin Biao, "Long Live the Victory of People's War," *The Lin Piao Affair*, Michael Y.M. Kau, ed., White Plains, N.Y.: International Arts and Sciences Press, 1975, 265–319. The underlying significance of Lin's essay has been widely debated. As Peter Van Ness pointed out, Lin's essay has been interpreted as Mao's equivalent of Hitler's *Mein Kampf*, as a contribution to the internal leadership debate over China's response to the U.S. escalation in Vietnam, and as a message to Hanoi and the Viet Cong that Chinese support would be limited. *Revolution*, 67. Most analysts agree, however, that one purpose of the essay was to present a clear statement of Maoist strategy for the overthrow of U.S. influence and eventual triumph of socialism throughout most of the world. Regarding the significance of Lin's essay, see David P. Mozingo and Thomas W. Robinson, *Lin Piao on People's War: China Takes a Second Look at Vietnam*, RM-4814-PR, Santa Monica, Calif.: Rand Corporation, 1965; Samuel B. Griffith, *Peking and the People's War*, New York: Praeger, 1966.

21. Among Hanoi's moves were formation of special units to infiltrate men and material into South Vietnam, strengthening VWP control over southern armed units, and seizing control of a district of Laos just west of the seventeenth parallel demilitarized zone between North and South Vietnam. See Ralph B. Smith, *An International History of the Vietnam War: Revolution versus Containment 1955–61*, New York: St. Martin's Press, 1983, 170–76; William J. Duiker, *The Communist Road to Power in Vietnam*, Boulder, Colo.: Westview Press, 1988, 169–234. Regarding VWP views on the relation between the revolution in North and South Vietnam, see Le Duan, *The Vietnamese Revolution*, New York: International Publishers, 1971.

22. Brian Shaw, "China and North Vietnam: Two Revolutionary Paths," *Current Scene* (Hong Kong) Part I, vol. 9, no. 11 (November 1971), 1–12, and Part II, vol. 9, no. 12 (December 1971), 1–12; King C. Chen, "Hanoi vs. Peking: Policies and Relations—A Survey," *Asian Survey*, vol. 2, no. 9 (September 1972), 806–17; John C. Connell and Melvin Gurtov, *North Vietnam: Left of Moscow, Right of Peking*, P-3794, Santa Monica, Calif.: Rand Corporation, February 1968; Zagoria, *Vietnam Triangle*; Jay Taylor, *China and Southeast Asia: Peking's Relations with Revolutionary Movements*, New York: Praeger, 1974, 1–27.

23. Regarding the Sino-Indonesian entente, see Sheldon W. Simon, *The Broken Triangle: Peking, Djakarta, and the PKI*, Baltimore: Johns Hopkins Press, 1969; David P. Mozingo, *Chinese Policy Toward Indonesia, 1949–1967*, Ithaca, N.Y.: Cornell University Press, 1976; Justus M. van der Kroef, "The Sino-Indonesian Partnership," *Orbis*, vol. 8, no. 2 (Summer 1964), 332–56.

24. Donald Hindley, "The Indonesian Communist Party and the Conflict in the International Communist Movement," *China Quarterly*, no. 19 (July–September 1964), 99–119; Antionie C.A. Dake, *In the Spirit of the Red Banteng: Indonesian Communists Between Moscow and Peking, 1954–1965*. The Hague: Mouton, 1973.

25. United States Central Intelligence Agency, *Indonesia: 1965, the Coup That Backfired*, Research Study, December 1968, 130, 173–74.

26. Ibid., 289.

27. See Anwar H. Syed, *China and Pakistan: Diplomacy of an Entente Cordiale*, Amherst: University of Massachusetts Press, 1974, 109–28; J.P. Jain, *China, Pakistan, and Bangladesh*, New Delhi: Radiant Publishers, 1974, 95–116; William J. Barnds, *India, Pakistan, and the Great Powers*, New York: Praeger, 1972, 188–223.

28. Some scholars argue that foreign policy issues were primary in the factional struggles culminating in the Cultural Revolution. See Andrew Hall Wedeman, *The East Wind Subsides: Chinese Foreign Policy and the Origins of the Cultural Revolution*, Washington, D.C.: Washington Institute Press, 1987. The more mainstream view is that domestic issues were primary.

29. *On Khrushchev's Phoney Communism and Its Historical Lessons for the World*, Beijing: Foreign Languages Press, 1964, 16.

30. Ibid., 17.

31. Ibid., 18–19.

32. Ibid., 29.

33. Ibid., 31.

34. Klaus Mehnert, *Peking and the New Left: At Home and Abroad*, Center for Chinese Studies, China Research Monograph, Berkeley: University of California, 1969, 61–68.

35. Armstrong, *Revolutionary Diplomacy*, 90–92.

36. Van Ness, *Revolution*, 224–26; Robert A. Holmes, "The Sino-Burmese Rift: A Failure for China," *Orbis*, vol. 16, no. 1 (September 1972), 211–36.

37. Van Ness, *Revolution*, 208–37.

38. Melvin Gurtov, "The Foreign Ministry and Foreign Affairs During the Cultural Revolution," *China Quarterly*, no. 40 (October–December 1969), 65–102.

39. Stephen Fitzgerald, "Overseas Chinese Affairs and the Cultural Revolution," *China Quarterly*, no. 40 (October–December 1969), 103–26.

40. Gurtov, "The Foreign Ministry," 65–102. A fascinating firsthand account of Red Guard anti-foreignism, including the burning of the British chancellery, is Anthony Grey, *Hostage in Peking*, Garden City, N.Y.: Doubleday, 1971.

41. O. Edmund Clubb, *China and Russia: The Great Game*, New York: Columbia University Press, 1971, 480–88.

42. C.P. Fitzgerald, "A Revolutionary Hiatus," *Bulletin of Atomic Scientists*, vol. 25, no. 2 (February 1969), 54.

Chapter Seven

The Retreat from Revolutionism

"CHAIRMAN MAO'S REVOLUTIONARY DIPLOMATIC LINE"

China's decision in 1970 to tilt toward the United States to check Soviet pressure led to a redefinition of the world revolutionary process. According to the new interpretation, the chief cleavage in world politics was between the two superpowers and all other countries of the world. The two superpowers, sometimes in collusion and sometimes in contention, were trying to dominate other countries. Consequently, all other countries of the world, and especially the small and medium-sized countries and the developing countries of the Third World, were struggling against the hegemonistic domination of one or the other superpower. In this situation, "revolution" meant overturning the old international order founded on dual superpower hegemony, and creating a new, qualitatively different international order based on absolute equality of all nations, and strict respect for the Five Principles of Peaceful Coexistence. The prospects for creating such a new international order were excellent, Beijing argued. The hegemonic power of the United States was declining and that of the Soviet Union was meeting increasing resistance. The old world order was characterized by great disorder and turmoil, as the small and medium-sized countries increasingly resisted superpower efforts at domination. China should do everything possible to encourage and support this global systemic transformation.

These views were elaborated more fully in 1974, in the form of the Three Worlds Theory unveiled by Vice Premier Deng Xiaoping during a speech to a special session of the United Nations General Assembly in April.[1] Deng defined the First World as made up of the United States and the USSR (the two superpowers), who colluded and contended for global hegemony. The Second World was made up of all industrially developed countries other than the superpowers; i.e., Western and Eastern Europe, Canada, and Japan. The Third World was made up of the developing countries. The central dynamic of world politics was the clash between the hegemonistic efforts of the First World and the efforts of the Second and Third worlds to achieve full independence and sovereignty. The Second and Third worlds should unite to create a new international order based on the full equality of all nations, regardless of size, strength, or social system. But because the countries of the Third World were most oppressed by the existing international order, they were the key force working to overthrow that order. The Third World was the "great motive force pushing forward the wheel of history."[2]

The Three Worlds Theory provided an ostensibly revolutionary justification for China's new diplomatic orientation. China's rapprochement with the United States met with considerable criticism within the CCP. Many comrades experienced "ideological confusion" regarding China's seeming abandonment of the world revolutionary struggle. The Three Worlds Theory addressed these doubts by explaining that China had not abandoned the struggle for a new international order. Mao Zedong played a key role in formulating the theory. After his death, in the CCP's authoritative 1981 summation of the positive and negative aspects of Mao's rule, the Three Worlds Theory was specifically identified as one of Mao's positive contributions—one of his few positive post-1949 theoretical contributions.[3]

The Three Worlds Theory differed from the old interpretation of the world revolutionary process by taking countries, rather than classes or national liberation movements, as the main agent of change in the international system. Social revolution within countries was no longer the sine qua non of achievement of a just international order. This was an extremely important departure. Relatedly, intergovernmental diplomacy played a much more important role, and armed struggle a much reduced role. While the old anti-imperialist analysis had not precluded diplomacy and the Three Worlds Theory did not preclude occasional resort to armed struggle, there was a very important difference in emphasis. Still another difference was that the Three Worlds Theory could be directed against either superpower. Even during Beijing's anti-United States period, Chinese condemnation of the Soviet Union had sometimes been more bitter than its condemnation of the United States. But as long as Beijing professed to uphold leftist social revolution in foreign countries, this created problems, since Moscow frequently supported such revolutions while Washington opposed them.

Moscow lost few chances to point out such contradictions between China's professed ideology and its practice. Indeed, this was a mainstay of Soviet exposés of Chinese "opportunism." This problem was eliminated by the Three Worlds Theory.

The new anti-Soviet orientation founded on the Three Worlds Theory brought China into conflict with many leftist revolutionary movements. The first and most important of these was North Vietnam's VWP. From Hanoi's standpoint, Sino-U.S. rapprochement, the cornerstone of the new anti-hegemony united front, worked against the interests of Vietnam's national liberation struggle. The improvement of Sino-U.S. ties greatly eased U.S. fears of possible Chinese entry into the Vietnam war, lessening constraints that had previously limited the scope of U.S. attacks on North Vietnam. This was revealed in May 1972, when in response to North Vietnam's massive conventional invasion of South Vietnam, the United States mined Haiphong harbor, and again in December 1972, when B-52 bombers struck at military targets in Hanoi and Haiphong for the first time. Hanoi believed that Washington would not have dared to take such actions if it had not known that China would not respond. During the 1972 peace negotiations, Beijing also pressured Hanoi to accept a compromise peace with the United States by dropping its demand that the United States remove South Vietnamese leader Nguyen Van Thieu and suspending for several years its armed struggle to liberate South Vietnam. Beijing wanted Hanoi to grant Washington a face-saving exit from Vietnam, thereby avoiding a humiliating U.S. defeat that might undermine American power throughout Asia and open the door to the expansion of Soviet influence.

Did Mao Zedong and Zhou Enlai still desire a VWP takeover of South Vietnam in 1972? We lack conclusive evidence to answer that question. A decade later, Hanoi charged that they did not, and instead favored continued division of Vietnam. According to a subsequent Vietnamese exposé, in November 1971, during discussions with North Vietnamese representatives, Mao drew an analogy between South Vietnam and Taiwan and urged Hanoi to be patient:

> The United States has many old friends that it could not afford to forsake....The Taiwan question is a long-term one. Probably it cannot be solved in a few years. Between a quick solution and a delayed one, I'm inclined to choose the latter....Where the broom cannot reach, the dust is not swept away.[4]

Richard Nixon agrees with Hanoi on this issue. Nixon argues that Mao and Zhou had concluded that a U.S. presence in South Vietnam at a substantially reduced level, but continuing for an indefinite period of time, was preferable to an ignominious U.S. defeat and Soviet-supported VWP takeover of the South.[5] Others have argued, however, that Mao fully expected Hanoi to conquer South Vietnam and that at most he wanted Hanoi to allow an interval of several years between the United States' exit and final VWP takeover of the South.[6] This issue will probably be debated for a long time.

Less debatable was Hanoi's anger with Beijing. To Hanoi, Beijing's new orientation amounted to nothing less than betrayal of the Vietnamese and world revolutions. Hanoi ultimately accepted Beijing's advice regarding the terms of a settlement with the United States and agreed to the South Vietnamese government's continuation in office. Nor did Hanoi publicly criticize China's new orientation. Yet Hanoi's leaders were extremely bitter. The seeds were laid for the rapid deterioration of Sino-Vietnamese relations after Hanoi's final victory over the United States in 1975.[7]

Within the CCP there was shock that China had made friends with the United States while U.S. forces were still ravaging North Vietnam. Vietnam had been extolled, after all, as the vanguard of the revolutionary struggle in Asia for almost twenty years. To help legitimize the new orientation, it was given Chairman Mao's imprimatur, becoming "Chairman Mao's revolutionary diplomatic line."

DECLINE OF REVOLUTIONARY ACTIVISM

China's anti-hegemony orientation did not immediately lead to a decline in support for foreign insurgencies. As China expanded diplomatic ties in the 1970s, it followed what it called a "dual-track" approach, separating government-to-government and party-to-party ties. According to this approach, ties at the two levels should be conducted independently of each other. This meant that China claimed the right to maintain party-level ties with foreign revolutionary movements (conducted through the CCP's International Liaison Department), even while maintaining state-level diplomatic relations with the government of a particular country. On the basis of this dual-track approach, China established diplomatic relations with Malaysia in 1974 and Thailand and the Philippines in 1975. This arrangement was far from satisfactory to the foreign governments concerned. As long as the CCP supported insurgencies in these countries, state-level relations were unlikely to become cordial. This question was debated within the CCP, and Maoist radicals, led by Mao's wife Jiang Qing, were opposed to any reduction in China's support for foreign revolutionary movements for the sake of improved state-level ties.[8]

Several factors pushed China toward reducing its support for foreign revolutions in the late 1970s. First, there was a change in China's leadership following Mao's death in September 1976 and the subsequent purge of radicals. Second, China became increasingly desirous of Western diplomatic and economic support. Beijing's growing apprehension over Moscow's aggressive moves in the 1970s was discussed in Chapter Three. As Beijing's fear of Soviet hegemonism mounted, it became increasingly desirous of a strong, vigilantly anti-Soviet Western alliance. This was reflected in Deng Xiaoping's October 1977 comment that China would not like to see the Communist parties of France, Italy, or Spain come to power or even participate in government, since they would carry out a "policy of appeasement" toward Moscow.[9] As China began its drive for economic modernization in the late 1970s, Beijing also became more desirous of Western trade, loans, and technology. China's involvement with foreign revolutionary movements stood in the way of those goals.

In Southeast Asia, the deterioration of Sino-Vietnamese relations in the late 1970s pushed Beijing toward disengagement from insurgent movements. As Sino-Vietnamese relations soured, both Beijing and Hanoi began courting the non-Communist governments of Southeast Asia. In the process, both severed or reduced links with insurgent movements.[10] In November 1978, as the Sino-Vietnamese confrontation neared the point of war, Deng Xiaoping visited several Southeast Asian countries to rally support for China. Deng's visit came shortly after a similar tour by Vietnamese Premier Pham Van Dong, in which Dong had pledged that Vietnam would not support foreign insurgencies. Deng refused to make a similar promise, but argued that China would not let party-to-party ties interfere with the improvement of state relations. In February 1981, Premier Zhao Ziyang went a step further during a visit to Bangkok, saying that CCP relations with Southeast Asian Communist parties were only "political and moral," and that China would "make efforts" to ensure that relations with these parties "would not affect our friendship and cooperation with ASEAN countries."[11] Zhao returned to Southeast Asia in August 1981 and went further still. China "would do its utmost to see that the problems left over from the past" would not hinder development of China's relations with Southeast Asian countries.[12]

The decline of the Communist Party of Thailand (CPT) provides an excellent example of the workings of these factors. In 1978, when the Sino-Vietnamese conflict became acute, the CPT stood at the height of its power. It had 15,000 guerrillas and exercised influence in 5,000 villages spread over fifty-two of Thailand's seventy-two provinces. Its ranks had been swelled by an influx of new recruits following a military coup d'état in October 1976. U.S. troops (some 23,000) had been withdrawn from Thailand in 1975 and 1976 following the collapse of the U.S.-supported regime in Indochina and a change of government in Bangkok. Thailand had been one of the prime "dominos" in the domino theory that led the United States to intervene in Vietnam, and by 1978 it seemed that the Thai domino might well fall. The Sino-Vietnamese conflict was a major factor preventing this.[13]

The Vietnam-China conflict put the CPT in a quandary. China provided it with training facilities in south China, a clandestine radio station based in south China, political support, and (probably) arms and cash. Vietnam provided it with safe sanctuary in Laos (which was under Vietnamese control after 1975) and allowed men and materials to cross Laos from China to the CPT. Hanoi also probably supplied arms and cash to the CPT. Since both Hanoi and Beijing supported the CPT, it is not surprising that the CPT initially attempted to remain neutral in the Sino-Vietnamese dispute. But this quickly proved impossible.

Vietnam's desire to reassure Thailand in late 1978, as preparations to invade Cambodia intensified, together with the pro-Beijing sympathies of many CPT leaders, led Hanoi to expel the CPT from its bases in Laos in November. This was a severe blow to the CPT and severed the CPT's supply lines from China. After China invaded Vietnam in February 1979, the CPT came down squarely on Beijing's side. But CPT support for China was not adequate to prevent further Chinese downgrading of ties. In July 1979, the clandestine CPT radio in south China ceased broadcasting. The CPT leadership also split over China's policy of quasi-alliance with the United States, with some CPT leaders believing that struggle against the United States was still primary. The CPT declined steadily in strength throughout the 1980s. In 1985, it finally abandoned armed struggle and the last of its fighters laid down their arms and accepted Bangkok's amnesty. The Communist Party of Malaya, another long time comrade of the CCP, abandoned armed struggle in December 1989.

Beijing continued to support a few foreign insurgencies during the 1980s and early 1990s. The Khmer Rouge guerrillas in Cambodia and the Mujahadeen in Afghanistan were the two major ones. By 1990, China gave the Khmer Rouge an estimated $100 million per year. Chinese support for the Mujahadeen ended with the withdrawal of Soviet forces from Afghanistan in March 1989. China's support for the Cambodian and Afghan insurgencies was rooted in national security considerations. Marxist-Leninist objectives played no role, a point indicated by the fact that both governments targeted for overthrow were socialist, albeit of a pro-Soviet variety. In terms of support for anti-Western insurgent movements, China's relation with the Palestine Liberation Organization was an exception. Even when there were relatively successful and explicitly Maoist insurgencies, such as those in the New People's Army in the Philippines or the Shining Path guerrillas in Peru, China avoided involvement.

In the 1970s, the United Nations General Assembly (UNGA) emerged as a major forum in which Beijing attempted to catalyze its "revolutionary" anti-superpower united front in accordance with the Three Worlds theory. It was fortuitous for Beijing that its entry into the United Nations coincided with the increasing assertiveness of the developing countries within that body. Indeed, to some extent, the manner of Beijing's admission can itself be seen as a manifestation of that growing assertiveness. Beijing saw this growing Third World assertiveness as a manifestation of the inevitable tide of history.

In the United Nations Beijing stressed three separate but mutually complementary dimensions of the Third World's anti-hegemony struggle: the revision of the UN Charter to increase the role of Third World and smaller countries in the workings of that body; the drafting of new law of the sea so as to minimize superpower influence and control; and the establishment of a New International Economic Order (NIEO).[14]

The push for a NIEO represented the most comprehensive aspect of China's new effort to transform the existing global order. As such it was the closest heir to the PRC's revolutionary aspirations of the 1950s and 1960s. There is also a fit between the NIEO and elementary Marxism, which teaches that economic power is inextricably intertwined with political power. If economic power forms the basis of political power, a redistribution of global wealth implies redistribution of global political power.

NIEO is a cluster of proposals advanced by the developing countries in the early 1970s, aimed at redistributing world wealth in favor of the developing countries. Its key elements involve the terms of trade for primary commodities versus manufactured goods, the expansion of global markets for the exports of developing countries, the alleviation of the debt burden of developing countries, and the provision of greater amounts of development assistance. China did not initiate the notion of a NIEO, nor was it involved in formulating the basic elements of that concept. Rather, the vanguard role was played by the Group of 77, a group of developing countries within the United Nations Conference on Trade and Development (UNCTAD). (Initially numbering seventy-seven nations, this group later expanded to over 100, but retained its original designation.) Beijing gave enthusiastic support to the Group of 77's NIEO proposals.[15]

China played a prominent role in the Sixth Special Session of the General Assembly, which kicked off the push for a NIEO in April 1974. During that session members of the PRC delegation made four speeches (including the one by Deng Xiaoping unveiling the Three Worlds theory) and played an active role in the committees discussing ways of implementing the NIEO, while Chinese media devoted considerable attention to the session's activities. At the conclusion of the Special Session, Beijing characterized it as a "major victory of the Third World's united struggle against hegemonism." The PRC's performance at the Sixth Special Session was, however, something of an exception. More typically the PRC preferred to keep a low profile. With very few exceptions, China did not initiate proposals. Its UN representatives made few speeches and avoided criticizing countries other than the two superpowers. It avoided the details of various proposals, and especially procedural and legal issues, preferring instead to expostulate on the general principles of anti-hegemony. As a rule, it did not participate in major UN committees dealing with the implementation of the NIEO, nor in the major international conferences held for the same purpose. China also declined an invitation, made shortly after its 1971 entry into the UN, to join the Group of 77. Nor did Beijing join the political equivalent of the Group of 77—the non-aligned movement (NAM). According to Samuel Kim, Beijing preferred to play the role of "a partisan spectator who cheers, moralizes, and votes, when necessary, rather than an active, not to say leading, player in the game of global politics."[16]

A major consideration underlying this approach appears to have been a concern for Third World unity. If China had immersed itself in intra–Third World politics, it would invariably have had to take sides, alienating some countries in the process. The harder China pushed for what it took to be the "correct" approach, the greater such alienation would have been. Many countries were already suspicious that China might harbor hegemonist ambitions—a suspicion the Soviet Union did everything possible to encourage in the 1970s and early 1980s. China playing a prominent role would have increased these apprehensions. Rather than alienating Third World countries and exacerbating suspicions about China's motives, Beijing opted to stand on the sidelines and support whatever proposals the rest of the Third World produced. Beijing may also have wished to avoid obligating itself to support proposals that conflicted with its own interests. It is also possible that China's leaders, in their heart of hearts, placed China in the same category as the United States and the Soviet Union, as a potential great power, and felt that to join such groups as the Group of 77 and NAM would detract from China's great-power status.

THE END OF THE CHINESE REVOLUTION

Revolutions eventually end: not in the sense that the core values and institutions created by the revolution disappear, but in the sense that society returns to a more routine, institutionalized, and relaxed functioning. Gradually both ordinary people and elites tire of the continual exertions demanded by the quest for a utopian society. People cease to believe in the attainability of the utopian vision that inspired the revolution and become less willing to bear sacrifices. As these processes occur, demands mount for a return to routine, order, and normality.[17] Such demands were quite strong in China by the mid-1970s but were held in check by the immense power of Mao Zedong. Mao's death in September 1976 opened the way for forces favoring a reroutinization of society. Those forces won a decisive political victory at the Third Plenum of the Eleventh Central Committee in December 1978.

China's foreign policy has undergone a process of deradicalization corresponding to the ebbing of revolutionary fervor within China. This process of socialization to the established international system has been gradual. One important step was the PRC's entry into the United Nations and the U.S. abandonment of the policy of containing China. With these moves, China was no longer excluded from the family of nations, and to the extent that China's revolutionism was a response to U.S. containment, it became unnecessary. Another milestone was Beijing's shift from supporting armed national liberation struggles to state-to-state diplomacy as the way to achieve change in the international system. In a sense this departure was equivalent to a revolutionary party laying down its arms and opting to seek its program of social change via the legal processes of the society within which it functions.

The move of greatest significance in terms of China's socialization to the international order was its voluntary integration into the world capitalist economic order in the early 1980s, a decision symbolized by the PRC's entry into the International Monetary Fund and the World Bank in 1980. By deciding to expand rapidly a broad range of international economic cooperation and open China to a variety of international influences, its leaders signaled that they believed that the processes of the world capitalist economy could be manipulated to their nation's benefit. Many of them still believe that existing global processes and institutions are unjust and should ultimately be changed. Nonetheless, China decided that it should work within the framework of the existing international system. Increasingly it stressed independence and self-reliance *within* the existing system, rather than struggle to transform the system itself.[18]

China's integration into the world economic system has also meant that Beijing increasingly finds its own interests in conflict with those of other developing countries. China now finds itself competing with other Third World countries for a share of the markets of the developed countries and for low-interest loans from international development agencies. It also finds that its interests on particular issues differ from those of other developing countries. Unlike most developing countries, for example, China is a major importer of primary commodities and exporter of light manufactured goods. Its economic interests would not necessarily be served, therefore, by programs altering the terms of trade between these two categories of commodities, as is advocated by many other developing nations.

China's revolutionary heritage and Marxist-Leninist ideology continues to have an impact on its foreign relations. Although there has been a substantial professionalization of the analysis of international relations during the 1980s, with the establishment of research centers and journals dealing with international relations, Marxist-Leninist terminology and ideas are still influential—especially among the conservative leaders who took charge after June 1989.

This lingering ideological influence was manifest in China's attitude, if not its overt response, to the 1989 collapse of Communist rule in various Eastern European countries. The East German and Romanian regimes had been among the most supportive of Beijing's military repression of the pro-democracy demonstrations in June 1989. As the process of Eastern European liberalization began to accelerate in late 1989, Romanian leader Nicolai Ceausescu proposed forming a front upholding Communist principles and trying to stem the tide of further reform. Beijing declined. As the Communist regimes of Eastern Europe collapsed, Beijing took a low-profile public approach. Official spokesmen refused to pronounce judgment, pro or con, on developments there. Those developments were, they said, purely internal affairs of the countries concerned and arose out of the specific conditions of those countries. Initially, Chinese media minimized the significance of the changes in Eastern Europe, stressing that the Communist Parties were still in control and had not given up socialism. By mid-1990, however, such understatement was no longer tenable, yet Beijing continued to minimize the significance of the European upheaval for Marxism-Leninism. According to one authoritative appraisal: "There is nothing strange in terms of the twists and turns arising in the course of socialism. These twists and turns do not mean its failure but are merely whirlpools in the long river of history. We believe that socialism will succeed eventually."[19] Internal CCP documents issued after the Eastern European revolution and designed to "unify the whole party's thinking and prevent possible confusion" stressed the differences between conditions in China and Eastern Europe.[20] *Renmin Ribao* and other authoritative sources carried lengthy defenses of the successes of socialism in China. There is little doubt, however, that these efforts were, at best, only partially successful. The demise of Communist rule and socialism in Eastern Europe has hastened the erosion of ideological faith in China. It has also deepened the siege mentality dominant among China's leaders after June 1989.

As the confrontation between liberal reformers and neo-stalinist conservatives deepened in the USSR in 1990 and 1991, the CCP did what it could prudently do to assist the CPSU's hard-liners. CCP support for the CPSU hard-liners took three forms: delegation diplomacy with the CPSU; a visit by CCP Secretary General Jiang

Zemin to Moscow in June 1991; and a $720 million commodity credit in early 1991.

Regarding delegation diplomacy, between the time of the May 1989 Deng-Gorbachev summit and the failed Soviet coup of August 1991, there was a steady stream of top-level delegations traveling between Beijing and Moscow. Fifteen high-level Soviet leaders visited China during this period. Virtually all of the Soviet visitors were prominent hard-liners. Two were subsequently members of the eight-man State Emergency Committee set up by the August 1991 coup. It was the Soviet hard-liners who pushed these exchanges in an effort to use the CCP to counter their liberal opponents within the CPSU. But the CCP responded enthusiastically to the CPSU hard-liners' bid. CCP leaders understood the game being played, and played it well. By their comments and actions during visits to the USSR, Chinese leaders made clear their support for continued Communist rule in that country. The high point of CPSU-CCP delegation diplomacy was CCP Secretary General Jiang Zemin's visit to Moscow in May 1991. The context of Jiang's visit was a shift in the CCP's evaluation of Gorbachev. Following Gorbachev's "betrayal" of Eastern Europe in 1989, Beijing cancelled a visit by Jiang to Moscow originally scheduled for mid-1990. Following Boris Yeltsin's abandonment of the CPSU at that Party's 28th Congress in July 1990, however, the CCP concluded that the real alternative to Gorbachev was likely to be Yeltsin and that the prime task was to block the anticommunist Yeltsin radicals. Thus, Gorbachev should be united with. This led to the rescheduling of Jiang's Moscow visit. The meeting of Jiang with his counterpart, Gorbachev, was a symbolic endorsement of the latter. In his talks with Soviet leaders, Jiang again conveyed the CCP's hope that the Soviet Union would adhere to the socialist road and the leadership of the communist party.

The $720 million commodity credit extended in February 1991 came just as Western nations were imposing economic sanctions on the USSR in response to a crackdown against secessionists in the Baltic states. In this context, Beijing's move was a strong demonstration of support for Moscow in its renewed confrontation with the West.

When CPSU hard-liners moved against Yeltsin and Gorbachev in August with their attempted coup d'etat, the CCP was warmly enthusiastic. No official statement was made endorsing the coup—although one had reportedly been prepared and was stopped from release only by the rapid unraveling of the coup. When the final collapse of the USSR came in December 1991, Beijing responded pragmatically, quickly recognizing the successor states lest Taiwan move to exploit PRC hesitation. By that point there was nothing further Beijing could do to bolster the CPSU's "progressive" forces.

The collapse of the CPSU regime and the USSR appeared to CCP rulers as calamities of epic proportions. In the first instance, the "proletariat's loss of state power" in a major state and the demise of the world's first socialist state was a major setback for the revolutionary struggle of the world's working classes. This development would further undermine Marxist-Leninist ideology through which CCP rule was legitimized. Moreover, the victory of imperialist subversion in the USSR could well lead to an intensification of imperialist efforts to overthrow Communism. At the global level, the radical improvement in Russian-American relations that came about in 1992, together with Russia's growing orientation toward the Western community of nations, has meant a major augmentation of U.S. global influence. Not only is Beijing much less able to play Moscow and Washington against one another, but it faces the increased possibility of Russian-American collaboration in ways antithetical to Chinese policy interests. Soviet-American "collusion" against China is more likely on issues ranging from territorial disputes in the South China Sea, to Korean unification, to Taiwan.

It is ironic that the CCP, which set out to transform the international system to its advantage via revolution, has found that system indeed transformed by revolution, but to its disadvantage and in ways never predicted by its ideology.

NOTES

1. "Chairman of Delegation of the People's Republic of China Teng Hsiao-ping's Speech at Special Session of the United Nations General Assembly," *Peking Review,* supplement to no. 15 (April 12, 1974), i–v. Regarding the origin of the anti-hegemony theme, see Joachim Glaublitz, "Anti-Hegemony Formulations in Chinese Foreign Policy," *Asian Survey,* vol. 16, no. 3 (March 1976), 205–15.

2. A revised version of the theory was promulgated in 1977. It was more firmly rooted in quotations from Marx and Engels, more clearly differentiated between the United States and the Soviet Union, with the latter being clearly identified as the most aggressive superpower, and paid greater attention to the Second World while still maintaining that the Third World was the key. See "Chairman Mao's Theory of the Differentiation of the Three Worlds Is a Major Contribution to Marxism-Leninism," *Peking Review,* vol. 20, no. 45 (November 4, 1977), 10–41. Regarding the relation between China's Three World theories and the world systems of dependency theory, see Edwin A. Winckler, "China's World-System: Social Theory and Political Practice in the 1970s," *The World-System of Capitalism: Past and Present,* Walter L. Goldfrank, ed., Beverly Hills, Calif.: London: Sage, 1979, 53–67.

3. "On Questions of Party History," *Beijing Review,* vol. 24, no. 27 (July 6, 1981), 10–39.

4. *The Truth About Vietnam: China Relations Over the Last Thirty Years,* Hanoi: Ministry of Foreign Affairs, Socialist Republic of Vietnam, 1979, 41–42.

5. Richard M. Nixon, *No More Vietnams,* New York: Arbor House, 1988, 146, 150, 176.

6. Peter Van Ness, "Richard Nixon, the Vietnam War, and the American Accommodation with China: A Review Article," *Contemporary Southeast Asia,* vol. 8, no. 3 (December 1986), 231–45.

7. See John W. Garver, "Sino-Vietnamese Conflict and Sino-American Rapprochement," *Political Science Quarterly*, vol. 96, no. 3 (Fall 1981), 445–64.

8. "Chiang Ch'ing's Address to Diplomatic Cadres," *Issues and Studies*, vol. ix, no. 7 (July 1975), 91–96.

9. Cited in *China Quarterly*, Chronicle, no. 73 (March 1978), 220.

10. Regarding the decline of Chinese support for Southeast Asian revolutionary movements, see William R. Heaton, "China and Southeast Asian Communist Movements: The Decline of Dual Track Diplomacy," *Asian Survey*, vol. 22, no. 8 (August 1982), 774–99; Donald E. Weatherbee, "Communist Revolutionary Violence in the ASEAN States: An Assessment of Current Strengths and Strategies," *Asian Affairs*, vol. 10, no. 3 (Fall 1983), 1–17; *China and Asia: An Analysis*, Library of Congress Report, 1979, 31–33; Yuan-li Wu, *The Strategic Land Ridge: Peking's Relations with Thailand, Malaysia, Singapore, and Indonesia*, Stanford, Calif.: Hoover Institution Publications, 1975, 13–55.

11. *FBIS,DRC*, February 2, 1981, E12.

12. *FBIS,DRC*, August 12, 1981, E2–4.

13. Regarding China and the development of the Thai revolutionary movement; see Daniel D. Lovelace, *China and "People's War" in Thailand, 1964–1969*, Berkeley: University of California Press, 1971.

14. Regarding China's UN diplomacy, see Samuel S. Kim, *China, the United Nations, and World Order*, Princeton, N.J.: Princeton University Press, 1979, 429–65; Samuel S. Kim, "China and the Third World: In Search of a Neorealist World Policy." in *China and the World: Chinese Foreign Policy in the Post-Mao Era*, Samuel Kim, ed., Boulder, Colo.: Westview, 1984, 178–211; Hungdah Chiu, "China and the Law of the Sea Conference," in *China in the Global Community*, James C. Hsiung and Samuel S. Kim, eds., New York: Praeger, 1980, 191–211. Other studies of China's role in international organizations include Gerald Chan, *China and International Organizations: Participation in Non-Governmental Organizations Since 1971*, New York: Oxford University Press, 1989; Harold K. Jacobson and Michel Oksenberg, *China's Participation in the IMF, the World Bank, and the GATT: Towards a Global Economic Order*, Ann Arbor: University of Michigan Press, 1990.

15. Kim, *China, the United Nations*, 242–307.

16. Ibid., 262.

17. Regarding the "end of revolution" phenomena, see Isaac Deutscher, *The Prophet Unarmed, Trotsky: 1921–1929*, New York: Vintage, 1959; Herbert Marcuse, *Eros and Civilization: A Philosophical Inquiry into Freud*, New York: Vintage, 1955.

18. Kim, "China and the Third World," 186–87.

19. *FBIS,DRC*, August 29, 1990, 1–3.

20. *FBIS,DRC*, December 13, 1989, 7–8.

Part Four

China's International Economic Relations

Chapter Eight

China's Search
for a Development Model

CHINA'S THREE PATHS

The CCP came to power determined to create a socialist China. Within a few years, the transition to socialism was well underway. Yet the dominant patterns of global economic activity were organized on the basis of capitalist principles and dominated by capitalist powers. To China's Communist rulers, the global capitalist system was closely tied to China's experience of national humiliation. The aggression China had suffered, its disunity, and its poverty were all traceable to imperialism and inextricably linked to the global capitalist economy, CCP leaders believed. The CCP thus faced a basic problem: What was to be the relation between socialist China and the global capitalist economy?

There were, and remain, three basic choices open to socialist China. First, it could withdraw from the international capitalist economy and strive together with other socialist countries to build an alternative, socialist international economic order. Second, it could withdraw from the global capitalist economy and seek to go it alone, pursuing a path of autarky. Third, it could actively participate in the established international economic order, manipulating it to China's maximal benefit while filtering out anti-socialist influences.

The PRC has pursued each of these choices in a roughly sequential fashion. During the 1950s, China saw itself as part of a socialist community and deliberately reoriented its international economic activity toward that community while limiting its relations with capitalist states. By the 1960s, Mao Zedong had decided that the revisionist policies of the Soviet Union under Nikita Khrushchev signaled the de facto impossibility of creating a global socialist countereconomy. China then embarked on a path of autarky. By the late 1970s, China's post-Mao leaders had concluded that autarky was unsatisfactory and moved to enmesh China with the global capitalist economy.[1]

Within each of these three paths, certain common economic problems had to be addressed. Several of these problems touched on China's economic relations with other countries. We shall analyze these common functional aspects shortly, but first we will review in greater detail the PRC's progression through these three stages.

THE SOVIET PERIOD OF DEVELOPMENT, 1949 TO 1960

The founding of the PRC led to an abrupt and drastic reorientation of China's international economic relations. Preliminary moves included the expulsion of foreign expatriates from the customs service; the establishment of centralized control over foreign trade; and the creation of a central bank, the People's Bank of China, with responsibility for all international financial transactions. Redirection of trade soon followed. Over the previous decades, China's trade had been oriented toward Japan and North America. Trade between China and the Soviet Union had been relatively small. Trade with the Eastern European countries was smaller yet. Within a few years of the PRC's establishment, however, China's trade was oriented toward the Soviet Union and Eastern Europe.

Western businesses in China were also eradicated. Prior to World War II, all of China's iron ore production, 70 percent of its coal production, half of all public utilities, and 35 percent of all manufacturing were foreign owned, while 90 percent of foreign trade was handled by foreign firms. About half of this massive foreign investment was Japanese-owned and was confiscated by the Nationalist government during and after the war. Nonetheless, in 1948 there was still US$1.5 billion in foreign investment in China. Most of this was British and American, and centered in Shanghai.[2]

According to the Marxist-Leninist ideology of the CCP, this foreign presence was part and parcel of imperialist domination of China. As the CCP consolidated power, foreign firms were squeezed out by such means as imposition of onerous taxes, bureaucratic restrictions, and instigation of employee strikes demanding higher wages and benefits. According to Beverley Hooper's detailed study of this period, such indirect means were adopted because CCP leaders realized that direct nationalization would, under international law, incur a heavy debt for compensation. Indirect means, on the other hand, could force foreign businesses to throw up their hands in exasperation, abandoning their enterprises to liquidate mounting losses and extricate hostage expatriate employees from China. By the time the Korean War broke out in June 1950, most foreign businesses had been eliminated through such indirect means.

Hooper's work indicates that the CCP's decision to eliminate direct foreign business presence in China was not a function of hostile policies of the Western powers toward the new PRC. Had the PRC's leaders desired to continue economic cooperation with the West, they could have done so through Britain. London early on broke with the U.S. policy of economic embargo of the PRC, and in October 1949 indicated a willingness to recognize the People's Republic. It did so in January 1950. Moreover, British firms deliberately tried to work with the new Communist authorities. Yet British firms, like their American counterparts, were quickly squeezed out of existence.[3] Again, this suggests that Communist leaders were not merely responding to Western hostility, but acted on the basis of an underlying ideological interpretation of the role of foreign capitalist presence in China. Hooper suggests that China's new Communist leaders hoped to continue trading with the Western countries even while eradicating the Western presence *within* China.

Not all analysts would accept the proposition that China's new Communist rulers more or less voluntarily brought about the dramatic reorientation of China's international economic relations. As the discussion in Chapter Two of the possibility of a "lost chance" for Sino-American cordiality indicated, some analysts maintain that American hostility, not CCP ideology, was the critical factor. According to this point of view, the economic embargo imposed on the PRC by Washington left Beijing no alternative but to seek new partners in the socialist camp.[4] Had it not been for U.S. hostility, they maintain, Beijing might have been willing to accept some level of Western economic presence in China. At least it would not have forced out the foreigners so abruptly.

However this may be, U.S. and Western economic sanctions were clearly one factor shaping China's international economic relations during the 1950s. Early in 1949, well before the conclusion of the PRC-USSR treaty or the outbreak of the Korean War, the U.S. government began to block U.S. exports of strategic and critical materials to CCP-controlled areas of China.[5] Once the PRC was established in October, it was treated as a Soviet satellite, subject to the licensing system recently established by the Commerce Department. Under this system, very few licenses were granted for exports to China. In January 1950, the embargo was broadened to include all petroleum products, all strategic metals, railway cars and locomotives, motor vehicles, and scientific and electrical apparatus and equipment. By March 1950, still prior to the beginning of the Korean War, the export of goods of any strategic significance to China had been stopped.[6] With the onset of the Korean War, Chinese assets in the United States were frozen and virtually all trade was prohibited. Restrictions on trade with China became stricter than those on trade with the Soviet Union. This adverse "China differential" lasted until 1957. The U.S. embargo remained in place and effectively prohibited Sino-U.S. trade until 1972.[7]

As the PRC's economic ties with the Western capitalist countries atrophied, its ties with the socialist countries burgeoned. In 1953 China began its first Five Year Plan—a program of rapid industrialization along the lines of the Soviet Union during the 1930s. The primary objective was to develop a comprehensive heavy industrial base in the shortest possible time. To this end, a huge proportion of China's national product (perhaps reaching 25 percent to 30 percent by 1958 and 1959) was channeled into heavy industry. Such rapid industrialization required extensive Soviet and Eastern European support. China simply lacked the indigenous capability to produce various types of machinery needed for the industries it sought to create. In 1949, for example, China did not manufacture electrical generators, trucks, automobiles, machine tools, aircraft, seagoing ships, oil field equipment, or chemical fertilizer, to name only a few essentials. If China was to incorporate such products into its emerging industry, it would have to import them. China also had to import machinery to make these products; that is, it had to build a machine-building industry. It was also necessary for Chinese personnel to master the processes upon which these machines were based. All of this required Soviet support.[8]

A major reason why PRC leaders decided to ally with the Soviet Union in 1950 was to help persuade Moscow to provide large-scale assistance to China's industrialization. This was also one reason why China stressed the unity of the socialist camp and Moscow's duty as the head of that camp. As Mao Zedong explained to his newly appointed ambassador to the USSR in September 1954, it was extremely important to strengthen Sino-Soviet friendship because "China needs development; we need Soviet support in every field."[9]

The Soviet Union gave the PRC substantial economic assistance during the 1950s. Between 1950 and 1962, the Soviet Union supplied China with $3 billion in machinery and equipment. Moscow assisted in the construction of 211 major factories, spanning the entire spectrum of heavy industry: machine tool lathes, diesel engines, boring machines, automobiles, locomotives, chemicals, instruments, ferrous and non-ferrous metals, metal-working machinery, petroleum drilling and refining equipment, plastics, and so on. Three large iron and steel complexes—at Anshan in Liaoning, at Wuhan in Hubei, and at Baotou in Inner Mongolia—were equipped, or reequipped, entirely with Soviet machinery. Between 1952 and 1960, nine-tenths of China's machinery and equipment imports came from the Soviet Union and Eastern Europe. The Soviet Union supplied some 51 percent of all capital investment during China's first Five Year Plan. Most Soviet equipment supplied to China came with complete blueprints and technical specifications; altogether some 10,000 sets. This greatly facilitated Chinese mastery and reproduction of the technology. The more industrialized Eastern European socialist countries—Czechoslovakia, East Germany, Hungary, and Romania—also rendered "fraternal assistance" to China's development. Ten thousand Soviet and 1,500 Eastern European technical experts worked in China between 1950 and 1960. Some of these personnel assisted China's development of an indigenous research and development capacity. Industrial and scientific research institutes of various sorts were set up with Soviet advice, instruments, equipment, and training. The work conducted in these institutes was often quite advanced.[10]

The Soviet–Eastern European effort to assist China's industrialization in the 1950s was massive and successful. In the opinion of Chu-yuan Cheng, it constituted one of the largest international transfers of technology in history, rivaling U.S. assistance to Western Europe under the Marshall Plan. As a result of that effort, China developed a substantial indigenous metallurgical and machine-building capacity. Moreover, Soviet technology was typically of a high level, and replication and dissemination of this technology gave a substantial boost to China's overall technological level.

Soviet assistance was not free. Most Soviet assistance was financed by loans—totaling $2.25 billion between 1950 and 1957, for all purposes. Although these loans were low-interest, they had to be repaid. The Soviet Union also demanded payment for many things that China's leaders thought should have been given gratis: the buyout of Soviet shares in the Manchurian and Xinjiang joint-stock companies forced on China in 1950; equipment installed by Japan in Manchuria from 1931 to 1945, carted away by the Soviet army in 1945, and returned to China as part of Soviet assistance in the 1950s; and military equipment used by Chinese forces during the Korean War.

Repayment of Soviet loans began in 1954. Between 1955 and 1960, payments amounted to $200 million per year, a very substantial sum. Moscow also attempted to pressure China through the latter's indebtedness. As Sino-Soviet relations deteriorated in 1962, Moscow began pressing for repayment of outstanding loans, then totaling some $1.75 billion. Beijing decided to accelerate repayment, even though China was in the midst of a severe economic crisis. Imports were cut drastically, creating surpluses used to liquidate China's Soviet debts. In 1963, China paid $270 million to Moscow; in 1964, $360 million. By 1965, China had liquidated its financial obligations to the Soviet Union.[11]

Disagreement over levels of assistance was a major source of tension within the Sino-Soviet alliance. China's needs were immense, while the means of the Soviet Union were limited. The USSR was still recovering from the devastation of World War II and was far from being a highly industrialized country. Moreover, the Soviet Union had to provide assistance to the Eastern European countries. Thus, the levels of Soviet assistance were far below what China's leaders desired. During his 1949 and 1950 negotiations with Mao Zedong, Stalin was very miserly. As noted in Chapter Two, post-Stalin Soviet leaders realized that such stinginess risked alienating China, and they agreed to substantial increases in Soviet assistance. In October 1954, Moscow agreed to assist fifteen additional Chinese projects. In April 1956, forty-four more were added. But still China's leaders felt that Soviet assistance was inadequate. They noted that Soviet aid to China was below that to Eastern Europe—totaling only 58 percent of Soviet aid to East Germany, 86 percent of aid supplied to Poland, and only 16 percent larger than Soviet assistance to Outer Mongolia during the period from 1945 to 1962. Perhaps most galling of all, Soviet aid to China was 3 percent less than total Soviet assistance to non-socialist India from 1954 to 1962. That the Soviet Union should give more aid to a bourgeois country such as India, a rival of China's to boot, grated on Chinese sensibilities.[12]

On the Soviet side, consumers were increasingly demanding the goods they had been denied for a generation. Moreover, the demands on the Soviet Union from all the socialist countries were already heavy. China alone took 9 percent of Soviet heavy machinery and 14 percent of precision instrument output during the 1950s. Once the Great Leap Forward began, Soviet leaders began to doubt whether Soviet aid was being used wisely. Did it make sense for the Soviet Union to supply precious capital when China followed such irrational and wasteful policies, Soviet leaders asked themselves. Finally, Beijing's rejection of Soviet proposals for closer military cooperation in 1958 made Chinese calls for greater bloc solidarity ring hollow. Chinese "solidarity" was a one-way street, Soviet leaders thought. China wanted "solidarity" in economic areas that benefited it, but not in military areas that would strengthen the Soviet Union. Moscow's abrupt suspension of its aid programs and withdrawal of its advisers in 1960 was an effort to pressure and punish China. Although the suspension of Soviet aid merely exacerbated an already severe economic crisis brought on by natural calamities and failures of radical policies of the Great Leap, it added to China's heavy burdens.

Moscow's suspension of economic assistance was a traumatic and pivotal event. It taught China's leaders that big powers will be tempted to use their economic relations with China to force it to accept domination. It also graphically demonstrated the risks entailed by economic dependency. In so doing, it helped move China toward policies of economic autarky. "Never again," vowed China's leaders, would their country become so dependent on another country. The bitter experience of Moscow's economic blackmail created the psychological ground for Maoist policies of Self-Reliance.

The Sino-Soviet economic relation of the 1950s also left a positive legacy. Soviet assistance helped China create a substantial industrial base that gave it a much greater capability to sustain industrialization on its own. Without the base built with Soviet assistance in the 1950s, China could not have undertaken its path of autonomous industrialization in the 1960s. Moreover, Soviet plants, technology, and machinery provided the core of many Chinese industries well into the 1980s.

China's sweeping adoption of the Soviet model of economic organization during the 1950s had a profound and lasting impact on China's international economic relations. As Alexander Eckstein pointed out, the institutions of Soviet-style socialism are biased against foreign trade. The skills demanded of managers for effective operation in a system of comprehensive material planning are very different from those demanded by a system responsive to market indicators. Success or failure is determined by fulfillment of assigned production quotas, not by the sale of goods on markets. International commerce, however, requires understanding of market techniques, and this puts Chinese managers, trained in Soviet techniques, at a handicap. Moreover, since international economic market trends are very difficult to predict, they make planning difficult. Since accomplishment of planned objectives is the raison d'être of executives in a Soviet-style system, these executives will tend to minimize reliance on international markets, since to do otherwise risks non-fulfillment of quotas.

Firms operating within a Soviet-style system also have little incentive to seek profits, let alone profits from foreign trade. Such firms are typically not allowed to participate directly in foreign trade, the latter being conducted by centralized trading monopolies. This sharp separation between production and marketing made it difficult for firms to respond to the needs of foreign consumers. It was the responsibility of the state trading company to learn the demands of foreign consumers for goods of a particular type, quality, and style, and then to consult with the central economic planners who would then assign the appropriate quotas during the next planning cycle. This is a cumbersome system that leaves each of the three participants little direct incentive to cater to foreign tastes. If in spite of these restrictions a firm managed to earn a profit through some international transaction, it would be compelled to surrender it to the state.

As long as China oriented its trade toward other socialist countries with Soviet-style systems, the disadvantages of these structural peculiarities were minimized. But once it decided in 1978 to adopt a strategy of export promotion, Soviet-style economic institutions became a major obstacle. Under such circumstances, reform became imperative.

THE PERIOD OF MAOIST SELF-RELIANCE, 1961 TO 1976

The rapid assimilation of Soviet techniques and institutions in the 1950s was probably the most radical, all-out Westernization in Chinese history. Many things about the period grated on Chinese sensibilities. Soviet aid came with strings attached. Soviet advisers often seemed condescending. The propaganda theme of the Soviet Union as "big brother" exacerbated Chinese resentment. Some of the institutions imported from the Soviet Union—for example, those having to do with industrial management and agricultural organization—soon seemed inappropriate. Conversely, Chinese felt considerable nationalist pride when the break with the Soviet Union gave them the opportunity to develop a distinctively Chinese model of socialism.

Again analysts disagree over the extent to which China's turn to autarky in the 1960s was self-imposed. U.S. containment remained in effect, and some analysts have argued that as relations with Moscow deteriorated China had nowhere to turn but inward. The problem with this interpretation is that key U.S. allies—Japan, West Germany, France, and Britain—broke with the U.S. embargo shortly after the Korean War. By 1964, Western European and Japanese exports to China were rising rapidly, only to be cut back sharply by the Cultural Revolution. Moscow, too, soon realized its mistake and began trying to repair economic relations with China. Beijing rejected these options, preferring instead to develop along self-sufficient lines.

The Maoist concept of *zili gengsheng*, or "Self-Reliance" (literally, "regeneration via one's own effort"), emerged in 1961 and had a great influence on China's international relations thereafter. It became a touchstone of China's international economic relations. Its precise meaning shifted over time, but there were strands of continuity. Some of these emerged during the 1950s: rapid all-around industrialization, import substitution, and concentration of foreign exchange earnings on key projects designed to achieve major advances. After 1960, minimal foreign indebtedness, diversification of trading partners, and exclusion of negative foreign influences that might accompany foreign technology became important tenets of Self-Reliance.

During the period between 1960 and 1978, Self-Reliance was given a distinctively Maoist cast. It never meant, at least in official pronouncements, the complete absence of foreign trade, but during those years, and especially from 1966 to 1976, it came close to being a doctrine of genuine autarky.

Many of the attributes of Maoist Self-Reliance of the period from 1966 to 1978 were related to Marxist debates about the interaction between means of production and relations of production. Marx taught that the development of the forces of production determined the course of historical development, but his model of revolution was also based on the possibility of particular relations of production becoming a "fetter" on the development of the forces of production. His theory thus allowed for the possibility that changes in relations of production might, sometimes, be the determinant factor in social development. Moreover, Marx predicted that the overthrow of capitalism and the institution of socialism would lead to very rapid development of the forces of production. In other words, more progressive, socialist types of relations of production would stimulate development of the means of production, or so Marx taught.

Maoist theoreticians found in Marx's assertions the key to self-reliant development. Politics had to be put in command. Progress toward "higher," more "progressive" forms of socialism-Communism would produce more motivated workers who would seek ways to improve production. Breaking down the division between mental and manual labor, by involving engineers in physical labor and blue-collar workers in management and engineering, would give all workers greater insight into productive processes. This insight would combine with greater enthusiasm, and with the understanding provided by correct Maoist theory, to produce a "spiritual atomic bomb." Rapid industrial and technological advances would follow. Enthusiastic, enlightened workers would work harder and think up new ways to improve machines and productive processes. Chinese scientists and engineers, fired with revolutionary zeal and guided by correct dialectical theory, would make great strides. The powers attributed to workers inspired by Mao Zedong Thought were truly miraculous. At times it was claimed that such correct revolutionary ideology allowed workers to build powerful rockets or ocean-going ships, grow especially sweet watermelons, or perform new and complex surgical operations.

China's Maoists believed that to a substantial degree, indigenous sources of technological innovation could substitute for import of foreign technology. They were not entirely opposed to acquisition of foreign technology, but felt that with a genuine revolutionalization of social relations, foreign technology could play a much smaller role. At times, Maoists argued that the technological advance unleashed by these forces would outstrip that derived from import of foreign technology. This was a tenuous position, however, and Maoists usually fell back on the more defensible argument that a somewhat slower rate of growth in the short run was an acceptable trade-off for achievement of "higher" social relations that would propel China ahead of the capitalist countries over the long run.[13]

In practice, "politics in command" was a doctrine of isolationism. In order to mold new human material, corrupting foreign influences had to be kept out. Reliance on foreign technology would also sap Chinese self-confidence. "Fawning over foreign things," "tailing along behind foreigners at a snail's pace," and "a belief that Chinese are not capable of producing good things"—attitudes that the Maoists attributed to those who favored broader acquisition of foreign technology—all ran counter to the enthusiasm, confidence, and inspiration that could conquer new heights. Such notions probably tapped deep xenophobic strains of China's tradition.

Maoist Self-Reliance resurrected another element of China's tradition in the form of the Canton trade fair. The Canton system that regulated China's sea-borne foreign trade prior to the Opium War was discussed in Chapter One. As China closed itself off in the 1960s, Canton was once again designated as the sole site for Sino-foreign trade. A semiannual trade fair was established in Canton in 1957 to handle China's trade with the non-socialist world. After 1960, its role increased. Foreign merchants came to the Canton fair by invitation only to negotiate with representatives of various Chinese trading monopolies. The fair was primarily export-oriented, but Chinese representatives also undertook negotiations regarding purchases. The movements of foreign participants were typically restricted to Canton. The Canton trade fair system had the advantage of greatly limiting foreign "contamination" while keeping open an avenue for acquisition of essential goods. During the 1960s, participation in the Canton trade fair numbered a few thousand annually. Attendance grew during the 1970s as China's foreign trade revived. By the late 1970s, annual foreign attendance was about 30,000.[14]

The question of the role of foreign technology was closely tied to the Maoist doctrine of "walking on two legs." "Walking on two legs" meant that China should develop both large-scale industry equipped with modern, largely foreign-derived machinery, *and* small- and medium-scale industry equipped with more simple, indigenously manufactured machinery. According to Robert Dernberger, one of the key attractions of this notion was that the equipment utilized by the second "leg" was indigenous—built by rural machine shops according to blueprints supplied by national or provincial design bureaus that had reverse-engineered and simplified imported machinery. In other words, the machinery employed in the second, small-scale "leg" was nationalized technology.[15]

The second "leg" built upon nationalized technology had other ideological advantages as well. Because it involved smaller-scale, more labor-intensive modes of production, and because the machinery used was relatively simple, technocratic and hierarchical control of production was less important. This meant a greater role for party activists, a less specialized division of labor, and greater ability to rely on non-material, moral incentives—all indications of "higher" forms of social relations from a Maoist point of view. The first, modern "leg," on the other hand, required bureaucratic control, technocratic supervision, and reliance on material incentives to achieve regularity, assumption of responsibility, and acquisition of skills. In the first "leg," industrial organization was comparable to that of capitalist factories, while within the second "leg," strides could be made toward equality and toward eliminating the gap between mental and manual labor.

The central point for our purposes is that notions of efficiency and productivity, and the organizational forms derived from those concepts, appeared to the Maoists as foreign and anti-revolutionary. The Maoist emphasis on "walking on two legs" can therefore be viewed as an attempt to adopt Western "things" (technology) in ways that accorded with the Chinese "essence" (revolutionary values). It also involved rejection of the idea that there is an organizational imperative embedded in modern technology. China's Maoists insisted that sophisticated foreign technology had to be used in ways that conformed with Communist ideals and rejected the contention that China could simply copy Western organizational forms along with foreign technology. Some pragmatic leaders were more willing to copy the efficient organizational forms of Western industry. They were less concerned with preserving the distinctive character of Chinese society and more concerned with rapid economic development.

The conflict between the putative organizational imperative of modern technology and Maoist ideological goals was central to the politics of China from 1958 to 1978. Western factories and firms might operate more efficiently, China's radicals argued, but the workers laboring in them were exploited. Workers motivated by desires for material goods might perhaps produce more, but they had weak revolutionary consciousnesses. China could not advance toward Communism if it copied bourgeois forms of economic organization. Rather, China had to adhere to its own revolutionary forms of organization. In short, the radicals feared that reliance on imported technology and organizational forms would lead to the atrophy of the quest to create a new Communist man and society.

With the beginning of the Great Leap Forward in 1957, China's Maoists began trying to devise genuinely revolutionary forms of economic organization. The severe depression resulting from the Great Leap persuaded many leaders that there was, after all, a particular rational way to organize a modern industrial society, and made them increasingly skeptical of Maoist nostrums. As Maoist influence and especially the influence of Mao Zedong himself waned in the early 1960s, increased emphasis was placed on economic rationality and efficiency. Then, in reaction, the Cultural Revolution renewed the drive for more Communist-like forms of organization. These policies more or less remained in place until 1977 and 1978.

NOTES

1. Regarding the three paths open to the PRC, see Bruce Cumings, "The Political Economy of China's Turn Outward," in *China and the World: Chinese Foreign Policy in the Post-Mao Era*, Samuel S. Kim, ed., Boulder, Colo.: Westview, 1984, 235–39. Also, Edward Friedman, "On Maoist Conceptualizations of the Capitalist World System," *China Quarterly*, no. 80 (December 1979), 806–37. Regarding the impact of these three broad alignments on the interests of various bureaucracies within China, see Kenneth Lieberthal, "Domestic Politics and Foreign Policy," *China's Foreign Relations in the 1980s*, Harry Harding, ed., New Haven, Conn.: Yale University Press, 1984, 43–70.

2. Regarding the scope of the foreign economic presence in China prior to 1949, see Albert Feuerwerker, "The Foreign Presence in China," *The Cambridge History of China*, vol. 12 (Republican China 1912–1949), Part I, John K. Fairbank, ed., New York: Cambridge University Press, 1983, 128–207; G.C. Allen and Audrey G. Donnithorne, *Western Enterprises in Far Eastern Economic Development: China and Japan*, London: Allen and Unwin, 1954. For analysis of the impact of foreign investment on China's development, see Chi-ming Hou, *Foreign Investment and Economic Development in China, 1840–1937*, Cambridge: Harvard University Press, 1965; Rhoads Murphey, *The Treaty Ports and China's Modernization: What Went Wrong?* Ann Arbor: Michigan Papers in Chinese Studies, no. 7, 1970; Robert F. Dernberger, "The Role of the Foreigner in China's Economic Development, 1940–1949," *China's Modern Economy in Historical Perspective*, Stanford, Calif.: Stanford University Press, 1975, 19–47. For an account by a PRC citizen working for a foreign firm in China after 1949, see Nien Cheng, *Life and Death in Shanghai*, New York: Grove Press, 1987. Regarding the eradication of the foreign presence, see Beverley Hooper, *China Stands Up: Ending the Western Presence, 1948–1950*, London: Allen and Unwin, 1986, 9; Thomas N. Thompson, *China's Nationalization of Foreign Firms: The Politics of Hostage Capitalism, 1949–1957*, Baltimore: School of Law, University of Maryland, 1979, Occasional Papers/Reprint Series in Contemporary Asian Studies, no. 6.

3. Regarding Anglo-Chinese relations through the early 1960s, see Richard Harris, "Britain and China: Coexistence at Low Pressure," *Policies Toward China: View From Six Continents*, A.M. Halpern, ed., New York: McGraw-Hill, 1965, 13–41; Robert Boardman, *Britain and the People's Republic of China, 1949–74*, London: Macmillan, 1976.

4. For example, Percy Timberlake, "China as a Trading Nation," *China's Road to Development*, Neville Maxwell, ed., New York: Pergamon, 1979, 259–77.

5. "Statement by Honorable William L. Thorp, Assistant Secretary of State for Economic Affairs," "Statement of Honorable Harold F. Linder, Deputy Assistant Secretary of State Economic Affairs," "Statement by Loring K. March, Deputy Director, Office of International Trade, Department of Commerce," in *U.S. Foreign Policy and the East-West Confrontation*, Committee on Foreign Relations, Selected Executive Hearings of the Committee, 1951–1956, vol. XIV, U.S. House of Representatives, Historical Series, 1980, 9–19, 31–32.

6. Some analysts have mistakenly argued that the imposition of U.S. sanctions began with the outbreak of the Korean War.

7. Regarding the U.S. embargo, see "Statement of Alexander Eckstein on the Economic Situation in China," *U.S. Policy with Respect to Mainland China*, Hearings Before the Committee on Foreign Relations of the United States Senate, 89th Congress, 2nd Session, March 1966, 337–42; Oliver M. Lee, "U.S. Trade Policy Toward China: From Economic Warfare to Summit Diplomacy," in *China's Trade with the West: A Political and Economic Analysis*, Arthur A. Stahnke, ed., New York: Praeger, 1977, 33–87; A. Doak Barnett, *China's Economy in Global Perspective*, Washington, D.C.: Brookings Institution, 1981, 262–63.

8. Alexander Eckstein, *China's Economic Revolution*, Cambridge: Cambridge University Press, 1977, 233–76; Alexander Eckstein, *Communist China's Economic Growth and Foreign Trade*, New York: McGraw-Hill, 1966, 87–134.

9. Liu Xiao, *Chu Shi Sulian Banian* (Eight Years as Ambassador to the Soviet Union), Beijing: Zhonggong dangshi ziliao chubanshe, 1986, 3.

10. Regarding the Soviet aid effort to China, see Chu-yuan Cheng, *Economic Relations Between Peking and Moscow, 1949–1962*, New York: Praeger, 1964; Sidney Klein, *The Road Divides: Economic Aspects of the Sino-Soviet Dispute*, Hong Kong: Green Pagoda Press, 1966; Roy F. Grow, "Soviet Economic Penetration of China, 1945–1960; 'Imperialism' as a Level of Analysis Problem," in *Testing Theories of Economic Imperialism*, Steven J. Rosen and James K. Kurth, eds., Lexington, Mass.: D. C. Heath, 1974, 261–81; O.B. Borisov and B.T. Koloskov, *Sino-Soviet Relations*, Moscow: Progress, 1975, 4–93; O. Edmund Clubb, *China and Russia: The Great Game*, New York: Columbia University Press, 1971, 391–95, 417–25; M. Gardner Clark, *The Development of China's Steel Industry and Soviet Technical Aid*, Ithaca, N.Y.: Cornell University School of Industrial and Labor Relations, 1973. A fascinating account by a Soviet adviser in China in the 1950s is Mikhail A. Klochko, *Soviet Scientist in Red China*, New York: Praeger, 1964.

11. Chu-yuan Cheng, *Economic Relations*, 69; Barnett, *China's Economy*, 1981, 213–14.

12. Klein, *The Road Divides*, 66, 68; Allen S. Whiting, "Chinese Politics and Foreign Policy," *China's Trade with the West*, 11.

13. Regarding the Maoist arguments on technology, see "Opposing Chairman Mao's Instructions Concerning the Export of Crude Oil, and the Import of Complete Sets of Equipment and Ships," in *Issues and Studies*, vol. xv, no. 5 (May 1979), 92–98. Also E. L. Wheelwright and Bruce McFarland, *The Chinese Road to Socialism*, New York: Monthly Review Press, 1970, 162–80; C.H.G. Oldham, "Science and Technology Policies," *China's Developmental Experience*, Michel Oksenberg, ed., New York: Praeger, 1973, 80–94; Genevieve C. Dean, "Science, Technology and Development: China as a 'Case Study,'" *China Quarterly*, no. 51 (July–September 1972), 520–34; Richard P. Suttmeier, "Science Policy Shifts, Organizational Change and China's Development," *China Quarterly*, no. 62 (June 1975), 207–41.

14. Daniel Tretiak, "The Canton Fair: An Academic Perspective," *China Quarterly*, no. 56 (October–December 1973), 740–48; Frederick M. Kaplan and Julian M. Sobin, *Encyclopedia of China Today*, New York: Eurasia Press, 1980, 259–60.

15. Robert F. Dernberger, "Economic Development and Modernization in Communist China: The Attempt to Limit Dependency on the Transfer of Modern Industrial Technology from Abroad and to Control Its Corruption of the Maoist Social Revolution," *Issues in East-West Commercial Relations*, A Compendium of Papers Submitted to the Joint Economic Committee, Congress of the United States, 95th Congress, 2nd Session, January 12, 1979, Washington, D.C.: U.S. Government Printing Office, 1979, 91–124.

Chapter Nine

The Opening
to the Outside World

The late 1970s saw a dramatic reorientation of China's international economic relations. The PRC began participating in the international capitalist economy to an unparalleled degree. It began drawing on foreign inputs of all sorts to foster the Four Modernizations. In Chinese this new orientation was called the *dui wai kaifang zhengze*: the "policy of opening to the outside world."

The policy of opening can be traced to a group of influential leaders centered around Zhou Enlai and Deng Xiaoping, who began arguing in 1974 that China's isolation was a major cause of its weakness. These leaders are usually referred to as "pragmatists" by foreign analysts. Throughout China's history, the pragmatists argued, China's self-isolation from the world had led to continuing weakness. Self-confident interaction with the world, on the other hand, had contributed to Chinese strength and vigor. The isolationist later Ming and Qing dynasties, for example, were periods of stagnation and humiliation, while the cosmopolitan Tang dynasty saw China at the height of its power. By isolating itself from the world, China was unable to draw on developments in science and technology that were the common heritage of humanity.[1]

The pragmatists were particularly struck by remarkably rapid growth of Japan, South Korea, Taiwan, Hong Kong, and Singapore during the 1960s and 1970s. Chinese analysts studied these newly

193

industrialized countries (NICs), and noted that they succeeded through shrewd integration into international markets. China's pragmatists were also struck by the contrast between the slow rate of Chinese technological innovation and the technological revolution taking place in Western countries. Increased international travel by China's leaders during the 1970s had made them aware of the growing technological gap between China and the West. Aside from key defense-related sectors, such as rockets and nuclear weapons that had received generous funding and priority allocations of resources, there had been minimal technological advance in China during the years of Maoist isolation. The technological level of China's industry had virtually stagnated while the Western economies were in the midst of the microelectronic revolution. China's technology was increasingly outdated. Unless China rejoined the world, unless it began assimilating the scientific and technological discoveries of the West, the pragmatists argued, China would fall further and further behind. In short, continued isolation condemned China to weakness and poverty.

The heart of the pragmatist program was priority commitment to economic development—the Four Modernizations, referring to the modernization of industry, agriculture, science and technology, and national defense. The Four Modernizations was conceived as an intense, sustained drive to transform China into a wealthy, modern, powerful socialist country by the end of the twentieth century. Zhou Enlai outlined the goals of the Four Modernizations in a work report to the National People's Congress in January 1975—to "turn a poverty-stricken and backward country into a socialist one with the beginnings of prosperity in only twenty years or more." Implementation of this program would, Zhou proclaimed, ensure that China would "be advancing in the front ranks of the world" by the twenty-first century.[2] After Zhou's speech, Deng Xiaoping supervised the drafting of documents implementing the Four Modernizations. The program was shelved under Maoist pressure in 1976, but was revived in 1978.

The Four Modernizations was closely tied to the opening to the outside world and to transition from extensive to intensive modes of development. With extensive development, production is expanded by duplicating existing patterns of production, and by channeling increased inputs (labor, machinery, energy, raw materials, etc.) into the production process. If the objective is to increase output of a particular good, more factories producing that good are built, more machinery installed, more workers employed, and so on. This entails accelerated accumulation of capital; that is, it requires that a greater portion of socially produced wealth be saved and used to increase society's stock of capital goods. This, in turn, creates strong pressure to keep levels of consumption and spending on infrastructure (housing, transportation, education, etc.) low so that high rates of capital accumulation can be achieved.

Intensive development deals with these problems differently. With intensive development, the key to expanding production is not increasing inputs, but more efficient utilization of resources by cutting costs and increasing productivity. Rather than building more factories, the output of existing factories would be increased. Rather than employing more workers, the amount that each worker produced would be increased. There are two main ways of achieving such increase in factor productivity: (1) increased rationalization of the labor process and (2) improvements in technology. Either by improving labor efficiency through motivation, discipline, or better organization, or by adopting more advanced machines, production may be expanded without proportional increases in inputs. Since the levels of capital accumulation necessary to make this possible are lower than with extensive modes of production, there is less pressure to hold down social consumption. Indeed, increased consumption may be useful in increasing labor productivity by providing greater material incentives.

From 1949 through 1979, China followed essentially an extensive mode of development. During the 1950s, large Soviet loans helped sustain high rates of capital accumulation and investment. After the break with Moscow, continued high levels of accumulation were made possible by the spartan living standards imposed by Maoism. Levels of social consumption were held to a bare minimum and all possible resources were channeled into expanding production.

The introduction of modern Soviet machinery during the 1950s did lead to a substantial and rapid increase in capital productivity, rising, as Table 9–1 indicates, from an index of 84.9 in 1952 to 100 in 1957 (the base year). The Great Leap Forward saw the beginning of a decline in capital productivity that continued throughout the 1970s. Overall labor productivity continued to increase, reaching an index of 165.6 in 1978, due to greater mechanization. But the costs of acquiring that machinery were so great, and its productivity so low, that total factor productivity (labor and capital combined) declined steadily throughout the 1960s and 1970s.[3]

The Soviet-style system adopted by China in the 1950s was very effective at mobilizing resources for extensive development, but provided few incentives for the efficient utilization of those resources. Resources were used with little thought to costs or productivity. Indeed, there were strong incentives to waste resources, since the more inputs necessary, the larger the volume of inputs assigned by the central planners. By the late 1970s, China had one of the lowest rates of return on capital investment of all Third World countries. Moreover, as the scale of production expanded, the amount of capital investment needed to achieve a given increment of increased output grew. It became steadily harder to maintain a given rate of industrial growth. But it should also be recognized that while extensive development approach imposed heavy

Table 9–1   Factor Productivity of State-Owned Industry

Measure	1952	1957	1978
1. Net output	37.6	100	673.3
2. Labor input	68.2	100	406.6
3. Capital input	44.3	100	948.7
4. Labor productivity (1 ÷ 2)	55.1	100	165.6
5. Capital productivity (1 ÷ 3)	84.9	100	71.0
6. Total factor productivity	69.8	100	89.6

[1957 = 100]

Source: World Bank, *China: Long-Term Development Issues and Options,* Baltimore: Johns Hopkins University Press, 1985, 111.

burdens on the Chinese people from the 1950 to the 1970s, it did allow China to develop a large and comprehensive industrial base in the face of American and later Soviet efforts to prevent this.

Politically, the denial of popular desires for adequate housing, transportation, varied diets, and consumer durables became less and less acceptable during the 1970s. During the first two decades of the PRC, there was a greater public willingness to forgo consumption for the sake of the revolution; a willingness rooted, perhaps, in a belief in the imminent attainability of the utopian goals proclaimed by the Maoists. But as skepticism and disillusionment increased, so did disgruntlement with the hardships of daily life. Moreover, as the ideological conviction underlying moral incentives eroded, so did the effectiveness of those incentives as instruments for motivating the workforce. Morale declined. By the mid-1970s, there was widespread bitterness and passive resistance to CCP rule. These forces were held in check by authoritarian means, but at the cost of sullenness that further reduced the quality of work. Moreover, there were risks of spontaneous outbursts of resistance that could be repressed only at substantial cost.

China's pragmatic leaders saw large-scale assimilation of Western technology and managerial techniques as a way of dealing with problems of declining factor productivity. By drawing broadly on advanced foreign technology, China could shift from its nearly exclusive reliance on extensive development to more intensive modes. Through technological improvements factor productivity could be increased, allowing industrial growth to be sustained with reduced levels of capital accumulation, allowing a diversion of resources from investment to consumption. Increased abundance of consumer goods would boost morale, enhancing productivity further while rallying popular support for the regime.

The pragmatic program met strong opposition from radical leaders led by Mao's wife Jiang Qing. These radicals were not opposed to all trade, but wanted to keep it as limited as possible. To align with the U.S.

imperialists internationally to help check the Soviet social imperialists was one thing, they argued; allowing the imperialists to infiltrate the sinews of Chinese society was quite another. Allowing capitalist businessmen and bourgeois specialists into the country would be letting the wolf inside the house, the radicals charged. By tying China's economy to foreign capitalist markets, pragmatic policies would allow the imperialists to pressure China. Most fundamentally, the radicals defined ideological conviction as the essence of Chineseness and saw (correctly, as it turned out), that a proliferation of foreign contacts and an emphasis on productivity would lead to erosion of revolutionary ideology.

The arrest of the Jiang Qing and her cohorts shortly after Mao's death in September 1976 led to a consensus among the top leadership that a major expansion of trade was necessary. There was still debate as to what form that trade should take, over extensive versus intensive development, and over the extent to which the values and institutions bequeathed from the Maoist years should be scrapped in favor of organizational forms more conducive to rapid economic growth. Gradually the Maoists lost out. The victory of the pragmatists at the Third Plenum of the 11th Central Committee in December 1978 marked a decisive defeat for Maoist radicalism. But even then an influential group of leaders, represented by Hua Guofeng, worked to minimize the corrosive impact of foreign trade on China's revolutionary values and social structure. This group was purged in February 1980, and Deng Xiaoping appointed Hu Yaobang and Zhao Ziyang as a pragmatic leadership duumvirate. This led to a fuller opening to the outside world.

COMPONENTS OF THE OPENING TO THE OUTSIDE WORLD

In the 1980s, China once again opened itself to Western influences, though in a more restricted fashion than it had in the 1950s. During the 1950s, Western, Soviet models were applied across a very broad range of Chinese society. During the 1980s, however, Beijing made strenuous efforts to restrict Western, capitalist influences to the economic-technological sphere. Repeated campaigns were conducted to limit Western, bourgeois influence in ideological and cultural spheres. In this regard, the opening of the 1980s was nearer to the center of China's political spectrum.

A drive to improve relations with the United States from 1978 to 1981 was an important component of the opening to the outside world. Economic motives reinforced the strategic concerns discussed in Chapter Three. Beijing wanted broad and generous U.S. support for the Four Modernizations and moved to improve relations with the United States to achieve this. A united front with the United States against hegemonism was expected to provide the political basis for such support, just as the alliance with the Soviet Union in the 1950s had provided a political basis for comprehensive Soviet support.

China desired several things from the United States. One was access to the vast and relatively open U.S. market. The successful development of the East Asian newly industrialized countries was a powerful demonstration of the importance of access to the U.S. market that influenced China's pragmatic leaders. The high quality of U.S. technology was also a consideration. China's leaders hoped to leapfrog stages of development passed through other countries, and this required acquisition of the most advanced technology; in many areas, this meant U.S. technology. This meant persuading Washington to ease restrictions on Chinese access to Western high technology. Still another consideration had to do with securing U.S. private investment and official U.S. support in multilateral lending institutions such as the World Bank, International Monetary Fund, and United Nations agencies. Beijing also hoped to persuade Washington to allow Chinese personnel unlimited access to U.S. higher education. In sum, for a myriad of reasons Beijing wanted sympathetic U.S. support for the Four Modernizations.

The normalization of Sino-U.S. relations on January 1, 1979, led to the rapid creation of an institutional and legal framework for expanded economic cooperation.[4] A critical gain came in July 1979, when Washington agreed to extend most favored nation (MFN) status for the PRC. Prior to that time, MFN status for China had been linked to comparable status for the USSR. The Carter Administration's decision to uncouple Soviet and Chinese treatment was a conscious U.S. effort to align with China against the USSR. Further gains came in September 1980 and August 1983, when agreements were signed setting generous quotas for Chinese textile exports to the United States. A rapid expansion of Chinese textile exports to the United States followed. In 1980 PRC exports of cotton textiles to the United States were only 5 percent of those of Hong Kong and 71 percent of Taiwan's. By 1987, they were 7 percent *above* Hong Kong's and 6.8 times Taiwan's. Between 1980 and 1987, PRC cotton textile exports to the United States grew at an annual rate of 14.2 percent, compared with 0.64 percent for Hong Kong and 1.68 percent for Taiwan. In effect, Washington allowed PRC textile exports to expand at the expense of such traditional textile exporters as Hong Kong, Taiwan, and South Korea.[5]

Another gain came as the United States gradually liberalized Chinese access under COCOM controls.[6] The rise and decline of various U.S. and Western restrictions on trade with the PRC is illustrated by Table 9–2.

A geographic opening of China was an another important aspect of the opening to the outside world. In 1979, special economic zones (SEZs) were set up at Shenzhen across the border from Hong Kong, Zhuhai opposite Macao, Xiamen across from Taiwan, and at Shantou on the coast of northern Guangdong. Within these enclaves, special tax and tariff incentives were given to foreign investors. The local Chinese government provided infrastructure and a trained labor force, and allowed foreign firms to operate within the enclaves according to more capitalist-like methods of management. These SEZs were modeled after the export processing zones that had been so successful in Taiwan and South Korea.[7]

The SEZs were designed to import high technology, increase exports, earn foreign exchange, create jobs, assimilate foreign managerial and entrepreneurial skills, and attract foreign investment. Beijing believed that China's low labor costs would be a major attraction to foreign capitalists and hoped that foreign firms would flock to the

Table 9–2 U.S./COCOM Restrictions on Trade with China

October 1949	COCOM regulations regarding USSR applied to China.
January 1950	U.S. embargo extended to wide range of strategic goods.
December 1950	Complete embargo. PRC placed in COCOM category Z (total embargo). All commercial dealings prohibited. Chinese assets frozen.
August 1951	U.S. aid prohibited to any country following less stringent embargo policies than the United States.
March 1952	COCOM sets up more restrictive "special list" for PRC. By end of Korean War, restricted China list twice size of that for USSR.
1957–59	Western European countries and Japan increasingly ignore U.S. embargo restrictions.
July 1969	U.S. citizens allowed to bring $100 in Chinese goods into the United States.
December 1969	Foreign subsidiaries of U.S. firms allowed to sell non-strategic goods.
April 1970	Selective licensing of goods for export to PRC.
July 1970	The United States approves Italian sale of trucks with U.S. engines.
April–June 1971	1950 embargo ended. The United States eases currency controls, allows U.S. vessels to enter PRC ports, and announces long list of exportable goods.
February 1972	PRC placed in COCOM category Y (same category as USSR).
July 1972	The United States approves sale of Boeing 707 aircraft.
June 1978	The United States authorizes sale of sophisticated scientific equipment.
January 1980	PRC given most favored nation status. Sale of dual-use technology authorized.
April 1980	PRC placed in special one-country COCOM category P.
June 1981	The United States announces sale of weapons on a case-by-case basis. Technological level of exports to China to be twice that approved for export to USSR.
May 1983	PRC placed in COCOM category V, "friendly, non-allied."
June–July 1989	Sales of military equipment suspended, and lending by international organizations put on hold.
July 1990	Japan resumes foreign aid after approval by Group of Seven.
September 1991	COCOM cuts by half number of goods requiring export licenses.

SEZs to process, assemble, or manufacture goods for re-export to Western markets. The SEZs also provided a relatively isolated laboratory in which could be conducted experiments that were too market-oriented for the rest of China. The authorities could then select useful things for application elsewhere in China, while preventing the undesirable influences from spreading beyond the boundaries of the SEZs. The SEZs in effect acted as filters through which foreign things and influences might be strained. Finally, the SEZs were a product of regional politics. Guangdong especially pushed for SEZs as a way of expanding its access to foreign markets and its independence from Beijing.

The geographic opening soon expanded beyond the four SEZs. In April 1984, fourteen coastal cities and Hainan Island were opened to foreign business operations. Like the SEZs, these cities were authorized to use such incentives as lower taxes, streamlined procedures, exemptions from customs duties, and lower land use fees to attract foreign investment. Pressures from interior provinces led within several months to action conferring special foreign currency privileges on twenty-four inland cities, thereby facilitating their participation in foreign trade and investment. With this, virtually every province and autonomous region had a share in the opening.[8]

The sixth Five Year Plan, adopted in December 1982, had indicated that China's entire coastal area would be allowed to draw on its "advanced capabilities" and orient itself toward foreign trade. Over the next several years a coastal-led development strategy gradually emerged. According to this strategy, the coastal belt with its population of 200 million was to be intimately tied to the emerging Pacific Rim economy, generate exports and draw in foreign capital and technology, and lead China's national development into the twenty-first century. Not surprisingly, this concept met with considerable opposition from the non-coastal areas. With the retrenchment that followed the upheaval of 1989, the coastal development strategy was downgraded and emphasis was placed on particular industries, rather than on territorial units. The effect was much the same, however, since investment was still concentrated in industries in Shanghai and the lower Yangtze valley. The Yangtze and Pearl river deltas and Fujian Province are, moreover, still designated as special export-oriented regions.[9]

Utilization of foreign investment was a central component of the open door. Such investment was anathema during the first thirty years of PRC history, but in 1979 a law on foreign investment was promulgated. Over the next several years restrictions on the type, size, and operations of foreign investment were progressively relaxed. The permissible forms of foreign investment eventually included compensatory trade, processing of materials, assembly, joint ventures, and complete foreign ownership.

Overseas Chinese were among the most enthusiastic respondents to

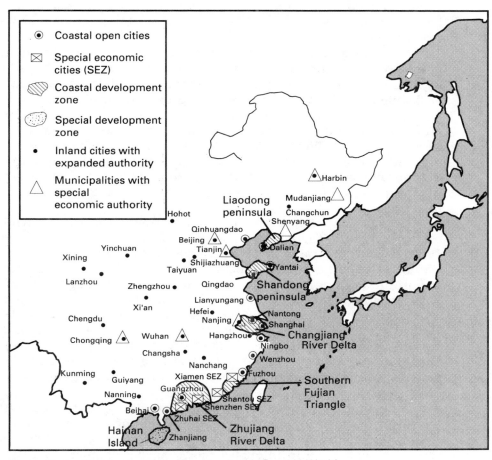

Figure 9–1   Geography of the Opening to the Outside World

Beijing's calls for foreign investment. Often they did so as much for patriotic as for economic reasons. In the case of Hong Kong businessmen, who topped the list of foreign investors, calculations of political expediency having to do with post-1997 developments sometimes played a role. There was also much enthusiasm, almost a sort of euphoria, about the China market among non-Chinese Western businessmen during 1978 and 1979. As in earlier periods of history, visions of a market of hundreds of millions of consumers, each purchasing one small item, became popular.[10] By 1980, cooler heads began to prevail as Western business began to appreciate the real difficulties of doing business in China. Beijing's efforts to cut imports and hold down domestic investment also contributed to the cooling of foreign interest. Foreign businesses increasingly realized that while

China's needs were immense, its ability to pay was limited, and that foreign purchases would still be constrained by central priorities and regulations.

In 1983 and 1984, Beijing took additional steps to encourage potential foreign investors. One aspect of this was strengthening the legal system. The 1979 foreign investment law was fleshed out with a set of detailed regulations. Laws regarding patents, trademarks, taxation, foreign ownership of land, advertising, and the enforcement and arbitration of contracts were promulgated. Investment protection treaties were signed with Western countries.[11] Such moves had some impact, but renewed retrenchment by central authorities in 1986 and the 1989 Beijing massacre again dampened foreign interests. By early 1992, however, foreign interest in China had fully revived and was stronger than ever.

Beijing maintains that its efforts to attract foreign investment have been successful—though less so than originally hoped. By the end of 1988, 16,325 contracts involving foreign capital had been signed and US$47.34 billion actually dispersed to China. Seventy percent of this was in the form of loans, 24 percent in the form of direct investments. This foreign capital was equivalent to about 10 percent of all domestic investment in state-owned fixed assets during the period from 1979 to 1988. It came from forty countries, with Hong Kong and Macao, Japan, and the United States leading the way, and five international organizations. About a quarter of it was invested in the SEZs. Seventy percent was contributed by overseas Chinese, including Hong Kong Chinese.[12]

Still another dimension of China's opening had to do with the reform of domestic structures on the basis of decentralization and greater use of markets. While a desire to increase productivity and to shift from extensive to intensive modes of development were the key motives underlying these reforms, several more foreign-related goals also played a role. These were: (1) expanding exports, (2) facilitating the absorption of foreign technology, and (3) encouraging foreign businesses to undertake operations in China.[13]

Regarding export promotion, as we saw earlier, the system of industrial organization adopted from the Soviet Union created a number of obstacles to exporting. A substantial devolution of decision-making power, fiscal responsibility, and reward to the enterprise level in the early 1980s eased some of these obstacles. Many enterprises were given powers to contract directly with foreign firms and to retain a portion of the profits and foreign currency generated by these operations. Central controls over foreign currency were relaxed and firms were given greater powers to mobilize and use foreign currency. These changes gave enterprises greater incentives to seek out foreign business and to adapt to the style and quality demands of foreign consumers. Municipalities and provinces were also given increased autonomy in accepting foreign investment and conducting foreign trade. Central approval was made unnecessary for foreign investment deals below a certain size, and sub-national units were allowed to retain a portion of any foreign exchange earned.

Market-oriented domestic reforms were also linked to the absorption of foreign technology. Technology transfers were now initiated and decided upon at the enterprise level, making it more likely that any technology acquired would be appropriate and fully utilized. Direct interactions between Chinese enterprises acquiring technology and foreign firms selling it also facilitated technical training by the foreign partner. Assumption of financial responsibility for payment along with partial retention of profits and foreign currency earnings by the Chinese enterprise also created incentives to get the most out of foreign technology.

Market-oriented domestic reforms also were intended to encourage foreign business to undertake operations by providing a more economically rational and less bureaucratized environment in which foreign businesses could operate. Together with the rebuilding of the judicial and legal system, these reforms were intended to help create a more predictable environment for foreign businesses.

SUCCESSES AND FAILURES OF THE OPENING TO THE OUTSIDE WORLD

The policies of opening to the outside world produced mixed results. On the positive side, China's average annual rate of growth increased from 6.64 percent between 1953 and 1978 to 9.29 percent between 1979 and 1988. There were also substantial increases in the factor productivity of industry. There were, however, major limitations on the success of opening. Exports did not expand as rapidly as anticipated. Overvalued currency discouraged exports and encouraged imports. An irrational price structure also meant that enterprises often found it more profitable to sell within China than on foreign markets. The portion of foreign currency earnings that Chinese enterprises were allowed to retain was too small to create powerful incentives to export. Moreover, enterprises were required to deposit any retained foreign currency earnings with the Bank of China and could use them only after formal application and approval.

Levels of foreign investment also remained lower than China's economic planners had hoped for. Problems continued to nag Sino-foreign economic cooperation. Many foreign businesses felt that there was still a strong underlying hostility toward foreign operations in China. Foreign capitalists were still viewed as fair game to be milked to the greatest extent possible. Various sorts of miscellaneous and arbitrary fees and taxes were imposed on foreign firms. Such firms were often forced to pay exorbitant prices for goods and services supplied by government monopolies. As a consequence, while Chinese wages were nominally low, the cost of doing business in China was often very high. By the late 1980s, for example, Beijing was one of the world's most expensive cities in which an international company might maintain an office.

Foreign businesses also found repatriation of profits extremely difficult. Foreign businesses were typically required to balance foreign currency accounts. Foreign currency earnings could be remitted only if counterbalanced by an inflow of exchange or new investment, or by export of foreign currency earning goods. When China's trade went into deficit, controls over foreign exchange tightened, and the repatriation of earnings and the acquisition of foreign currency to finance needed imports became even more difficult. Foreign firms were allowed limited access to China's internal market. They also found it very difficult to fire Chinese employees, even if those employees were lazy or incompetent. Consequently, featherbedding was common. Chinese firms also had great difficulty in meeting the standards of quality and prompt delivery required by foreign firms.

Foreign firms were often confronted with unilateral Chinese decisions on critical matters. A foreign firm might, for example, be informed that it would now be required to use Chinese components, even though those indigenous components were of inferior quality and would greatly reduce the competitiveness of the resulting products on international markets. Dealing with the Chinese bureaucracy proved very difficult. At best, it was time consuming. At worst, it was corrupt and arbitrary. And hanging over all was uncertainty over China's future. What would happen after Deng died? Would China again turn inward? In sum, the costs and risks associated with doing business in China were very high. Foreign investors did not flock to China.

Nor did the SEZs prove to be the success that their architects had hoped. Relatively little foreign investment in the SEZs was in high technology. Most was in real estate, processing, and labor-intensive light manufacturing. Overseas Chinese were the major investors, a fact that suggested that, to some degree, the SEZs were redirecting foreign investment rather than attracting capital that would not otherwise have come to China. Government infrastructural spending in the SEZs was also much higher than anticipated. Yet investors still complained of shortages of skilled labor, inadequate physical facilities, and isolation from major cities where conditions were better. Instead of stimulating exports, SEZs tended to become avenues of import procurement for Chinese firms, with imports outweighing exports 5 to 1. Such problems led to a sharp debate among Chinese leaders over the SEZs between 1984 and 1985. Eventually a compromise was reached, whereby the

SEZs were continued but central support was cut back and measures were taken to encourage exports and discourage imports.

The failure of many Chinese sent overseas for education to return to China—a "brain drain"—has been another nagging problem, especially in exchanges with the United States where it was relatively easy for determined Chinese students to find ways of remaining in the country. Throughout the 1980s, Beijing sought means of dealing with the brain drain. Tighter restrictions were placed on who could go abroad. Older students and scholars were selected, on the assumption that they were more likely to return. It became more difficult for spouses and children to accompany their partner, on the grounds that family remaining in-country was a good guarantee of return. Patriotic counseling was required prior to departure, and once overseas, personnel were required to maintain contact with the nearest Chinese consulate. Publicly financed students were required to sign statements specifying the length of their intended stay and pledging to return. All of these measures had only limited success.

One of the major reasons for non-return of Chinese personnel is that they frequently are not be able to use their newly acquired skills at home. The units to which they are assigned may lack the necessary equipment. They may find no colleagues familiar with the advanced methods they have recently studied abroad. There is always a possibility that they may simply be assigned to a job that is unrelated to their new skills. Governmental units responsible for cultivation of high-level technical personnel have taken a number of moves to address these problems. Counseling centers have been established to help returnees find appropriate jobs. Specially equipped research centers have also been established to ease transition back into Chinese society.

As with other aspects of the open policy, the brain drain became a subject of sharp debate within China. Some people have advocated further restrictions on those sent abroad, and/or a redirection of educational exchanges from the United States to other countries— Europe, Japan, or the Soviet Union. Others have taken a longer-term view, arguing that even if large numbers of highly trained Chinese remain in the United States, they will constitute a reservoir of top-quality talent on which China can draw in future decades. They are likely to maintain an affinity with China and return at some point to serve the motherland. When they do, so the argument runs, they will constitute the highest-quality talent. In the meantime, these people will serve lesser but still useful purposes—sending remittances back to China, organizing and hosting exchanges, sending useful technical information back home, and assisting covert collection operations.

The absorption of foreign technology by Chinese industry also encountered difficulties that diminished the payoffs of the open policy. Skilled workers and technical personnel necessary to utilize sophisticated foreign machinery were often in short supply. Telecommunications, transportation, and energy infrastructure upon which the full use of modern equipment often depended was both inadequate and very expensive to develop. This frequently meant that expensive imported equipment was used at only a fraction of its capacity. Such problems plagued even critical defense industries that have privileged access to personnel and resources. In more run-of-the-mill factories, the problems were even greater, frequently insurmountable.[14]

The integration of China into the global economy also subjected China to new economic forces. The most important of these was an import boom-bust cycle. It worked this way. The relaxation of central controls gave firms greater autonomy to enter into foreign contracts. The newly liberated enterprises proved very innovative in finding ways of mobilizing foreign currency to finance imports. They were less concerned with correspondingly expanding exports to cover those imports. After all, balancing the national trade account was not their responsibility. The result was large trade deficits and mounting foreign debt. As deficits and debt mounted, Beijing would reimpose central control to bring trade into balance. Imports then fell sharply.

There have been four import boom-bust cycles since the opening: in 1978, in association with the Ten Year Plan; in 1980, with the initial relaxation of central controls; in 1985, with a decentralization of the banking system and relaxation of foreign currency controls; and in 1990, with the retrenchment following Zhao Ziyang's ouster. In 1985, for example, imports increased by 54 percent, while exports increased only 5 percent. In each case the central authorities were dismayed by the mounting trade deficits, and reimposed central controls. Yet the reimposition of such controls conflicted with the increased entrepreneurship that was the genesis of decentralizing reforms in the first place.[15] The effectiveness of centrally imposed cutbacks in imports after 1989 (down by 12 percent in 1990) combined with continued growth in exports to produce a large trade surplus. This became a major problem in Sino-U.S. relations.

Capital goods have usually been the object of China's import booms. Chinese firms continue to desire expansion, and when given leeway, they have proved very eager to acquire foreign machinery. On occasion, however, consumer goods have been imported for resale on domestic markets. The most notorious example of this involved Hainan Island in 1985, when Hainan authorities mobilized US$570 million by drawing on their official foreign currency allotment from the central treasury, by retaining earnings of the island's exports, and by purchasing foreign currency on the black market in other localities with *Renminbi* borrowed from local banks. This money was then used to import 90,000 autos, 3 million televisions, 250,000 videotape players, and 120,000 motorcycles, which were resold on the domestic market as "used" goods at two or three times their import price.

Still another problem of the open policy from Beijing's perspective has been the tendency of Chinese enterprises and regions to compete with one another for foreign deals. Regions might try, for example, to attract foreign investment by offering lower taxes or lower prices than some other region. While economically rational from the standpoint of each firm or region, from the standpoint of China's central economic planners such inter-Chinese competition diminished the overall advantage accruing to China. A centrally administered cartel arrangement seemingly made more *national* economic sense, and in 1988 and 1989 measures were implemented to lessen such competition.

A final aspect of the opening that worried China's leaders was what they referred to as "spiritual pollution." This term refers to a wide range of ideas and practices that became common in China as the controls of the Maoist era were lifted: corruption, consumerism, a decline in the spirit of self-sacrifice, pornography, hedonism, declining belief in Marxism-Leninism and in the superiority of the socialist system, and increased willingness to challenge the leadership of the CCP. The forces that produced these phenomena were extremely complex. To some degree they did arise from China's increased contacts with the outside world.

Increased exposure to foreign media, tourists, and businessmen; increased travel abroad; and an increased honesty in China's own media made the Chinese increasingly aware of their country's poverty. During the Maoist years, many Chinese had believed that their country was among the most advanced in the world. They believed, as the Chinese media told them, that the Western countries were plagued with massive unemployment, racial violence, and inflation, with the working classes of those countries living under brutal repression and in deep economic hardship. While aware that China was technologically behind the West, most Chinese simply did not know just how far behind it was. They simply did not realize the fabulous level of wealth that the industrialized capitalist democracies had produced. This changed with the opening to the outside world. New ways of looking at things emerged, and expectations began to rise. Many Chinese found attractive Western ideas of liberty, freedom, and democracy, and became increasingly critical of the lack of these things in China. China's Communist rulers chose to focus on such putative Western "flies and insects" as pornography and corruption that supposedly came in through the "open door." They were at least as concerned, however, with the erosion of habits of obedience to the CCP, critical attitudes subsumed under the term "bourgeois liberalism." Repeated campaigns were carried out to suppress these undesirable influences. Beijing's repression of the democracy movement in 1989 was one such campaign.

STRATEGIC EQUIDISTANCE AND THE FOUR MODERNIZATIONS

The policy of opening to the outside world applied initially to the Western countries. Trade continued between China and the Soviet Union, but at levels far below those with the Western countries. Until the mid-1980s, China looked overwhelmingly to the West for the critical foreign inputs for the Four Modernizations. Beginning in 1983, however, there was a slow but steady expansion of Sino-Soviet economic cooperation. A visit by first deputy chairman of the Soviet Council of Ministers Ivan Arkhipov to China in 1984 led to Soviet agreement to help refurbish some of the factories built with Soviet assistance in the 1950s. By 1990, the Soviet Union had become China's fifth largest trading partner.

Important economic considerations underlay the Sino-Soviet rapprochement of the late 1980s. There was strong pressure from China's western and northwestern provinces to expand the opening to the outside world to include the Soviet Union. The location of these provinces excluded them from maritime interaction with the West. Much more than mere jealousy was involved. At stake were claims to central budgetary allocations, access to foreign currency, and imported technology. Western provinces saw an opening to the Soviet Union as a way of getting a bigger share of the budgetary and foreign currency pie, as a way of accelerating economic growth.

A large infusion of Soviet technology would also be very useful to Chinese industry. Much of Chinese heavy industry was equipped with Soviet machinery from the 1950s or with Chinese copies of those machines. In many cases the Soviets had improved the original machinery, and Soviet assistance in upgrading corresponding Chinese equipment would be very useful. Many Chinese personnel were familiar with Soviet equipment and would find it considerably easier to utilize updated Soviet equipment than Western equipment. The fact that China had large numbers of unskilled or semi-skilled workers and a corresponding shortage of skilled personnel also meant that relatively simple Soviet technology could be assimilated more easily than complex Western equipment.[16]

Soviet industrial equipment also had the advantage of being cheaper than Western equipment. The Soviet machine tool industry also had considerable excess capacity, while Soviet consumers eagerly purchased Chinese foodstuffs and consumer goods. Moreover, many Chinese goods exported to the Soviet Union were of too low quality to be sold on Western markets, or Western markets were simply too crowded. Nor did expanded trade with the Soviet Union interfere with Sino-Western trade. Until 1990, Sino-Soviet trade was usually barter, not requiring China to draw on its hard currency reserves. Chinese enterprises frequently found Soviets much easier to deal with than Western businesses—less picky about style and quality, and more tolerant of the bureaucratic procedures of a socialist economy. China also had an abundance of labor, which was in short supply in the Soviet Union. In terms of maximizing foreign inputs into the Four Modernizations, cordial relations and broad economic cooperation with *both* the United States and the Soviet Union made sense.

NOTES

1. Regarding the debate between the radicals and the pragmatists over this issue, see Michael Baron, "Uneasy Truce: Political Trends in Post-Mao China and Their Implications for Foreign Trade," in *China Trade, Prospects and Perspectives*, David C. Buxbaum, ed., New York: Praeger, 1982, 22–45; Jurgen Domes, "The 'Gang of Four' and Hua Kuo-feng: Analysis of Political Events in 1975–76," *China Quarterly*, no. 71 (September 1977), 478–81; A. Doak Barnett, *China's Economy in Global Perspective*, Washington, D.C.: Brookings Institution, 1981, 122–32; Harry Harding, *China's Second Revolution*, Washington, D.C.: Brookings Institution, 1987, 40–69; James T.H. Tsao, *China's Development Strategies and Foreign Trade*, Lexington, Mass.: D.C. Heath, *Development Strategies and Foreign Trade*, Lexington, Mass.: D.C. Heath, 1987.

2. Alexander Eckstein, *China's Economic Revolution*, Cambridge: Cambridge University Press, 1977, 240–41.

3. Other studies reach similar conclusions. See Robert F. Dernberger, "Communist China's Industrial Policies: Goals and Results," *Issues and Studies*, vol. 17, no. 7 (July 1981), 34–75; Y.Y. Kueh and Christopher Howe, "China's International Trade: Policy and Organizational Change and Their Place in the 'Economic Readjustment'," *China Quarterly*, no. 100 (December 1984). 813–48; Robert M. Field, "Slow Growth of Labour Productivity in Chinese Industry, 1952–81," *China Quarterly*, no. 96 (December 1983), 641–64.

4. For a list and synopsis of agreements signed in 1979, see Thomas Fingar and Victor Li, eds., "United States–China Relations in 1979: Agreements, Protocols, Accords, and Understandings," *Chinese Law and Government*, vol. xiv, no. 1 (Spring 1981), 1–126.

5. Joseph Pelzman, "PRC Textile Trade and Investment: Impact of the U.S.-PRC Bilateral Textile Agreements," *China's Economy Looks Toward the Year 2000*, vol. 2: Economic Openness in Modernizing China, Selected Papers Submitted to the Joint Economic Committee, Congress of the United States, 94th Congress, 1st Session, May 21, 1986, 400, 412–13.

6. Regarding the relaxation of COCOM restrictions, see Madelyn C. Ross, "Export Controls: Where China Fits In," *China Business Review* (May–June 1984), 58–62; Office of Technology Assessment, *Technology and East-West Trade*, Washington, D.C.: U.S. Government Printing Office, 1979.

7. Regarding the SEZs, see Victor C. Falkenheim, "China's Special Economic Zones," *China's Economy Looks Toward the Year 2000*, vol. 2, 348–70; Michael Oborne, *China's Special Economic Zones*, Paris: Development Center of the OECD, 1986; Jan Prybyla, "China's Special Economic Zones," *ACES Bulletin*, vol. xxvi, no. 4 (Winter 1984), 1–24; Ai Wei, "The Special Economic Zones in Mainland China, An Analytic Study," *Issues and Studies*, vol. 21, no. 6 (June 1985), 117–35; Y.C. Jao and C.K. Leung, ed., *China's Special Economic Zones: Problems and Prospects*, New York: Oxford University Press, 1986. Regarding the decision to form the SEZs, see A. Doak Barnett, *The Making of Foreign Policy in China: Structure and Process*, SAIS Papers, International Affairs, Boulder, Colo.: Westview, 1985, 20–25.

8. Madelyn C. Ross, "China's New and Old Investment Zones," *China Business Review*, November–December 1984, 14–18.

9. Kazuo Yamanouchi, "China's Coastal Region Developmental Strategy," *Japan Review of International Affairs*, vol. 3, no. 1 (Spring–Summer 1989), 27–42. Zhao Ziyang was a major proponent of this strategy. See "Zhao on Coastal Areas Development Strategy," *Beijing Review*, February 8–14, 1988, 18–23.

10. Regarding this myth in an earlier era, see Paul A. Varg, "The Myth of the China Market, 1890–1914," *American Historical Review*, vol. xxiii, no. 3 (February 1968), 742–58. For a study of the impact of this notion on U.S. foreign policy, see Thomas J. McCormick, *China Market, America's Quest for Informal Empire, 1901–1983*. Chicago: Quadrangle Books, 1967.

11. Regarding efforts to elaborate the legal system, see Stanley B. Lubman, "Technology Transfer in China: Policies, Practice, and Law," *China's Economy Looks Toward the Year 2000*, vol. 2, 287–308. Regarding Chinese efforts to attract foreign investment, see Nigel Campbell and Peter Adlington, *China Business Strategies: A Survey of Foreign Business Activity in the PRC*, New York: Pergamon, 1988, 11–15; Samuel P.S. Ho and Ralph W. Huenemann, *China's Open Door Policy: The Quest for Foreign Technology and Capital*, Vancouver: University of British Columbia Press, 1984.

12. State Statistical Bureau, "The Utilization of Foreign Capital: 1979–1988," *Beijing Review*, vol. 32, no. 10 (March 6–12, 1989), 26–29; *FBIS,DRC*, October 20, 1989, 38.

13. Regarding the reform of China's economic structures, see Harding, *China's Second Revolution*, 70–170; Dwight H. Perkins, "Reforming China's Economic System," *Journal of Economic Literature*, vol. xxvi, no. 2 (June 1988), 601–45; Elizabeth J. Perry and Christine Wong, "The Political Economy of Reform in Post-Mao China: Causes, Content, and Consequences," *The Political Economy of Reform in Post-Mao China*, Elizabeth Perry and Christine Wong, eds., Cambridge: Harvard University Press, 1985, 1–27; Wolfgang Klenner and Kurt Wiesgart, *The Chinese Economy: Structure and Reform in the Domestic Economy and in Foreign Trade*, New Brunswick, N.J.: Transaction Books, 1985.

14. Office of Technology Assessment, *Technology Transfer to China*, OTA-ISC-340, Washington, D.C.: U.S. Government Printing Office, July 1987, 40–41.

15. Ryosei Kokubun, "The Politics of Foreign Economic Policy-making in China: The Case of Plant Cancellations with Japan," *China Quarterly*, no. 105 (March 1986), 19–44.

16. Regarding the economic underpinnings of the Sino-Soviet rapprochement of the 1980s, see John W. Garver, "Peking's Soviet and American Policies: Toward Equidistance," *Issues and Studies*, vol. 24, no. 10 (October 1988), 55–77; Roy Medvedev, *China and the Superpowers*, New York: Basil Blackwell, 1986, 202–21.

Chapter Ten

International Components of China's Development

ACQUISITION OF FOREIGN TECHNOLOGY

Within each of the three possible development paths, China has had to confront several fundamental problems. One has been the acquisition of foreign science and technology (S&T). The transfer of technology from one country to another takes two broad forms: embodied transfers involving the acquisition of machinery, equipment, or physical systems of technology; and disembodied transfers involving the transfer of information via the minds of people without movement of goods. There are many different forms of embodied and disembodied technology transfer, and the PRC has made liberal use of virtually all forms. A major task of Chinese leaders and their advisers has been to determine which form of technology acquisition most benefits China.[1]

Industrial exhibitions, in which foreign countries or firms are invited to display their wares, have been one important and inexpensive way of acquiring foreign technology. A few such exhibitions were held in the 1960s, prior to the Cultural Revolution. They were resumed in 1971 and became increasingly common during the 1980s. Such exhibitions have typically attracted large numbers of foreign participants, who demonstrated their most modern products, conducted educational seminars, showed films, and distributed glossy catalogues and technical data extolling their goods. Such fairs make comparison shopping easy for Chinese personnel. They allow the Chinese to become familiar with the state of foreign technology and to collect large amounts of useful technical information, all at virtually no cost to China. The commercial returns to foreign firms from such fairs were usually very limited. As often as not, the only sales were of discounted display models at the end of the fair. Nonetheless, an abiding faith in the potential of the China market virtually ensures large numbers of foreign participants.[2]

Another important form of disembodied transfer involves the participation of Chinese specialists in the international communities of their field by reading foreign journals, attending international conferences, and so on. This demands that foreign languages be widely taught in China. It also requires effective systems to distribute the foreign-derived information: libraries, specialized publications, circulation networks, and electronic data banks. Foreign specialists may be invited to China to teach or advise, or to participate in conferences. According to China's 1987 White Paper on science and technology, for example, over 3,000 Chinese attended 2,000 international science and technology symposia in 1986, and over 100 international symposia were convened in China.[3] Research centers must be set up to replicate the foreign knowledge and apply it to China's own needs.

Study abroad by Chinese is another important form of disembodied technology transfer; indeed, it is probably the most effective method of international transfer of knowledge. Some 36,000 Chinese students studied in the Soviet Union during the 1950s. Tens of thousands of workers received specialized training in Soviet factories. During the Maoist years few Chinese went abroad for study. This inflicted heavy losses on China's technological advance. With the opening to the outside world, foreign study was revived. In March 1978, the State Commission on Science and Technology announced plans to send Chinese scholars abroad once again, and to welcome foreigners to China for academic and scholarly purposes. Soon afterwards educational exchange agreements were signed with France, Italy, West Germany, Great Britain, the United States, and Japan.

The United States rapidly emerged as the largest recipient of Chinese scholars—hosting some 56,000 between 1978 and 1988. There were several reasons for this. First, the highly decentralized nature of higher education in the United States made it easier for Chinese scholars to secure support from U.S. sources. Exchanges with Western European countries and Japan were usually regulated by governmental agreements specifying numbers and sources of support. The absence of such agreements in the case of the United States meant that there were no absolute limits on the numbers of Chinese who could be admitted to American universities and that they were free to seek out financial assistance from their U.S. host schools. A second reason had to do with U.S. leadership in many areas of science and technology. Still another factor was the large community of Chinese in the United States. Chinese-Americans often took the initiative to establish exchange programs between U.S. and Chinese institutions. They sponsored Chinese scholars in the United States and facilitated the study, research, or living arrangements of Chinese scholars. The Chinese communities in Europe and Japan were tiny in comparison with that of the United States.[4] As Table 10–1 indicates, China's post-1978 opening involved the most extensive outflow of students in China's modern history.

Governmental agreements providing for S&T exchanges between official and quasi-official agencies is yet another mechanism of technology transfer. Such exchanges proliferated with socialist countries in the 1950s; with the Western countries in the 1980s; and, by the late 1980s, again with the socialist countries. Shortly after the normalization of Sino-U.S. relations in 1979, Beijing and Washington signed an S&T cooperation agreement, and by the end of 1986, over 500 projects had been carried out under this agreement. A similar agreement was signed with Japan in 1980, and twenty-seven projects were carried out through 1986. The Japanese International Cooperation Agency sponsored another thirty-two projects. Twelve S&T exchange agreements were concluded with Western European governments between 1978 and 1986. In 1986, exchanges were resumed with the Soviet Union.

China has also looked to international organizations for S&T. In the words of China's 1987 S&T White Paper, "China attaches great importance" to such specialized United Nations agencies as the UN intergovernmental Council on Promotion and Development of Science and Technology, Science and Technology Center, UN University, UN Industrial Development Agency, UN Food and Agricultural Organization, and UN Economic and Social Commission for Asia and the Pacific. A number of non-governmental Chinese organizations also play important roles in S&T acquisition. The Chinese Academy of Sciences, for example, signed "seventy-odd" agreements with counterparts in fifty countries between 1978 and the end of 1986, while the Chinese Association of Science and Technology (roughly equivalent to the American Council of Learned Societies) had concluded twenty agreements with organizations

Table 10–1 Estimates of Chinese Students Abroad

Period	Number Abroad
1854–1953	21,000 to the United States, long term
1900–1937	34,000 to Japan, long term
1900–1940s	100,000 to Japan, including short term
1949–1959	36,000 to the USSR (based on Soviet figures)
1979–1989	Over 60,000 regular students to Western countries (including Japan)
1983–1988	150,000 total Chinese departures on student visas

Source: James R. Townsend, "Reflections on the Opening of China," in *Perspectives on Modern China: Four Anniversaries*, Kenneth Lieberthal, ed., New York: M.E. Sharpe, 1991, p. 401. Reprinted with permission of M.E. Sharpe.

in sixteen countries. The Chinese S&T Exchange Center had concluded thirty-four agreements with 100 organizations in twenty countries.[5]

As far as embodied forms of technology transfer, probably the most important has been import of foreign industrial machinery and equipment (hereafter abbreviated M&E) imports. (Equipment refers largely to transport and construction equipment.) Regarding M&E imports, it is important to distinguish between imports that upgrade China's technological level and imports that merely expand the capital stock at an already existing technological level. As noted earlier, especially during the 1980s, Chinese economic planners have emphasized improvements in factor productivity, and hence import of advanced technology that will achieve this. During the 1950s, when many types of industries simply did not exist in China, M&E imports creating those industries usually represented a technological advance. Even once China developed an indigenous ability to produce a particular type of M&E, the domestic machine building industry often could not satisfy demands created by ambitious industrialization targets. The consequent M&E imports did not necessarily boost China's technological level, but they did expand mechanization, which also increased the productivity of labor.

Table 10–2 shows China's M&E imports. There have been several periods of rapid growth in M&E imports. The first came during the Sino-Soviet alliance in the 1950s, when M&E imports grew rapidly during the first Five Year Plan and continued to rise during the Great Leap Forward, reaching a peak in 1959 with an annual total of US$933 million. The break with Moscow in 1960 had a devastating impact on M&E imports, which fell from an annual average of $889 million between 1953 and 1960 to a low of $100 million in 1963, before recovering to an average of up to $312 million between 1961 and 1971. After the break with Moscow, revival of M&E imports began in 1964 as recovery from the Great Leap collapse got underway. This was interrupted by the Cultural Revolution. Growth resumed in 1970. Renewal of whole plant imports pushed the level past the 1959 peak in 1974. The largest and most sustained boom began in 1978 with the adoption of the Ten Year Plan. After a slowdown between 1980 and 1982, growth resumed and continued throughout 1989.[6]

Between 1952 and 1960, 90 percent of M&E imports came from the Soviet Union and Eastern Europe. After 1960, imports from the Soviet Union collapsed, but they continued from Eastern Europe. Between 1961 and 1973, half of China's M&E imports came from Communist countries—East Germany and Romania being the major suppliers. The other half came from Western countries other than the United States. As noted earlier, Japan, France, West Germany, and Britain broke with U.S. embargo policy shortly after the end of the Korean War. Chinese imports from those countries remained low until after the recovery from the

Table 10–2 China's Machinery and Equipment Imports, 1953–1988

Year	U.S. $ Billions	As % of Imports	Year	U.S. $ Billions	As % of Imports
1953	.762	56.6	1971	.484	21.9
1954	.697	54.2	1972	.557	19.5
1955	1.088	62.8	1973	.788	15.3
1956	.837	53.5	1974	1.585	20.8
1957	.790	52.5	1975	2.406	32.1
1958	.850	45.0	1976	2.037	30.9
1959	1.120	52.8	1977	1.277	17.7
1960	.970	49.7	1978	1.903	17.5
1961	.330	22.8	1979	3.957	25.2
1962	.172	14.6	1980	5.375	27.5
1963	.122	9.6	1981	5.105	26.2
1964	.169	10.9	1982	3.394	19.4
1965	.358	17.6	1983	3.254	17.6
1966	.502	22.3	1984	5.196	20.5
1967	.406	20.1	1985	10.965	31.9
1968	.303	15.6	1986	12.292	37.2
1969	.217	11.9	1987	10.803	32.3
1970	.369	15.8	1988	10.818	27.2

Source: *Zhongguo duiwai jingji maoyi nianjian 1989* (Yearbook of China's Foreign Economic Relations and Trade, 1989), Beijing: Zhanwang chubanshe, n.d., p. 309.

post–Great Leap Forward depression, that is, until about 1964. Then for several years M&E imports from Eastern Europe and the Western countries were roughly balanced. Around 1973, a major shift from Eastern Europe to the developed capitalist countries occurred. This shift was based primarily on an increased recognition of the superior technological level of Western M&E and on the improved relations with the West resulting from China's strategic alignment with the United States against the Soviet Union.

Import of prototypes for copying and of complete plants have been two important types of M&E imports. Regarding prototypes, China has often purchased one or several items to be studied, reverse engineered, and copied. This method has the advantages of being relatively cheap and conforming with the dictates of import substitution. It was used extensively during the 1960s and continues to be important in the 1990s. There are, however, major drawbacks to prototype copying. At best, reverse engineering is a very time-consuming process, sometimes taking decades. Moreover, if the technological level of the foreign model is too advanced, determination of exact composition and processes may be beyond the capacity of the Chinese engineers. This became a major problem with the microelectronic revolution of the past twenty years. It was relatively easy to copy most machines of the 1950s. It is more difficult to see how digitally controlled machines of the 1990s work, for example, or to determine the precise composition of modern composite materials. Even when Chinese engineers succeed in reproducing sophisticated foreign machines, copies are often brought into domestic production only after long delays and at very great cost.

Import of whole plants may be a form of prototype copying. That is, the intention may be to replicate the facility for expanded domestic use. This tended to be the case with the few whole plant imports during the 1960s. On the other hand, in a few instances substantial numbers of plants have been imported to rapidly expand production of critical goods. This was the case during the 1950s and 1970s. Import of whole plants declined in importance with the 1980s reforms.

Import of complete plants offers a number of advantages. In contrast to the usual purchases of single items of M&E, whole plants come with complete technical specifications and blueprints. The Chinese side acquires considerable organizational knowledge and learns exactly how the parts and processes fit together. There will also be a uniformity of equipment. All of these factors mean that China is more likely to get the full benefits of the acquired technology. Of course, there are also disadvantages to whole plant purchases. One is cost. A second is the violation of the principle of import substitution; inevitably, some items will be imported that China could manufacture indigenously. A third drawback is the high risk. If the project does not work out, losses can be huge.

Still another form of technology transfer involves cooperative ventures with foreign firms. During several periods this has been an important form of technology transfer. During the 1950s, China drew on the technical expertise of Eastern European enterprises. During the 1980s, China sought joint ventures with firms from virtually all industrialized and industrializing capitalist countries—Western Europe, Japan, North America, Australia, and the "newly industrializing countries" of the Pacific Rim.

Finally, covert collection is another important form of Chinese technology transfer. PRC intelligence services apparently focus many of their covert operations of this type on the United States—probably because of the unusually open and porous nature of U.S. society, the leading role of U.S. technology in many areas, and a calculation that Washington's strategic interest in China will lead it to turn a blind eye to these activities. In any case, by 1989 the U.S. Federal Bureau of Investigation estimated that Chinese covert technology collection operations in the United States exceeded those of the Soviet Union. Technologies denied to China by U.S. and/or COCOM regulations are major targets of Chinese intelligence agencies.[7]

China's intelligence agencies often utilize ethnic Chinese. They maintain close contact with the thousands of Chinese scientists, engineers, and students working in universities and laboratories across the United States. They cultivate people within the Chinese community in the United States and try to persuade them to find ways of circumventing restrictions to ship restricted goods to China. China also relies on Hong Kong firms to get access to restricted technology. PRC enterprises are sometimes encouraged to seek cooperative ventures with particular Hong Kong firms that have access to certain types of foreign technology. These covert collection operations have probably greatly increased in scope and effectiveness since China's opening.

Acquisition is only the first and in many ways the least difficult step in utilizing foreign technology. Next must come mastery of that technology by Chinese personnel, its full integration into production processes, and the diffusion of that technology throughout the Chinese economy—all part of the process of absorption. Unless Chinese personnel can learn to operate and repair foreign machinery, it will not be used fully and may not be used at all. Unless Chinese engineers and scientists can learn the principles underlying sophisticated foreign machinery, China will be unable to replicate it. If this happens, the foreign technology may remain an isolated enclave in Chinese industry, with its benefits not passed on to other enterprises.

China has faced huge problems with absorption. The educational level of many Chinese workers is low. The depreciation of education (and especially higher education) during the Maoist years, combined with the rapid growth of Chinese industry, has meant that skilled workers, let alone engineers and technicians, are in very short supply. Bottlenecks in energy and transportation have also hindered utilization of foreign technology. So too has the hodgepodge nature of China's capital stock: A single plant often incorporates equipment from Eastern Europe, Japan, and the United States, with equipment design perhaps spanning a period of fifty years. Most basic, however, has been the absence of strong incentives for enterprises to utilize capital, domestic or foreign, efficiently and with maximum results. China's difficulty in absorbing foreign technology was reflected in the conclusions of a study that found that of nine large and medium-sized industrial projects imported from abroad and completed between 1980 and 1982, six had poor economic results.[8]

GENERATION OF FOREIGN CURRENCY

Generation of foreign currency is the counterpart of technology transfer. With a few exceptions such as covert collection or gratis developmental assistance, foreign technology, whether in the form of student tuition or the purchase of whole plants, must be paid for. Sometimes this may be done via barter. More commonly, China must pay for its technology acquisitions with foreign currency. Earning foreign currency is thus a central component of China's drive for modernization.

Like technology acquisition, this can be done in many ways. One way is to borrow money from foreign lenders. During the 1950s, the PRC relied heavily on this method. As noted in Chapter Eight, between 1950 and 1957 China borrowed the equivalent of $2.25 billion from the Soviet Union. Although this borrowing helped finance the large-scale import of Soviet machinery during the 1950s, it imposed a heavy repayment burden on China. In 1964, nearly 20 percent of China's export earnings went to pay interest and principal on Soviet loans.

Since the Sino-Soviet split, China has been a very cautious borrower. Throughout the 1960s, avoidance of foreign debt was extolled as one of the hallmarks of Self-Reliance.[9] This was modified in the 1970s, when China began using commercial credits to import various commodities, including whole plants financed through deferred, medium-term (five-year) repayment schemes. Some of these deferred payment plans involved explicit interest charges. A critical change of attitude toward foreign borrowing came in 1974, when Deng Xiaoping redefined Self-Reliance in terms of China's ability to repay loans, rather than complete avoidance of foreign debt or keeping debt at some low level. Once Deng consolidated power in 1978, China began negotiating large lines of credit with Western bank syndicates and governments, especially Japan. It was remarkably cautious in drawing on these credits, however, preferring instead to keep its level of foreign debt low.

As Table 10–3 shows, the PRC's level of indebtedness is small compared with that of other developing countries; only about one-fifth the debt of Brazil or Mexico, for example. China's debt burden is also small in terms of the ratio of total outstanding debt to annual export earnings or as a percent of GNP. Maintaining a low level of foreign debt remains a central tenet of the doctrine of Self-Reliance in the 1990s.

China has preferred to borrow from governments and international organizations rather than from commercial lenders, who usually expect a higher return. In 1979, China began to seek money from organizations such as the International Development Association, the World Bank, and the U.N. Development Program. It had previously denounced such organizations as instruments of capitalist exploitation. By 1982, China had become the largest recipient of multilateral development aid. In order to bolster its claim to the concessional assistance, in 1979 and 1980 Beijing released relatively complete economic statistics. These figures revealed China's poverty but thereby increased its eligibility for concessionary aid while simultaneously reducing its annual UN assessment. Throughout the 1980s, most of China's borrowing was concessional or semiconcessional. The foreign good will upon which this success depended may, however, have been one of the casualties of the repression of 1989. Lending to China by

Table 10–3 Comparative Levels of Foreign Indebtedness

	China	Brazil	India	Indonesia	Egypt	Mexico
Total international debt, U.S. $ millions	42,015	114,592	57,513	52,600	49,970	101,567
Debt as percent of exports	88%	340%	394%	267%	1,111%	492%
Debt as percent of GNP	11%	35%	24%	63%	146%	58%

Source: *World Bank, World Development Report 1990*, New York: Oxford University Press, 1990, 168, 218.

foreign governments fell by half in the year after the Beijing massacre. Loans by international financial organizations, however, doubled during the same period.

Since 1979, China has also generated substantial foreign currency through tourism. From 1949 to 1979, foreign tourism to China served essentially political purposes. Limited numbers of foreigners (some 5,000 to 10,000 per year in the 1950s) were invited to China for various political reasons: to propagate Marxist-Leninist ideology; to foster a favorable image of China, which would help win friends and counter U.S.-imposed isolation; and to enhance China's reputation in the Third World. As part of China's effort to win over its "foreign guests," the activities of these guests were carefully controlled to direct their experience in China toward "correct" conclusions. While breaking down trade barriers was among the secondary goals of this "cultural diplomacy," earning foreign currency from the pockets of the foreign guests was not. Indeed, the in-country expenses of most pre-1979 visitors to China were usually paid by the Chinese government, or at least substantially subsidized, as part of the effort to win their sympathy.[10]

This changed in 1978. Realizing that foreign curiosity about China could attract large numbers of tourists, Beijing reorganized tourism along commercial lines. Now virtually anyone with a few thousand dollars to spend was welcome to visit China. Infrastructure necessary to accommodate large numbers of foreign tourists was built. Interpreters were trained. Western-style hotels were built. Air-conditioned tour buses were imported. Scenic and historic sites were restored and opened to foreigners. "Friendship shops" were established at strategic points and provided with adequate supplies of goods. Even the Anglers Guest House (diaoyu tai binguan) in Beijing and the Kun Lun excursion steamer on the Yangtze River, both luxury facilities previously reserved for use by Chinese leaders and visiting foreign dignitaries, were turned over for use by wealthy foreign tourists.

Tourism rapidly became a major source of foreign currency. From

1.8 million tourists spending $263 million in 1978, it grew to 31.7 million tourists spending $2.22 billion in 1988. This was the equivalent of about 5 percent of all export earnings, and one-third of all non-trade foreign currency earnings. By the mid-1980s, China had become the No. 1 worldwide destination for tourists. Most of those tourists (94 percent in 1988) came from Hong Kong, Taiwan, and Macao.[11] Moreover, non-economic elements continued to govern treatment of these "compatriots" as Beijing sought to court their loyalties via special "compatriot" prices. Nonetheless, even "compatriots" from Hong Kong and Taiwan brought in foreign exchange.

Remittances by overseas Chinese has also been an important source of foreign currency. People of Chinese extraction in many countries, but especially in Southeast Asia, routinely send money to relatives living in China. Such remittances can be used in many ways by their immediate recipients—to build better houses, or for marriages or funerals. Remitting money also allows overseas Chinese to demonstrate respect toward their ancestors and benevolence toward their ancestral village. While private individuals are usually the immediate recipients of these remittances, because of foreign currency controls most of these foreign monies end up in the state treasury. In fact, the monies are usually transferred through special foreign currency–denominated accounts offered by the Bank of China. Scarce goods often unobtainable for *Renminbi* (People's money) are often available with special foreign currency–convertible money, the *waihuichuan* (foreign currency certificate).

The volume of remittances by overseas Chinese has been quite significant. Although Beijing does not provide exact figures, they probably constitute the single largest invisible item in China's capital accounts, being large enough in the mid-1980s to offset substantial deficits in China's merchandise trade accounts.[12]

Not surprisingly, the flow of remittances has been linked to shifts in China's policy toward the overseas Chinese. Generally, Beijing has sought to foster links with communities of overseas Chinese while maintaining cordial relations with the governments ruling those populations, a course which had as one of its primary objectives facilitating the flow of remittances to China. The exception to this approach was during the Cultural Revolution, when overseas Chinese were viewed as corrupting influences on revolutionary China. During these years Chinese who had contact with overseas Chinese were often considered tainted by the reactionary ideology of their relatives. Moreover, the money remitted to China, or the property purchased with that money, was often confiscated by Red Guards or by radical local governments. As one would expect, the level of remittances fell substantially. After 1977 Beijing moderated its policies so as to revive the flow of remittances. Chinese with overseas relatives were prime beneficiaries of policies restoring wealth illegally confiscated during the radical years. The new emphasis on material incentives and the greater acceptance of economic inequality meant that remitted monies could again be enjoyed by their Chinese recipients. The general opening to the outside world also meant that foreign contacts were less suspect. Overseas Chinese were once again treated as honored guests during their visits to the motherland. And once again, as in the 1950s, special banking procedures were set up to facilitate remittances to China.[13]

China's foreign aid program also touches on its earning of foreign currency. To a degree, China's dispersal of military and economic development assistance to other countries required expenditures of foreign exchange by China. More typically, however, Chinese foreign aid has been aid in kind; that is, the direct provision of goods or services to a country paid for by the Chinese government in *Renminbi*. From this perspective China's foreign aid program did not involve a direct diversion of foreign exchange from China's technology acquisition efforts. It could, however, have diverted goods or services that might have otherwise been sold on foreign markets. It also involved a diversion of resources away from China's own development efforts.

The PRC's foreign aid program began as soon as the PRC was established with shipments of munitions to the Vietminh in French Indochina and to North Korea during the Korean War. It was expanded to include non-Communist countries in 1956 as Beijing sought to counter U.S. containment. In line with this, most aid in the late 1950s went to Asian countries neighboring China. Levels of aid increased during the early 1960s, with radical Africa states and Albania becoming favored recipients. Disbursements were virtually suspended during the Cultural Revolution, but resumed in 1970 and soon reached new peaks. Total commitments between 1970 and 1974 were more than double the total for the period between 1956 and 1969. Two-thirds of this money went to Africa, and much of this to finance the Tanzam railway project linking Zambia to ports in Tanzania (thereby lessening Zambia's dependency on Apartheid-dominated South Africa). The Tanzam railway may have cost China as much as $2.6 billion.[14]

North Vietnam, North Korea, and Albania were the largest recipients of Chinese aid, receiving somewhere between $3 billion and $20 billion, $1 billion and $8 billion, and $0.5 billion and $5 billion, respectively. Excluding aid to Communist countries, between 1956 and 1977 China distributed a total of some $2.26 billion, or an average of over $100 million per year for twenty-two years. This was a very heavy burden for a poor country. It was also an impressive testament to the determination of China's leaders to play an important role in world affairs. Non-Communist recipients of Chinese aid of $100 million or more include (in rank order): Pakistan,

Tanzania, Zambia, Nepal, Sri Lanka, Egypt, Somalia, North Yemen, and Indonesia.[15]

The level of China's foreign aid declined dramatically after 1978, when China suspended aid to its largest recipients, North Vietnam and Albania. Political exigencies influenced the decline of aid, but an underlying concern was a determination to focus resources on China's own development. China continued to give some foreign assistance during the 1980s and 1990s—Pakistan and Cambodia's Khmer Rouge insurgents being the major recipients. But by and large, China's leaders decided to concentrate resources on the Four Modernizations rather than lavishing them on other developing countries. This decline did not appear in official PRC aid statistics, because only a small portion of China's aid was ever officially announced, and it seems to have been largely the unannounced portion that has been shelved.[16]

While cutting back on its aid to foreign countries, the PRC has itself drawn increasingly on foreign aid. Between 1979 and 1988, for example, China received nearly $400 million in gratis assistance from United Nations agencies and developed countries.[17] It received over $7.5 billion in various types of official development assistance.[18] As noted earlier, lending to China by international organizations doubled in the year after the Beijing massacre, according to Chinese statistics.

CHINA'S FOREIGN TRADE

Export of goods and services is a key way of earning foreign currency to pay for technology acquisitions. Until the late 1980s, PRC foreign trade was "import driven." That is, China's economic planners made decisions about development targets and then calculated the amounts and types of producer goods, raw materials, and so on, necessary to achieve these targets. They then determined which of these inputs could not be produced domestically and would have to be imported. They then decided what to export in order to pay for these imports. Thus, a decision to increase the rate of investment in industry led to increased demand for imported capital goods and/or raw materials. This led, in turn, to increased exports to cover the costs of those imports.[19]

The decentralization of economic authority during the 1980s undermined the import-driven nature of export. When localities and enterprises were given wide latitude to export independently of central regulation, rapid export growth resulted. When central controls were reimposed in 1988 and 1989 as the economy overheated, those controls affected mostly imports. Central investment and growth objectives were scaled back, and demand for foreign M&E fell correspondingly—just as had been the case earlier. Tightened central controls over foreign currency also reined in Chinese demand for foreign M&E. Exports, however, continued to surge. One result was huge trade surpluses, which became a major source of friction with China's trading partners.

A second characteristic of Chinese foreign trade has been import substitution. As noted earlier, a central component of Self-Reliance has been "all-around industrialization." To this end, Beijing has typically allowed the import of only those goods that could not be manufactured indigenously. Its objective was to conserve as much foreign currency as possible for key development projects and for imports of advanced technology. Strenuous efforts were also made to develop indigenous industry, and as Chinese industry could meet demand, foreign imports were progressively excluded. It is difficult to characterize this practice as protection of infant industry against foreign competition. Protection it certainly was, but in many cases the industry being protected was hardly "infant" after several decades of growth. Moreover, indigenous industry faced little if any domestic competition. Competition, domestic or foreign, was not part of China's socialist economy until, within limits, the 1980s.

Import substitution became somewhat less rigorous with the decentralization of economic authority during the 1980s. Import of strategic, high-tech imports was still the overall objective, and export earnings were still intended to cover the cost of imports, but no longer was this to be achieved via central planning and direction. Rather, macro controls, especially control over access to foreign currency, were used to ensure that import substitution was generally achieved.

Another traditional pattern of China's foreign trade has been that, in aggregate, China has enjoyed a substantial trade surplus with other developing countries and a deficit in its trade with industrialized countries. In effect, China has used the foreign currency it earns from trade with developing countries to finance imports from the developed countries. This triangular pattern of China's trade arises from the logic of China's development effort. In terms of imports, China wants sophisticated machinery, equipment, and technology, which is available chiefly from the developed countries. At the same, its low-quality manufactured goods have limited appeal to consumers in developed countries, but are welcomed by consumers in the developing world.

This triangular pattern of trade emerged after the rupture with the Soviet Union in 1960. China conducted substantial trade with Third World countries in the early 1950s—buying raw cotton and jute from Pakistan, copra from Indonesia, rubber from Ceylon, and rice from Burma, and paying for these goods primarily with cotton textiles. In the mid-1950s, a combination of political and economic motives led Beijing to launch a major campaign to promote trade with Third World countries. The break with Moscow and the desperate effort to find foreign currency sources to replace Soviet assistance led to another push in the early 1960s to expand exports to the developing countries. By then China had industrialized sufficiently to be able to export a broader range of manufactured goods, including textile machinery, cement, paper, and transport equipment. A renewed export push came with the need to pay for whole plant imports in the early 1970s. China's trade surplus with the Third World rose from $235 million in the early 1970s to $407 million in 1976, the latter figure comparing with an overall deficit of $4.257 billion in trade with non-Communist industrial countries. This triangular pattern became even more pronounced during the 1980s. By 1988, China enjoyed a $2 billion surplus in trade with developing countries against a nearly $6 billion deficit with the developed countries. The pattern of China's trade is illustrated by Table 10–4.

The triangular pattern of trade creates a degree of conflict between China and other developing countries. As noted in Chapter Seven, in many cases China's economic interests more closely approximate those of the developed countries. Regarding the terms of trade between primary and manufactured goods, for example, China imports from the Third World largely primary commodities (e.g., copper, cobalt, zinc, phosphates, rubber, timber, cocoa, cashew nuts, and tobacco) while exporting mainly manufactured goods to those countries. Thus the shift of terms of trade in favor of manufactured goods during the 1980s has benefited China, just as it benefited the developed countries. Some analysts have suggested that China's vociferous pro–Third World propaganda and its aid to Third World countries are explained, in part, by a desire to offset, or obfuscate, this pattern of selling to the developing countries and buying from the developed countries.

As Table 10–5 indicates, China's foreign trade has gone through two periods of especially rapid expansion: the 1950s and the 1980s. During the 1950s, the growth of Chinese foreign trade was one of the most rapid of all Asian countries, second only to Japan. During that decade, trade declined only in 1952 (because of the Korean War–related embargo and disruption due to internal political campaigns) and in 1957 (because of over-investment in industry and a poor farm harvest the previous year).

Table 10–4 The Pattern of Chinese Trade

	1978 (In millions U.S. $)			1988 (In millions U.S. $)		
	Exports	*Imports*	*Balance*	*Exports*	*Imports*	*Balance*
Developing countries	1,908	1,501	+407	6,327	4,287	+2,040
Industrialized countries	3,644	7,901	−4,257	16,164	22,114	−5,950
Hong Kong and Macao	2,667	75	+2,592	13,210	9,399	+3,811
Centrally planned economies	1,489	1,416	+73	3,556	3,839	−283

Source: Zhongguo duiwai jingji maoyi nianjian 1989 (Yearbook of China's Foreign Economic Relations and Trade, 1989), Beijing: Zhanwang chubanshe, n.d., p. 311.

Table 10-5 China's Aggregate Foreign Trade, 1950–1990

Year	Millions U.S. $	Year	Millions U.S. $
1950	1,130	1971	4,850
1951	1,960	1972	6,300
1952	1,940	1973	10,900
1953	2,370	1974	14,570
1954	2,440	1975	14,750
1955	3,140	1976	13,440
1956	3,210	1977	14,800
1957	3,110	1978	20,640
1958	3,870	1979	29,340
1959	4,380	1980	38,140
1960	3,810	1981	44,030
1961	2,940	1982	41,610
1962	2,660	1983	43,620
1963	2,920	1984	53,550
1964	3,470	1985	69,600
1965	4,250	1986	73,850
1966	4,620	1987	82,650
1967	4,160	1988	102,790
1968	4,050	1989	111,680
1969	4,030	1990	115,440
1970	4,590		

Sources: Zhongguo tongji nianjian 1989 (China Statistical Yearbook 1989), Beijing: State Statistical Bureau, n.d., 633; *Beijing Review*, October 1–7, 1990, 20; *China Statistics Abstract 1991*, Beijing: State Statistical Bureau, 1991, 106.

Trade rose sharply in 1958 and again in 1959, as investment targets were boosted during the Great Leap Forward, only to collapse in 1960. It declined further between 1960 and 1963, as Sino-Soviet relations deteriorated and imports were cut to pay off Soviet loans, and as investment was shifted from industry to agriculture. Investment in agriculture generated less of a demand for imported capital goods than did investment in industry. Economic recovery brought modest trade growth between 1964 and 1966, but this was aborted by the Cultural Revolution. Trade began to revive in 1970, surpassing in that year the previous 1959 peak. It slowed again in 1975 and declined sharply in 1976, primarily because of opposition by Maoists within the central leadership. Then in 1978 the second takeoff began and it continued, with a temporary slowdown in 1982 and 1983, throughout the decade. Foreign sanctions following the upheaval of 1989 had no impact on China's exports. Tightened central controls did, however, reduce imports, a situation that led to ballooning trade surpluses, as noted earlier.

Several major factors have influenced the level of China's foreign trade. One has been the size of the annual agricultural harvest, or more precisely, the rate of increase of agricultural production relative to population growth. China must feed its huge and expanding population. Since levels of investment in agriculture have been a major determinant of growth in agricultural production, slowing food production relative to population growth has typically led China's planners to shift investment from industry to agriculture. This in turn has led to decreased demand for imported capital goods, which is linked, as we have seen, to industrialization targets. Moreover, since agricultural products are among China's major export items, good harvests have meant more goods to export, poor harvests fewer goods to export.[20] Offsetting this tendency to some degree was the need for increased food imports when harvests were poor. When harvests were good, levels of trade could be cut (this was a factor in the 1975 slowdown), or funds could be shifted back to imports of capital goods and technology. In this regard, the institution of the household responsibility system in agriculture after 1977 has had a substantial effect on China's foreign trade. By boosting rates of agricultural growth, the decollectivization of agriculture lessened the need to purchase foreign foodstuffs, thereby freeing foreign currency resources for import of capital goods and technology. In this way, the success of the post-1978 agricultural reforms has been a major factor permitting machinery and equipment to rise as a share of total imports during the 1980s. The increased proportion of manufactured goods in China's exports has also lessened the negative impact of agricultural downturns on levels of overall exports.[21]

A second factor influencing levels of trade has been planning cycles and shifts in investment priorities. The promulgation of new plans, or the alteration of industrialization goals under an established plan, led to changes in levels of imports and exports. The ambitious industrialization targets of the first Five Year Plan (1953–1957), the Great Leap Forward, the fifth Five Year Plan (1971–1975), and the short-lived Ten Year Plan of 1978 (1978–1979) led to substantial growth in foreign trade, while the retrenchments of 1960 through 1963 and 1980 led to declines. Levels of military spending also affect decisions regarding levels of industrial investment and therefore foreign trade. To the extent that resources are channeled into defense, less is available for basic industrialization, leading to lower demands for foreign capital goods. Cuts in military spending in the 1970s and again in the 1980s were one factor underlying the expansion of trade during those decades, while heavy defense spending during the 1960s hobbled trade.

Another basic determinant of China's foreign trade has been the quality of its political relations with various countries. This has greatly influenced both levels and directions of trade. After 1960, for example, Sino-Soviet trade fell as Beijing deliberately directed trade away from the Soviet Union. Sino-American rapprochement in 1971 opened the door to expanded trade between those two countries. Loss of MFN status with the United States in the 1990s would lead to a large decline in Sino-American trade.

A final factor influencing foreign trade has been ideological debate and factional conflict within China's elite—a topic discussed in Chapter Eight. Radical leaders have sometimes insisted on trade restrictions, and at times have been able to impose their views to a substantial degree; e.g., from 1966 to 1969 and again from 1974 to 1976.

The composition of PRC imports and exports has changed substantially since 1949.[22] Regarding imports, one basic change was the fall of food imports as China approached self-sufficiency in food production during the 1980s. Foodstuffs constituted only 2 percent of imports in the late 1950s, then skyrocketed to 21 percent in 1961, and remained high (from 13 percent to 26 percent) through the mid-1970s. Then they began to fall with the success of agricultural reforms of the late 1970s, and by 1986 constituted only 4 percent of imports. Conversely, the share of M&E in total imports has risen dramatically in the 1980s. Imports of industrial raw materials have also increased with industrialization.

Regarding exports, in 1953 traditional agricultural products such as soybeans, textile fibers, tung oil, tea, eggs, and tobacco made up 55.8 percent of exports.[23] Agricultural items continue to be important PRC exports, but their relative share has fallen steadily, from an average of 33.1 percent in 1965 to 22.6 percent by 1988. As the share of agricultural products fell, the percentage of manufactured goods rose. Exports of light industrial products, such as bicycles, sewing machines, cameras, radios, and watches, began to increase in the 1960s. Exports of machinery and equipment also rose, from between 2 percent and 5 percent during the 1950s to over 6 percent in 1987. A substantial part of China's M&E exports were linked to its foreign aid program, but some Chinese machine tools also proved commercially attractive to buyers in Africa and South Asia. Exports of heavy industrial products rose from 17 percent of total exports in 1953 to 23 percent in 1988. Textiles have also grown in importance, rising from 6.1 percent in 1953, to 20 percent in 1965, to nearly 23 percent in 1988. Figure 10–1 illustrates the changing composition of China's exports.

The addition of petroleum as a major export item is the most important change in Chinese exports over the past two decades. Prior to 1970, China imported petroleum. Such purchases represented about 10 percent of all Chinese imports, and the third largest Soviet export to China during the 1950s. The Soviet Union also gave China extensive assistance in developing its petroleum industry in the 1950s, and exploration, drilling, and development of refining capacity proceeded rapidly with Soviet (as well as East German, Romanian, Polish, and Hungarian) help. The discovery of major oil fields at Daqing in northern

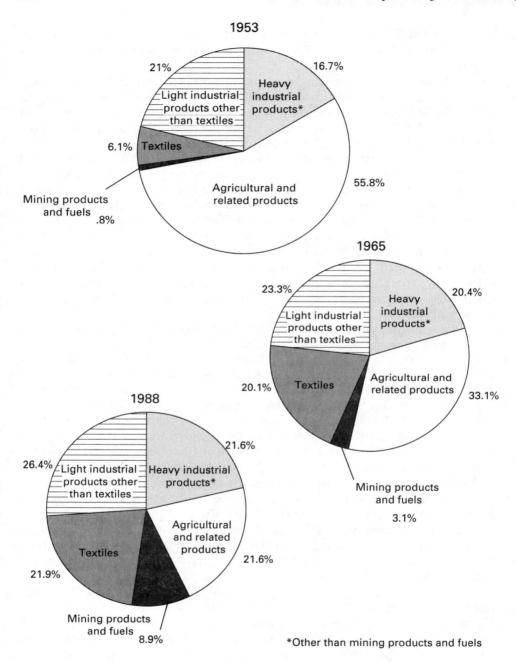

Figure 10–1   Changing Composition of PRC Exports

Manchuria in 1959 and in the Gulf of Bohai in the early 1970s dramatically altered China's oil picture. By the late 1970s, the PRC was a major petroleum exporting country. By 1988, China was the world's fourth largest producer of petroleum, ranking behind the USSR, the United States, and Saudi Arabia, but ahead of Mexico, Iraq, and Iran.[24] The growth of China's petroleum exports is illustrated in Table 10–6.

It was China's good fortune that the growth of its petroleum industry occurred just as the Organization of Petroleum Exporting Countries (OPEC) was pushing up the price of oil on the international market (from US$3.39 per barrel in 1973 to $34.50 in 1980). China did not join OPEC, but it followed OPEC's lead, benefiting tremendously therefrom.[25] Conversely, the precipitous decline of international oil prices between 1985 and 1988 (reaching an average price of $14.50 in 1988) substantially cut China's export earnings, greatly contributing to trade deficits that appeared in those years.[26]

The volatility of oil prices notwithstanding, China will remain a major petroleum exporter. Indeed, it has considerable potential in this regard. China has minimized its domestic oil consumption by relying on coal—of which it has the largest proven reserves in the world. China's proven reserves of bituminous coal are 4.5 times the size of combined Soviet *and* Eastern Europe reserves, and 5.2 times as large as combined U.S. *and* Canadian reserves. Burning coal may become less attractive as environmental pollution mounts, but China will probably remain one of the major petroleum exporters well into the next century.

Weapons were another significant addition to China's commercial exports during the 1980s. From 1949 to 1978, Beijing sent large amounts of munitions to socialist allies such as North Korea, North Vietnam, and Albania. Smaller amounts went to select non-Communist countries. Between 1970 and 1978, Chinese deliveries of military equipment to the non-Communist Third World totaled US$855 million. Pakistan was the largest single recipient of this aid. These exports served political rather than economic ends, however. Almost all arms aid was free or transferred through credits that were later canceled.[27]

In 1978, arms exports were put on a commercial basis. As part of China's export promotion campaign, Chinese representatives began peddling arms to the Third World, where the cheapness, ruggedness, and relatively simple design of Chinese arms often proved attractive. Sales expanded rapidly, from 1 percent of all Chinese exports in 1978 to 5 percent between 1982 and 1986. Between 1983 and 1987, China sold some $6.5 billion in weapons, making it the world's sixth largest arms merchant, ranking behind the Soviet Union, the United States, France, Britain, and West Germany. In 1987, China sold 28 percent of all

Table 10–6 China's Petroleum Exports (in thousands of U.S. $)

1970	1975	1980	1985	1987
7,465	862,475	4,124,728	6,821,850	4,019,189

Source: CIA, *China: International Trade Annual Statistical Supplement,* EA 89-10007, IR 89-10009, February 1989, 2.

weapons purchased by developing countries, making it the largest arms exporter among developing countries (well ahead of the runner-up Brazil).[28] Purely commercial objectives were sometimes mixed with political ends, however. The sale of Silkworm anti-ship missiles to Iran in 1985 and 1986, for example, was influenced by a desire to firm up the Sino-Iranian link, and the sale of CSS-2 intermediate range ballistic missiles to Saudi Arabia in 1987 was influenced by a desire to lure away one of Taiwan's few remaining significant international supporters.[29] But even in these cases, the commercial motive was strong. Arms sales to Iran alone totaled $1.8 billion during the 1979–1989 Iran-Iraq war.[30]

The sale of labor services also became a significant source of foreign exchange during the 1980s. In 1979, the China Construction Engineering Corporation, set up in 1957 to oversee China's foreign aid projects, was reorganized and began marketing Chinese labor power abroad. Beijing hoped to replicate the successful experience of Korean, Pakistani, and Thai construction companies in the Middle East by drawing on China's abundance of cheap labor. By 1986, the earnings from such projects and service sales represented about 3 percent of all export earnings.

The expansion of China's merchant marine has been still another method of generating foreign exchange. Having Chinese ships carry more of China's exports saved foreign exchange, while carrying goods for foreigners—their exports to China, for example—earned exchange. The PRC began to build up its merchant marine began shortly after the break with the Soviet Union. Between 1961 and 1975, China added 150 ships to its fleet. Expansion accelerated sharply in the late 1970s. Between 1976 and 1978, China purchased 228 foreign ships. The growth of China's merchant fleet is illustrated by Table 10–7.

The Four Modernizations and the opening to the outside world have turned China into a major trading country. This is apparent when China's foreign trade is viewed as a percent of national income. In these terms, trade did not grow much between 1950 and 1980. During the 1980s, however, the importance of trade increased rapidly, rising from 15.6 percent in 1980 to 32.5 percent in 1988. This is illustrated by Table 10–8.

It is highly probable that China will continue to expand its foreign trade well into the twenty-first century. China's rich endowment of natural resources, its large industrial base, and its low labor costs give it strong comparative advantages. China will almost certainly be a major trading power in the emerging Pacific Rim economy.

Table 10–7 China's Merchant Fleet (in thousands of gross registered tons)

1975	1977	1978	1979	1980	1981	1982	1983	1984	1985
2,828	4,245	5,168	6,337	6,874	7,653	8,057	8,675	9,300	10,568

Source: United Nations, *Statistical Yearbook, 1985/86*, New York: U.N., 1988, 721.

Table 10–8   Foreign Trade as Percent of National Income

Year	Merchandise Trade*	National Income (N.I.)*	Trade ÷ N.I.
1952	6.46	58.9	11.0
1957	10.4	90.8	11.4
1959	14.9	122.2	12.2
1962	8.1	92.4	8.8
1966	12.7	158.6	8.0
1970	11.3	192.6	5.9
1975	29.0	250.3	11.6
1980	57.0	368.8	15.6
1985	206.7	740.0	29.4
1988	382.2	1177.0	32.5

*In billions *Renminbi*

Source: *Zhongguo tongji nianjian 1989* (China Statistical Yearbook 1989), Beijing: Guojia tongjiju, 1989, 29.

HONG KONG

The British Crown Colony of Hong Kong is the PRC's single largest source of foreign currency, providing 30 percent to 40 percent of all foreign exchange earnings. The continuation of this lucrative income source is a major Chinese concern in the 1990s.

The island of Hong Kong was ceded by China to Britain at the conclusion of the Opium War in 1842. Kowloon peninsula was ceded in 1860, and the New Territories were leased (but not ceded) to Britain for ninety-nine years in 1898. When the 1898 treaty expired in July 1997 the New Territories were to return to China. Without that hinterland, Hong Kong island and Kowloon peninsula would not be viable.

Hong Kong remained an economic backwater until after the Communist victory in 1949, when capital and human talent moved there from Shanghai and Canton. Throughout the post-1949 period, a combination of efficient, pro-business British colonial rule and Chinese entrepreneurial spirit and work ethic produced remarkable growth. By 1982, when negotiations between China and Britain on the status of Hong Kong began, Hong Kong had an affluent annual per capita income of about $6,000 and had emerged as one of the manufacturing, banking, and transport centers of the Pacific Basin.

The PRC derives foreign currency from Hong Kong in several ways. First, it sells large amounts of foods and miscellaneous manufactured goods to Hong Kong for freely convertible Hong Kong dollars. A large part of the foodstuffs, household commodities, electricity, and even water consumed by Hong Kong's 5.7 million inhabitants (as of 1988) came from the PRC. As one adage had it, Hong Kong is a very efficient machine for turning Chinese chickens and pigs into pounds sterling.

Hong Kong also serves as a major transit point for trade between China and other countries. Sixty percent of Chinese exports to Hong Kong were reexported in 1987, while 75 percent of China's imports from Hong Kong were from third countries.[31] In some cases political sensitivities precluded direct trade; e.g., as with South Africa, Israel, and until the late 1980s, South Korea and Taiwan. In other cases companies in Hong Kong can obtain sensitive items unavailable to China under COCOM regulations. As noted earlier, Hong Kong figures prominently in the PRC's technology acquisition efforts. In still other cases, repackaging in Hong Kong allows Chinese goods to enter crowded third country markets, such as the U.S. textile market, under Hong Kong labels and quotas.[32] Transshipment via Hong Kong also allows China to draw on the marketing expertise and experience of Hong Kong's astute businessmen.

As Table 10–9 indicates, Hong Kong is the PRC's largest trading partner, taking 36 percent of all China's exports in 1987 with a two-way trade of $22.8 billion. This compared to $16.5 billion in two-way trade with Japan, China's second largest trading partner. Moreover, China enjoys a large surplus in its trade with Hong Kong. The importance of Hong Kong to China are indicated by calculations by Y.C. Jao, according to which if Hong Kong were excluded from China's trade, between 1950 and 1980 China would have run deficits in twenty-five out of thirty years, totaling $15 billion. With Hong Kong, however, China showed deficits in only thirteen years, totaling $3 billion.[33]

Hong Kong Chinese remit substantial amounts of foreign currency to relatives in the PRC. Hong Kong businessmen also provide the single largest bloc of external investment in the PRC. Eighty percent of all foreign investment in China is by overseas Chinese, mostly from Hong Kong. PRC banks also operate actively in Hong Kong and transfer a significant portion of their foreign currency accounts to China. In 1986, for example, some 20 percent of U.S. dollar deposits in Hong Kong were

Table 10–9   China's Major Trading Partners, 1987

Imports	U.S. $ Billions	As % of Total	Exports	U.S. $ Billions	As % of Total
Japan	10.1	23%	Hong Kong	14.2	36%
Hong Kong	8.6	20	Japan	6.4	16
United States	4.8	11	United States	3.0	8
West Germany	3.1	7	West Germany	1.2	3
Soviet Union	1.3	3	Soviet Union	1.2	3

Source: CIA, *China: Economic Performance in 1987 and Outlook for 1988*, EA 88-10018, May 1988.

held by the Bank of China. Exact figures on the invisible flow of funds from Hong Kong to China are not available. Christopher Howe estimated, however, that in 1982 such invisible transfers amounted to $3.2 billion.[34] By 1992 that flow was certainly much larger.

The economic benefits derived by the PRC from Hong Kong are substantial and argue in favor of maintenance of the status quo. But Chinese policy toward Hong Kong is also subject to nationalist sentiments that work in the opposite direction. From a nationalist perspective, Hong Kong is a piece of Chinese territory seized by imperialists during China's century of humiliation. Now that China has "stood up," this blot on its national honor and sovereignty must be removed. Such sentiments were stated succinctly by Xinhua after British Prime Minister Margaret Thatcher's September 1982 discussions with Chinese officials in Beijing:

> Xianggang (Hong Kong) is a part of China's territory. The treaties in relation to the Xianggang area were concluded by the old British government and the Chinese government in the Qing Dynasty were unequal ones which have never been accepted by the Chinese people. It is a sacred mission of the Chinese government and people to claim sovereignty over Xianggang. This has consistently been the just stand of the Chinese people.[35]

Nationalist sentiments probably underlay the tough line followed by Beijing in its 1982–1984 negotiations with London over Hong Kong. During a meeting with Margaret Thatcher in September 1982, Deng Xiaoping told the British prime minister that agreement would have to be reached within two years, otherwise the PRC would unilaterally announce its plans for dealing with Hong Kong. Over the next two years Beijing forced London to negotiate on the basis of China's plan and timetable. London initially pushed for a continuing British administrative role after 1997, based in part on its contention that the 1842 and 1860 treaties had ceded Hong Kong island and Kowloon peninsula to Britain in perpetuity. Beijing insisted it would resume full sovereignty over *all* of Hong Kong after 1997, thereby ruling out any residual role for Britain. Beijing refused to accept the validity of any of the relevant treaties because (1) they had been imposed on China by military force and against its will and (2) they conferred completely unequal benefits and obligations on the signatory countries. (This doctrine of the invalidity of "unequal treaties" is not widely accepted by Western countries, but has won some support from Third World countries.) Britain successively acceded to Beijing's demands. Nor were the people of Hong Kong allowed to directly express their sentiments via a referendum. Critics of British negotiating behavior subsequently charged that London failed to play its ace—that is, to make clear a willingness to walk away from Hong Kong, leaving it entirely in Chinese hands, thereby triggering the probable rapid economic decline of Hong

Kong. Britain failed to do this, these critics charge, because it did not want to lose access to markets in the PRC by angering Beijing.[36] Defenders of British actions pointed out that London had no real choice given that Beijing insisted on Hong Kong's return and that Hong Kong was dependent on China for even its food and water.

Beijing was quite cognizant of the possibility that too inflexible an approach endangered continuation of the economic benefits China derived from Hong Kong. The prospect of Communist administration of Hong Kong could easily precipitate a flight of talent and capital that could send the economy into a tailspin. About 20 percent of Hong Kong's population are refugees from the PRC and have no wish to return to Communist rule. Middle-class professionals were concerned that CCP rule might mean loss of personal freedoms and professional independence. Many of Hong Kong's capitalists trusted the Communists once before, at the time of the "liberation" of Shanghai and Canton in 1949, only to experience the rapidity with which Communist pledges of cooperation with "patriotic capitalists" were forgotten once power was in Communist hands. Nor did prospects seem particularly good for making profits as usual under Communist rule.

The fact that a large portion of Hong Kong's capital assets are kept in liquid form is an indication of the readiness of many Hong Kong entrepreneurs to flee. Twice during the Anglo-Chinese negotiations when prospects for agreement dimmed, there were flights of capital from Hong Kong to offshore banking centers; sharp declines in the value of the Hong Kong dollar, real estate, and stocks; and sharp increases in emigration from Hong Kong. These panics were stabilized by joint British-Chinese actions, but the possibility of more grave repetitions remained. There are powerful economic and psychological factors that could easily cause flight from Hong Kong to snowball. Economically, once the exit from Hong Kong began, those who delayed too long could have to liquidate assets at very low prices. Selling out earlier might minimize losses, but each action made it likelier that others would follow suit. A panic psychology could set in. In other words, Hong Kong's prosperity is built on a fragile foundation. There was, and remains, the possibility that CCP actions would kill the goose that lays the golden egg.

Beijing attempted to reconcile its conflicting economic and nationalist interests through the concept of One Country, Two Systems, promulgated in May 1984. The central idea of this doctrine is that while the PRC is socialist, parts of it that for historic reasons are not currently under Beijing's administration, and thus are not socialist, might retain their existing capitalist social-economic systems for a long period of time after their incorporation into the PRC. Hong Kong and Taiwan were intended as the principal objects of this doctrine. Regarding Hong Kong, Beijing hoped to reassure its populace and foreign business that the return of Hong Kong to China in 1997 would not mean the suppression of capitalism and subjugation of Hong Kong to the rigors of Communist rule.

The concept of One Country, Two Systems was implicit in the December 19, 1984, Anglo-Chinese "Joint Declaration" on Hong Kong. This declaration consisted of a set of unilateral Chinese declarations, a unilateral British declaration, and several annexes. This arrangement was demanded by Beijing since it deemed Hong Kong a purely domestic matter and felt that regulation of those affairs by treaty was inappropriate. In its declaration, Beijing affirmed its intention to assume sovereignty over Hong Kong in 1997, but also to establish Hong Kong as a Special Administrative Region (SAR) of the PRC. The Hong Kong SAR was to enjoy a high degree of autonomy, with legislative, executive, and judicial powers exercised by "local inhabitants" approved by the central government. The Hong Kong SAR would also remain an economic entity separate from the PRC, with its own freely convertible currency, free port operating under separate customs laws, foreign consular representation, and immunity from taxation by the central government. Hong Kong's social and economic system and its lifestyle would remain unchanged for fifty years.[37]

The mechanisms through which the Hong Kong SAR was to be governed were laid out in a Basic Law drafted by a special committee of the National People's Congress (NPC) of the PRC. This committee began operations in July 1985. After several drafts and extensive consultation with people from Hong Kong, the committee finally promulgated the final Basic Law in February 1990.[38]

While containing many declarations about Hong Kong's future autonomy, the Basic Law provided few institutional safeguards of such autonomy. Only 20 percent (later to be expanded to 30 percent) of the sixty-member legislative council are to be directly elected. Hong Kong's governor is to be appointed by Beijing after selection by an 800-member election commission, about the origins of which the Basic Law said nothing. It is very likely that Beijing will exercise decisive influence on the composition of this governor election commission and the indirectly elected portion of the legislative council. The governor appoints and removes judges. The Standing Committee of China's NPC has the power to veto any law passed by the legislative council, to nullify any law in force in Hong Kong prior to 1997, to interpret and amend the Basic Law, and to decide to enforce particular PRC laws in Hong Kong. The governor is also empowered to remove any matter from the jurisdiction of Hong Kong's courts. Contacts between Hong Kong political groups and foreign organizations are prohibited, and key government posts may be held only by Hong Kong Chinese who do not have right of permanent residence in a foreign country. Nor were Deng Xiaoping's comments on the type of Hong Kong person who will be acceptable post-1997 administrators reassuring. Speaking to a delegation of prominent Hong Kong industrial and commercial leaders in June 1984, Deng said:

> Some requirements and qualifications should be established with regard to the administration of Hong Kong affairs by the people of Hong Kong. It must be required that patriots form the main body of administrators; that is, of the future government of Hong Kong....Who are patriots? The qualifications for a patriot are respect for the Chinese nation, sincere support for the motherland's resumption of sovereignty over Hong Kong, and a desire not to impair Hong Kong's prosperity and stability. Those who meet these requirements are patriots, whether they believe in capitalism or feudalism or even slavery.[39]

To skeptics, such words meant that a patriot was whoever Deng Xiaoping or his successor said was a patriot. In short, Hong Kong's post-1997 government is likely to be very responsive to Beijing's will, and Hong Kong's post-1997 autonomy will rest on that will.

While the Basic Law was being drafted, the CCP strengthened its organization in Hong Kong and increased its encouragement of, support for, and liaison with Communist and pro-Communist groups. Beijing also warned that Hong Kong would not be allowed to become a base for activities in opposition to the central government. Hong Kong would continue to enjoy freedom of the press, Beijing said, so long as it did not use that freedom to "harm China's sovereignty." The Xinhua News Agency office in Hong Kong was transformed into a shadow government, with ten departments corresponding to the organization of the Hong Kong government. This apparatus was apparently intended to take over should Hong Kong collapse before 1997.

The greatest danger to Hong Kong's future autonomy probably comes not from China's top leaders, who understand full well that Hong Kong is a goose that lays golden eggs, but from China's bureaucracies, which are prone to pursue narrower interests without regard to China's broad interest in maintaining Hong Kong's autonomy. A good example of this is the allocation of airline routes between Hong Kong and Chinese cities by the Civil Aviation Administration of China (CAAC). As China's aviation regulatory body, CAAC allocates air routes between Hong Kong and Chinese cities. Because of the large volume of travel between Hong Kong and China, these routes are typically quite lucrative. Unfortunately for CAAC and the Chinese airlines tied to it, many foreign travelers are reluctant to fly on PRC airlines because of poor safety and irregular service, and if allowed a choice, will choose a non-Chinese carrier. Such competition has been held to a minimum, however, by CAAC's refusal to increase the flights by Hong Kong–based airlines (primarily Cathay Pacific) into China, even though as of early 1989 flights by Chinese airlines between Chinese cities and Hong Kong outnumbered comparable flights by Hong Kong–based airlines by 8 to 1. This was in spite of the fact that Cathay Pacific flights operated at full capacity, while Chinese flights carried far fewer passengers. CAAC's objective, of course, is to earn additional foreign currency. In effect, PRC airlines are given an officially sponsored quasi-monopoly.[40] While understandable from the interests of CAAC, such practice raises concerns about the future of the free-market economy that has underlain Hong Kong's prosperity. If such cases proliferate with the growth of PRC influence in Hong Kong, it is easy to imagine how Hong Kong's market economy could be stifled by bureaucratic control as numerous Chinese agencies milk Hong Kong. Rather than try to function in such an environment, many of Hong Kong's capitalists would move elsewhere.

Beijing's handling of the Hong Kong issue has done little to assuage the fears of Hong Kong people. Emigration continues to mount. Between 1980 and 1986, an annual average of 20,600 people emigrated from Hong Kong. By 1990, the figure had risen to 54,000. If the flight of people and capital from Hong Kong accelerates as 1997 approaches, this will contribute to a decline of the Hong Kong economy.

CHINA'S DEVELOPMENT IN INTERNATIONAL PERSPECTIVE

China's development record is impressive when compared to those of other large, low-income countries. As Table 10–10 indicates, between 1960 and 1987 China achieved an average annual increase in per capita real output of 5.1 percent, a full percent higher than its nearest rival, Brazil. In terms of industrialization, China's performance is even more outstanding, having sustained per annum industrial growth of over 10 percent for several decades. Few other developing countries, large or small, have achieved this, and of those few, only Thailand and Nigeria had populations of over 25 million.[41] The success of China's industrialization effort is reflected in the proportionally larger size of its industrial sector.

When indicators of the quality of life of the ordinary person are considered, China's performance is more mixed. China's socialist system has enabled it to provide basic health services to broad segments of the population, a fact reflected in a substantially lower infant mortality rate and longer life expectancy than in other large, low-income countries. China has also achieved average levels of caloric intake approaching the satiated levels of developed countries. Yet it has also been characterized by periods of widespread famine.[42] In terms of enjoyment of consumer durables, China has also lagged behind most other large, low-income countries—a fact directly related to its rapid industrial growth. Education has been another area of weak Chinese performance. While ranking ahead of India and Egypt in basic literacy, China falls substantially behind Brazil, Indonesia, and Mexico.

Table 10–10 China's Development in International Perspective

	Average Annual Growth, Per Capita Real Product, 1960–87	Average Annual Growth, Total Real Product, 1960–87	Industrial Activity as % of GNP	Agriculture as % of GNP	Percent of Population That Is Urban	Illiteracy	Life Expectancy at Birth	Infant Mortality Rate Per 1,000 Live Births	Radio Receivers in Use Per 1,000 Population	Telephones Per 1,000 Population	Population Per Physician
China	5.1	7.1	40	41	21.1	30.7	69.4	32.5	140	.7	1,769
Brazil	4.1	6.6	29	10	75.4	22.2	64.9	63.2	365	8.8	1,632
India	1.6	3.8	19	28	27.1	59.2	57.9	98.8	78	.5	2,545
Indonesia	4.0	6.3	26	26	27.5	25.7	56	74.0	118	n.a	11,740
Egypt	3.6	6.0	31	19	47.9	55.5	60.6	85.3	313	2.8	760
Mexico	2.7	5.8	35	9	72.5	9.7	67.2	46.7	197	9.6	2,136

Sources: United Nations Conference on Trade and Development, *Handbook of International Trade and Development Statistics, 1988,* New York: UN, 1989, 514–17, 520–23, 430–33; United Nations, *Statistical Yearbook, 1985/86,* New York: U.N., 764–65.

Another distinctive characteristic of Chinese development is a comparatively low degree of urbanization despite a relatively high degree of industrialization. Seventy-eight percent of China's population is rural, while 41 percent of its gross national product is generated by agriculture. Most other comparable countries have seen a much greater shift of population from rural to urban areas. China has prevented such a shift through strict controls over residency. These controls have enabled China to avoid the large urban slums that plague other low-income countries, but have also contributed to massive rural underemployment and stunted the growth of the urban service sector, the latter being a major source of inconvenience to urban dwellers. China's control over population movement can also be seen as a denial of basic freedoms. In spite of the harsh conditions people face in urban slums, movement to those slums is often an economically rational choice for impoverished rural dwellers. There is little question that were residence controls lifted in China, large slums would soon appear around China's cities. That this has not happened may be seen as a denial of one road to self-betterment that many Chinese peasants would undoubtedly choose were that choice open to them.

Another relevant comparison is between PRC growth and growth rates achieved by other developed powers during their years of rapid industrialization. During the years from 1850 to 1890, Britain averaged annual real growth of 2.3 percent. During the years from 1891 to 1931, the United States averaged real growth of 3.3 percent per year. Between 1870 and 1910, Germany averaged 2.8 percent annually. Between 1928 and 1968 (excluding the war years), the Soviet Union averaged 6.5 percent annual real growth. Japan between 1946 and 1986 achieved annual real growth of 7.8 percent. According to Chinese statistics, between 1952 (when recovery from the civil war was basically completed) and 1988, the real value of China's total economic output grew at an average annual rate of 8.8 percent.[43]

The leaders of the PRC are proud of the relative success of China's development efforts. Beijing also touts this success to increase the appeal of Chinese advice and, during certain periods, of the Chinese model of development, to other developing countries. But the real standard against which China measures itself is not other Third World countries, but the advanced countries of the West. Overtaking these countries is the goal the PRC has set for itself. China's objective is to stand shoulder to shoulder with the most advanced countries of the world. This is a tall order.

When the PRC's aggregate economic output is compared with the developed countries, China lags far behind. As Table 10–11 indicates, in 1988 China's GNP was about 6.4 percent of U.S. GNP, 10.7 percent of Japan's, and 12.1 percent that of the Soviet Union. China's aggregate GNP was 43 percent larger than India's and 6 percent larger than

Table 10–11   Relative Size of PRC Economy, 1988

	PRC	USA	Japan	USSR	India	Brazil
GNP [U.S. $ Billions]	286	4,486.2	2,664	2,356.7	200	270
Per capita GNP	$280	$18,400	$21,820	$8,375	$250	$1,880
Total crude steel production (million metric tons)	52.2	80.2	98.3	161	11.1	21.4
Steel production (Kg/capita)	49	330	870	569	14	153
Total electricity production (million Kwh)	490,000	2,779,279	670,000	1,660,000	190,000	192,950
Electricity production (Kwh/capita)	460	11,430	5,490	5,675	240	1,310

Source: CIA, *The World Fact Handbook, 1988*, CPAS WF 88-001, May 1988, 31, 48, 108, 122, 216, 245.

Brazil's. In terms of per capita GNP, China registered 1.5 percent of the United States, 1.3 percent of Japan, and 3.3 of the Soviet level, but 12 percent higher than India. Brazil's per capita GNP was 6.7 times that of China. In terms of levels of production of basic industrial goods, China does somewhat better. In 1988, China's crude steel production was 65 percent of the U.S. level, 53 percent of Japan, 32.4 percent of the USSR, but 2.4 times Brazil's, and 4.7 times India's output. In terms of electricity production, China produced 17.6 percent, 73 percent, and 30 percent respectively of the U.S., Japanese, and Soviet levels, and about two-and-a-half times as much as either India or Brazil. In per capita terms, China's electrical production fell far behind the developed countries and Brazil, but was nearly double that of India.

ECONOMIC AND NATIONAL POWER

Creating propitious conditions for development has consistently been one of the overriding foreign policy goals of the PRC's leaders. This objective has profoundly influenced China's foreign relations. But Beijing has also had to balance the goal of economic development against other, often conflicting objectives, usually those having to do with national security or broad diplomatic goals. Moreover, PRC diplomacy is replete with instances in which Beijing sacrificed economic objectives to other interests. The decision to push through the rupture with the Soviet Union in the early 1960s, for example, inflicted heavy costs on China's development effort. The drive to create a China-led Third World revolutionary front in the 1960s, while it can be rationalized in terms of long-run Maoist-style development, certainly entailed major sacrifices of at least short-term economic interests. The commitment of substantial resources to foreign aid or the development of nuclear weapons also indicates the primacy of political over developmental objectives.

The most recent example of the primacy of political over narrowly economic concerns was the decision to use military force to crush the democracy movement in 1989, in spite of an anticipated adverse Western reaction. The adverse foreign reaction to the bloody repression of 1989 apparently exceeded the expectations of Deng Xiaoping. Nonetheless, he and other leaders had anticipated some negative reaction yet decided to use military force to crush dissent. Confronted by a challenge to their power, they decided to use all necessary force to crush that challenge. The negative economic consequences of that decision, whatever they were, would be tolerated.

The primacy of political over strictly economic goals is related to the relative ineffectiveness of foreign economic sanctions against China. U.S. containment inflicted heavy burdens on China's economy during the 1950s, but China refused to moderate its policy as sought by the United States. Instead it adopted even more radical, anti-United States policies. Ironically, U.S. containment policy achieved its fundamental objective of undermining the Sino-Soviet alliance. But, again ironically, by breaking with the USSR, Beijing again demonstrated the futility of economic sanctions (in this case Soviet) against China. Other, more limited, foreign efforts to pressure China via economic means have also failed. The U.S. effort between 1981 and 1982 to use Beijing's desire for U.S. economic support (and U.S. strategic support against the Soviet Union) to force China to accept an upgrading of relations between the United States and Taiwan backfired. Nor did Western sanctions following the June 1989 events in China lead to a reorientation in China's policy toward internal dissent.

China's relative invulnerability to economic pressures is rooted in the huge size and relatively self-contained nature of its economy. China needs foreign inputs to grow, but if it is willing to accept a somewhat lower rate of growth, it is able to get along well enough. Nationalist pride and revolutionary ideology, in turn, help create such a willingness to accept lower rates of growth.

But one should avoid simple answers. Arguably, U.S. containment worked over the long run. A desire to break out of containment and expand economic relations with the West was certainly one factor influencing China's abandonment of support for foreign revolutions. And while Beijing refused in 1981 and 1982 to countenance the reestablishment of official United States–Taiwan ties, it nonetheless accepted a formula that allowed indefinite continuation of U.S. arms sales to Taiwan. And if Beijing did not suspend the executions of dissidents in mid-1989 in response to Western pressure, at least it began conducting those executions secretly. China will also become increasingly vulnerable to economic pressure as it internationalizes its economy—as trade increases as a percentage of GNP, as imported technology and foreign capital play a greater role, and so on. Indeed, the fact that increased interdependence means increased vulnerability may well be one of the prime grounds on which China's conservatives oppose increased participation in the global economy.

The prospects for China's development are generally quite good. Dwight Perkins concluded that the PRC was positioned to replicate the development successes of such East Asian countries as Japan, Taiwan, South Korea, Singapore, and Hong Kong. In 1949, China's human resource endowment (a productive and education-seeking population with commercial instincts) was comparable to that of the other East Asian successes. Moreover, China's government instituted equalizing economic and social reforms—a key element of the successful East Asian model of development, according to Perkins. There were critical differences in 1949, however. The PRC's per capita income was much lower, and the government had only a weak commitment to outward-oriented economic policies and did not give top priority to economic development. By the late 1970s, however, China's per capita income and level of capital formation were roughly comparable to those of Taiwan and South Korea in the 1950s and to Japan in the early 1900s. Moreover, the Four Modernizations and the opening to the outside world meant adoption of policies comparable to those used by earlier East Asian successes. Important differences remain, notably China's socialist system and central planning. Yet the changes were adequate to enable China to roughly double its GNP between 1977 and 1985—an annual growth rate of about 8 percent. This was comparable to the 9 percent to 10 percent achieved by the other East Asian successes from the 1950s to the 1970s. Given the continuation of present policies, Perkins concludes that these rates of growth can be sustained, and that China will indeed become Asia's next "economic giant."[44]

Greater economic power will allow China to wield greater international influence. While still far behind the Western countries in terms of per capita wealth, China's aggregate wealth will, for example, be great enough to permit the maintenance of substantial armed forces. As Deng Xiaoping pointed out in 1984, given recent rates of growth, if China spent only 5 percent of its GNP on defense by the year 2000, that would amount to $50 billion. At that point, Deng said, "China will be truly powerful, exerting a much greater influence in the world."[45]

How will China use its growing economic power to achieve national objectives? It will almost certainly use foreign aid, trade, and investment to influence the policies of other countries. In the past China sometimes used these instruments in a coercive fashion. Albania provides a good example of this. Albania was one of China's closest allies throughout the 1960s. During the 1970s, however, Albania's ruler Enver Hoxa became critical of China's deepening relation with the United States and, more importantly from Albania's position, Beijing's moves toward rapprochement with Yugoslavia. As Albanian criticism of Chinese foreign policy grew, Beijing began slowing aid deliveries. When Albanian criticism became public, Chinese aid was suspended. Hoxa commented in his diary in September 1976:

> We want, we have tried, and we shall go on trying to have friendship with China, but friendship on the Marxist-Leninist road and no other. We reject friendship under slavery, under pressure, under blackmail, whether with China or anyone else. The Chinese leaders are acting like the leaders of a "great state." They think, "The Albanians fell out with the Soviet Union because they had us, and if they fall out with us, too, they will go back to the Soviets." Therefore they say: "Either with us or the Soviets, it is all the same, the Albanians are done for." But to hell with them! We shall fight against all this trash, because we are Albanian Marxist-Leninists and on our correct course we shall always triumph![46]

China has also used trade to achieve political ends. The clearest and most important example of this involved relations with Japan in the late 1950s. As Chinese foreign policy entered its moderate period in 1954 and 1955, Beijing showed increased interest in expanding ties with Japan. The Liberal Democratic governments of prime ministers Ichiro Hatayama and Tanzan Ishibashi responded positively, and Sino-Japanese trade began to expand rapidly—from $53 million in 1953 to $150 million in 1956. Beijing systematically manipulated this trade to pressure the Japanese government to increase the level of political-diplomatic relations with China. Simultaneously it expanded its people-to-people diplomacy to the same end.[47]

In 1957, Nobusuke Kishi was elected prime minister. Kishi favored expanded trade with China, but he also favored strengthened ties with the United States. Even more objectionable from Beijing's point of view, Kishi favored closer relations with Nationalist China. When Kishi visited Chiang Kai-shek in Taiwan, Beijing's reaction was extreme. It cancelled plans to hold a trade fair in Japan and stalled negotiations for a new trade agreement. Chinese pressure increased as Japan approached new general elections in May 1958. Contracts were cancelled. Japanese fishing vessels were harassed. Sino-Japanese trade plummeted and Chinese propaganda intensified in a clear Chinese effort to influence the outcome of Japan's elections. When Kishi and the LDP won the 1958 elections, Beijing continued its efforts to punish Japan. It encouraged a boycott of Japanese goods in Southeast Asia, while stepping up export of its own goods to that region in an effort to displace Japanese goods. Beijing's campaign against Japan continued until Kishi resigned as prime minister in 1960. The apparent intent of these activities was to discredit Kishi and the LDP, help the Japan Socialist Party (JSP), and force the LDP government to substantially revise its foreign policy. Beijing's actions backfired. Support for the JSP and for various pro-PRC lobbies in

Japan began to decline and Japanese attitudes toward China hardened.

Even without such outright use of economic instruments to influence other countries, China's growing economic power and its growing involvement in the world economy will create many conflicts of economic interest. Chinese goods will increasingly compete with those of other low–labor cost, exporting countries. Its claim on the resources of multilateral international organizations will increase, diminishing the resources available to other Third World borrowers. Its cycles of import boom and retrenchment will continue to inflict hardships on foreign traders and investors. China will continue to push for unlimited access to U.S. and Western technology—even for a dismantling of the COCOM structure. The expansion of China's trade will also make it more vulnerable to foreign protectionism. Protectionism poses perhaps the greatest danger to China's continued rapid development, and Beijing will strenuously oppose all efforts to limit Chinese access to foreign markets, even while continuing to narrowly limit Chinese access to its own markets.

There is also the question of how China will relate to the emerging Pacific Basin economy. As Japan emerges as the dominant economic power in the Western Pacific, and as interdependency among all the capitalist countries of the Pacific Basin increases and takes organized forms, China will have to sort out its relations with the other nations of the Pacific community. China will almost certainly participate in this emerging community. But the extent of participation will be controversial within China, and conditions of participation will be difficult for China and its foreign partners to agree upon.[48]

NOTES

1. Regarding the general problem of foreign technology and Chinese economic development, see Richard P. Suttmeier, *Science, Technology and China's Drive for Modernization*, Stanford, Calif.: Hoover Institute Press, 1980; E. E. Buyer, *China Takes Off: Technology Transfer and Modernization*, Seattle: University of Washington Press, 1986; Huang Fangyi, "China's Introduction of Foreign Technology and External Trade: Analysis and Options," *Asian Survey*, vol. xxvii, no. 5 (May 1987), 577–94; Denis F. Simon, "The Evolving Role of Technology Transfer in China's Modernization," *China's Economy Looks Toward the Year 2000*, vol. 2, Economic Openness in Modernizing China, Selected Papers Submitted to the Joint Economic Committee, U.S. Congress, 99th Congress, 2nd Session, May 21, 1986, 254–86.

2. Hans Heymann, Jr., "Acquisition and Diffusion of Technology in China," *China: A Reassessment of the Economy*, A Compendium of Papers Submitted to the Joint Economic Committee, Congress of the United States, 94th Congress, 1st Session, July 10, 1975, 680–81, 696–707; William W. Whitson, "China's Quest for Technology," *Problems of Communism*, vol. 12, no. 4 (July–August 1973), 16–29.

3. State Science and Technology Commission of the PRC, *Guide to China's Science and Technology Policy*, 1987, White Paper on Science and Technology no. 2, Beijing: International Academic Publishers, New York: Pergamon, 1988, 354.

4. Regarding Sino-U.S. educational exchanges, see David M. Lampton, *A Relationship Restored: Trends in U.S.-China Educational Exchange, 1978–1984*, Washington, D.C.: National Academy Press, 1986; Leo Orleans, *Chinese Students in America: Policies, Issues, and Numbers*, Washington, D.C.: National Academy Press, 1988; Harold W. Jacobson, *The Educational System and Academic and Technological Exchanges of the PRC*, May 6, 1980, United States Information and Communications Agency.

5. *Guide to China's Science and Technology Policy*, 351–54.

6. P.S. Ho and Ralph W. Hunenemann, *China's Open Door Policy: The Quest for Foreign Technology and Capital*, Vancouver: University of British Columbia Press, 1984, 13–20.

7. "Enigmatic Espionage by Old Pros," *Insight*, March 14, 1988, 30–31. Other sources on Chinese covert operations include Nayan Chanda, "Diplomatic Tit-for-Tat," *FEER*, January 19, 1989, 22; Simon, "The Evolving Role of Technology Transfer in China's Modernization," 264; Jeffrey T. Richelson, *Foreign Intelligence Organizations*, Cambridge, Mass.: Ballinger, 1988, 297–99.

8. World Bank, *China: Long-Term Development Issues and Options*, Washington, D.C.: World Bank, 1985, 112–14. Regarding China's problems of absorption see Office of Technology Assessment, *Technology Transfer to China*, OTA-ISC-340, Washington, D.C.: U.S. Government Printing Office, 1987; Heymann, "Acquisition and Diffusion of Technology in China."

9. Regarding China's borrowing policies during the Maoist years, see David L. Denny, "International Finance in the People's Republic of China," *China: A Reassessment of the Economy*, 653–77.

10. Regarding China's political use of tourism, see Herbert Passim, *China's Cultural Diplomacy*, New York: Praeger, 1962.

11. "Foreign Trade and Tourism," *Beijing Review*, vol. 32, no. 7–8, (February 13–26, 1989), 28–31.

12. One source dealing with this issue is A. Doak Barnett, *China's Economy in Global Perspective*, Washington, D.C.: Brookings Institution, 1981, 220.

13. Regarding the shifts in policy toward the overseas Chinese in the late 1970s, see C.Y. Change, "Overseas Chinese in China's Policy," *China Quarterly*, no. 82 (June 1980), 281–303. Regarding Chinese policy toward the overseas Chinese more generally, see Stephen Fitzgerald, *China and the Overseas Chinese*, Cambridge: Cambridge University Press, 1972; Leo Suryadinata, *China and the ASEAN States: The Ethnic Chinese Dimension*, Singapore: Singapore University Press, 1985.

14. George T. Yu, *China and Tanzania: A Study in Cooperative Interaction*, Berkeley: University of California Press, 1970. Regarding the Tanzam railway, see Martin Bailey, *Freedom Railway: China and the Tanzania-Zambia Link*, London: Collins, 1976. Regarding Chinese aid to Africa generally, see Wei Liang-tsai, *Peking Versus Taipei in Africa, 1960–1978*, Asia and World Monograph Series, no. 25 (April 1982), Taibei: The Asia and World Institute.

15. Sources on China's foreign aid include Milton Kovner, "Communist China's Foreign Aid to Less Developed Countries," *An Economic Profile of Mainland China*, vol. 2, External Economic Relations, Studies Prepared for the Joint Economic Committee, Congress of the United States, 90th Congress, 1st Session, February 1, 1967, 609–20; Leo Tansky, "Chinese Foreign Aid," *People's Republic of China: An Economic Assessment*, A Compendium of Papers Submitted to the Joint Economic Committee of the U.S. Congress, 92nd Congress, 2nd Session, May 18, 1972, 371–82; Carol Fogarty, "Chinese Relations with the Third World," *Chinese Economy Post Mao*, A Compendium of Papers Submitted to the Joint Economic Committee, Congress of the United States, 95th Congress, 2nd Session, vol. I, November 9, 1978, 851–59; John F. Copper, *China's Foreign Aid: An Instrument of Peking's Foreign Policy*, Lexington, Mass.: D.C. Heath, 1976; John F. Copper, "China's Foreign Aid Program: An Analysis and Update," *China's Economy Looks Toward the Year 2000*, vol. 2, 499–519; Wolfgang Bartke, *China's Economic Aid*, London: C. Hurst, 1975; King C. Chen, "Communist China's Relations with the Third World," *The Foreign Policy of China*, King C. Chen, ed., Roseland, N.J.: East-West Who?, 1972, 406–9; Harry Harding, "China and the Third World," in *The China Factor: Sino-American Relations and the Global Scene*, Englewood Cliffs, N.J.: Prentice Hall, 1981, 273–75. For documents regarding the principles underlying PRC aid in the 1950s and 1960s, see Weinberg Chai, *The Foreign Relations of the People's Republic of China*, Toronto: Capricorn, 1972, 210–34.

16. See Copper, "China's Foreign Aid," *China's Economy Looks Toward the Year 2000*, vol. 2, 501–2.

17. "China's Foreign Trade in Past 40 Years," *Beijing Review*, vol. 32, no. 40, October 2–8, 1989), 11.

18. World Bank, *World Development Report 1990: Poverty*, New York: Oxford University Press, 1990, 216.

19. Alexander Eckstein, *Communist China's Economic Growth and Foreign Trade*, New York: McGraw-Hill, 1966, 87–91; Nai-Ruenn Chen, "China's Foreign Trade, 1950–1974," *China: A Reassessment of the Economy*, 617–52. Other sources on foreign trade are Feng-hua Mah, *The Foreign Trade of Mainland China*, Chicago: Aldine-Atherton, 1971; Robert L. Price, "International Trade of Communist China, 1950–1965," *An Economic Profile of Mainland China*, vol. 2, 579–608; A.H. Usack and R.E. Batsavage," "The International Trade of the People's Republic of China," *The People's Republic of China: An Economic Assessment*, 335–70; Gene T. Hsiao, *The Foreign Trade of China: Policy, Law, and Practice*, Berkeley: University of California Press, 1978.

20. Eckstein, *Communist China's Economic Growth and Foreign Trade*, 89–90. Also Y.Y. Kueh, "China's New Agricultural Policy Program: Major Economic Consequences, 1979–1983," *Journal of Comparative Economics*, vol. 8, no. 4 (December 1984), 353–75. Regarding China's food imports, see Y.Y. Kueh, "China's Food Balance and the World Grain Trade: Projections for 1985, 1990, and 2000," *Asian Survey*, vol. xxiv, no. 12 (December 1984), 1247–74.

21. Harry Harding, *China's Second Revolution*, Washington, D.C.: Brookings Institution, 1987, 140.

22. Regarding the changing composition of China's trade, see Nai-Ruenn Chen, "China's Foreign Trade, 1950–1974,"; A. Doak Barnett, *China's Economy in Global Perspective*, Washington, D.C.: Brookings Institution, 1981, 171–83; Harding, *China's Second Revolution*, 139–49.

23. Regarding China's pre-1949 trade, see Foster Rhea Dulles, *The Old China Trade*, Boston: Houghton Mifflin, 1930; Albert Feuerwerker, "Economic Trends, 1912–1949," *The Cambridge History of China*, vol. 12, Republic China 1912–1949, Part I, John K. Fairbank, ed., Cambridge: Cambridge University Press, 1983, 116–27; William Burke, *The China Trade*, Federal Reserve Bank of San Francisco, Monthly Review Supplement/1972, 3–15.

24. Regarding the international politics of China's petroleum industry, see Kim Woodard, *The International Energy Relations of China*, Stanford, Calif.: Stanford University Press, 1980; Selig S. Harrison, *China, Oil, and Asia: Conflict Ahead?*, New York: Columbia University Press, 1977; Tatsu Kombara, "The Petroleum Industry in China," *China Quarterly*, no. 60 (December 1974), 699–719; Chu-yuan Cheng, *China's Petroleum Industry: Output Growth and Export Potential*, New York: Praeger, 1976; Feredian Fesharaki and David Fridley, *China's Petroleum Industry in the International Context*, Boulder, Colo.: Westview, 1986.

25. Regarding Chinese policy toward OPEC, see Woodard, *International Energy Relations of China*, 242–50.

26. For OPEC prices, see Central Intelligence Agency, *Economic and Energy Indicators*, DI, EEI, 84-016, August 3, 1984, 11, and CIA, *International Energy Statistical Review*, DI IESR, 89-007, July 25, 1989, 13.

27. Regarding Chinese arms transfers during the pre-1978 period, see John F. Copper, "China's Military Assistance," in *Communist Nations Military Assistance*, John Copper and Daniel S. Papp, eds., Boulder, Colo.: Westview, 1983., 96–125; National Foreign Assessment Center, *Communist Aid Activities in Non-Communist Less Developed Countries, 1979 and 1957–1979*, October 1980, ER-80-10318U; U.S. Arms Control and Disarmament Agency, *World Military Expenditures and Arms Transfers, 1966–1975*, USACDA document 90, Washington, D.C.: U.S. Government Printing Office, 1976.

28. Regarding the post-1978 period, see U.S. Arms Control and Disarmament Agency, *World Military Expenditures and Arms Transfers, 1988*, Washington, D.C.: U.S. Government Printing Office, 1989, 10–11, 111; Stockholm International Peace Research Institute

(SIPRI), *SIPRI Yearbook 1989: World Armaments and Disarmament*, New York: Oxford University Press, 1989, 199; Anne Gelks and Gerald Segal, *China and the Arms Trade*, New York: St. Martin's Press, 1985; Ya-chun Chang, "Communist China's Arms Exports," *Issues and Studies*, vol. 23, no. 9 (September 1987), 8–11.

29. *The New York Times* October 23, 1987, 1; *Christian Science Monitor*, March 30, 1988, 11. Regarding the CSS-2 sale, see Yitzhak Shichor, *East Wind Over Arabia: Origins and Implications of the Sino-Saudi Missile Deal*, China Research Monograph no. 35, Berkeley: University of California Press, 1989.

30. SIPRI, *Yearbook*, 21. Other sources give higher estimates of Chinese arms sales to Iran. The Far Eastern Economic Review, *Asia Yearbook 1989*, 17, for example, says that they may have amounted to US$1 billion per year throughout the war. North Korean exports may account for some of the discrepancy. North Korea was Iran's major weapons supplier, and some of the arms it sold were Chinese manufactured.

31. "Hong Kong and China's Trade Interdependence," *Asian Wall Street Journal*, December 22, 1986.

32. This is a source of conflict between China and the United States. According to the United States, Chinese goods reexported through Hong Kong are considered PRC exports. According to this point of view, China enjoys a $2.1 billion dollar surplus in its merchandise trade with the United States. According to Beijing, goods exported by Hong Kong companies are Hong Kong goods. PRC exports are considerably lower according to this method of calculation and, using it, the PRC has a $2.01 billion dollar deficit in its merchandise trade with the United States.

33. Y.C. Jao, "Hong Kong's Role in Financing China's Modernization," in *China and Hong Kong: The Economic Nexus*, A.J. Youngson, ed., Hong Kong: Oxford University Press, 1983. Other sources regarding economic ties between Hong Kong and China include Colina MacDougall Lupton, Hong Kong's Role in Sino-Western Trade," in *China's Trade with the West*, 175–208; Robert G. Sutter, "Hong Kong's Future and Its Implications for the United States," in *China's Economy Looks Toward the Year 2000*, vol. 2, 371–84; Chalmers Johnson, "The Mousetrapping of Hong Kong: A Game in Which Nobody Wins," *Asian Survey*, vol. xxiv, no. 9 (September 1984), 887–909.

34. Christopher Howe, "Growth, Public Policy and Hong Kong's Economic Relationship with China," *China Quarterly*, no. 95 (September 1983), 529–33.

35. "China's Stand on Hong Kong," *China and the World*, no. 3, Beijing: Beijing Review, 1983, 90–100. Regarding Chinese policy toward Hong Kong in an earlier period, see Gary Catron, "Hong Kong and Chinese Foreign Policy, 1955–1960," *China Quarterly*, no. 51 (July–September 1972), 406–24.

36. Jurgen Domes and Yu-ming Shaw, eds., *Hong Kong: A Chinese and International Concern*, Boulder, Colo.: Westview, 1988; Hungdah Chiu, et al., ed., *The Future of Hong Kong: Toward 1997 and Beyond*, New York: Quorum Books, 1987. George L. Hicks, *Hong Kong Count-Down*, Hong Kong: Writers and Publishers Cooperative, 1989. Regarding the early rounds of the Hong Kong negotiations, see David Bonavia, *Hong Kong 1997*, Hong Kong: South China Morning Post, 1983.

37. *The New York Times*, September 27, 1984, A 14.

38. The text is in *China Quarterly*, no. 122 (June 1990), 372–400.

39. Deng Xiaoping, *Fundamental Issues in Present-Day China*, Beijing: Foreign Languages Press, 1987, 52.

40. Michael Westlake, "Rights of Passage," *FEER*, February 23, 1989, 68–70.

41. World Bank, *China: Socialist Economic Development*, Annex D: Challenges and Achievements in Industry, Washington, D.C.: World Bank, 1983, 11.

42. Nick Eberstadt, "Material Poverty in the PRC in International Perspective," *China's Economy Looks Toward the Year 2000*, vol. 1: The Four Modernizations, Selected Papers Presented to the Joint Economic Committee, Congress of the United States, May 21, 1986, 263–324.

43. Xie Minggan, *Zhongguo jingji fazhan sishi nian* (Forty Years of Chinese Economic Development), Qinhuangdao: Renmin chubanshe, 1990, 25. Some economists question the veracity of Chinese economic statistics. The figures for other countries are from standard handbooks of economic statistics.

44. Dwight H. Perkins, *China: Asia's Next Economic Giant?* Seattle: University of Washington Press, 1986.

45. Cited in Harding, *China's Second Revolution*, 245.

46. See Enver Hoxa, *Reflections on China, II. 1973-1977: Extracts from the Political Diary*, Tirana: The 8 Nentori Publishing House, 1979, 277-78. Vol. I covers the 1962-1972 period. For Beijing's view of its escalating dispute with Albania, see "Huang Hua's Report on the World Situation," (July 30, 1977), *Issues and Studies*, vol. xiii, no. 12 (December 1977), 81-85. Also regarding the cutoff of aid to Albania and Vietnam, see John F. Copper, *China's Economic Aid in 1978*, Occasional Prints/Reprints Series in Contemporary Asian Studies, University of Maryland Law School, no. 8, 1981. Regarding the Sino-Albanian relation generally, see Elez Biberaj, *Albania and China: A Study of an Unequal Alliance*, Boulder, Colo.: Westview, 1986.

47. Regarding China's economic offensive against Japan in the late 1950s, see A. Doak Barnett, *China and the Major Powers in East Asia*, Washington: Brookings, 1977, 101-3; Jerome Alan Cohen, "Chinese Law and Sino-American Trade," in *China Trade Prospects and U.S. Policy*, Jerome A. Cohen, et al., ed., New York: Praeger, 1971, 170; Shigeharu Matsumoto, "Japan and China, Domestic and Foreign Influences on Japan's Policy," *Policies Toward China: Views from Six Continents*, A.M. Halperin, ed., New York: McGraw-Hill, 1965, 132-34.

48. Regarding the implications of China's growing economic power, see Nicholas R. Lardy, *China's Entry into the World Economy: Implications for Northeast Asia and the U.S.*, New York: University Press of America, 1987; Dwight H. Perkins, "The International Consequences of China's Economic Development," in *The China Factor*, Richard Solomon, ed., New York: Prentice Hall, 1981, 114-36.

Part Five

China's National Security

Chapter Eleven

China's International Use of Military Force

THE POLITICAL OBJECTIVES SOUGHT BY MILITARY MEANS

This part of the text is concerned with the circumstances under which PRC leaders have decided to use military force as an instrument of foreign policy and the ways in which such force was employed. China's leaders have decided a dozen or so times to employ military force to influence China's relations with foreign countries. This has taken various forms, ranging from month-long punitive expeditions against India and Vietnam, to protracted high-intensity but geographically limited war with the United States in Korea, to mobilizations on China's borders with Laos, India, and Vietnam to influence developments in those regions, to amphibious operations across the high seas to seize contested territory in the South China Sea. These decisions to use military force have not been made recklessly, but they were made readily enough. China's leaders have viewed military force as an indispensable instrument of foreign policy, and when they have concluded that the risks and costs of military inaction were greater than those of military action, they have been ready to order military moves. Instances of PRC use of military force are listed in Table 11-1.

In many instances China's military moves have been closely tied to diplomatic negotiations. Beijing has frequently viewed military action and negotiation as complementary instruments. During the last two years of the Korean conflict, for instance, military offensives by Chinese forces were closely linked to armistice talks underway at Panmunjom. As we saw in Chapter Two, the decision to bombard Quemoy in 1958 was rooted in Beijing's desire to puncture the American arrogance perceived at the ambassadorial talks in Warsaw. The mobilization opposite Laos in 1962 was designed to bolster China's efforts at the Geneva conference to negotiate a neutralization of Laos. And the entire chronicle of military pressure on India has been part of Beijing's efforts to negotiate a satisfactory territorial settlement with that country.

China's leaders maintain, as do those of virtually every country, that they have acted in an entirely defensive manner and resorted to military force only in self-defense. Of the times when China has used force, Beijing argues, in only two instances did Chinese forces enter foreign, non-Chinese, territory; i.e., in Korea from 1950 to 1953 and in Vietnam in 1979. In both of those cases, China faced a clear and imminent danger to its national security from a hostile superpower. In all other cases China's forces have not left Chinese territory, albeit, in some cases, that Chinese territory was occupied by foreign forces—in the Taiwan Straits, along the Sino-Indian and the Sino-Soviet borders, and in the South China Sea. This self-perception of China as a pacific, non-threatening country that wishes nothing more than to be allowed to live in peace with its neighbors is extremely common in China, among both the elite and ordinary people.

Several authoritative American analysts have agreed that China has used military force in an essentially defensive fashion. These analysts

Table 11–1 China's International Use of Military Force

1950–1953	Three-year war with United States/United Nations in Korea
1954, 1958	Artillery bombardment of Quemoy and Matzu in circumstances certain to involve the United States
1960–1961	Unpublicized incursions into Burma against KMT remnants with consent of Burma government
1961–1968	Extensive military construction of roads and anti-aircraft protection of roads in northern and eastern Laos
1962	Mobilization in South China to force "neutralization" of Laos
1962	One-month war with India
1965	Mobilization on Indian border to relieve Indian pressure on Pakistan during Indo-Pakistani war
1964–1970	Confrontation with United States over Vietnam; large deployment to North Vietnam
1969	Border confrontation with the Soviet Union
1974	Seizure of western Paracel Islands from South Vietnam
1978	Deployment of armed fishing vessels to Japanese-held Sengaku islands during treaty negotiations with Japan
1979	One-month war with Vietnam
1962–1988	Border confrontation and sporadic skirmishes with India
1979–1988	Border confrontation and sporadic skirmishes with Vietnam
1988	Seizure of islands in Spratly archipelago

argue that China's leaders have been deeply influenced by memories of foreign aggression against China during the century of National Humiliation and have spoken exclusively in terms of national defense. With few exceptions, China's use of military force against other nations has been closely tied to perceptions of threat to China. Moreover, the military doctrine and force structure of the PLA has consistently been defensive in orientation, geared to dealing with foreign invaders. The PLA has had very limited capability to conduct operations beyond China's borders. Finally, China's leaders were very cognizant of the overwhelming superiority of the American and Soviet forces confronting China, and moved cautiously to avoid a confrontation with either superpower. Only when pushed to the wall did China strike back.[1]

The image of an essentially defensive China contrasts starkly with the image of an aggressive "Red China" dominant in the United States in the 1950s and 1960s. Nor are the perceptions of a benign, defensive China uniform among its neighbors. At least as common among China's neighbors are deep fears of Chinese power and the belief that such fears are justified by the PRC's past behavior.

China's past revolutionism is one reason for this regional fear of China. As we saw in Chapter Six, while China has not employed its own military forces as agents of foreign revolution (except as occasional advisers and trainers), for a long time it did provide substantial assistance to insurgencies in various South and Southeast Asian countries.

Regional fears of China are also grounded in the large disparity between China's military capabilities and those of its neighbors, a gap illustrated in Table 11–2. While China's military capabilities have been dwarfed by those of the superpowers, they have towered over other regional actors. This, together with Beijing's pragmatic willingness to use military force, inspires apprehension in capitals across Asia.

The fact that China has often taken the initiative in its military conflicts with other nations—the fact that its forces sometimes "shot first"—has also strongly influenced foreign perceptions. In the Taiwan Strait in 1954 and 1958, in the 1962 war with India, in the confrontation on the Ussuri River in 1969, and again in the confrontation with Vietnam in 1979, China took the initiative in opening at least the expanded stage of the conflict. But again the situation is not simple. Since the 1930s, CCP military thinking has been dominated by the concept of "active defense," which consists of taking tactically offensive action within a strategically defensive situation. According to this concept, the best way to prevent attack by an aggressor, or to defend against an aggressive invasion once it is underway, is to undertake limited offensive operations designed to disrupt the aggressor's preparations while wearing down his strength. This should be done by creating tactical circumstances favorable to successful

Table 11–2 Relative Conventional Military Capabilities

	PRC	Taiwan	India	Vietnam	Japan
Total size of armed forces	3,030,000	370,000	1,262,000	1,052,000	249,000
Size of reserves	1,200,000	1,657,500	460,000	4–5 million	48,400
Size of army	2,300,000	270,000	1,100,000	900,000	156,200
Number of tanks	9,200	584	3,250	1,600	1,222
Artillery (towed, self-propelled, and multiple rocket launchers)	18,300	1,375	4,120	n.a.*	870
Combat aircraft	5,894	536	833	250	473
Major naval combatants	55	34	27 (including 2 aircraft carriers)	7	68
Submarines	93	4	19	0	15
Naval infantry	6,000	30,000	1,000	27,000	0

*n.a. = not available.

Source: *The Military Balance 1990–1991*, London: International Institute of Strategic Studies, 1991.

conduct of quick-decision battles that sap the aggressor's strength, shake his confidence, and force him to restock and replenish his own forces while adding to the material stockpiles of the defending forces. The opposite of active defense is passive defense, which entails merely preparing to resist an aggressor's attack.[2]

The concept of active defense has deeply influenced PRC efforts to deter foreign attacks. Beijing has frequently acted upon the assumption that the best way to deter is not by passively awaiting enemy attack, but by inflicting controlled blows designed to exploit the aggressor's vulnerabilities and keep him off balance. Sharp controlled blows, executed in carefully engineered situations in which China's forces enjoy local superiority, may cause a potential aggressor to stop and come to his senses. Passivity, on the other hand, will probably be taken for weakness, further emboldening the aggressor. Thus, tactically offensive moves initiated by China may, from the Chinese perspective, be essentially defensive. In line with this idea, China's leaders maintain that all of their international uses of military force have been defensive. More important than who opened fire on a particular day, they would argue, is the question of who is attempting to encroach on whose national territory. In all cases, Beijing maintains, it has been China's territory that has been threatened by other states.

A topology more complex than two categories of aggression and defense is required to analyze China's decisions to use military force. In terms of the goals underlying China's use of military force, five categories can be identified: (1) deterring superpower attack against China; (2) defending Chinese territory against encroachment; (3) bringing "lost"

Chinese territory under Beijing's control; (4) enhancing regional influence; and (5) enhancing China's global stature. These categories are not mutually exclusive. Several have been simultaneously involved in most Chinese decisions to use force.

Although Beijing has settled territorial conflicts with many of its neighbors by peaceful means, in several instances it has employed military force in attempts to recover territory that it deems Chinese. The bombardment of the Offshore Islands in 1954 and 1958 was partially motivated by the desire to prepare conditions for the liberation of Taiwan by driving a wedge between the Nationalists and the United States. The 1974 and 1988–1989 operations in the South China Sea also fall into this category. China's maritime claims, especially those in the South China Sea, will probably be among those pressed most vigorously by Beijing during the 1990s.

Figure 11–1 shows China's extensive maritime claims. In the Yellow and East China seas these claims are based on the continental shelf principle, which holds that the submarine natural prolongation of land territory to the outer edge of the continental margin belongs to the contiguous state. This principle places China's maritime territory well beyond the mid-line claimed as the international boundary by the Koreas and Japan. In the South China Sea, China claims virtually all of the twenty large islands, and 2,500 reefs, shoals, sandbanks, and cays, as well as the entire seabed, on the basis of historical use and administration. The claims and counterclaims in all of these seas are highly contentious because of the rich petroleum resources that lie under those sea floors.[3]

A desire to enhance regional influence has frequently entered into Beijing's decisions to use or threaten to use force. Beijing has sought to demonstrate its ability to help its foreign friends, thereby demonstrating China's value as an ally. The decision for war with Vietnam in 1979 (discussed more fully shortly), for example, involved a desire to punish Vietnam for toppling China's Cambodian clients and to encourage Thailand to oppose Vietnam's occupation of Cambodia by demonstrating China's credibility as a protector against Vietnam.

Efforts at regional influence have often involved threats to use force. The mobilization of Chinese forces in south China to influence events in Laos from 1960 to 1962, again during the Indo-Pakistan war of September 1965 to help Pakistan by preventing India from shifting forces from its eastern front to the western front, and again adjacent to North Vietnam in 1965 and 1966 are examples of this. Such efforts at regional influence have gone beyond considerations of countering superpower threats to China—although such considerations have sometimes been involved. The support for Pakistan in 1965, for example, was rooted in a desire to maintain a favorable balance of power in South Asia, while the push for Laotian neutralization in 1962

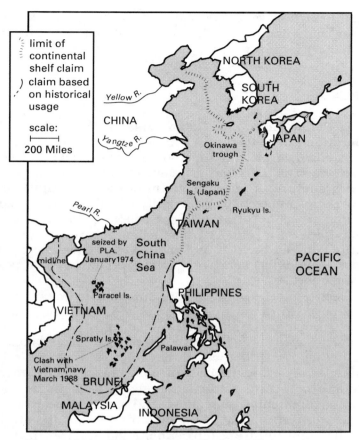

Figure 11–1   China's Maritime Territorial Claims

was linked to the desire to sustain the momentum of the revolutionary advance in South Vietnam.

Enhancement of global status has been an amorphous but important objective. China's historical experience has convinced its leaders that the established international order is a rough-and-tumble place where possession of substantial force and demonstrated willingness to use it is a prerequisite for securing respect—especially respect from the imperialist powers that seek to impose their will on China. Beijing's willingness to use military force has, in fact, made other powers respectful. China's decision to fight a prolonged and costly war against the United States in Korea greatly influenced later American and Soviet policy toward China. During the 1965–1966 Sino-American confrontation over Vietnam, for example, U.S. decision makers moved cautiously to avoid a second Sino-American war. China's leaders believe it imperative that foreign powers take China seriously, know that China means what it says, and understand that it is not bluffing when it says it is ready to use military force.

DETERRING THE SUPERPOWERS

In relations with the superpowers, China's use of force has involved mainly considerations of deterrence. The level of threat to China's security posed by either of the two superpowers far exceeds that posed by regional powers such as India and Vietnam. The PLA has been able to overcome powers such as India and Vietnam by a combination of quantitative superiority and technological parity, but China simply could not hope to match the concentrated forces of either superpower. So overwhelming has been Soviet and American military power, so great has been the disparity between the PLA and the forces of the superpowers, that among the nations of the world, only the superpowers could pose a mortal danger to the PRC.

China has been compelled to deal with superpower threats from a position of weakness. In doing this it has relied on three principal means: diplomacy, people's war, and nuclear weapons.

Efforts to deter superpower threats via diplomacy have taken two key forms: one, to align with the less threatening superpower to help check the other; two, orchestration of a broad range of forces, including state and non-state actors, to challenge, divert, tie down, confuse, and tire a threatening superpower. (These were dealt with in parts Two and Three, respectively.) One should note that the strategy of deterrence through counterencirclement via wars of national liberation can be linked to the concept of active defense, designed to keep the enemy off balance and preoccupied. More broadly, some analysts have argued that Chinese notions of deterrence differ fundamentally from Western notions. Whereas Westerners tend to believe that deterrence rests on superior material strength, the Chinese, according to this interpretation, draw on their ancient strategic tradition, stressing the role of psychological factors in persuading a potential aggressor not to attack. Accordingly, a potential aggressor is not restrained primarily by the balance of military power (although that is important), but by a series of psychological factors. If a hostile power thinks its potential victim will fight like a tiger, it will hesitate to attack even though it enjoys military superiority. Likewise, if the enemy is preoccupied elsewhere, or has many worries and concerns, it will be reluctant to attack. One may therefore deter a more powerful enemy by presenting an image of toughness and willingness to fight, and by keeping the enemy off balance.[4] The fact that both superpowers have been very cautious in confronting China in spite of their overwhelming military superiority suggests that there is some merit to this view.

The doctrine of people's war has been China's main military response to superpower threats. People's war is a military strategy designed to turn weaknesses into strength by utilizing China's vast size and manpower to wage a war of attrition against an invader. It arose out of Mao Zedong's analysis of the CCP's guerrilla war against Japan. According to Mao, Japan's primary advantages were superior firepower and mobility. China's advantages were the superior number of units it could deploy and extensive space for maneuver. Mao concluded that the way to utilize these advantages was to wage quick-decision offensive warfare on exterior lines of movement. That is, China's forces should maneuver about those of Japan, outflanking or encircling them, preferably while Japan's forces were on the move. By employing rapid movement along exterior lines, it was possible for China to engineer situations in which it enjoyed local superiority and surprise. Once combat was joined, China's forces should seek a quick decision, overwhelm the enemy, and withdraw before Japanese reinforcements could be brought up. China would thus utilize tactically offensive operations within a situation of overall strategic defense. Japanese strength would be lessened while Chinese forces would replenish their stockpiles with material scavenged from the battlefield. Gradually the balance of forces would shift. Japanese strength and confidence would be sapped, while that of China would grow. Eventually a crossover point would be reached, and China's forces could go on the strategic offensive. Such a crossover point was never reached during the war against Japan, but it was during the post–World War Two struggle against the Nationalists.[5]

People's war was applied with some success against U.S. forces in the opening stages of Chinese intervention in the Korean War. Once U.S. and United Nations forces managed to stabilize the front line, however, it proved much less successful. It produced huge casualties for Chinese forces and was not successful, with a few exceptions, in overwhelming U.S. positions. Experience of the shortcomings of people's war in Korea led to efforts to modernize the PLA.

During the mid-1950s, the PLA was reorganized along the lines of the Soviet Red Army. As this process proceeded, the PLA's earlier guerrilla strategies were set aside and the PLA reconfigured to fight a positional war against a mechanized enemy with modern firepower. This move away from people's war also reflected the fact that the PLA now had responsibility for defending China's urban industrial centers. Under the strategy of people's war, particular areas might be defended against enemy assault, but the retention of none was essential to the continuation of the war effort and all could be abandoned to the enemy in order to maintain the strategic principle of fluidity and maneuver.

This made sense when the PLA was a lightly armed infantry force based in the vast expanses of China's countryside. It made less sense once the PLA was responsible for the defense of China's industrial centers, which now produced munitions for the PLA's more heavily armed forces.

The viability of the strategy of conventional warfare adopted in the mid-1950s was dependent, however, on continuing access to Soviet spare parts, fuel, ammunition, and weapons. As Sino-Soviet relations deteriorated, China could no longer count on this. Mao Zedong's solution was to revert to a strategy of people's war. From 1960 to about 1977, people's war again dominated PLA strategy. The PLA was again reconfigured to fight a protracted guerrilla war. Tens of millions of people were given rudimentary military training. Several million were given somewhat more advanced training and organized into militia. Preparations for war were undertaken, including construction of fortifications and stockpiling of critical materials.

The essence of people's war as deterrence was to convince a would-be superpower invader that an invasion of China would mean a costly, inconclusive land war in which technologically superior forces would be worn down through protracted struggle by numerically superior, determined Chinese fighters. The PLA would not try to halt invading superpower forces at China's frontiers but would allow them to advance deep into China's interior. Then guerrilla and mobile war would be developed against the foreign occupiers on a vast scale. Superpower forces might be able to win victories over the PLA, but they would suffer heavy casualties in the process and would not be able to defeat China. The war would become one of attrition and eventually the superpower invader would be exhausted.

This strategy would work only if the hostile superpower occupied Chinese territory. If the hostile superpower were content to use nuclear weapons to destroy Chinese military forces or cities from afar without sending its own armies across China's borders, people's war would be of little use. This problem led to certain practical modifications in the concept. During confrontations with the Soviet Union in 1969 and with the United States over Indochina in 1964–1965 and 1970–1971, China threatened to retaliate to superpower air or missile attacks with large-scale infantry attacks against Siberia or, in the U.S. case, Laos and Thailand, which China's superpower opponent would have to use its own infantry forces to check. While Beijing used the term "people's war" to describe such threats, this considerably stretched the meaning of that term. More importantly, such operations would deprive the PLA of many key advantages offered by a more pure form of people's war: fighting on China's own terrain with the support of the surrounding populace and along lines of exterior movement. Its viability in strictly military terms was questionable. In terms of creating uncertainty in minds in Moscow or Washington, it made more sense.

Throughout the period from 1960 to 1977, China invested heavily in the development and production of modern weapons such as tanks, trucks, artillery, aircraft, rockets, and atomic and nuclear bombs. The technological level of these indigenously produced weapons was not high, but they still had major implications for the doctrine of people's war. As the PLA acquired modern weapons, it became more important for China to defend the industrial base that produced and replenished those weapons and the modern means of transportation that moved them to the battlefield. This meant that the PLA had to defend critical industrial and transportation centers. Less and less could the PLA abandon any point without critically weakening itself. Less and less could it rely on battlefield scavenging to meet logistic needs. A secure industrial base became increasingly essential.

During the 1960s, China addressed this problem by moving much defense industry to regions far from the frontier. Retreat into China's interior, as called for by the doctrine of people's war, would still mean, however, abandonment of the major industrial bases in Manchuria and along the coast. This meant that the PLA's qualitative level would fall rapidly after the opening stages of any superpower invasion. Moreover, even once it abandoned the coastal areas the PLA would still have to defend its inland industrial bases. Given the deep-penetration aircraft and precision rockets increasingly deployed by the superpowers, this was problematic.

The growing technological sophistication of superpower forces also increased doubts about the effectiveness of people's war tactics. The increased mobility and firepower of superpower infantry; increased use of close air support; and greatly improved command, control, and communication technology all gave a potential superpower invader a greater ability to coordinate actions on multi-front battlefields and to shift forces quickly from one place to another. The repeated failure of North Vietnamese and Viet Cong forces to overrun U.S. units in South Vietnam illustrated the limitations of mobile and guerrilla tactics against modern superpower forces, even in situations where there was no stabilized battle front. The growing mobility of superpower forces also meant that the PLA would no longer enjoy exterior lines of maneuver as it had against the Japanese. Instead, it would increasingly find itself outmaneuvered and compelled to fight defensive battles.

While Mao lived, China's military leaders were not able to address the mounting problems with the doctrine of people's war. Within a year of Mao's death, however, a reevaluation began with the promulgation of the doctrine of "people's war under modern conditions." This doctrine was elaborated over the next several years. According to it, the PLA would no longer retreat into the interior, abandoning China's population and industrial centers to enemy occupation. Rather, it would prepare in-depth defenses near the frontier to meet, wear down, and eventually stop an invading enemy. The PLA would defend key strategic positions, while waging aggressive mobile operations against enemy supply lines. The deeper the enemy advanced into China, the more vulnerable his logistic lines would become to PLA strategic counterattacks. This remains China's strategic doctrine against superpower threat in the 1990s.[6]

CHINA'S NUCLEAR FORCES

Threatened use of nuclear weapons has been China's third response to perceived superpower threats. The CCP Politburo launched China's nuclear weapons program in January 1955. According to John Lewis and Xue Litai, this decision was greatly influenced by repeated U.S. threats of atomic attack.[7] In the weeks following Chinese intervention in the Korean War, the U.S. government considered the use of atomic bombs against Chinese columns marching toward the thirty-eighth parallel in Korea. During the Eisenhower administration's efforts to force a cease-fire in Korea during 1953, the U.S. threatened to use atomic weapons unless the war was brought to a quick end. A year later, when Washington was considering intervention to rescue the besieged French garrison at Dien Binh Phu in northwestern Vietnam, consideration was again given to use of atomic weapons. Chairman of the U.S. Joint Chiefs of Staff Arthur Radford urged such a course with the understanding that Chinese counterintervention would also be met with nuclear weapons. The general contours of these deliberations were leaked to the press shortly afterwards.[8] Finally, during the Taiwan Strait crisis in 1954, U.S. leaders again threatened to use atomic weapons if Beijing expanded the conflict. Faced with America's atomic diplomacy, CCP leaders decided that China had to acquire its own atomic and nuclear weapons within the shortest possible time.

Considerations of national pride also played a role in China's nuclear decision. As Foreign Minister Chen Yi told Japanese newspapermen in October 1963, "Atomic bombs, missiles, and supersonic aircraft are reflections of the technical level of a nation's industry. China will have to resolve this issue within the next several years; otherwise, it will degenerate into a second-class or third-class nation."[9] The head of China's strategic weapons program, Marshal Nie Rongzhen, later recalled the emotion he felt in October 1966 when China first tested a nuclear armed rocket: "I was proud of our country, which had long been backward but now had its own sophisticated weapons."[10] Soviet and U.S. efforts to prevent China's acquisition of nuclear weapons confirmed to China's leaders the importance of such weapons in achieving international preeminence in the modern world.

A desire to increase China's political influence was also a factor in the decision to go nuclear. Their reading of China's experience in the century after 1840 convinced PRC leaders that the international order was dominated by imperialism and was a predatory system in which justice unbacked by power counted for little. The imperialists understood only power, and until China was militarily powerful, its voice would go unheeded. Atomic and thermonuclear weapons were the dominant weapons of the modern era, and if the imperialist powers had them, China would have to acquire them too. Only then would it be taken seriously; only then would it no longer be ignored and humiliated. As Foreign Minister Chen Yi told a CCP conference of July 1961, which decided to press forward with the nuclear weapons program even though the country was racked by famine and severe depression, China should build nuclear weapons, "even if the Chinese had to pawn their trousers for this purpose....As China's minister of foreign affairs, at present I still do not have adequate backup. If you succeed in producing the atomic bomb and guided missiles, then I can straighten my back."[11] China's leaders were determined to establish the PRC as a great power, and by the 1950s it was apparent to them that great-power status required the possession of nuclear weapons.

Still another aspect of China's nuclear decision was a determination to pursue goals for which it could not count on Soviet nuclear support. Primary among these was probably the desire to liberate Taiwan. There was also a subtle link between China's nuclear weapons program and its revolutionary aspirations. A nuclear China would be more secure against imperialist attack and thus more able to render support to foreign revolutionary movements. It would also be more able to give effective deterrent support to revolutionary states such as North Vietnam.

As we saw in Chapter Two, China's nuclear program enjoyed substantial Soviet support for the first several years. That support ended in 1959, at which point China's leaders decided to persevere without Soviet assistance. By concentrating resources in this area, and at huge costs to overall economic development, China was able to test an atomic bomb in 1964 and a hydrogen bomb in 1967. In October 1966, a rocket test delivered an atomic warhead to a target 800 kilometers away. By the end of the 1960s, China had an arsenal of several dozen atomic and hydrogen bombs and a few medium-range missiles capable of delivering them.

During the 1970s, China rushed the development of medium-range and intermediate-range missiles. By 1980, several hundred of these had been deployed against the Soviet Union. In May 1980, China launched its first ICBM able to reach all of European Russia or the continental United States. By 1990, the PLA possessed 100 to 150 medium- and intermediate-range missiles, plus twenty ICBMs. It also possessed MIRV technology, enabling its rockets to carry multiple independently targeted warheads. (France and Britain also have MIRV capability.) By 1990, China was the world's third nuclear power, ranking ahead of France and

Britain. Its nuclear capabilities were dwarfed, of course, by those of the USSR and the United States. The composition of China's strategic forces is depicted in Table 11–3.

China was slow to develop a doctrine regarding the use of its strategic forces. Even during the early 1970s, while the PLA was deploying increased numbers of nuclear weapons, people's war continued to be China's military doctrine. Exactly how nuclear weapons would be coordinated with a widespread guerrilla war against an enemy occupying China's urban areas was never explained. According to Paul Godwin, this was probably due to the hidebound nature of Mao Zedong's military thinking and the reluctance of other PLA leaders to dabble in the domain of military strategy that Mao considered to be his bailiwick.

In practice, China has consistently followed a strategy that Western analysts would call minimal deterrence. According to this doctrine, a lesser nuclear power can effectively deter nuclear attack by a superior nuclear power by threatening to retaliate to a nuclear first strike with an attack adequate to devastate a number of the industrial and population centers of the superior power. It is not necessary that the deterring power have an arsenal large enough to destroy the more powerful aggressor. All that is required is that the inferior nuclear power, in this case China, be able to retaliate by destroying several enemy cities—or, in the case of the United States in the 1950s, U.S. military bases in various East Asian countries. While China would suffer destruction far heavier than it inflicted on its superpower enemy, the losses suffered by the

Table 11–3 China's Strategic Forces in International Comparison

Country	Weapon System	Number Deployed	Year Deployed	Range (Km)	Warhead Yield	Number in Stockpile
PRC	bombers					
	B-5 (Il-28)	15–30	1974	1,850	20 KT	15–30
	B-6 (Tu-16)	100	1966	5,900	20 KT–3 MT	100–130
	IRBM					
	DF-2 (CSS-1)	30–50	1966	1,450	20 KT	30–50
	DF3 (CSS-2)	75–100	1970	2,600	1–3 MT	75–100
	ICBM					
	DF-4 (CSS-3)	<10	1971	4,800–7,000	1–3 MT	—
	DF-5 (CSS-4)	<10	1979	13,000	4–5 MT	—
	SSBN					
	Xia class	1 with 12 tubes	1983	2,800	200 KT–1 MT	—
France	Mirage IVP bombers	18	1988	930	45 KT	24
	IRBM	18	—	3,500	1 MT	—
	SSBN	6 with 96 tubes	—	3,000–6,000	150 KT–1 MT	—
Britain	SSBN	4 with 64 tubes	—	4,600	200 KT	—

Source: SIPRI Yearbook 1989, World Armaments and Disarmament, New York: Oxford University Press, 1989, p. 20. *The Military Balance, 1990–1991,* London: International Institute for Strategic Studies, 1991.

superpower would also be heavy and might critically weaken that superpower in its rivalry with the other superpower. This would be adequate to deter a potential nuclear aggressor.[12]

In line with this doctrine of minimal deterrence, China's public statements regarding the possible use of its nuclear weapons have consistently stressed that China would never be the first to use nuclear weapons. It would not hesitate, however, to retaliate in kind to a nuclear strike against China.

The ability of China's nuclear force to serve as a minimal deterrent is predicated on its ability to survive a preemptive enemy first strike. To ensure a second-strike retaliatory capability, the PLA has gone to great lengths to conceal its missiles, positioning them in caves or in other widely dispersed, carefully camouflaged positions. Superpower satellite reconnaissance and electronic monitoring capabilities are very good, and Soviet and American leaders could be confident that they have targeted most, if not all, of China's strategic sites. They cannot be confident, however, that no Chinese rockets would survive a preemptive first strike. A central thrust of China's strategic program in the 1980s was to enhance the survivability of its nuclear force by the development of submarine-launched ballistic missiles. The first test launch of a missile from a submerged Chinese submarine took place in September 1982, but as of 1992 no operational SLBMs had been deployed.

Deterrence rests not only on numbers of nuclear missiles, but on each side's perception of the willingness of the other to use those weapons. Given the huge disparities in the size of American and Soviet versus Chinese nuclear arsenals, it would never make sense for China's leaders to order the launch of Chinese rockets against American or Soviet cities. To do so would invite massive retaliation and destruction far exceeding anything that China could remotely hope to inflict on its superpower opponent. Moreover, since China's missiles are inaccurate, they could not be effective against small targets such as military bases, but only against big targets such as cities. Yet if China launched a nuclear attack on American or Soviet cities, it would invite a much more massive counterstrike against Chinese cities, a countervalue strike.

There are two chief solutions to the problem of credibility, and China has adopted both. One is to develop more accurate missiles that could be fired against military targets in retaliation for a superpower first, counterforce strike against Chinese strategic sites. In line with this, improvement in accuracy was a key thrust of PRC rocket development in the 1980s. The second solution is to convince opponents that, whether rational or not, China will retaliate in kind to a nuclear strike. Some analysts have suggested that China's proclamations in the 1960s that it did not fear nuclear war and was confident it would survive such a war are best interpreted as this sort of calculated irrationality. If American and Soviet leaders could be convinced that Chinese leaders genuinely did not fear nuclear war—that is, if they could be convinced that China's leaders were irrational—then the superpowers would be less tempted to launch a preemptive strike on the basis of a calculation that Chinese retaliation to such a strike would be irrational.

The credibility of China's nuclear retaliatory force is also endangered by the development of sophisticated anti–ballistic missile technologies by other powers. If China's rivals developed effective anti–ballistic missile systems or space-based strategic defense systems— such as those originally projected under the U.S. Strategic Defense Initiative, for example—China's small retaliatory force could be rendered useless. The small size of China's missile force would mean that it could not hope to overwhelm such defenses, as either of the superpowers might. Nor could it hope to develop a credible strategic defense system of its own, at least not for many decades. China would have poured immense funds into the development of a modest retaliatory force, only to find the deterrent value of that force eroded by the technological leaps of the United States, Russia, or other technologically-advanced powers.[13]

NOTES

1. Allen S. Whiting, "The Use of Force in Foreign Policy by the People's Republic of China," *The Annals of the American Academy of Political and Social Sciences*, July 1972, no. 402, 55–66; Angus M. Frazer, "Use of the PLA in Foreign Affairs," *Problems of Communism*, vol. 24, no. 6 (November–December 1975), 13–25.

2. Paul H.B. Godwin, "Mao Zedong Revised: Deterrence and Defense in the 1980s," in *The Chinese Defense Establishment: Continuity and Change in the 1980s*, Paul Godwin, et al, ed., Boulder, Colo.: Westview, 1983, 28–29. General studies of China's national security strategy include Arthur Huck, *The Security of China: Chinese Approaches to Problems of War and Strategy*, London: International Institute of Strategic Studies, 1970; Angus M. Frazer, *The People's Liberation Army*, New York: Crane, Russak, 1973; Gerald Segal, *Defending China*, New York: Oxford University Press, 1985.

3. Regarding China's claims, see Marwyn S. Samuels, *Contest for the South China Sea*, New York: Methuen, 1982; Chi-Kin Lo, *China's Policy Towards Territorial Disputes: The Case of the South China Sea Islands*, London: Routledge, 1989; Hongdah Chiu, *Chinese Attitude Toward Continental Shelf and Its Implications on Delimiting Seabed in Southeast Asia*, Occasional Papers/Reprint Series in Contemporary Asia Studies, School of Law, University of Maryland, 1977, no. 1; Donald E. Weatherbee, "The South China Sea: From Zone of Conflict to Zone of Peace," *East Asian Conflict Zones*, Lawrence E. Grinter and Young Whan Kihl, eds., New York: St. Martin's Press, 1987, 123–48. A. James Gregor, *In the Shadow of Giants, the Major Powers and the Security of Southeast Asia*, Stanford, Calif.: Hoover Institution Press, 1989. Regarding China's naval power and diplomacy, see David G. Muller, *China as a Maritime Power*, Boulder, Colo.: Westview, 1983. Bruce Swanson, *Eighth Voyage of the Dragon, A History of China's Quest for Seapower*, Annapolis, MD: Naval Institute Press, 1982. An analysis of the 1974 Paracels operation is in Segal, *Defending China*, 197–210. Regarding petroleum interests in the South China Sea, see the sources cited in note 24 of Chapter Ten.

4. Michael Pillsbury, "Strategic Acupuncture," *Foreign Policy*, no. 41 (Winter 1980–1981), 44–61.

5. Godwin, "Mao Zedong Revised," 26–30. Mao Zedong's classic statement of people's war is "On Protracted War," in *Selected Military Writings of Mao Tse-tung*, Beijing: Foreign Languages Press, 1966, 187–265. See also other writings in that volume, plus Lin Biao, "Long Live the Victory of People's War," *Peking Review*, no. 36 (September 3, 1965), 9–30; Peter Van Ness, *Revolution and Chinese Foreign Policy*, Berkeley: University of California Press, 1971; Chalmers Johnson, *People's War: An Autopsy*, Berkeley: University of California Press, 1973. Regarding the revision of people's war doctrine in the 1980s, see Harland W. Jenks, "People's War Under Modern Conditions: Wishful Thinking, National Suicide, or Effective Deterrent?" *China Quarterly*, no. 98 (June 1984), 305–19; Ellis Joffe, "People's War Under Modern Conditions: A Doctrine for Modern War," *China Quarterly*, no. 112 (December 1987), 555–71.

6. Godwin, "Mao Zedong Revised." Also Paul H.B. Godwin, "Changing Concepts of Doctrine, Strategy, and Operations in the Chinese People's Liberation Army, 1978–87," *China Quarterly*, no. 112 (December 1987), 572–90.

7. John Wilson Lewis, Xue Litai, *China Builds the Bomb*, Stanford, Calif.: Stanford University Press, 1988, 11–34.

8. Regarding the possible U.S. use of atomic weapons in 1954, see Stanley Karnow, *Vietnam*, New York: Penguin Books, 1984, 197; Bernard Fall, *Hell in a Very Small Place: The Siege of Dien Bien Phu*, New York: Da Capo, 1967, 299, 306–7; Melvin Gurtov, *The First Vietnam Crisis*, New York: Columbia University Press, 95.

9. Quoted in Alice Langley Hsieh, "The Sino-Soviet Nuclear Dialogue: 1963," *Sino-Soviet Military Relations*, Raymond L. Garthoff, ed., New York: Praeger, 1966, 164.

10. Quoted in Wilson and Xue, *China Builds the Bomb*, 238.

11. Ibid., 130.

12. Regarding China's nuclear strategies, see Morton Halpern, *China and the Bomb*, New York: Praeger, 1965; Alice Langley Hsieh, *Communist China's Strategy in the Nuclear Era*, Englewood Cliff, N.J.: Prentice Hall, 1962; Jonathan Pollack, "Chinese Attitudes Towards Nuclear Weapons, 1964–1969," *China Quarterly*, no. 50 (April–June 1972), 244–71; P.R. Chari, "China's Nuclear Posture," *Asian Survey*, no. 18 (August 1978), 817–28; Chong-pin Lin, *China's Nuclear Weapons Strategy: Tradition Within Evolution*, Lexington,. Mass.: Lexington Books, 1988.

13. Bonnie S. Glaser and Banning N. Garrett, "Chinese Perspectives on the Strategic Defense Initiative," *Problems of Communism*, vol. 35, no. 2 (March–April 1986), 28–44; John W. Garver, "China's Response to the Strategic Defense Initiative," *Asian Survey*, vol. 26, no. 11 (November 1986), 1220–39.

Chapter Twelve

External Threat and Internal Security

THE ETHNIC FACTOR

Beijing's perceptions of external threat have been profoundly conditioned by geographic and demographic factors that impinge on China's internal security. For Beijing, the gravest external threats were those that threatened to link up with internal opponents of the regime. Indeed, Melvin Gurtov and Byong-moo Hwang have argued that virtually all of Beijing's decisions to use force against other states were due to a conjuncture of external threat and internal instability.[1]

Especially in Xinjiang and Tibet, demographic, geographic, and historic factors have combined to make Beijing sensitive to threats to internal security. According to China's official 1982 census, 60 percent of the 13 million people of Xinjiang were non-Han, mostly Uighurs, Mongols, and Uzbeks. Ninety-five percent of Tibet's 1,863,000 people are Tibetans.[2] These peoples have cultures quite different from that of China's majority Han. They speak and write languages distinct from Chinese. Their religions have been Islam and Lamaist Buddhism, rather than the Confucianism, Mahayana Buddhism, or Marxism-Leninism practiced by the Han. Han have viewed many of the customs of these non-Han peoples as backward. The non-Han have, by and large, reciprocated those sentiments.

Beginning in 1957, Beijing adopted a policy of forced assimilation of non-Han minorities. It tried to force these peoples to abandon nomadic pastoralism and adopt settled agriculture, to use the Latin script rather than the more common Persian or Arabic to write their local languages, and to adopt Han/Maoist political rituals. Religion was also repressed.

Assimilationist policies continued through the 1970s and bred much discontent with Chinese rule.[3]

Great distances and rugged terrain combine with an underdeveloped transportation system to exacerbate the difficulties Beijing faces in controlling the outlying, non-Han regions. Overland routes between central China and Xinjiang and Tibet are few, long, and difficult. There is only one route from China proper into Xinjiang—via the narrow Gansu corridor. Access to Tibet requires crossing extremely rugged mountains in Qinghai or western Sichuan. A half dozen roads have been carved through these mountains, but most are made of crushed rock and wash out frequently. It still takes two weeks to travel by road from Lhasa to rail heads in western Sichuan. There is only a single motor road entering Tibet from the west, across the Aksai Chin plateau which is claimed by India and is the crux of the Sino-Indian territorial dispute. There is only one railway (built in the 1950s and opened for traffic in 1962) running into Xinjiang. Tibet has no railways at all. Because of geographic difficulties, access to these regions has historically been more convenient from Russia or India than from China proper.

Plans have been laid out for the construction of rail lines into Tibet and Xinjiang. In 1959, a line from Lanzhou to Xining in Qinghai was opened. Plans called for extending this line westward into central Qinghai, then south over the Kun Lun Mountains to the Tibetan plateau and thence to Lhasa. By 1991, this line had reached Geermu in central Qinghai. There were also plans to extend the line further west from Geermu along the south rim of the Tarim basin to Kashgar in western Xinjiang. This line would then link up with a line coming south from Urumqi to form a circuit around the entire Tarim basin. During the late 1960s, a railway from Chengdu to Lhasa was planned. As of 1992, all of these lines were incomplete. Work has been slow because of extremely difficult terrain, high costs, and competing demands. Figure 12–1 illustrates the transportation network of Tibet and Xinjiang, areas affected by anti-Beijing rebellions, and the Sino-Indian territorial conflict.

Several decades hence, when China's economy is more developed and it can afford to build more railroads and highways, Beijing will be able to reduce the impact of natural barriers. Until then, Beijing's hold on these outlying regions will remain tenuous.

Beijing's security fears regarding these regions are also based on a history of intrigue by Russian and British Indian governments who looked on Xinjiang and Tibet respectively as spheres of influence. Russian involvement in Xinjiang was overwhelming until it was uprooted by the Nationalists in 1942; so great was this involvement that the region effectively became a Soviet satellite in the 1930s. Then from 1944 to 1949, Moscow supported a Turkic secessionist regime in western and

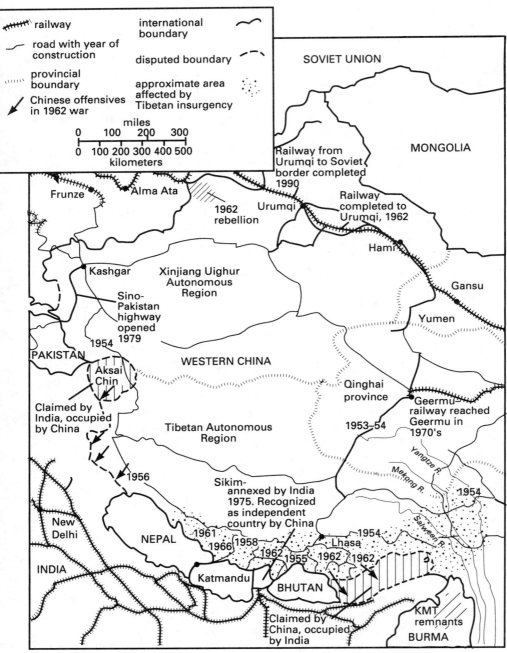

Figure 12–1   Transportation and Insurgency in Western China

northern Xinjiang. Regarding Tibet, the decline of Qing power in the late nineteenth century translated into a steady growth of British-Indian influence. Britain continued to recognize China's suzerainty over Tibet in order to minimize Russian influence, but until 1950 the authority of China's central government was nominal while British-Indian influence was substantial. Not until Tibet was occupied by the PLA in 1950 was Indian influence eradicated and effective Chinese authority established.[4]

Foreign-supported rebellions in Xinjiang and Tibet have been one of Beijing's major concerns. The Tibetan insurgency of the 1950s and 1960s was the most serious of these revolts.[5] This rebellion was based primarily among the Khamba Tibetan tribes inhabiting the rugged mountain fastness between the Sichuan basin and the Tibetan plateau. Small uprisings began in this region in 1954 and developed into a full-scale uprising by late 1955. U.S. and Taiwanese intelligence services began covert assistance to the rebels in 1956, with training being supplied at camps in Taiwan (and later in Colorado), and arms and other supplies being parachuted to the rebels in Tibet. The main air bases for these air supply operations were in Thailand. By 1957, the Khamba rebels were strong enough to launch a concerted campaign against isolated PLA garrisons in eastern Tibet. By mid-1958, the rebels controlled most of southeastern Tibet and were attacking PLA garrisons within twenty-five miles of Lhasa. In January 1959, the rebels nearly overran a PLA garrison of 3,000 men only thirty miles from Lhasa. Two months later the rebellion spread to Lhasa. The Lhasa revolt of March 1959 was crushed by 15,000 PLA troops, but Tibet's Lamaist Buddhist leader, the Dalai Lama, fled to India with CIA assistance along with thousands of his followers. In India many of the refugees acquired arms and recrossed the border to fight the PLA. Tibetan refugee camps often became bases of support for guerrilla operations inside Tibet.[6]

Following the Lhasa revolt the PLA launched a brutal but effective counterinsurgency campaign. By late 1960, PLA pressure and CIA advice prompted the insurgents to shift their base of operations further west, to south central Tibet, opposite Nepal. PLA pressure continued and a year later the insurgents moved again, this time to the desolate Mustang plateau of central Nepal. From there they ambushed PLA convoys moving along the Xinjiang-Tibet highway. Revolt flared periodically in eastern Tibet and in the central Lhasa valley, but it was suppressed. The insurgency had lost its strength by the late 1960s, but sputtered on until 1974. U.S. support for the insurgency was suspended by Richard Nixon in 1970 as part of his bid for rapprochement with China.[7]

Concern with control over Tibet was central to Beijing's decision for war with India in 1962. This decision involved multiple factors: seeming Indian complicity in the Tibetan rebellion, Soviet and American relations with India and China, and the bilateral Sino-Indian territorial dispute.

As mentioned earlier, the Aksai Chin plateau on the western Xinjiang-Tibet border was the crux of the territorial dispute. As insurgency mounted in eastern Tibet in 1955, the PLA began turning an old caravan trail across Aksai Chin into a motor road in order to provide an alternate route into Tibet. China announced its road construction activities in 1958, prompting an Indian protest in October of that year. Negotiations ensued without result. Beijing felt it absolutely imperative to hold on to Aksai Chin, and proposed that China relinquish its claim to lands on the southern slope of the eastern Himalayan Mountains as a quid pro quo for Indian recognition of Chinese ownership of Aksai Chin. Such a trade of Chinese claims in the eastern sector for Indian claims in the western sector seemed eminently reasonable to Beijing. India, however, felt that not only was Aksai China Indian territory, but since Tibet's local government had previously agreed (at a conference at Simla, India, in 1914) that the boundary in the eastern sector ran along the crest of the Himalayan mountains, there was no basis for an east-west swap. China denied that it had ever agreed to the crest-line principle in the eastern sector, saying that the acceptance of this by Tibet's representative at the Simla conference was invalid. The Tibetan insurgency and the support it received from across the Sino-Indian border helped persuade Beijing that it was essential to establish effective control over that border. Following discovery of the Chinese road through Askai Chin, the Indian government of Jawaharal Nehru had also decided to establish effective control up to the line that it claimed as the boundary. With Chinese and Indian troops moving into the same contested areas, clashes were inevitable. The first occurred in August 1959. As the crisis slowly escalated during 1960 and 1961, both sides sought a negotiated solution, but neither was willing to abandon its claim to Aksai Chin.

Beijing also suspected India of complicity in U.S.-KMT operations supporting the Tibetan insurgency. New Delhi allowed the Tibetan refugees to establish camps in India and seemingly turned a blind eye to CIA activities with the refugees in India. Then in the winter of 1961–1962, Indian forces began implementing a "forward policy" intended to assert Indian control up to the line claimed by India. This coincided with increased Tibetan raids against the Xinjiang-Tibet highway in south central Tibet. Meanwhile, Indian-American relations were increasingly cordial as New Delhi finally became responsive to Washington's warnings about the Chinese threat. To Beijing all this looked like a conspiracy to destabilize Chinese rule in Tibet.

Beijing felt that India's policy was rooted in a perception of Chinese weakness. With the Sino-Soviet alliance collapsing, confronted by a mounting insurrection in Tibet and with deepening confrontations with the United States over Laos and in the Taiwan Strait, and with its economy in collapse in the aftermath of the Great Leap Forward, China could not afford to adopt a forceful policy—or so China's leaders reconstructed India's calculations. Beijing concluded that only a firm blow would disabuse India's leaders of that idea. Rather than back down before Indian advances into contested border areas, Beijing decided on a short but intense war against India. Beijing's decision for war was probably made after the United States informed PRC representative Wang Bingnan at the Warsaw talks on June 23 that the United States would not support a Nationalist invasion of southeast China, and after the resolution of the Laos crisis via the conclusion of the Geneva conference on Laos on July 25—developments that are discussed shortly. Diplomacy at Warsaw and Geneva thus minimized chances that the upcoming conflict with India would spread. Before striking at India, Beijing also reached an understanding with Moscow, trading Chinese support for the USSR over Cuba (where the missile crisis was underway) for Soviet support against India.

In the months preceding its attack, China issued increasingly strong warnings to India and underlined these warnings with low-scale military moves. When New Delhi ignored these warnings, the PLA launched an intense one-week attack in northwestern Aksai Chin near the Karakoram Pass on October 20. Four days later the PLA halted and ceased fire, while Beijing proposed an armistice and mutual withdrawal. According to Allen Whiting, this attack on the twentieth was intended as a final, strong warning to New Delhi. When India ignored this warning and continued its forward policy, the PLA launched a second, much larger offensive on November 16. Table 12–1 illustrates the gradual hardening of Chinese warnings to India.[8]

The PLA achieved a decisive military victory in the 1962 war. New Delhi's forward policy had not been backed up by adequate military force. The PLA had carefully marshaled overwhelming local superiority. In some sectors Indian defenses collapsed within days. In the western end of the eastern sector, Chinese forces conquered virtually the entire southern slope of the Himalayan range and stood on the threshold of the Assam plain. North India was gripped by panic and fears that the PLA would march into the heart of the subcontinent. Beijing's objectives were limited, however. On November 22, the PLA halted and began a unilateral withdrawal to a line that Beijing claimed was twenty kilometers north of the line of actual control on November 7, 1959; that is, before India began implementing its forward policy. One reason for the PLA's withdrawal was a desire to avoid another, larger battle with India the following spring. The Himalayan passes were also about to be closed by snow.

The 1962 Sino-Indian war had a profound impact on Indian perceptions of China. The view of China as a fraternal Third World country previously prevalent in India disappeared. After 1962, most Indians saw China as a warlike country pursuing a policy of territorial expansion. India had bent over backward to befriend China during the

Table 12–1 Chinese Protests Preceding the 1962 War

	Ministry of Foreign Affairs Protests to India	
Date	*Area*	*Warning*
July 22	Ladakh	"The Chinese Government *can by no means sit idle* while its frontier guards are being encircled and annihilated by aggressors."
August 27	Ladakh	"The Chinese side *will have to resort to self-defense.*"
September 5	Ladakh	". . . Seriously urges the Indian Government to give careful consideration to the grave consequences that may arise from such acts of playing with fire. . . . One should be aware that *whoever plays with fire will hurt himself.*"
September 13	Ladakh	"*He who plays with fire will eventually be consumed by fire.* . . . Chinese border defense forces are duty-bound to defend their territory."
September 21	NEFA	"The situation is extremely dangerous and *flames of war may break out there.*"
September 25	NEFA	"In the face of the increasingly frantic armed attacks by the aggressive Indian troops, the Chinese frontier guards cannot but take resolute measures of self-defense."
October 3	NEFA	"*Whenever India attacks, China is sure to strike back.*"
October 11	NEFA	"*Should the Indian side still not rein in before the precipice but continue to spread the flames of war*, the Indian Government must bear full responsibility for the resulting casualties on both sides and all other consequences that may ensue."

(Italics added.)

Source: Allen S. Whiting, *The Chinese Calculus of Deterrence: India and Indochina.* Ann Arbor: University of Michigan Press, 1975. Reprinted with permission of University of Michigan Press.

1950s, most Indians believed, but China had betrayed India's friendship. The overwhelming power of Chinese forces also deeply shocked the Indians. The result was an Indian military buildup that continued into the 1990s. India also began looking for superpower support against China. The Soviet Union proved more willing than the United States to support India against China, and a durable Indian-Soviet bond emerged, based on parallel interests vis-à-vis China. Beijing responded by forming an entente cordiale with India's other nemesis, Pakistan.[9]

As of 1992, Beijing remains extremely sensitive to threats to its control of Tibet. The relaxation of political controls in Tibet and the influx of foreign journalists and tourists during the 1980s encouraged Tibetans to air their grievances against Chinese rule. When these protests erupted into demonstrations, riots, and open calls for Tibetan independence during October 1987 and again in March 1989, Beijing used force to maintain internal security. Martial law was also imposed, but lifted in May 1990 as part of China's effort to avoid suspension of most favored nation status by the United States.

Beijing's problems of control in Tibet are exacerbated by the existence of a sizable group of Tibetans in foreign exile—some 1 million altogether, with 100,000 of those concentrated in India. The Tibetan refugees in India have generally maintained their own ethnic identity and refused to take Indian citizenship or otherwise assimilate into Indian society. A "Tibetan refugee association" headed by the Dalai Lama functions as a quasi-government over the refugee community. The Dalai Lama himself retains considerable prestige within Tibet. The refugees in India constitute a standing pool of recruits for potential subversive operations inside Tibet or terrorist actions against Chinese interests in third countries. The latter development is unlikely as long as the pacifist Dalai Lama maintains control over the refugee community and as long as no nation is willing to antagonize China by sponsoring a Tibetan "national liberation" organization. Nonetheless, it remains a potential threat. A desire to insure against Indian support for anti-government Tibetan activities was one (secondary) reason Beijing desired better relations with India in the late 1980s. When Indian Prime Minister Rajiv Gandhi visited China in December 1988, Beijing was careful to secure guarantees from India. In the words of the joint communiqué signed at the conclusion of Gandhi's visit: "The Indian side reiterated its recognition of Tibet as an autonomous region of China and said that anti-China political activities by Tibetan elements are not permitted on Indian soil."[10]

In Xinjiang, too, Beijing has faced problems of foreign threat combined with internal insecurity. As in Tibet, in Xinjiang the radicalism of Chinese policy after 1957 led to mounting discontent with Han rule. The Uighurs and Tajiks of Xinjiang often retained close ties with their ethnic kin across the border in the USSR, and by the early 1960s there was a swelling tide of Soviet-encouraged emigration to the USSR. After initially acquiescing to this exodus, Beijing ordered a clampdown in the spring of 1962. This led to demonstrations in Yili that were put down with heavy loss of life. Riots and disturbances then spread to other regions of Xinjiang. Beijing suspected that the entire affair was the result of Soviet machinations.

From the mid-1960s to the early 1980s, Moscow fanned popular discontent in Xinjiang. Soviet radio stations broadcast anti-Beijing propaganda to Xinjiang, condemning, for example, the "cultural genocide" being carried out under Chinese rule and contrasting the poverty and regimentation of Chinese Uighurs and Uzbeks with the prosperity and freedom enjoyed by their brethren just across the border in Soviet Central Asia. Moscow did not attempt to incite an anti-Chinese uprising in Xinjiang, but Chinese authorities were apprehensive about such a possibility. Emigrés from Xinjiang were active in Soviet subversive efforts. Even more ominously, in the mid-1960s an exile "Free Turkistan Army" based in the Soviet Union was organized. Reportedly numbering 50,000 by the late 1960s and headed by an Uighur military figure who had played a prominent role in the Soviet-sponsored anti-Chinese rebellion in western Xinjiang in the 1940s, this Free Turkistan Army figured in Soviet radio broadcasts to Xinjiang. During periods of high Sino-Soviet tension, Moscow occasionally hinted elliptically that the Soviet Union might support a move by the Turkic peoples of Xinjiang to seek independence from China.[11] In the 1970s and early 1980s, many Western analysts believed that if Moscow decided on war with Beijing, one probable objective would have been seizure of Xinjiang. In this eventuality, Moscow could have used the Xinjiang "liberation movement" as the nucleus of a satellite regime.

The disintegration of the USSR at the end of 1991 and the independence of the central Asian republics—especially Kirghizia, Tadzhikistan, and Kazakhstan which border on China—has great significance for the internal security threat Beijing faces in Xinjiang. The collapse of the USSR gave a great fillip to anti-Communist Islamic fundamentalism by demonstrating that the "godless Communist tyrants" could be overthrown. It is also possible that the post-Soviet successor regimes in Central Asia will be unwilling or unable to control Islamic fundamentalism activities directed against Xinjiang. The threat thus emerges that militant anti-Communist Islam will spread from South Asia and Central Asia into Xinjiang.

The nature of the Islamic fundamentalist threat to China's control over Xinjiang was illustrated by an article entitled "Eastern Turkistan not Xinjiang" published in April 1990 by the Hezbi-i-Islam, the most important Afghan Mujahadeen group.[12] The article bitterly condemned Chinese Communist rule in Xinjiang and called for the liberation of that area so that its Muslims could participate fully in the Islamic community. "Islam has survived in Eastern Chinese-held Turkistan despite the dominance of the blood-stained bayonet of Yellow Communism," the article said. Chinese Communist rule "has not brought any good for Eastern Turkistan." Rather, "Communism's gifts to the people of Eastern Turkistan have been hunger, prison, torture, and indiscriminate massacres." The Chinese Communist regime had tried by every means to repress Islam, but has failed, according to the article. Mosques were being reopened and refurbished. There were now more than 200 mosques in Xinjiang where Muslims prayed five times a day. Imams used loudspeakers to read the Qur'an. Islamic books and audio-cassettes with recitations from the Qur'an were available everywhere. Uighur and Arabic were increasingly replacing the Chinese language. As to the path of liberation, "[The] Afghan Jihad is regarded as a minaret of light." This article was noted by the Chinese embassy in Islamabad.

The seriousness of the Islamic fundamentalist threat to Chinese control of Xinjiang was illustrated by an uprising at Baren township just south of Kashgar in western Xinjiang in April 1990. According to official

Chinese reports, a group of "religious fanatics" linked to a secret, underground organization, called "the Islamic Party of Eastern Turkistan," attempted to launch a Jihad to establish an independent Islamic state.[13] The Baren episode arose out of a local dispute over the construction of a mosque. Because of difficulties in obtaining a construction permit from the local Han cadre, local Muslims constructed a mosque without a permit. Before work was complete, however, local officials forbade further work and moved to demolish what had already been completed. A mob gathered. When two higher level officials were sent in to mediate the dispute, they were seized by the mob and killed. Army troops then moved in, but met coordinated resistance which included the use of automatic weapons. When the military eventually reestablished control, thousands of Muslim activists reportedly fled to the mountains. Following the uprising at Baren, Chinese authorities closed western Xinjiang to foreigners and cracked down on "separate activities" throughout Xinjiang. According to diplomatic sources several other uprisings had been planned to occur simultaneously with the Baren episode, but failed because of the Islamic insurgents' inadequate communications.

Xinjiang's borders with Pakistan, Afghanistan, Khrizia, and Khazkistan are extremely rugged and remote. They are also honeycombed with mountain tracks passable by men on foot and mules. Between the Karakoram Pass and the Sino-Afghan-Pakistan triborder juncture, for example, there are fourteen passes. While infiltration over these routes is slow and arduous, it is possible. Moreover, because of the decade-long war in Afghanistan that region of the world is awash with light arms, uprooted people, and men fully familiar with the techniques of guerrilla war against a fully modern army with superior firepower and mobility.

This helps explain the shift in the Chinese policy on the Afghanistan war after Soviet forces withdrew in February 1989. At that point China terminated its material support for the Afghan Mujahideen and began supporting a negotiated settlement involving a role for Najibullah, then head of the Soviet-installed Kabul government. While primarily related to the overall improvement in Sino-Soviet relations associated with the Gorbachev-Deng Xiaoping summit of May 1989, this shift was also influenced by a desire to see the end of the "Klashkinov culture" fostered by the Afghan war and threatening to seep into Xinjiang.

To deal with the threat of Islamic fundamentalist infiltration of Xinjiang, China will have to strengthen its control over its borders. It will also need to develop good relations with the new Central Asian countries to secure their cooperation with Beijing's efforts to prevent or acquire intelligence about subversive activities directed against Xinjiang.

Early in 1992 China quickly recognized the independent successor states of Central Asia. China may well be positioned to develop relations with several of those ex-Soviet successor regimes that are crypto communist and favor a state run economy, tend toward secularism, and fear Islamic fundamentalism. With these predilections, China could emerge as a natural partner of some of the new Central Asian states. China may well agree to extend economic development assistance to these new states as part of an effort to cultivate cooperative relations. Simultaneously, China's diplomatic missions to the new Central Asian states will probably cultivate contacts with various Islamic groups, including, perhaps especially, fundamentalist ones, in hopes of keeping tabs on possible anti-CCP activities.

Beijing's attempts to cope with the new, unstable, potentially dangerous situation in Central Asia will also rely on China's entente cordiale with Pakistan. China's link with Pakistan has proved remarkably durable, remaining strong in spite of regime changes in both countries, catastrophic defeats in war (Pakistan's 1971 defeat and dismemberment), and basic changes in alignments among the great powers. This stability is testament to the utility of the relationship to governments in both Islamabad and Beijing.

From Beijing's perspective, the most fundamental geopolitical utility of the link with Pakistan is, as suggested above, the two front threat that link presents to India. A strong Pakistan, independent of and hostile to India, severely constrains India's ability to concentrate its forces against China in the event of a major India-China war. Indian defense planners assume that Pakistan would enter a large-scale India-China war. In the event of such a war India would thus have to keep a substantial portion of its forces deployed in the west away from China. But Beijing's entente cordiale with Pakistan serves many other Chinese purposes as well. One important purpose is dealing with the threat of Islamic subversion to Xinjiang.

This works along several dimensions. First, Pakistan is a major power in the Islamic world and is willing to use its influence to facilitate good relations between China and the rest of the Islamic world. Following the Iranian revolution in 1979, for example, Iran's ruling Allatolas felt considerable hostility and suspicion toward Communist China. Not only were they atheistic and oppressors of the Muslims within China's borders, but Beijing had had cordial relations with the Shah's regime and was involved in a quasi-alliance with the Great Satan America. Once the Iran-Iraq war began, however, Tehran needed munitions and China was a ready supplier. More to the point, Pakistan mediated Sino-Iranian relations at this juncture, persuading their Iranian brethren that China was a reasonable, non-aggressive power that could be worked with. More recently, Pakistan played a role in the normalization of Sino-Saudi Arabian relations. If China enjoys good relations with the major Islamic countries, it is less likely that those countries would support or tacitly condone subversive activities directed against China.

Second, Pakistan has considerable influence with Afghan Islamic fundamentalist groups because of its front-line role in sustaining the Afghan Jihad and because it was the immediate quarter-master of that struggle. Moreover, because of Pakistan's role in the Afghan Jihad, no one can doubt Islamabad's credentials as "good Muslims." Since Islamabad is apparently willing to use its influence with the Mujahadeen to check anti-China activities, it is thus well positioned to persuade various Islamic groups to desist from activities against China.

Third, Beijing's link with Pakistan helps convince China's own Muslims that China's CCP regime is not "anti-Muslim" and is acceptable to other "good Muslims." Chinese Muslims make the Haj (pilgrimage) to Mecca by passing through Pakistan, either by air to Karachi or overland. In Pakistan Chinese Hajji (pilgrims) are treated as guests, with Pakistani visas being granted routinely and relatively swiftly. Pakistan has set aside special facilities for their housing. Completion of the Haj is, of course, one of the fundamental duties of Muslims. Chinese Hajji can see that their government has facilitated their journey (via good relations with Pakistan), while Beijing can be fairly confident that Pakistani authorities will see to it that Chinese Hajji are not subjected to subversive indoctrination while in Pakistan.

Fourth, the expansion of Pakistani Islamic influence in Central Asia would be relatively benign in terms of China's interests, and might have the useful effect of keeping out more dangerous influences. For a series of doctrinal and practical reasons, Pakistan's brand of Sunni Islam would be less likely to take anti-Chinese forms than other brands. Moreover, to the extent that Central Asian Muslims looked to Islamabad for support and guidance, they might be less inclined to look to Moscow, Istanbul, or Washington. The expansion of Indian influence into Central Asia could also be antithetical to Chinese interests, and a Pakistani presence would also have the useful effect of minimizing Indian presence.

Of course, Islamabad's willingness to provide all these services for Beijing is premised on the utility of its bond with China in dealing with India and in securing Chinese support for Pakistan's economic and military development. Because of China's substantial contributions to Pakistan in these regards, Islamabad is willing to help Beijing in other areas of peripheral concern to it, but of some significance to Beijing.

It should also be noted that Beijing's desire to court foreign Islamic opinion constrains its efforts to repress Islamic fundamentalism within China. To the extent that Beijing uses overt force against Islamic activists within Xinjiang, it will undermine its ability to count on a sympathetic hearing in foreign Islamic capitals.

Beijing's long-term solution to its ethnicity-based security problems in Tibet and Xinjiang will probably be to change the demography of these regions through settlement of Han Chinese. Although Beijing has hotly denied that it is pursuing a policy of sinicization via immigration, an ethnic transformation of several frontier regions has, in fact, occurred. In 1949, perhaps 6 percent of Xinjiang's population were Han. By 1982, that figure had increased to 40 percent, according to the official census. An equally dramatic transformation occurred in Inner Mongolia, where the percentage of Han rose from 25 percent in 1949 to 84 percent in 1982.

The strategy of securing frontier territories to China via Han immigration stretches far back into Chinese history.[14] It was used successfully by the Qing and Republican governments to consolidate Chinese sovereignty over such one-time non-Han areas as Manchuria and Inner Mongolia. Manchuria, the homeland of the Qing dynasty that ruled China from 1644 to 1911, was closed to Han settlement until the 1890s. When Russian-Japanese rivalry in that region began intensifying, however, the imperial Qing opened Manchuria to Han immigration. One of the great migrations of modern history resulted, and the ethnic composition of Manchuria rapidly changed. By 1911, 90 percent of Manchuria's population of 15 million to 17 million were Han. This indisputably "Chinese" character of Manchuria played a major role in its return to China in 1945.

The policy of sinicization via demographic inundation has been less successful in Tibet. The climate of Tibet is so severe that Han from China's lower-elevation provinces have great difficulty adapting to it. Pregnant Han women in Tibet, for example, frequently miscarry because of the high elevation. Tibet is so poor (it is China's poorest province), its customs so different, and the animosity between the Han and the Tibetans so great that most Han compelled to live in Tibet are extremely disgruntled. This creates additional problems of internal security.

The policy of sinicization via immigration eased with the relaxation of social controls during the 1980s. Nonetheless, it continues at a reduced rate. This will lead to short-term problems of internal security as the non-Han peoples of Xinjiang and Tibet watch their homelands being inundated by Han Chinese. Beijing must ensure that the more militant of these indigenous peoples do not turn to any foreign power for support of their efforts to stem the tide of Han migration.

REVOLUTION AND COUNTERREVOLUTION

Another important factor conditioning Beijing's perceptions of foreign threats involves the revolutionary origins and aspirations of the CCP regime. As Lenin noted, a revolution involves one class in society imposing its will upon another class by force of bayonets. Those people thus imposed upon provide a natural constituency for counterrevolution. In the first instance, there are people from the privileged classes of the pre-revolutionary society. There are also many ordinary people who were not part of the privileged classes, but who were victimized by the unpredictable campaigns that swept across China. Finally, the demands imposed on the Chinese people by their Communist rulers in the pursuit of the Communist millennium have been heavy: long labor with minimal reward; constant surveillance; demands to remold one's thought, to inform on family and friends, and so on. One consequence of this has been that there were many Chinese who would have welcomed the demise of the Communist regime.

Just how widespread this sentiment was during various periods will probably never be known. It is clear, however, that the leaders of the PRC took the danger of counterrevolution very seriously. Several quite violent campaigns were directed against opponents of the regime in the early 1950s.[15] A comprehensive system of social control was set up to help guard against counterrevolutionary activities. This system was backed up by efficient police work. Behind the police stood the PLA.

The danger of internal counterrevolution has been exacerbated by the Nationalist regime on Taiwan, which has constituted a unique threat to the PRC's security. Since 1949, the Nationalist government has been a rival government of China, maintaining that the PRC government is an illegal, bandit regime that has temporarily usurped power over the Chinese mainland through rebellion against duly constituted authority. This remains KMT doctrine as of 1992. Since 1949, the Nationalist objective has been nothing less than the destruction of the Communist regime; that is, the destruction of the People's Republic of China and the reestablishment of the Republic of China on the mainland. This idea of a "return to the mainland" to restore "legitimate authority" was understood to entail a major invasion of the mainland by Nationalist armed forces. After initial Nationalist victories over the PLA, the people of the mainland would rise up against their Communist oppressors and rally to their Nationalist liberators. The doctrine of "return to the mainland" remained an important component of Nationalist policy throughout the 1950s and 1960s.

Given the disparities in strength between Nationalist Taiwan and Communist mainland China, without superpower support Nationalist activities did not constitute a major threat to the PRC. With superpower backing, however, the threat from Taiwan might become quite substantial. During the early 1950s, some U.S. leaders were inclined to support a Nationalist invasion. These people were critical of the containment policy developed by the Truman administration, seeing it as passive and leading only to eventual Communist victory. They proposed, instead, an active policy of "liberation" or the "rollback" of Communist rule from China. Nationalist forces were typically assigned a central role in these schemes.

General Douglas MacArthur was the first prominent U.S. official to favor U.S. support for a Nationalist invasion of the mainland. After Chinese entry into the Korean War, MacArthur urged such a course on the grounds that it would divert Chinese forces from Korea and greatly complicate Chinese logistic problems. President Truman rejected this proposal, but the debate over it leaked into the media and figured into Beijing's security calculations. When ordering Chinese forces to intervene in Korea, for example, Mao Zedong warned that the most disadvantageous situation for China would be a protracted, stalemated war that would tempt the United States to bomb China's industrial centers and would "create discontent among the national bourgeoisie and a section of the people."[16]

Shortly after Dwight Eisenhower took office in January 1953, he "unleashed" the Nationalists as a way of signaling to Beijing the possibility of U.S. support for a Nationalist invasion if a Korean armistice was not signed soon. Chiang Kai-shek was hopeful, and in May and June of 1953, as Korean armistice negotiations entered a crucial stage, he pushed his American allies to support an invasion of the mainland by sixty Nationalist divisions.[17]

The Korean armistice led to the shelving of the Nationalists' proposal for a U.S.-supported invasion. It was revived almost immediately, however, in the context of discussions about how to deal with what Washington perceived as "Chinese Communist aggression" in French Indochina. Again in November 1956, after the anti-Communist uprising in Hungary and after Eisenhower's landslide second-term election, Chiang called on Eisenhower to authorize a Nationalist invasion.[18]

The last time U.S. officials considered authorizing a Nationalist invasion was during China's economic collapse in the early 1960s. In 1962, Chiang Kai-shek's son Chiang Ch'ing-kuo (then Taiwan's defense minister) traveled to Washington to try to persuade U.S. officials that, with China in the midst of deep economic crisis and with Beijing stepping up its support for revolution in Laos, the United States should fight fire with fire by supporting a Nationalist invasion. Beijing was extremely concerned about this possibility and deployed an additional 100,000 troops to Fujian and Zhejiang.[19]

U.S. officials listened to but ultimately rejected each of Chiang Kai-shek's proposals for an invasion of the mainland. At each juncture a few top American officials supported an invasion, arguing that since war with Communist China was inevitable, the United States should choose the circumstances of that conflict. The mainstream of U.S. officialdom, however, rejected a Nationalist invasion on the grounds that it would involve the United States in a war with China without the full support of the American people or U.S. European allies. It would also undermine U.S. efforts to draw China away from the Soviet Union. For most U.S. leaders, a full-scale Nationalist invasion was something to be held in reserve for the contingency of a full-scale Sino-U.S. war. In such a contingency, a Nationalist invasion would constitute a major weapon against the Communists.

Until the moment for a Nationalist "return" arrived, the political ground had to be prepared. This meant psychological warfare operations against the mainland. Covert Nationalist military operations against Communist China also increased the pressure on Beijing in line with U.S. containment policy. Such operations also provided useful intelligence about Communist China, while helping build the Nationalist military into an effective force that would be an important asset in the event of a Sino-U.S. war. Allowing the Nationalists to wage covert operations against the mainland was also a concession to Chiang Kai-shek's demands for action against the Chinese Communists, thereby keeping alive the Nationalist hope for an eventual return to the mainland. This, in turn, helped prevent a collapse of Nationalist morale, which U.S. leaders feared might open the door to Communist takeover of Taiwan and loss of Taiwan as a link in the U.S. chain of containment. Thus throughout the 1950s and 1960s, the United States supported small-scale, clandestine Nationalist actions against the PRC. Nationalist agents infiltrated into the mainland to conduct sabotage and espionage operations. They conducted periodic raids along China's coasts. Their aircraft flew reconnaissance missions over China. Nationalist advisers trained anti-Communist insurgents from eastern Tibet. They were active with anti-Communist forces in Laos. All the while, Nationalist radio stations broadcast subversive propaganda to the mainland.[20]

After Sino-U.S. rapprochement in 1972 and after the death of Chiang Kai-shek in 1975, the Nationalist policy of "return to the mainland" increasingly became an empty slogan. Possible link-ups between the KMT and the Soviet Union continued, however, to figure in PRC national security considerations. During the early 1980s, for example, Chinese spokesmen warned that under no circumstances would China accept a Soviet presence in Taiwan.[21]

The 1989 upheaval in China saw a revival of the Nationalist subversive threat. PRC media charged that the Nationalists were working with American hegemonists to subvert Communist rule in China as part of the global U.S. offensive against socialism.

We are able to talk fairly knowledgeably about earlier Nationalist-U.S. efforts to subvert the PRC because of the freedom of press and inquiry that U.S. scholars enjoy. Since this has not been the case in either the Soviet Union or China, comparable evidence about Soviet subversive operations efforts in China is very limited. Yet there are grounds for believing that Moscow has also attempted covertly to influence events within China through pro-Soviet agents and factions within the CCP elite.[22] This is a murky but probably important area.

During the Sino-Soviet alliance of the 1950s, the Soviet Union enjoyed broad access to Chinese officials in the PLA and in military-related heavy industry. Many thousands of Chinese studied in the Soviet Union. Given KGB standard operating procedures in Eastern Europe, it would be remarkable if the Soviets did not recruit agents of influence among these Chinese. The major divisions among CCP leaders over policy, and the extent to which Mao Zedong's interpretation of Marxism-Leninism differed from the orthodox Soviet brand, also suggest that China would have provided fertile ground for Soviet recruitment. There is also evidence that Moscow attempted to influence intra-CCP developments. According to Nikita Khrushchev's memoir, during the early 1950s northeastern CCP leader Gao Gang reported regularly to the Soviet Union on developments within the CCP, including the anti-Soviet sentiments of various Chinese leaders. Later, Defense Minister Peng Dehuai very probably had at least implicit Soviet support when he launched his criticism of the Great Leap Forward in 1959. Finally, Defense Minister Lin Biao was alleged to have counted on Soviet support during in his 1971 attempt to seize power.[23]

Mao Zedong took the danger of Soviet subversion seriously. Indeed, during the 1960s he became almost obsessed with it, seeing the Soviet Union behind virtually all opposition to him. Mao's fear of Soviet subversion was a major factor shaping his struggle against domestic and foreign revisionism in the 1960s, and one reason why he and his followers wished to keep the Soviet Union at arm's length. Soviet subversion was especially dangerous, Mao felt, because it spoke the language of Marxism-Leninism, allowing its agents to worm their way into the party.

According to Kenneth Lieberthal, during the early 1970s one group of radical CCP leaders argued that the danger of Soviet subversion constituted the primary threat to revolutionary China. Many counterrevolutionary revisionist elements opposed to the Maoist policies instituted during the Cultural Revolution and seeking a return to Soviet-style policies still remained hidden within the CCP, these radicals argued. Moscow was seeking to link up with these hidden revisionists to effect a seizure of power. Once in power, it was inevitable that these revisionists would reject Mao's revolutionary line and turn China into a satellite of Moscow. To guard against this danger, persistent and intense class struggle had to be waged. In this way, enemies hidden within the ranks of the party and the people could be identified, isolated, and destroyed. This analysis of the Soviet threat neatly dovetailed with the radicals' preferences regarding domestic policy. It also exemplified what many Chinese leaders felt was the internal security component of the Soviet threat.[24]

NOTES

1. Melvin Gurtov and Byong-moo Hwang, *China Under Threat: The Politics of Strategy and Diplomacy*, Baltimore: Johns Hopkins University Press, 1980.

2. Official Chinese statistics overstate the number of Han in Tibet by including in that figure soldiers and the transient Han population of Lhasa.

3. For a review of CCP minorities policy through the mid-1970s, see June T. Dreyer, *China's Forty Millions*, Cambridge: Harvard University Press, 1977. Regarding Xinjiang, see W.A. Douglas Jackson, *The Russo-Chinese Borderlands: Zone of Peaceful Contact or Potential Conflict*, London: Van Nostrand, 1962; Lowell Tillett, "The National Minorities Factor in the Sino-Soviet Dispute," *Orbis*, vol. 21, no. 2 (Summer 1977), 241–60; Donald H. McMillen, *Communist Power and Policy in Xinjiang, 1949–1977*, Boulder, Colo.: Westview, 1979. Regarding Tibet, see A.T. Grunfeld, *The Making of Modern Tibet*, Armonk, N.Y.: M.E. Sharpe, 1987.

4. Regarding Russian involvement in Xinjiang, see Allen S. Whiting and Sheng Shih-ts'ai, *Sinkiang: Pawn or Pivot?*, East Lansing: Michigan State University Press, 1958; John W. Garver, *Chinese-Soviet Relations, 1937–1945: The Diplomacy of Chinese Nationalism*, New York: Oxford University Press, 1988, 153–81; Linda K. Benson, *The Ili Rebellion: The Moslem Challenge to Chinese Authority in Xinjiang, 1944–1949*, Armonk, N.Y.: M.E. Sharpe, 1989. Regarding the British role in Tibet, see Michael C. van Walt van Praag, *The Status of Tibet: History, Rights, and Prospects in International Law*, Boulder, Colo.: Westview, 1987; R. Dhanalaxmi, *British Attitude to Nepal's Relations with Tibet and China (1814–1914)*, Chandigarh: Bahri Publishers Private Limited, 1981.

5. Regarding the origins of the rebellion, see George N. Patterson, "China and Tibet: Background to the Revolt," *China Quarterly*, no. 1 (January–March 1960), 97–99; George N. Patterson, "The Situation in Tibet," *China Quarterly*, no. 6 (April–June 1961), 81–86; Dawa Norbu, "The 1959 Tibetan Rebellion: An Interpretation," *China Quarterly*, no. 77 (March 1979), 74–93.

6. Regarding the Tibetan insurgency and foreign involvement in it, see Michel Peissel, *The Secret War in Tibet*, Boston: Little, Brown, 1973; L. Fletcher Prouty, "Colorado to Kolo Nor," *Denver Post, Empire Magazine*, February 6, 1972; Gurtov and Hwang, *China Under Threat*, 123–26; Victor Marchetti and John D. Marks, *The CIA and the Cult of Intelligence*, New York: Knopf, 1974, 115–17, 138–39.

7. Regarding PLA counterinsurgency operations in Tibet, see "Insurgency in China," *Indian Defence Review* (New Delhi), January 1988, 99–104; "Studies in Low Intensity Conflict: The Tibetan Rebellion," *Indian Defence Review*, July 1988, 67–75.

8. The standard study of Chinese maneuvering in the pre-war period is Allen S. Whiting, *The Chinese Calculus of Deterrence*, Ann Arbor: University of Michigan Press, 1975, 1–169. For an analysis of Indian policy, see Neville Maxwell, *India's China War*, New York: Anchor Books, 1972. For a treatment of the link between internal security and external threat, see Gurtov and Hwang, *China Under Threat*, 99–152. Regarding the international politics of the 1962 war, see William J. Barnds, *India, Pakistan and the Great Powers*, New York: Praeger, 1972. G.W. Choudhury, *India, Pakistan, Bangladesh, and the Major Powers: Politics of a Divided Subcontinent*, New York: Free Press, 1975.

9. Regarding the Sino-Pakistan relation, see Anwar Hussai Syed, *China and Pakistan: Diplomacy of an Entente Cordiale*, Amherst: University of Massachusetts Press, 1974; Yaacov Vertzberger, *The Enduring Entente: Sino-Pakistan Relations, 1960–1980*, Praeger, 1983. The memoir of Pakistan's ambassador to China from 1978 to 1982 is also available: Mohammed Yunus, *Reflections on China: An Ambassador's View From Beijing*, Lahore: Wajidalis Limited, 1986. Documents relating to China-South Asian relations are available in R.K. Jain, ed., *China South Asian Relations, 1947–1980*, 2 volumes, Brighton, U.K.: Harvester Press, 1981.

10. The communiqué is in *FBIS, DRC*, December 27, 1988, 16.

11. For example, Victor E. Louis, *The Coming Decline of the Chinese Empire*, New York: Times Books, 1979.

12. Wahdat, "Eastern Turkistan not Xinjiang," *The Mujahideen* (Pershawar), April–May 1990, no. 2, 36–37. *The Mujahideen* is a high quality publication complete with glossy photographs and an illustrated cover. It is the main English language publication of the Hezbi-i-Islam headed by Gulbadin Hekmatyar.

13. Quoted in *Pakistan Times*, (Karachi), April 24, 1990.

14. Regarding the general strategy of sinicization, see Michael Hunt, "Chinese Foreign Relations in Historical Perspective," *China's Foreign Relations in the 1980s*, Harry Harding, ed., New Haven, Conn.: Yale University Press, 1984, 10–19.

15. Ezra Vogel estimated that in the province of Guangdong alone, between October 10, 1950, and August 10, 1951, some 28,332 people were executed in the course of the campaign to suppress counterrevolutionaries. *Canton Under Communism*, New York: Harper and Row, 1971, 64. Also Richard L. Walker, *The Human Cost of Communism in China*, U.S. Congress, Senate Subcommittee to Investigate the Administration of the Internal Security Act and Other Internal Security Laws of the Committee on the Judiciary, 92nd Congress, 1st Session, 1971. Amnesty International regularly publishes up-to-date reports on political repression in China.

16. Mao Zedong, *Mao Zedong junshi wenxian* (Mao Zedong Selected Military Writings), Beijing: Zhongguo renmin jiefangjun junshi kexue xueyuan, 1981, 346.

17. Chargé d'affaires Jones to State Department, May 27, 1953, *FRUS, 1952–1953*, vol. XIV, Part I, 197–98.

18. *FRUS, 1955–1957*, vol. II, 447–48.

19. Roger Hilsman, *To Move a Nation: The Politics of Foreign Policy in the Administration of John F. Kennedy*, New York: Delta, 1976, 314–18; Whiting, *Chinese Calculus*, 68–69.

20. Regarding these U.S.-Nationalist covert operations against the PRC, see Whiting, *Chinese Calculus*, 64–72; Gurtov and Hwang, *China Under Threat*, 75–83, 123–29. The *Pentagon Papers* also contains some information about U.S.-Nationalist covert operations against China. *The Pentagon Papers*, The Senator Gravel Edition, vol. 2, Boston: Beacon Press, n.d., 648–49. U.S. support for these operations was also the result of a compromise between the pro-containment and the pro-rollback forces within the United States. See Franz Schurmann, *The Logic of World Power*, New York: Pantheon, 1974, 161–65.

21. Deng Xiaoping, on his visit to the United States in January 1979, for example, told Senator Sam Nunn that China would use armed force against Taiwan only if the Soviets intervened in Taiwanese affairs or if the KMT refused to negotiate with the PRC over the long run. In 1985, foreign affairs adviser to the State Council Huan Xiang told foreign reporters that while he could not enumerate the factors that might force China to use military force against Taiwan, "it would not be tolerable if Taiwan entered into an alliance with the Soviet Union." *China Quarterly*, no. 78 (June 1979), 438; *China Report* (New Delhi), vol. 21, no. 5 (September–October 1985), 456.

22. Sources touching on Soviet covert operations against China include Kenneth G. Lieberthal, *Sino-Soviet Conflict in the 1970s: Its Evolution and Implications for the Strategic Triangle*, R-2342-NA, Santa Monica, Calif.: Rand Corporation, July 1978, 25–30; John Barron, *KGB*, New York: Bantam, 1974, 259.

23. Nikita S. Khrushchev, *Khrushchev Remembers: The Last Testament*, Boston: Little, Brown, 1974, 243–44. Other discussions regarding Soviet liaisons with CCP opposition to Mao include Philip Bridgham, "Factionalism in the Central Committee," *Party Leadership and Revolutionary Power in China*, John W. Lewis, ed., New York: Cambridge University Press, 1974, 203–35; Michael Y.M. Kau, *The Lin Piao Affair: Power Politics and Military Coup*, White Plains, N.Y.: IASP, 1975, 69–70, 84, 86; C.L. Sulzberger, *The Coldest War: Russia's Game in China*, New York: Harcourt Brace Jovanovich, 1974, 5, 10–11.

24. Lieberthal, *Sino-Soviet Conflict*, 76–86.

Chapter Thirteen

The Period
of Sino-American
Confrontation

DEALING WITH THE UNITED STATES

PRC security relations with the superpowers may be divided into three broad periods: from 1949 to 1969, when China's leaders believed that the threat posed by the United States exceeded that posed by the Soviet Union; from 1970 to 1985, when Beijing believed the Soviet threat exceeded the American threat; and the years after 1985, when Beijing believed that attack by either superpower was unlikely and concentrated instead on more likely contingencies of conflict with India or Vietnam.

The origins of the PRC's fear of the United States and alignment with the Soviet Union were examined in Chapter Two. Here we will merely recall that the conclusion of the Sino-Soviet alliance led to a major hardening of U.S. policy toward China. Since Beijing was now a close military-political ally of Moscow, Washington decided to extend the policy of containment to Asia. The formation of the Sino-Soviet bloc also figured prominently in the U.S. decision to intervene in 1950 to thwart Pyongyang's effort to conquer South Korea.

The Korean War militarized the Sino-American confrontation and locked it into place for more than a decade. The exact nature of China's role in the initial decision to launch the June 25, 1950, North Korean attack on South Korea is still unclear. This remains one of China's most closely guarded historical secrets. According to Nikita Khrushchev's memoirs, the initial decision was made by Stalin and Kim Il-sung during the latter's visit to Moscow in January 1950. Mao Zedong was also in

Moscow then (to negotiate the Sino-Soviet treaty), and Stalin informed him of the decision to liberate South Korea. Mao did not object, according to Khrushchev.[1] This was substantiated by North Korea's deputy chief of staff in 1950, who subsequently defected to the USSR.[2] Current Chinese writing also minimizes Mao's role in the initial decision for war. But circumstantial evidence suggests a less benign role for Mao. It does not make sense to conclude that Mao would let pass Stalin's comments about projected war in Korea without inquiring fully about how such an undertaking would affect China's interests. If fuller discussion ensued, should it be taken to indicate Mao's endorsement? Vietnamese leader Ho Chi Minh was also in Moscow at the same time as Mao and Kim. At about this time a number of important and interrelated decisions were made: to liberate South Korea, to liberate Taiwan, to step up Chinese assistance to the Vietminh's effort to liberate Vietnam, and to conclude the Sino-Soviet alliance. It is *possible* that Stalin, Mao, Kim, and Ho jointly made a decision in Moscow to step up the revolutionary struggle in Asia. Uncertainty will remain until Beijing and Moscow declassify the full transcripts of the Mao-Stalin talks.

Kim Il-sung's war objective was to unify all of Korea under his rule. Stalin's objective was probably to acquire warm-water ports in South Korea for the Soviet navy.[3] Stalin may also have been reacting to U.S. preparations to sign a peace treaty with Japan without Soviet participation.[4] Neither Stalin nor Kim expected U.S. intervention, since statements by top-level U.S. officials had explicitly excluded South Korea from the U.S. defense perimeter in Asia.

War between the United States and China resulted not from Kim Il-sung's initial invasion of South Korea, nor from U.S. intervention in South Korea to throw back that invasion, but from the U.S. decision to use its forces to reunify all of Korea under Seoul's control. After holding a beachhead around Pusan and then outflanking North Korean forces with a bold amphibious landing at Inchon on September 15, U.S.-UN forces pushed rapidly north. U.S. forces crossed the thirty-eighth parallel on October 7, 1950, pushed past the narrow waist of North Korea between Wonsan and Chyinnampo, and reached the Yalu River on October 26. As U.S. forces approached and then crossed the thirty-eighth parallel and marched toward the Yalu River, Beijing issued increasingly blunt warnings. On October 2, Zhou Enlai formally notified Indian Ambassador K.M. Panikkar that if U.S. forces entered North Korea, China would intervene in the war. As U.S. forces approached the Manchurian border, China's warnings became shrill.[5]

Washington noted Beijing's warnings but decided to push north anyway. U.S. Far Eastern Commander General Douglas MacArthur felt that China was bluffing. China was simply too weak to challenge the United States, MacArthur believed. After his dramatically successful landing at Inchon on September 15, MacArthur's opinions carried great weight in Washington. Figure 13–1 depicts the tides of war in Korea.

On October 1, Kim Il-sung requested Chinese intervention. The next day a special enlarged Politburo meeting convened in the Forbidden City to discuss Kim's request. According to Peng Dehuai, deputy commander of the Eighth Route Army during the war against Japan and soon to be appointed commander of Chinese forces in Korea, most participants at the conference were opposed to intervention, arguing that the industrial and military strength of the United States far exceeded that of China, and that the CCP had only begun to consolidate its control. Mao Zedong admitted these difficulties, but nonetheless favored intervention, saying: "Everything that you say makes sense. Nevertheless, if we just stand by while others are experiencing a national crisis, no matter what, it is very hard to accept."[6] Mao's view, supported by Peng Dehuai, prevailed.

Among the reasons for intervention cited by Peng were fears that unless pushed back, U.S. forces would be stationed along the Yalu, threatening Manchuria. A half-century earlier, Japan had used Korea

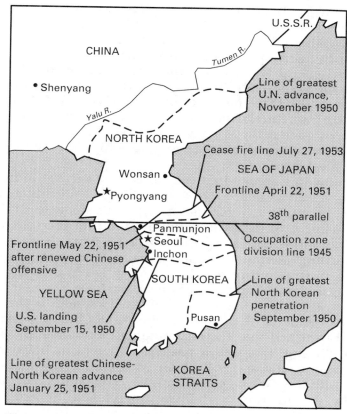

Figure 13–1   The Korean War

as a springboard from which to advance into Manchuria. Now, China's leaders feared, this process might be repeated. When it inherited Japan and Japan's Pacific empire, the United States also inherited Japan's geopolitical imperialist policy toward China. Mao also feared that failure to strike back at the United States would make it even more belligerent. In an October 2, 1950, order outlining the decision to send Chinese forces to Korea, Mao explained that if U.S. forces occupied all of Korea, the strength of the Korean revolution would suffer a basic defeat, further emboldening the U.S. aggressors.[7] Peng Dehuai expressed it more colorfully in his memoir: "Tigers eat people. Just when and how is determined by their appetites. To attempt to placate a tiger is not wise."[8]

Mao's perception of the U.S. threat was influenced by a belief that U.S. intervention in Korea reflected a more basic U.S. decision to intervene in the Chinese civil war on behalf of Chiang Kai-shek. During the last months of the civil war, Mao, oblivious to Truman's overly subtle policy of disengagement from the Nationalists, felt that U.S. intervention on behalf of Chiang Kai-shek was likely, and ordered appropriate countermoves.[9] When Truman ordered the U.S. Seventh Fleet to protect Taiwan two days after the Korean War erupted, and then deployed U.S. forces to Korea, Mao interpreted these as signs that U.S. leaders had finally decided to intervene in China to rescue the KMT. The bellicose statements by General MacArthur provided further evidence of this. Given the seeming inevitability of a PRC-U.S. confrontation, Mao concluded that of the three possible routes of U.S. attack (via French Indochina, along the central China coast opposite Taiwan, or via Korea), fighting in Korea offered the greatest advantages to China. There the PLA's logistic lines would be shorter and China's transportation infrastructure most developed.[10]

Allen Whiting has argued that even after they decided to intervene in Korea, China's leaders hoped that a war with the United States might be avoided by persuading Washington of the seriousness of China's intent and causing U.S. forces to withdraw south of the thirty-eighth parallel. Although Washington did not take China's verbal and diplomatic warnings seriously, a preliminary, limited military clash might cause it to stop and reconsider. Chinese forces thus briefly but forcefully engaged South Korean forces near the Yalu River on October 26 and U.S. forces on both the western and eastern sides of the Korean peninsula on November 2. Then on November 7, all Chinese forces broke off action and vanished into the surrounding mountains and forests. According to Whiting, this was a pattern of deterrent behavior that would be repeated in the 1962 clash with India, the 1964–1965 confrontation with the United States, and the 1969 border confrontation with the Soviet Union: After verbal warnings failed, limited military actions were used to signal China's serious intent to its adversaries. Faced with a hostile advance on China's borders, Beijing used carefully controlled military action to warn that continued encroachment would ultimately prove unacceptable to the aggressor because China was ready for battle and would not back down.[11]

Chinese scholars Hao Yufan and Zhai Zhihai, whose research was more closely based on access to Chinese leaders and classified documents than was Whiting's, have challenged the latter's thesis regarding Chinese signaling.[12] According to Hao and Zhai, the disengagement on November 7 was due to logistic difficulties and consequent depletion of supplies. Whatever the case, U.S. leaders, particularly General MacArthur, dismissed the attacks of late October and early November as bluff. On November 24, MacArthur ordered an offensive to "win the war" and "bring the boys home by Christmas." On November 26, 200,000 Chinese soldiers launched a counterattack that sent UN forces reeling southward.

Beijing sought to limit the Korean conflict by calling its interventionary forces "volunteers," thereby implying some sort of unofficial status. Nonetheless, once the Chinese People's Volunteers (CPV) entered the conflict in force, General MacArthur began agitating for substantial escalation, including bombing the bridges across the Yalu River and military bases in Manchuria, a Nationalist invasion of southeast China, and the use of atomic bombs against Chinese forces in Korea. Chinese leaders were undoubtedly relieved when Truman fired MacArthur in April 1951.

The Sino-U.S. war in Korea lasted from November 1950 until July 1953.[13] After the initial U.S. retreat from the Yalu in the winter of 1950–1951, the front line was stabilized around the thirty-eighth parallel in the spring of 1951. Chinese forces often resorted to human wave assaults in efforts to overcome U.S. firepower. Once a front was stabilized, these attacks were usually without much success and came at the price of huge casualties. Some 900,000 Chinese soldiers, including one of Mao Zedong's sons, died in Korea. According to the Chinese, the United States also employed chemical and bacteriological weapons against Chinese forces. As late as 1981, Peng Dehuai repeated this charge in his memoirs.[14] The U.S. government has consistently denied this, but some scholars maintain that it may nonetheless be true.[15] But even without biological and chemical weapons, the hatred engendered on both sides was adequate to color Sino-American relations for many years.

Dwight Eisenhower assumed the presidency in January 1953, determined to force an end to the Korean War by threatening to escalate it rather than accept an indefinite stalemate. To this end, he dropped hints at the truce talks in Panmunjom (begun in June 1951), via Indian diplomats, and through U.S. moves in the Taiwan Straits that "in the event that the Chinese refused to accede to an armistice in a reasonable time" the United States was prepared to escalate the war.[16] Implicit in this threat was the possible use of atomic weapons against military targets in China, a blockade of the China coast, or a Nationalist invasion of the Chinese mainland or Hainan Island. Mao took Eisenhower's threats seriously; on December 20, 1952, he ordered preparations for an invasion by seven U.S. divisions.[17]

We know less about China's decision for peace in Korea than about its decision to enter the war. One key issue in dispute during the arduous truce talks was the repatriation of prisoners of war.[18] The United States insisted that repatriation be voluntary, while China and North Korea insisted on across-the-board repatriation of all POWs regardless of individual wishes. This was a point that touched directly on China's national security, or more precisely, on the PLA's ability to maintain military discipline in a future conflict with the United States. If Chinese soldiers knew, as U.S. propaganda would ensure that they did, that they would not be returned to China against their will at the end of some future conflict, they would be much more likely to surrender or desert. That Beijing finally gave way on this important issue was probably a function of its fear of a wider war with the United States. Several other factors also played a role in Beijing's decision for peace. China had already achieved its initial objectives: saving the Communist regime in North Korea, driving U.S. forces away from Manchuria's borders, and showing the Americans that New China was a force to be reckoned with. Stalin's death in March 1953 may also have facilitated the decision for peace.

The United States came out of the Korean War determined to create a system of containment in Asia powerful enough to ensure that the Communist bloc would never again dare to risk war as it had in Korea. This policy of "a position of strength" included strengthening U.S. nuclear forces in the Far East. The doctrine of massive retaliation adopted by the Eisenhower administration was based on the premise that a repetition of the Korean War experience was best avoided by threatening nuclear strikes against any Communist power that initiated international aggression. Further Communist aggression would not be met by U.S. infantry as in Korea, but by nuclear weapons, used at times and places of U.S. choosing, and quite possibly directed against the ultimate source of the aggression. In line with this, more nuclear warheads, along with additional modern aircraft—F-84 and F-100 fighters, and B-47 and B-54 bombers—were deployed to the Far East. In 1957, Matador cruise missiles were added to the U.S. Far Eastern arsenal.

Beijing responded to the mounting U.S. pressure by consolidating its alliance with the Soviet Union and by linking the Sino-Soviet treaty to the Warsaw Treaty Organization comprised of the USSR and the Eastern European states. "Peace is inseparable": this was a major theme of Chinese propaganda in the mid-1950s.[19] Beijing hoped to convince

Washington that an attack on China would lead to a full-scale world war involving the entire socialist camp. Soviet leaders were willing to go along with this strategy, but felt that a corollary was that Beijing must act with utmost caution.

As Sino-Soviet relations deteriorated after the Taiwan Strait crisis of 1958, Beijing was forced to reconsider its national security policy. No longer could it rely on Soviet protection and support against the United States. It is important to note that although Soviet support for China weakened, Beijing did not adopt a more conciliatory approach toward Washington. Rather, China relied on three elements: (1) reorientation of the PLA to conduct a self-reliant people's war; (2) development of nuclear weapons; and (3) revolutionary offensive against U.S. imperialism in the Third World. People's war and nuclear deterrence were discussed in Chapter Eleven. The ideological-revolutionary aspects of the revolutionary offensive in the Third World were discussed in Chapter Six. The national security aspects of that offensive will be discussed here.

The theory of defending socialist countries via revolutionary offensives in the intermediate zone lying between the socialist and imperialist countries can be traced back to Mao's debates with Stalin during the Second World War. In 1940, Stalin urged Mao to restrain the Eighth Route Army's drive to expand Communist base areas behind Japanese lines because he feared that such activity would induce the Nationalists to come to terms with Japan, freeing Japanese forces for war with the Soviet Union. Mao countered by arguing that vigorous expansion of China's patriotic, anti-Japanese forces was the best way to keep China in the war against Japan. Again from 1946 to 1948, Stalin urged restraint on Mao out of fear that revolutionary upheaval in China might induce the United States to attack the Soviet Union. Mao again rejected Stalin's advice, arguing that a revolutionary offensive in China would in fact tie U.S. hands, preventing it from attacking the Soviet Union.[20]

As the Sino-Soviet alliance collapsed, Mao revived this theory of security of defending the socialist countries via revolutionary offensives in the intermediate zone. The most comprehensive statement of this theory of security via revolution was Lin Biao's September 1965 thesis entitled "Long Live the Victory of People's War." According to this tract, the proliferation of anti-imperialist wars of national liberation throughout the intermediate zone would steadily weaken U.S. imperialism, rendering it ever more passive. As U.S. forces attempted to stamp out the flames of people's war in one country after another, its forces would be dispersed, its strength sapped, opposition to it encouraged, and its will broken. Ultimately, U.S. imperialism would collapse before the combined assault of the people of the whole world.[21]

From the standpoint of China's security, wars of national liberation in the intermediate zone were the first line of defense. Dispersion of U.S.

military forces throughout the Third World to cope with revolutionary insurgencies made the U.S. less able to attack China. U.S. leaders would be preoccupied with pressing problems other than China. Broadly conceived, China's support for distant wars of national liberation can be viewed as a counterencirclement strategy outflanking U.S. containment.[22]

As noted in Chapter Six, from Beijing's perspective, Vietnam's was the most important revolutionary struggle against the United States in the 1960s. And it was in Indochina that the PRC next confronted the United States.

SINO-AMERICAN CONFRONTATIONS OVER LAOS AND VIETNAM

Because of geography, the "wars of national liberation" in Laos and South Vietnam were closely linked. Beijing had two major objectives in Laos, a country about twice the size of New York state with a population of only 2 million. First, as Laos was a state bordering China, Beijing wished to exclude an American or Nationalist Chinese military presence there and prevent Laos's integration into SEATO. Washington's policy toward Laos was premised on the doctrine of containment, and by the mid-1950s Washington was supplying economic and military assistance to the Royal Laotian government. (Responsibility for training the Lao army was assigned to France by the Geneva conference.) There were also remnants of several KMT divisions operating in the Laotian-Burmese border region where they had settled after 1949. The main activities of these remnant Nationalist forces were farming and smuggling, but they were occasionally involved in operations against China in association with Taiwanese and U.S. intelligence agencies.[23]

Beijing's second objective in Laos was to support the growing insurgency in South Vietnam. In 1959, Hanoi established special military units to infiltrate men and materiel into South Vietnam via the Laotian panhandle. As the insurgency in South Vietnam grew in 1960 and 1961, so did the importance of those supply lines. Success of the insurgency in South Vietnam thus depended on effective North Vietnamese control over the Laotian panhandle. A U.S. military presence or an actively anti-Communist Laotian government that would threaten this were unacceptable to Beijing. Salient features of the Indochinese situation in the 1960s are illustrated in Figure 13–2.

The Geneva conference of 1954 provided for the regrouping of military forces of Laos's Communist-led liberation movement, the Pathet Lao, into the two northeastern provinces of Phong Saly and Sam Neua, pending amalgamation with the national government via elections. These elections were held in May 1958 and resulted in strong Pathet Lao representation in the National Assembly and participation in a coalition

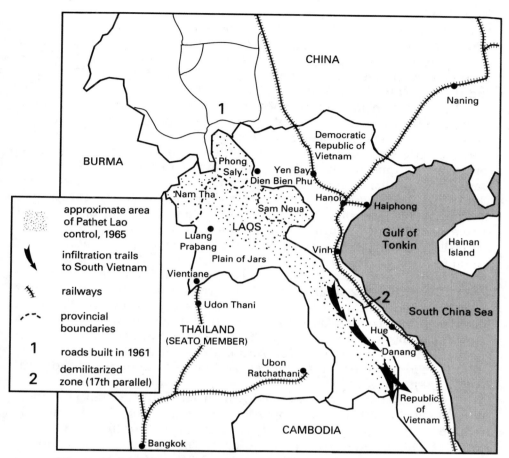

Figure 13–2   China, Laos, and North Vietnam, 1962–1965

government headed by neutralist leader Prince Souvanna Phouma.
Washington was dismayed by the growing leftist influence in Laos and
used its influence (which was substantial, since Washington was the
paymaster of the Laotian army) to oust Souvanna Phouma and bring to
power an anti-Communist government headed by Phoui Sananikone.
The new government began military moves against Pathet Lao areas and
U.S. soldiers (wearing civilian clothing in deference to the Geneva
agreements) began training the Laotian army.

Beijing was deeply concerned with the growing U.S. military
presence in Laos and with the increasingly anti-Communist orientation
of the Laotian government. In a statement of August 12, 1959 (just after
Sananikone replaced Souvanna), for example, Beijing charged that the
United States was orchestrating events in Laos: "In order to realize its
ambition to extend aggression and intervention in Indochina and

menace China...the United States has persistently sought to turn Laos into an American military base and drag it into...the aggressive SEATO bloc. This naturally poses a threat to China and Vietnam."[24] The statement demanded the dismantling of U.S. "military bases" in Laos and the withdrawal of U.S. military personnel.

The situation in Laos reached crisis proportions in August 1960, when a coup by neutralist military units brought Souvanna Phouma back to power. The restored neutralist government collapsed after two months, with Souvanna Phouma fleeing to Cambodia and the neutralist forces who supported him fleeing northward to join the Pathet Lao. Hanoi, meanwhile, strengthened the Pathet Lao with cadre and soldiers. The Pathet Lao then launched an offensive, rapidly expanding their area of control. By February 1961, they controlled the Plain of Jars and threatened Vientiane and the royal capital of Luang Prabang. The neutralist–Pathet Lao government established diplomatic relations with China in April 1961.

A fourteen-nation conference on Laos convened in Geneva from May 1961 till July 1962 against the background of a deepening Sino-American confrontation over Laos. China's representative, Foreign Minister Chen Yi, pushed for the withdrawal of all "foreign forces" from Laos, insisting that since the only "foreign forces" in Laos were those of the United States, the Chinese Nationalists, and other pro-Western nations, the question of a Chinese or North Vietnamese withdrawal simply did not arise.

As the Laotian crisis escalated, China strengthened its position in Laos. In October 1961, Beijing opened a consulate general in Phong Saly headed by a major general of the PLA, the ex-commander of the Kunming Military Region adjacent to Laos. The next month a high-level PRC economic and cultural delegation travelled to Laos to sign various agreements expanding relations. In January 1962, an agreement was signed providing for Chinese construction of roads from Yunnan into Phong Saly, and for the establishment of air links between China and Laos. PLA forces adjacent to Laos were also further reinforced. Foreign analysts interpreted these moves as preparation for direct military intervention.

The Laotian crisis reached its peak in the spring of 1962. In May of that year, after a three-month siege reminiscent of the battle of Dien Bien Phu, Nam Tha in northwestern Laos was overrun by four battalions of Pathet Lao. Washington interpreted the move as a Communist probe to test U.S. resolve in the final stages of the Geneva conference, and responded forcefully. The Seventh Fleet moved to the Gulf of Thailand, while U.S. troops and bombers deployed to Thailand. Washington was very concerned about the developing situation in Laos and seriously considered direct military intervention by U.S. forces to halt the Communist advance. Eventually, however, the United States decided that Laos' geographic remoteness and lack of modern transportation infrastructure made intervention impractical, and decided to work for an international agreement neutralizing Laos.

From Beijing's perspective, the Laotian situation was quite threatening. The U.S. buildup in Laos took place just as Taiwanese preparations for an invasion of the mainland were intensifying. The border conflict with India was also intensifying. KMT remnant units were active opposite Yunnan. Beijing thus faced threats along virtually the entire range of its southern borders.[25] On May 19, 1962, *People's Daily* warned Washington:

> U.S. aggressive moves in Southeast Asia are a serious threat to the security of China. The Chinese people cannot remain indifferent to this....The Chinese people firmly oppose U.S. imperialist armed intervention in Laos, and absolutely cannot tolerate the establishment by U.S. imperialism in areas close to China of any new military bridgeheads directed against this country....We must serve a fresh warning to the Kennedy Administration that it shall be held fully responsible for all grave consequences arising from its policy of playing with fire.[26]

While signaling its readiness for military action to defend its interests in Laos, Beijing moderated its negotiating position at Geneva, dropping its earlier demand for the dissolution of SEATO and agreeing to a more vigorous International Control Commission for Laos, rather than the ineffectual body it had originally sought. Beijing held, however, to its central objective: exclusion of a U.S. military presence in Laos and protection of the infiltration routes between North and South Vietnam. It achieved these through the particular type of neutralization of Laos agreed to by the 1962 Geneva conference.

The Geneva agreement on Laos had a substantial impact on subsequent U.S. strategy in the Vietnam War. It was one reason why the United States ruled out (until April 1971) land operations against North Vietnamese forces in southern Laos. By helping to minimize the U.S. presence in Laos, China helped North Vietnam defeat the United States.

It is still unclear whether PLA soldiers served with the Pathet Lao from 1961 to 1962. U.S. representatives at Geneva asserted that they did, but produced no hard evidence. China denied it. One evenhanded academic study concluded that a direct China role, while unproven, was likely.[27] In any case, China's direct role in Laos was much smaller than that of North Vietnam, which had several thousand cadre and soldiers serving with the Pathet Lao. Eventually, China's presence in Laos became one of its largest (but secret) foreign military involvements. The PLA continued to build roads into the northern provinces of Laos throughout the 1960s. Eventually some 20,000 Chinese soldiers protected by Chinese anti-aircraft batteries were deployed to Laos for road-building activities. During the early 1960s, these activities helped persuade U.S. leaders that China was attempting to expand into

Indochina. By the early 1970s, however, they had decided that China's presence in northern Laos was designed to counter North Vietnam.[28]

As the insurgency in South Vietnam intensified, so too did Sino-American conflict. From Washington's perspective, the facts that China was Hanoi's most vociferous foreign backer and its major supplier (at least by 1963 and until 1965) of military equipment, and that Hanoi took an increasingly pro-Beijing stance in the Sino-Soviet dispute, were proof that events in Vietnam were manifestations of Chinese expansionism. The insurgency in South Vietnam was, U.S. leaders concluded, a test case of the Chinese model of revolution. If it worked in Vietnam, other cases would follow. The challenge, therefore, had to be met. As the Northern-supported Viet Cong insurrection in South Vietnam mounted, more U.S. advisers were committed to bolster the Saigon regime.

By 1964, U.S. leaders had concluded that Hanoi had to be forced to stop supporting the Southern insurrection, and that this could be accomplished by threatening to bomb North Vietnam's newly built industrial facilities. From Beijing's perspective, both the viability of China's world revolutionary strategy and China's own national security were at stake. Regarding the former, Mao had argued in his debates with Khrushchev over the question of "peaceful coexistence" that the United States would not dare to attack the socialist countries for supporting wars of national liberation as long as the socialist countries remained firm. If the United States now attacked North Vietnam, it would prove Mao wrong. Regarding China's national security, North Vietnam was a Chinese ally on China's very borders. U.S.–North Vietnamese conflict would obligate China to assist its ally and tempt Washington to expand the war to China's borders or perhaps even into China.

As U.S. pressure on North Vietnam mounted during early 1964, Beijing stepped up its commitment to Hanoi in an effort to deter U.S. air attacks. These deterrent efforts failed in August, when U.S. war planes bombed North Vietnamese naval bases and gasoline storage facilities. When the direction of North Vietnamese policy did not change following those raids, the United States began preparing for sustained bombing of North Vietnam. Again China issued warnings. As in earlier crises, China's statements grew increasingly blunt and forceful. Verbal warnings were also backed up by military moves to underline the seriousness of Beijing's intent. New airfields were constructed in South China and China's air force was redeployed southward. Again China's attempts to deter U.S. attacks against North Vietnam failed.

The beginning of sustained U.S. bombing of North Vietnam and the introduction of U.S. combat units into South Vietnam (both in February 1965) brought the United States and the PRC into military confrontation. U.S. strategy was based on the belief that Hanoi could be persuaded by U.S. bombing to stop sending men and materiel into South Vietnam. It was unclear to U.S. leaders exactly how much bombing would be necessary to force Hanoi to reach such a decision. But at some level of pain and destruction, they believed, Hanoi would suspend its support for the Viet Cong.

From Beijing's perspective, U.S. moves threatened China's own security. The introduction of U.S. combat units into South Vietnam brought U.S. forces closer to China and raised the possibility of a U.S. invasion of North Vietnam or southern Laos. Washington might also decide to strike at airfields, rail lines, or supply depots in southern China that were supporting North Vietnam's war effort. Most serious of all was the possibility that the North Vietnam regime might collapse if the United States began unlimited bombing, perhaps destroying the dams and dikes upon which North Vietnam's agriculture depended; instituted a naval blockade of North Vietnam; or used nuclear weapons against North Vietnamese military concentrations or military choke points. China's credibility as an ally was also at stake. Had China done nothing, its regional influence would have suffered grievously.

China sought to limit U.S. attacks on North Vietnam by warning Washington that if U.S. escalation went too far, China would enter the war. Shortly after sustained U.S. bombing of North Vietnam began, Foreign Minister Chen Yi warned: "The Chinese people will exert every effort to send the heroic *South* Vietnamese people the necessary material aid, including arms and all other war material, and stand ready to dispatch their men to fight shoulder to shoulder with the *South* Vietnamese people whenever the latter require."[29] Chen's reference to *South* Vietnam was ominous, suggesting that China might enter the war even if U.S. military actions were confined to Vietnam. After the first dogfight between U.S. and Chinese aircraft over Hainan Island, Beijing warned:

> The Chinese Government and people have already solemnly declared that aggression by the United States imperialists against the Democratic Republic of Vietnam means aggression against China. The Chinese people will absolutely not stand idly by without lending a hand....The Chinese people have always been infinitely loyal in fulfilling their proletarian internationalist obligations, they have never spared any sacrifice whatever in this respect and always meant what they say. Both past and present struggles testify to this.[30]

By September 1965, Chen Yi warned that China would respond to a U.S. attack against Chinese territory by carrying the war to America's Asian allies, implying that China was ready to impose on the United States a costly land war in Southeast Asia. At the ambassadorial talks in Warsaw, China's representative Wang Bingnan warned that Washington would be committing a "grave historical blunder" if it underestimated the determination of the Chinese and Vietnamese peoples.[31]

These warnings were given substance by substantial Chinese military support for North Vietnam. According to Allen S. Whiting, there were five salient characteristics of this support.[32] First, it was sizable. By spring 1966, nearly 50,000 PLA troops were deployed to North Vietnam to man anti-aircraft guns, carry out logistic work, and repair rail lines destroyed by U.S. bombing. Between October 1965 and October 1968 (when PLA forces were withdrawn), a total of 320,000 Chinese troops served in North Vietnam, with the annual maximum reaching 170,000.[33] North Vietnam's air force was also allowed to use air bases in south China. An integrated radar grid, including stations in south China and covering all of North Vietnam, was established to provide intelligence about U.S. air operations to North Vietnam's air defense system. China's own air defenses in south China were also strengthened.

Second, PLA deployments were *not* conducted under conditions of maximum security. PLA units deployed to North Vietnam retained their normal unit designations, wore regular uniforms, and used non-secure methods of communications, thereby ensuring that Washington knew of China's moves and the seriousness of its intentions. To avoid locking itself into a situation that might escalate into a direct confrontation with the United States, however, Beijing did not officially acknowledge its military presence in North Vietnam.

Third, Chinese units in North Vietnam did not remain in a passive, reserve role but actively engaged U.S. forces. They shot down U.S. aircraft and suffered casualties from U.S. bombing. PLA aircraft based in China also scrambled on occasion and engaged U.S. aircraft that penetrated Chinese airspace during combat operations against North Vietnam. Several U.S. planes were shot down over China.

Fourth, Chinese units constructed a large, heavily fortified complex at Yen Bai on the Red River some 140 kilometers northwest of Hanoi. This complex, replete with a large runway and anti-aircraft guns placed in caves and mounted on railway tracks, seems to have been designed to serve either as a North Vietnamese redoubt in the event that a U.S.–South Vietnamese invasion overran Hanoi or as PLA headquarters in the event of Chinese intervention.

This particular configuration of Chinese support was intended to convey to Washington the seriousness of China's intent. The fifth and final characteristic of China's support for Hanoi was careful maneuvering to avoid war with the United States. While warning Washington not to go too far, Beijing also signaled that it hoped to avoid a Sino-American war. In April 1965, Zhou Enlai told Algerian leader Ahmed Ben Bella and Cambodian leader Norodom Sihanouk that China would not intervene in the Vietnam conflict unless there was a U.S. invasion north of the seventeenth parallel. Both statements were in CIA hands within several days, undoubtedly exactly as Zhou had intended.[34]

As U.S. bombing of North Vietnam escalated in 1965 and 1966,

Chinese and U.S. ambassadors in Warsaw discussed the Vietnam situation. Both sides sought to avoid a war by misperception and miscalculation as had happened in Korea. It is widely believed that these talks led to an understanding that, as long as U.S. forces did not invade North Vietnam or attack China, China would not directly enter the war.[35] Even if such an understanding was reached, however, it could have been undone by events. Both countries moved cautiously to avoid a second Sino-U.S. war.

The combination of Chinese threat and caution helped induce the United States to adopt the strategy of gradual escalation against Hanoi. A fundamental purpose of that strategy was to prevent Chinese intervention by keeping the level of violence directed against North Vietnam below the threshold that would spark full-scale Chinese intervention. Washington believed that Beijing would enter the war only if it concluded that the United States sought the occupation of North Vietnam or the destruction of North Vietnam's Communist regime. At the Warsaw talks, U.S. representatives assured China that U.S. aims were limited only to compelling Hanoi to forgo the conquest of South Vietnam. Limitation of levels of force used against North Vietnam was intended to demonstrate this. Moreover, since the exact threshold at which China would enter the war was unknown, gradual escalation would give the U.S. an opportunity to gauge China's reactions and draw back should there be signs of imminent Chinese intervention. Gradual escalation was also judged less likely to unnerve Beijing or cause it to miscalculate.

The China-induced U.S. strategy of gradual escalation was an immense boon to North Vietnam. It allowed Hanoi time to adjust to U.S. pressure and to find ways to circumvent U.S. moves. By helping to induce Washington to adopt this particular strategy, Beijing contributed substantially to Hanoi's eventual victory over the United States. But the PRC also benefited from Hanoi's struggle against the United States. The U.S. failure to impose its will on Hanoi gradually revealed the limits of U.S. power, and Washington began to reevaluate its policies toward China. The U.S. failure in Vietnam was an important factor inducing Washington to embrace rapprochement with China.

Western analysts have long believed that the onset of the U.S.–North Vietnam war precipitated a debate within the CCP over the nature of the threat posed by the United States and the optimal strategy for coping with that threat. There has been extensive research on the supposed strategic debate within China's elite at this juncture. Contributors to this debate have disagreed as to the exact nature of the issues and alignments involved, but are generally agreed that China's leaders were divided over national security issues at this juncture.

Donald Zagoria argued that there were three distinct factions within the Chinese elite, which he dubbed hawks, doves, and an in-between faction, the "dawks." The hawks, led by PLA Chief of Staff Luo Ruiqing, felt that there was an imminent danger of attack by the United States. Moreover, unless U.S. aggression against Vietnam was defeated, Luo argued, Washington would be tempted to employ similar means against China. Luo's policy prescription was reconciliation with the Soviet Union to deter U.S. escalation against North Vietnam and attack on China, or to fight the United States if deterrence failed again as it had in 1964 and 1965. China should repair its strained relations with the Soviet Union by accepting Moscow's proposal for united action in support of Hanoi.[36]

Zagoria's doves favored efforts to improve relations with both the Soviet Union *and* the United States, even if this meant leaving North Vietnam to fend for itself. China's paramount duty, they felt, was its own economic development. The centrist "dawk" faction was, in Zagoria's view, led by Lin Biao, but ultimately supported by Zhou Enlai and Mao Zedong. Dawks saw the United States as a grave threat to China, but they were even more concerned about the subversive danger posed by Soviet revisionism. Consequently, they felt that priority must be given to the struggle against revisionism within China. This ruled out rapprochement with Moscow. China should support North Vietnam, the dawks felt, but avoid actions that would lead to war with the United States. The extent of China's support for Vietnam was limited, the dawks said, by the very nature of revolutionary struggle. While enjoying a certain degree of international support, wars of national liberation in various countries were essentially self-reliant. It followed from this that war with the United States was not imminent, and, in turn, that China could pursue a domestic anti-revisionist agenda. This debate over foreign policy was tied closely to disputes over domestic policy, which are not the concern of this book.

By the end of 1965, the strategic debate, if indeed there was one, had been resolved. Luo Ruiqing was purged and united action with Moscow was rejected. Simultaneously, China prepared to wage a self-sufficient people's war with the United States should U.S. escalation go too far. The most important aspect of these preparations was a crash program to build up a military-industrial base in China's mountainous interior. This top-secret program, referred to as the Third Front, came in response to the breakdown of the Sino-Soviet alliance and the recognition that China could no longer count on Soviet support in the event of a war with the United States. It was also premised on the assumption that in the event of war with the United States, China's coastal industrial centers would be destroyed or occupied in the early stages of the conflict. A military industrial base therefore had to be constructed in the interior provinces of Sichuan, West Hubei, Guizhou, Yunnan, Qinghai, and Hunan. Begun in August 1964, as U.S. air attacks on North Vietnam began, Third Front construction was pushed forward with top priority. Resources from all over the country were poured in at a huge rate to build new military-industrial facilities. Rail lines were built to connect these plants and dams constructed to provide electricity. In order to minimize vulnerability to air attack, the plants were widely dispersed, and many were situated in caves or deep, narrow valleys.[37]

Initially intended to counter a U.S. invasion, in 1969 the Third Front program was reconfigured to cope with a possible Soviet attack. Defense bastions and industrial bases were prepared in the Wutai mountains in Shanxi. A large number of critical factories were moved out of Manchuria. New nuclear weapons facilities were begun in the deep interior, duplicating the original plants situated in China's now-vulnerable northwest.

The Third Front program was drastically curtailed in 1971 with the purge of Lin Biao and rapprochement with the United States. Mao Zedong and Zhou Enlai apparently felt that the added increment of security derived from ties with the United States could substitute for the immensely costly Third Front program. The Third Front program inflicted heavy costs on China's industrialization efforts. Projects were poorly planned and pushed forward with little regard for costs. Efforts continued for a decade to salvage some of the immense capital invested in these projects.

NOTES

1. Nikita Khrushchev, *Khrushchev Remembers*, Boston: Little, Brown, 1970, 367, 401.

2. According to the defector, Li Sang-jo, Kim Il-sung did not consult with Mao about his war plan during their day in Moscow in 1950. *North Korea News* (Seoul), no. 481, June 26, 1989. Several scholars have argued that the United States and/or South Korea initiated the war. See I.F. Stone, *The Hidden History of the Korean War*, New York: Monthly Review Press, 1952; Karunaker Gupta, "How Did the Korean War Begin?" *China Quarterly*, no. 52 (December 1972), 699–716.

3. Regarding Stalin's aims, see Robert Slusser, "Soviet Far Eastern Policy, 1945–1950: Stalin's Goals in Korea," in *The Origins of the Cold War in Asia*, Yonosuke Nagai and Akira Iriye, eds., New York: Columbia University Press, 1977, 123–46.

4. Harold C. Hinton, *China's Turbulent Quest: An Analysis of China's Foreign Relations Since 1949*, Bloomington: Indiana University Press, 1970, 41.

5. Allen S. Whiting, *China Crosses the Yalu*, Stanford, Calif.: Stanford University Press, 1960, 92–94, 116–17. Also Allen S. Whiting, *The Chinese Calculus of Deterrence*, Ann Arbor: University of Michigan Press, 1975, 196–223; Russell Spurr, *Enter the Dragon: China's Undeclared War Against the United States in Korea, 1950–51*, New York: Newmarket Press, 1988.

6. Peng Dehuai, *Peng Dehuai zishu* (Autobiography of Peng Dehuai), Shanghai: Renmin Chubanshe, 1981, 257.

7. Mao Zedong, *Mao Zedong junshi wenxian*, (Mao Zedong Selected Military Writings), Beijing: Zhongguo renmin jiefangjun junshi kexue xueyuan, 1981, 345.

8. Peng Dehuai, *Autobiography*, 259.

9. These precautionary measures included acceleration of the PLA advance so as to wipe out the KMT before U.S. leaders had time to intervene, rapid seizure of major ports that the Americans might use to land interventionary forces, and the stationing of large forces near Shanghai and Tianjin so as to deter a U.S. landing.

10. Hao Yufan and Zhai Zhihai, "China's Decision to Enter the Korean War: History Revisited," *China Quarterly*, no. 121 (March 1990), 94–115; Chen Xiaolu, "China's Policy Toward the United States, 1949–1955," *Sino-American Relations, 1945–1955: A Joint Reassessment of a Critical Decade*, Yuan Ming and Harry Harding, eds., Wilmington, Del.: SR Books, 1989, 184–97.

11. Whiting, *China Crosses the Yalu* and *Chinese Calculus*.

12. *Op. cit.*, note 10.

13. For a general account of the war, see Clay Blair, *The Forgotten War: America in Korea, 1950–1953*, New York: Doubleday, 1989. For the Chinese view of the war, see Anthony Farrar-Hockley, "A Reminiscence of the Chinese People's Volunteers in the Korean War," *China Quarterly*, no. 98 (June 1984), 287–304. For an analysis of the Chinese military performance, see Alexander L. George, *The Chinese Communist Army in Action: The Korean War and Its Aftermath*, New York: Columbia University Press, 1967. The memoir of the U.S. commander who succeeded Douglas MacArthur, Matthew Ridgeway, is also available: *The Korean War*, New York: De Capo, 1986. On Sino-Soviet relations during the war, see Robert R. Simmons, *The Strained Alliance: Peking, Pyongyang, Moscow and the Politics of the Korean Civil War*, New York: Free Press, 1975.

14. Peng Dehuai, *Autobiography*, 264.

15. Stephen L. Endicott, "Germ Warfare and 'Plausible Denial'," *Modern China*, vol. 5, no. 1 (January 1979), 79–104. See also the information about Department of Defense experiments with non-lethal but infectious bacteria in San Francisco in 1950, based on information obtained under the Freedom of Information Act and presented on the television program "60 Minutes," on February 17, 1980.

16. Dwight D. Eisenhower, *Mandate for Change, 1953–1956*, Garden City, N.Y.: Doubleday, 1963, 179.

17. Mao Zedong, *Selected Writings on Military Affairs*, 354–56.

18. For an account by the head of the U.S. negotiating team, see C. Turner Joy, *Negotiating While Fighting: The Diary of Admiral C. Turner Joy at the Korean Armistice Conference*, Stanford, Calif.: Hoover Institution Press, 1978. For an account by the secretary of the Chinese negotiating team, see Chai Chengwen, *Panmendian tanpan* (Panmunjom Negotiations), Beijing: Renmin jiefangjun chubanshe, 1989. A solid scholarly account is Rosemary Foot, *A Substitute for Victory: The Politics of Peacemaking and the Korean Armistice Talks*, Ithaca, N.Y.: Cornell University Press, 1990.

19. Robert G. Sutter, *China-Watch: Toward Sino-American Reconciliation*, Baltimore: Johns Hopkins University Press, 1978, 34–46.

20. Regarding the 1940 debates, see John Garver, *Chinese Soviet Relations, 1937–1945: The Diplomacy of Chinese Nationalism*, New York: Oxford University Press, 1988, 136–40. Regarding the post–World War II debates, see John Gittings, "New Light on Mao, His View of the World," *China Quarterly*, no. 60 (October–December 1974), 756–57.

21. Lin Biao, "Long Live the Victory of People's War," *Peking Review*, no. 36 (September 3, 1965), 9–30. For an analysis of the doctrine of people's war, see Peter Van Ness, *Revolution and Chinese Foreign Policy: Peking's Support for Wars of National Liberation*, Berkeley: University of California Press, 1972; Chalmers Johnson, *Autopsy on People's War*, Berkeley: University of California Press, 1973; John Gittings, *The World and China, 1922–1972*, New York: Harper, 1974.

22. Scott A. Boorman argued that this encirclement-counterencirclement strategy is derived from Chinese chess. See *The Protracted Game: A Wei-ch'i Interpretation of Maoist Revolutionary Strategy*, New York: Oxford University Press, 1969.

23. Regarding China's policies during the Laotian crisis, see Chae Jin Lee, *Chinese Communist Policy in Laos: 1954–1965*, University Microfilms, 1967; Brian Crozier, "Peking and the Laotian Crisis: An Interim Appraisal," *China Quarterly*, no. 6 (July–September 1961), 128–37; Brian Crozier, "Peking and the Laotian Crisis: A Further Appraisal," *China Quarterly*, no. 11 (July–September 1962), 116–23. Regarding the background of the Laotian crisis, see Hugh Toye, *Laos: Buffer State or Battleground*, London: Oxford University Press, 1968. Regarding China's positions and activities at the 1961–1962 Geneva conference, see Arthur Lall, *How Communist China Negotiates*, New York: Columbia

University Press, 1968. Lall was head of India's delegation to the conference. U.S. policy is summarized in Roger Hilsman, *To Move a Nation*, New York: Delta, 1976, 91–155.

24. *Concerning the Situation in Laos*, Beijing: Foreign Languages Press, 1959, 66.

25. Regarding this conjunction of threats, see Whiting, *Chinese Calculus*, 62–72.

26. "Hands Off Southeast Asia!" *Peking Review*, no. 21 (May 25, 1962), 9–10.

27. Crozier, "A Further Appraisal," 117. According to Crozier, U.S. advisers saw reinforcements and supplies for the Pathet Lao crossing the border from China into Laos in April 1962 but were unable to confirm whether the individuals sighted were of Chinese nationality.

28. Henry A. Kissinger, *Years of Upheaval*, Boston: Little, Brown, 1982, 58–59.

29. *Support the People of South Vietnam, Defeat United States Aggression*, Beijing: Foreign Languages Press, 1965, vol. I, 38. Cited in Frank E. Rogers, "Sino-American Relations and the Vietnam War, 1964–66," *China Quarterly*, no. 66 (June 1976), 293–314.

30. "Resolute and Unreserved Support for Viet Nam," *Peking Review*, April 23, 1965, 6–7.

31. Kenneth T. Young, *Negotiating with the Chinese Communists: The United States Experience, 1953–1967*, New York: McGraw-Hill, 1968, 272.

32. Whiting, *Chinese Calculus*, 170–95. Other sources regarding Chinese support for North Vietnam include Hoang Van Hoan, "Distortion of Facts About Militant Friendship Between Vietnam and China Is Impermissible," *Chinese Law and Government*, vol. 16, no. 1 (Spring 1983), 75–93; "On Hanoi's White Book," in *Chinese Law and Government*, vol. 16, no. 1 (Spring 1983), 69–74; "China's Role in Vietnam's Struggle," *China News Analysis* (Hong Kong), no. 1179 (April 25, 1980), 6–7; Daniel S. Papp, *Vietnam: The View from Moscow, Peking, and Washington*, Jefferson, Mo.: N.C. McFarland and Company, 1981, 73–82, 111–22; George M. Kahin and John W. Lewis, *The United States in Vietnam*, New York: Delta, 1969, 189–93, 227–38.

33. *Renmin ribao* (People's Daily), November 21, 1979, 4. Hanoi gives substantially lower figures.

34. CIA Intelligence Information Cables, April 10 and 29, 1965, in *CIA Research Reports, China 1946–76*, Reel II, frame 0245 and 0251, University Publications of America, Bethesda, MD.: 1982.

35. Young, *Negotiating with the Chinese Communists*, 268–75; Allen S. Whiting, "War with China?" *The New Republic*, May 20, 1972. Hanoi made this charge after its 1979 war with China. See Ministry of Foreign Affairs, Socialist Republic of Vietnam, *The Truth About Vietnam-China Relations Over the Last Thirty Years*, Hanoi, 1979, 32.

36. Donald Zagoria, *Vietnam Triangle: Moscow, Peking, and Hanoi*, New York: Pegasus, 1967, 63–98. Also Uri Ra'anan, "Peking's Foreign Policy Debate, 1965–1966," and Donald Zagoria, "The Strategic Debate in Peking," both in Tang Tsou, ed., *China in Crisis*, vol. 2, Chicago: University of Chicago Press, 1968, 23–71 and 237–68; Donald Zagoria, "On Kremlinology: A Second Reply," *China Quarterly*, no. 50 (April–June 1972), 343–50; Maury Lisann, "Moscow and the Chinese Power Struggle," *Problems of Communism*, vol. 18, no. 6 (November–December 1969), 32–41. Analysts questioning the conclusion that Luo desired to repair relations with Moscow include Harry Harding and Melvin Gurtov, *The Purge of Luo Jui-ch'ing: The Politics of Chinese Strategic Planning*, R-548-PR, Santa Monica, Calif.: Rand Corporation, 1971; Michael Yahuda, "Kremlinology and the Chinese Strategic Debate, 1956–66," *China Quarterly*, no. 49 (January–March 1972), 32–75.

37. Barry Naughton, "The Third Front: Defense Industrialization in the Chinese Interior," *China Quarterly*, no. 115 (September 1988), 351–86. Naughton argues that the Third Front refutes conventional wisdom about an intra-CCP debate over the gravity of the U.S. threat in 1964–1965.

Chapter Fourteen

The Period of Sino-Soviet Confrontation

THE RISE OF THE SOVIET THREAT

The emergence of the Sino-Soviet territorial issue in 1963 led Moscow to deploy more troops to border regions to insure against Chinese encroachment. Beijing responded in kind. By 1965, the previously non-militarized Sino-Soviet border was rapidly being transformed. Both sides constructed observation posts, patrol roads, and checkpoints and, somewhat further to the rear and at a somewhat later date, military bases, supply roads, rail spurs, and air fields.[1]

China's descent into the maelstrom of the Cultural Revolution during 1966 and 1967 led to further intensification of the Soviet threat. The disorder and factional conflict associated with that upheaval sorely tempted Soviet leaders to intervene on behalf of Mao's "revisionist" opponents. The new Soviet leadership, under Leonid Brezhnev and Alexi Kosygin, was critical of many of Khrushchev's Asian policies, but agreed with his skeptical appraisal of Mao Zedong. To Soviet leaders, the Cultural Revolution proved that Mao Zedong was not a Marxist, but a petty-bourgeois nationalist inclined toward adventurism and idealism. Mao's economic policies had nothing in common with correct principles of socialist construction, and his Cultural Revolution amounted to either a counterrevolutionary mass rebellion or a military coup against the CCP. In short, Mao's policies endangered the existence of socialism in China. In terms of foreign policy, Soviet leaders believed that Mao objectively assisted the forces of imperialism by disrupting and dividing the revolutionary camp. Perhaps most serious of all, the Maoists showed signs of willingness to improve relations with the United States. Mao's opponents, on the other hand, favored sounder policies. To Moscow, those CCP leaders that Mao called revisionists were China's "healthy, Marxist-Leninist forces." The Soviet Union had a proletarian internationalist duty to support such healthy forces.

In January 1966, the 1936 treaty of mutual security between Mongolia and the Soviet Union expired and was renewed. According to Beijing, the new treaty contained a secret protocol providing for stationing of Soviet troops in Mongolia. Within months, Beijing announced that large concentrations of Soviet troops and armor were being deployed to forward positions in Mongolia. Soviet deployments along the Chinese border steadily increased, and by the end of 1967, they numbered between 250,000 and 350,000. Moscow also indicated increasing readiness to use these military units in support of China's healthy forces. In February 1967, for example, the Soviet military paper *Red Star* announced that the Soviet Union was ready to take any action necessary, offensive or defensive, to help the Chinese people liberate themselves from Mao's rule. Other Soviet broadcasts called on genuine Communists in China to overthrow Mao, while Uighur language broadcasts to Xinjiang implied that Soviet assistance would be forthcoming if Xinjiang Uighurs rebelled against Chinese rule. In mid-1967, Soviet forces carried out large-scale maneuvers in the Soviet Far East.[2]

The chaos of the Cultural Revolution would have greatly facilitated Soviet intervention. With the PLA involved in domestic political and administrative duties, Chinese front-line resistance to a Soviet invasion would have been weakened. Moreover, many of Mao's opponents were fighting for their lives and might have been willing to work with Soviet forces to repress Maoist extremism. Finally, the ultra-militancy of China's Cultural Revolutionary diplomacy had isolated it from the international community. Most foreign governments looked upon China as a dangerously irrational power and would have had limited sympathy for the Maoist regime in the event of Soviet intervention to restore order—or at least so Soviet leaders might hope.

The Soviet intervention in Czechoslovakia in August 1968 and the promulgation of the Brezhnev Doctrine were extremely grave omens. According to the Brezhnev Doctrine, it was the "proletarian internationalist duty" of the Soviet Union to uphold the "gains of socialism" whenever those gains were threatened by the forces of domestic counterrevolution. This doctrine could readily be applied to China. Meanwhile, the buildup of Soviet military forces along China's borders continued.[3]

Steady escalation of the border conflict during 1967 and 1968 was one immediate cause of the Soviet military buildup. Moscow was determined to establish firm control over the full extent of what it felt was Soviet territory. In mid-1967, Soviet border guards began patrolling up to the boundary line claimed by Moscow; i.e., the Chinese banks of the Amur and Ussuri rivers. Beijing maintained that the boundary followed the *thalweg*, or central line of the main channel. This meant that both sides claimed some 600 islands on the "Chinese" side of the *thalweg*.

Beijing was determined not to acquiesce to de facto Soviet control over the disputed islands. Consequently, Chinese and Soviet patrols increasingly challenged one another in disputed areas, and the level of violence grew. The passing of patrols escalated to formal challenges of each side by the other. Next came pushing and shoving matches. Then rifles were unslung and their butts used as clubs. During summers, patrol craft maneuvered about one another, with larger boats attempting to capsize smaller craft. Fire hoses were aimed at opposing craft, and in retaliation the offending craft were boarded and their fire hoses cut with axes. Neither side was prepared to back down. An armed clash was inevitable. It came on March 2, 1969, at Zhenbao Island, called Damansky by the Russians, located about midway between Khabarovsk and Vladivostok on the Ussuri River. Figure 14–1 depicts Zhenbao Island.

There is a consensus among Western analysts that China took the initiative in the March 2 clash: Chinese soldiers may not necessarily have fired first on that day, but they did, Western analysts agree, take the initiative in engineering the episode on that day.[4] Confrontations at Zhenbao had begun in 1967, escalated gradually, and by February 1969, Soviet border guards were warning Chinese patrols that further intrusions into Soviet territory would be fired upon. Rather than stop patrolling, the Chinese moved to ensure that when the inevitable clash occurred, their forces would enjoy local superiority: Future Chinese patrols onto Zhenbao were covered by machine guns concealed along the Chinese bank. On the morning of March 2, a Chinese patrol crossed the ice of the frozen Ussuri toward Zhenbao. Challenged by Soviet troops, it withdrew onto the island. The Soviet patrol pursued and a firefight erupted. At this point the Chinese covering forces, previously undetected by the Soviets, opened fire from the Chinese bank. The Soviet patrol was caught in a cross fire. Seven Soviet soldiers were killed, and twenty-three wounded.

Most Western analysts agree that China's decision to stand at Zhenbao was made by Mao Zedong. Several factors were probably foremost in his mind. A refusal to stand firm would have meant allowing the establishment of a de facto boundary along the line claimed by Moscow. Moreover, Soviet pressure on China was mounting. There were indications that Moscow was considering a Czechoslovakia-style intervention in China. Standing firm at Zhenbao would demonstrate just how difficult a military engagement with China would be, and might make Moscow reconsider such a move. Failure to stand firm, on the other hand, would further embolden Moscow. China's initiative at Zhenbao is probably best understood as a limited local rebuff designed to discourage further Soviet encroachment. It was, in other words, a form of "active defense."

Mao may also have used the clash at Zhenbao to shift debate in favor of Zhou Enlai's policy of tilt toward the United States and to

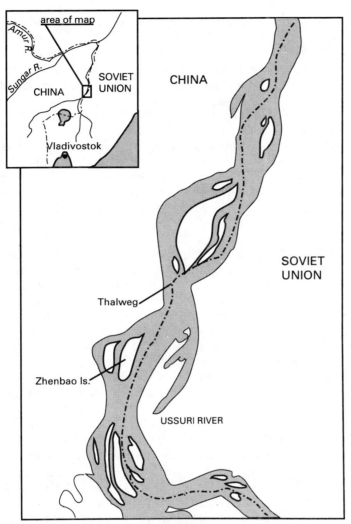

Figure 14–1 Zhenbao Island Area

inoculate China against a renewal of intimate ties with the Soviet Union. (The debates between Zhou and Lin Biao were discussed in Chapter Three.) Many Chinese still thought of the United States as China's prime enemy. By late 1968, however, Mao had concluded that the Soviet threat surpassed the American threat, and may have ordered the use of active defense at Zhenbao as a way of educating people about the true nature of the Soviet Union and creating conditions propitious for the implementation of Zhou's policy of rapprochement with the United States. Domestic considerations probably also entered into Mao's calculations over Zhenbao. Having unleashed the Cultural Revolution, in the late summer of 1968 Mao faced the task of restoring order. In this situation, a border crisis with the Soviet Union could be useful, encouraging people to rally around the PLA and the national government.

Whatever Mao's calculations, the clash at Zhenbao precipitated a crisis that took China and the Soviet Union to the brink of all-out war. After the initial clash at Zhenbao, the Soviets rushed reinforcements to the area and a second, much larger battle occurred on March 15. This time both sides employed artillery and the Soviets used armor. Clashes then erupted elsewhere along the disputed border.

Soviet ground forces also administered decisive defeats, what the Soviets called "firm rebuffs," to Chinese forces who challenged Soviet efforts to control contested territory. Moscow applied the heaviest pressure in western Xinjiang, where logistic and demographic factors favored the Soviet Union. In the Far East, Soviet supplies had to transit the already overloaded Trans-Siberian rail line, while Chinese population and industrial centers were nearby. In Central Asia the advantages were reversed. There Soviet industrial and population centers were closer and the Soviet railway system more developed, while China had to transport men and supplies from distant urban centers over the railway to Urumqi. In late August, Soviet forces moved forcefully to assert control over disputed territories in the Dzungarian region of western Xinjiang.[5]

Moscow also prepared large-scale military action against China. Additional Soviet divisions were deployed to positions strikingly reminiscent of those taken up by the Soviet army prior to its August 1945 assault on Japanese Manchukuo. Preparations were made for a surgical strike by Soviet aircraft carrying conventional bombs against China's uranium-enrichment plant at Lanzhou. Such a move would have severely crippled China's nuclear weapons program. Ominous hints that the Soviet Union might employ nuclear weapons against China appeared in Soviet media, were leaked to Eastern European and Pakistani diplomats, and were broached by the reputed KGB operative Victor Louis. In mid-March, for example, Radio Moscow warned that if Mao's provocations against the Soviet Union continued, millions of Chinese might die. The Chinese people should not believe their leader's assertions that the Soviet Union was a paper tiger:

> The whole world knows that the main weapon of the Soviet armed forces are its rockets...carrying nuclear warheads. What can Mao summon to counter the reply of the Soviet armed forces to a military venture against the Soviet Union? Does he have rockets capable of carrying nuclear weapons?[6]

According to Arkady Shevchenko, Soviet ambassador to the United Nations who defected to the United States in 1978, the Soviet Politburo seriously considered a preemptive strike against China in 1969. Defense Minister Andrei Grechko reportedly favored a large-scale attack on China with big thermonuclear bombs producing enormous amounts of radiation. This would solve Moscow's China problem for several generations, while further procrastination would make such resolute action impossible. War with China was inevitable, Grechko argued, and it was irresponsible not to strike while the USSR had the upper hand. The CPSU Politburo was stalemated for several months over the question of war with China, according to Shevchenko. Eventually fears regarding the possible U.S. response tipped the scales in favor of peace. Shevchenko recounts:

> Of the factors that dissuaded the Politburo from approving an attack on China, the important one was undoubtedly the warning that the United States would rebuff it vigorously....This knowledge cooled passions in the Politburo and strengthened Brezhnev's middle-of-the-road position: not to attack China but instead show Soviet power by stationing large contingents of troops armed with nuclear weapons along the entire length of the border.[7]

Paralysis arising from the deep divisions between Zhou Enlai and Lin Biao prevented Chinese diplomacy from attempting to exploit Soviet-American rivalries during the 1969 confrontation. Instead, Beijing relied on its own military capabilities to deter Soviet attack. First, it threatened to retaliate to a Soviet strike by imposing on the USSR a vast, costly, and unwinnable land war. If Moscow began a war, China would continue it on terms advantageous to China. While Moscow might strike with nuclear bombs, China would counterattack with infantry at times and places of its own choosing. Once war began, Beijing warned, it would cover a vast area and last a very long time. A PRC statement of October 7 warned: "China will never be intimidated by war threats, including nuclear war threats. Should a handful of war maniacs dare to raid China's strategic sites in defiance of world condemnation, that will be war, that will be aggression, and the 700 million Chinese people will rise up in resistance and use revolutionary war to eliminate the war of aggression."[8]

Beijing launched a campaign to prepare for war to give substance to Beijing's warnings about a protracted Sino-Soviet war. Domestic disorder was suppressed and PLA units reassembled. Additional divisions were deployed to the frontier. Bomb shelters were dug in cities across China and especially in north China. Critical government personnel evacuated Beijing. Critical materials were imported and/or stockpiled. Militia was called up and given accelerated training. Critical defense factories in Manchuria were dismantled and relocated in hardened underground positions or in China's interior.[9]

China also used its small and primitive nuclear force as a deterrent during the 1969 crisis. China then probably had a dozen or so atomic and hydrogen bombs. At the peak of the 1969 crisis in September, it tested a twenty-five-kiloton fission bomb and a three-megaton fusion bomb. The official announcements accompanying these tests were low-key but firm, reiterating that China's nuclear forces were exclusively for defense and that China would never be the first to employ such weapons. China would, however, the statement said, retaliate in kind to any nuclear attack.[10] Taken in context, these tests were statements of Chinese determination to use its nuclear weapons if forced to by Moscow. Interestingly, fear of Chinese nuclear retaliation was not a factor mentioned by Shevchenko as dissuading the Soviet leadership from embracing Grechko's hard-line approach in 1969.

The major delivery system for Chinese nuclear forces during the 1969 crisis was the Hong-6 bomber. These were Chinese copies of the Soviet Tupolev Tu-16 "Badger" first manufactured in China in August 1964. While the Hong-6's chances of penetrating Soviet air defenses were low, several might make it to Soviet Siberian cities such as Khabarovsk, Irkutsk, Chita, or Vladivostok. They did not, after all, have far to go. They were also dispersed and rotated among numerous airfields to increase chances of surviving a Soviet preemptive strike. China also had several CSS1 East Wind ballistic missiles with a range of some 800 kilometers. A CSS1 had test-delivered a twenty-five-kiloton fission bomb (about the size of the Hiroshima bomb) to the Lop Nor test range in October 1966. These were primitive, inaccurate, liquid-fueled missiles, quite vulnerable to Soviet preemption. But again, vulnerability to preemption was minimized by use of camouflage, decoys, and repositioning to new sites.[11]

Chinese firmness during the 1969 crisis was balanced by a willingness to compromise on critical issues. On June 13, Moscow demanded that border negotiations broken off in 1964 be resumed "within the next two or three months." In effect, this was an ultimatum. On September 11, two days before the deadline expired, Zhou Enlai met with Alexi Kosygin at the Beijing airport. Either at that meeting or through subsequent diplomatic exchanges, China dropped its previous demand for a withdrawal of Soviet forces from disputed areas *prior* to the beginning of negotiations. The Zhou-Kosygin meeting led to the beginning of negotiations in October. During the next year China also made a number of moves to restore a modicum of cordiality to Sino-Soviet relations.

DEALING WITH THE SOVIET THREAT

From 1969 to 1985, Chinese national security policy was directed at checking the Soviet threat. Until 1982, Beijing kept Moscow at arm's length. During the early 1970s, Beijing agreed to certain improvements in bilateral Sino-Soviet relations as a way of reducing the extreme tension generated by the border crisis. Such improvements were limited, however, and ties remained cool. Beijing continued the bilateral talks with Moscow begun in 1969 largely as a way of keeping alive Soviet hopes for future improvement in Sino-Soviet relations, thereby dissuading Moscow from resorting to force against China. But while the talks continued, they made no progress, in part because many of China's leaders feared that improvement in Sino-Soviet relations would embolden Moscow.[12]

There was disagreement within China's elite over the nature of the Soviet threat. As noted earlier in the discussion of internal security in Chapter Twelve, the CCP's radicals argued that the Soviet threat was primarily one of internal subversion. The radicals conceded that Soviet military power was far superior to China's, but felt that there was little danger of outright Soviet attack as long as China was prepared to wage a protracted people's war and as long as Moscow could not count on collaboration by hidden revisionists within China. A moderate faction led by Zhou Enlai and Deng Xiaoping was much more concerned with the possibility of a straight-out Soviet military attack. Zhou's group was more troubled by the great disparity between Soviet and Chinese military power than by the existence of unorthodox thought within China. Soviet power was so overwhelming, Zhou argued, that should Moscow choose to use it, the Chinese people would endure untold suffering. The best way to deal with the Soviet threat was reduce the industrial and technological gap between China and the Soviet Union, and the best way to do this was through a comprehensive and rapid program of economic development, the Four Modernizations.

Zhou's moderates differed among themselves about whether or not relations with Moscow should be improved in order to diminish the danger of Soviet attack. Most opposed such improvements for reasons described above. The moderates also disagreed among themselves as to how much stress should be placed on immediate improvements in China's military capabilities. Some favored major increases in defense spending. Others argued that such increases would make little difference over the short term, would alarm Moscow, and would be a drag on China's economic and technological development. Finally, some moderates argued for closer alignment with the United States in order to help deter a Soviet attack, secure Western support for China's development effort, and make unnecessary major increases in China's defense budget. This perspective was too bold for many moderates, let alone their radical opponents, during the early and mid-1970s. In the late 1970s, however, it was translated into policy. The death of Mao in September 1976, the purge of the extreme radicals shortly after his death, and the return of Deng Xiaoping to power in July 1977 represented a triumph for the moderate point of view.[13]

CHINA'S "SELF-DEFENSIVE COUNTER-ATTACK" AGAINST VIETNAM

All five types of political objectives enumerated in Chapter Eleven were involved in Beijing's decision for war with Vietnam in February 1979. In terms of deterring superpower threat, Beijing was dismayed by

Vietnam's deepening alignment with the Soviet Union. In September 1975, VWP secretary general Le Duan visited Beijing to solicit Chinese support for Vietnam's postwar development. Beijing tried to persuade Duan to endorse China's Three Worlds theory, which placed Soviet "social imperialism" on a par with "U.S. imperialism." Duan refused. Instead, during his speech in Beijing, Le Duan lauded the Soviet role in the defeat of U.S. imperialism, the common enemy of the people of the world. From Beijing's perspective, of course, Soviet hegemonism, not U.S. imperialism, was the arch-villain. Hanoi moved another step closer to Moscow the next month when Le Duan signed a joint communiqué in Moscow praising the Soviet policy of detente. To Beijing, detente was merely a smokescreen for Soviet hegemonist expansion. From the Chinese perspective, the Soviet-Vietnamese communiqué represented Vietnam's surrender to hegemonism. As a consequence, Chinese aid to Vietnam declined while Soviet aid increased.[14]

Vice Premier Li Xiannian enumerated China's grievances to Vietnamese Premier Pham Van Dong in Beijing in June 1977. Territorial issues were at the top of Li's list. China had proposed negotiations over the boundary issue in 1975. "But you," Li told Dong, "while stalling negotiations with us, continued to let your men enter Chinese territory illegally, claim[ing] this or that place as belonging to Vietnam. They even engaged in fistfighting and other acts of violence."[15] Vietnamese encroachment on Chinese territory, Li charged, had increased from 100 incidents in 1974 to 900 in 1976. Another territorial grievance had to do with the Paracels and Spratlys. During its war against the Americans, Vietnam had recognized China's sovereignty over those islands. But once the United States was defeated, Li told Dong during their 1977 meeting, Hanoi moved to seize the Spratly Islands and reneged on its earlier recognition of Chinese ownership.

Still another grievance put forth by Li had to do with Hanoi's policy toward ethnic Chinese in Vietnam. During the 1950s, Hanoi had promised Beijing that ethnic Chinese would be allowed to retain Chinese nationality if they so desired. The Hanoi-backed National Liberation Front gave similar guarantees regarding ethnic Chinese in South Vietnam. Early in 1976, however, all ethnic Chinese in South Vietnam were forced to accept Vietnamese nationality on pain of expulsion. Throughout 1977 and 1978, Hanoi adopted policies designed to break the economic and social power of the overseas Chinese in South Vietnam and to forcibly assimilate ethnic Chinese in both North and South Vietnam. During his meeting with Dong in June 1977, Li Xiannian severely rebuked Hanoi for its betrayal of promises regarding ethnic Chinese in Vietnam.[16]

Beijing's displeasure with Hanoi's harsh treatment of Vietnam's Chinese population was linked with efforts in the late 1970s to reestablish China's links to the 15 million overseas Chinese in Southeast Asia in order to draw on the contribution those overseas Chinese could make to the Four Modernizations. Had Beijing allowed Hanoi's moves to pass unchallenged, this would have been a severe blow to Beijing's prestige among the Southeast Asian overseas Chinese communities. Moreover, Chinese inaction might have encouraged other Southeast Asian countries to adopt similar drastic solutions to the "Chinese question" in their own countries.

Cambodia constituted another source of Sino-Vietnamese conflict. This issue was closely tied to the future of Chinese regional influence. Was Cambodia to remain a fully independent state with friendly ties with China? Or was it to enter into a special, close relation with Vietnam? The PRC had long enjoyed a special relation with Cambodia. After the Geneva conference in 1954, Cambodian ruler Norodom Sihanouk looked to China for protection against Cambodia's two traditional nemeses, Vietnam and Thailand. Sihanouk's neutralism rejected association with U.S. containment efforts and included cordial relations with China. When Hanoi began planning stepped-up infiltration into South Vietnam in the late 1950s, it sought Sihanouk's consent for the use of eastern Cambodia for such purposes. Beijing persuaded Sihanouk to accede to Hanoi's requests, promising that China would guarantee North Vietnam's withdrawal from eastern Cambodia after the war.[17]

Beijing also enjoyed close ties with the Cambodian Communists, the Khmer Rouge, who took power in April 1975. The Khmer Rouge were determinedly independent, but felt a strong ideological kinship with China's radical Maoists. Just as importantly, they looked to China for material support. They were also deeply suspicious of Vietnam and determined to liberate Cambodia from what they viewed as Vietnamese encroachments. As soon as the Khmer Rouge seized power, they began driving Vietnamese out of Cambodia and laying claim to Khmer-populated areas of South Vietnam—areas included in Vietnam by boundaries drawn by the French colonialists. As Cambodia's conflict with Hanoi intensified, the Khmer Rouge looked to China for support.

Hanoi was dismayed by the direction of Khmer Rouge policy. It felt that there was, or ought to be, a special relation between Cambodia and Vietnam. Vietnam had led the way to the liberation of all of Indochina, bearing the brunt of the fighting against the French and the Americans. Moreover, a friendly Cambodia was vital to Vietnam's security. Vietnam could not allow Cambodia to fall under the influence of a potentially hostile power such as China. Deep suspicions of China colored Hanoi's actions. Vietnam's leaders tended to see China's territorial claims in the South China Sea, its link with Cambodia, the influential position of the overseas Chinese community within South Vietnam, together with Beijing's support for those ethnic Chinese, the escalating conflict along the Sino-Vietnamese border, and the reduction in Chinese aid to Vietnam as parts of a campaign to pressure Vietnam. Beijing's objective, Hanoi believed, was to force Vietnam to become a satellite state.

The border conflict between Ca nb   i and Vietnam escalated throughout 1977, culminating in large   s in November. Le Duan then made a secret trip to Beijing to ask   i to use its influence with the Cambodian regime to compel it to   attacking Vietnam. No agreement was reached, and in Febru   1978, the Vietnamese leadership decided to get rid of the Pol Pot   ime one way or another. Hanoi decided, in other words, to oust C iina's closest client in Southeast Asia. Covert efforts would be made   o overthrow that regime, but if these failed, a large-scale invasion wou l accomplish the task. Shortly afterwards, and probably in preparation ior a confrontation with China, Hanoi decided to push through the "socialization of commerce" in South Vietnam—a move that fell most heavily on the ethnic Chinese who dominated the finance and commerce of pre-1975 South Vietnam.

Chinese intelligence soon learned of Hanoi's decision to invade Cambodia and, as Vietnamese preparations mounted, China signaled that it "would not stand idly by" while Vietnam attacked Cambodia. To counter Chinese support for Cambodia, Hanoi moved to secure Soviet support, and in November 1978 a Soviet-Vietnamese security treaty was signed.[18] From Beijing's perspective, the formation of a Soviet-Vietnamese alliance and a Soviet-supported Vietnamese attack on Cambodia were a part of Moscow's global strategy of a "drive to the south." While directed primarily toward seizing control over the raw materials and sea lanes upon which the West depended, the Soviet-Vietnamese bid for hegemony over Indochina represented a major advance for Soviet efforts to encircle China. With Vietnam in Moscow's orbit and a Soviet military presence in Vietnam, an entirely new component would be added to the Soviet military threat to China. Such national security considerations were commingled with a desire to expand China's own influence in Southeast Asia by supporting its Cambodian ally and by keeping Indochina divided into three independent states that would be more amenable to Chinese influence than a Vietnam-dominated Indochinese federation.

Beijing's decision for war with Hanoi was a type of "active defense" against Moscow's expansive "drive to the south." In Beijing's view, the way to avert a major war was to challenge Soviet advances, disrupt its strategic preparations, and keep it from achieving an advantageous position that might tempt it to launch a major war. Moscow's support for Hanoi was part and parcel of its global advance and had to be dealt with accordingly. Beijing was also urging the United States to increase vigilance and wage a "tit-for-tat" struggle against the Soviet hegemonists. If China stood up to Hanoi and Moscow in Indochina, it would help show other members of the global anti-hegemony united front how to struggle against the hegemonists. It would also enhance the stature of China as America's anti-hegemony partner.[19]

Finally, there was a strong emotional component to China's

decision for war with Vietnam. China's leaders were very angry with what they perceived as Hanoi's ingratitude and duplicity. From Beijing's perspective, China had given North Vietnam consistent, substantial, and critical support throughout its long struggle against the French and then against the Americans. Hanoi had gratefully accepted such assistance at the time, but once the Americans were defeated, Hanoi began implementing one anti-China policy after another.

The PLA's invasion of Vietnam began on February 17, 1979, with an initial invasion force of 100,000 and another 230,000 in reserve. Beijing had initially hoped to launch the attack to coincide with Vietnam's invasion of Cambodia in December 1978, in order to slow the Vietnamese advance into Cambodia and allow Cambodian forces time to organize resistance. This failed because the PLA was unable to move quickly enough and because Vietnamese forces occupied Cambodia more rapidly than Beijing had anticipated.[20]

The day after China's invasion began, Moscow issued a statement citing its treaty obligations to Vietnam, calling on China to "stop before it is too late," and demanding an immediate withdrawal of Chinese forces from Vietnam. Further Soviet warnings followed and were given substance by deployments of Soviet naval squadrons off Vietnam's coast and the mobilization of Soviet forces along the Xinjiang border. The Soviet Union also rushed vital military supplies, via India, to Vietnam, but otherwise took no substantive military action to assist Vietnam.

Two days after its attack began, China tried to minimize chances for Soviet intervention by declaring that its objectives were limited in time and space and that it would withdraw once those objectives were obtained. PLA forces along the Sino-Soviet border were also put on alert, and some 300,000 civilians evacuated from sensitive border areas. China's newly established diplomatic ties with the United States helped steel Beijing's nerves. Washington did, in fact, provide some deterrent support to China during its brief war with Vietnam. Deng Xiaoping's belligerent statements made from public platforms during his January 1979 visit to the United States were conspicuously not contradicted by Carter administration officials. Once the war was underway, the U.S. aircraft carrier *Constellation* deployed to the Gulf of Tonkin to monitor Soviet naval activities. Although Washington's support was considerably less firm than Beijing desired, the United States did use its power to a certain degree to protect China from Soviet intervention.

The PLA's performance during the 1979 war was not impressive. It moved slowly; its equipment and tactics were outdated; and communications and coordination of artillery fire were poor. Although it did not engage Vietnam's main force units, the PLA suffered huge casualties—some 26,000, according to Western reports. Yet the PLA succeeded by sheer weight of numbers in seizing its objectives. The heaviest fighting occurred in the vicinity of Lang Son and Lao Cai. The PLA mounted its final assault on Lang Son (about ten miles inside Vietnam) on March 3. On March 5 that city (along with Lao Cai, Ha Giang, Cao Bang, Dong Ke, That Ke, and Mon Cai) was in Chinese hands and Beijing announced that its forces would now withdraw. Beijing also warned Vietnam not to attack withdrawing Chinese forces, lest China renew the offensive. Hanoi heeded the warning. The withdrawal was completed by March 17, but not before the PLA systematically demolished the economic and transportation infrastructure in the area under Chinese occupation.

Military performance aside, Beijing largely achieved its political objectives. It punished Hanoi for ignoring Beijing's warnings about violating China's vital interests. It greatly increased the costs to Hanoi of its conquest of Cambodia. It demonstrated to the world that the Soviet Union and its allies could be successfully challenged. It maintained China's credibility as an ally; even after its client regime in Cambodia was ousted by Vietnam, China emerged as a credible ally of Thailand in a continuing confrontation with Vietnam. It was able to do this because of its willingness for war with Hanoi, which made Beijing a credible ally despite the ouster of its Cambodian clients.

Throughout the 1980s, Beijing kept up military pressure on Vietnam. Artillery bombardments and infantry probing actions along the border occurred sporadically, often in response to stepped-up Vietnamese military operations in Cambodia. Substantial PLA forces were stationed near Vietnam's northern borders and Beijing periodically threatened a second punitive attack against Vietnam. PLA naval actions in the South China Sea also increased. Beijing also sought to keep Vietnam and Moscow bogged down in their costly Cambodian quagmire. China cooperated with the United States, Thailand, and Singapore to support the anti-Vietnamese Cambodian resistance. It also did everything it could to isolate Vietnam from the international community, urging the United States to withhold diplomatic recognition and Japan to withhold economic relations from Vietnam as long as its forces remained in occupation of Cambodia. As noted in Chapter Three, cooperation with China in pressuring Vietnam became an important dimension of the Sino-U.S. strategic relation during the 1980s. Beijing also made Soviet pressure on Vietnam to withdraw from Cambodia one of its three demands for a "normalization" of Sino-Soviet relations. Given that Moscow had become Hanoi's major supplier of economic and military assistance, and since Moscow under Mikhail Gorbachev did ardently desire better Sino-Soviet ties, this created very substantial pressure on Hanoi.

The ASEAN countries also played an important role in China's anti-Vietnam strategy. Thailand was especially important for China, since it was the only ASEAN country geographically placed to provide sanctuary for the Cambodian resistance. It was largely because of Chinese and American guarantees of support in the face of probable Vietnamese pressure that Thailand decided in early 1979 to provide such sanctuary.

On the basis of this, an informal but important security relation developed between Thailand and China during the 1980s.

THE DECLINE OF THE SOVIET THREAT

By 1985, Beijing had concluded that the danger of Soviet attack was greatly reduced. The collapse of Soviet-American detente and the reinvigoration of U.S. containment put Moscow on the defensive. Simultaneously, the improvement in Sino-Soviet relations that began in 1982 undermined the arguments of Soviet hawks regarding the inevitability of Sino-Soviet conflict and the need to strike "before it was too late." In Afghanistan, Soviet forces were bogged down in a costly war. Since some of Moscow's major scenarios for war with China envisioned seizure of Xinjiang or Manchuria by Soviet forces, the difficulties experienced in pacifying Afghanistan made it unlikely that Soviet leaders would decide to undertake a similar task on a larger scale in China's northeast or northwest. Perhaps most important, the deterioration of the Soviet Union's domestic economy combined with the burdens of Moscow's foreign endeavors and loss of Western credits and technology to bring about a reorientation of Soviet thinking under Gorbachev. Chinese leaders concluded that with Gorbachev's program of domestic reform and economic development guiding Soviet policy, the risks of a Soviet attack on China were reduced even further.

Even into the late 1980s, Chinese security policy remained founded on the primacy, if not the immediacy, of the Soviet threat. The PLA was still primarily deployed and trained to deal with the contingency of a Soviet invasion of Xinjiang or Manchuria. The acquisition of anti-tank weapons designed to counter a Soviet invasion remained a major thrust of PLA modernization efforts. But a large-scale Soviet attack was now judged unlikely. Even smaller-scale Soviet attacks were deemed highly improbable. Nonetheless, the Soviet Union was still seen as the major long-term threat to China's security.

Regional powers such as Vietnam and India were seen as posing more immediate dangers. Significantly, both of those countries enjoy treaties of alliance with the USSR. Regarding Vietnam, naval-amphibious battles over islands in the South China Sea are the most probable form of conflict. Regarding India, the territorial conflict remains a festering source of tension. In 1987, dispute over control of a remote canyon just east of the trijuncture of the India-Bhutan-Chinese border in the eastern Himalayas took the two countries to the brink of war. The crisis was defused, but left the two sides eyeball to eyeball over the disputed frontier. The wide demilitarized strip that had separated the two sides since the 1962 war was obliterated during the crisis.

India's desire to prevent China from establishing security relations with India's South Asian neighbors is another major source of Sino-

Indian conflict. Twice during the 1980s, New Delhi acted forcefully to limit China's security links with South Asian nations: from 1984 to 1987, when it forced Sri Lanka to accept an Indian protectorate, and from 1989 to 1990, when it forced Nepal to respect the terms of the protectorate established in 1950.[21] From Beijing's perspective, these South Asian countries are China's neighbors, with whom China can establish and expand relations as it and the South Asian country concerned wish. For New Delhi to attempt to limit China's links with its neighbors constitutes a policy of regional hegemonism and smacks of the old containment policies of Washington and Moscow.

China's entente cordiale with Pakistan is another primary source of Sino-Indian tension. As noted earlier, China derives a wide range of important benefits from its relation with Pakistan. In security terms, a strong independent Pakistan confronts India with a two-front threat in the event of war with China. Indian defense planners assume that Pakistan would enter a major Sino-Indian war. This means that India has to keep a large part of its army facing Pakistan in the event of a war with China. If India were able to subordinate Pakistan, however, it would be able to concentrate its forces against China. From New Delhi's perspective, China's very substantial support for Pakistan's military development efforts encourages Pakistani recklessness. New Delhi believes that Pakistan supports secessionists in Punjab and Kashmir as part of a plot to destabilize and fragment India. Moreover, Pakistan's nuclear weapons program, which New Delhi believes Beijing is assisting, threatens South Asia with an accelerated arms race and nuclear war. It would be best, New Delhi believes, if Beijing cut its support for Pakistan's military development efforts. This Beijing has refused to do. There would be uncertainty regarding China's role in an Indian-Pakistan conflict if it seemed that India was about to decisively defeat Pakistan.

India's drive for preeminence in the Indian Ocean also poses a security dilemma for China. China has a large and rapidly growing merchant marine. A large part of China's international commerce flows across the Indian Ocean. In the event of a Sino-Indian border war, India might respond to defeat on land by severing China's sea lines of communications in the Indian Ocean. Such a move could create pressure for a larger Chinese land blow against India. Indian defense planners see Burma as the most probable avenue of a major Chinese attack against India. The terrain and climate of the Himalayas would make it too difficult for China to sustain a major war across those mountains. Chinese armies have twice sustained major operations in Burma, however, in 1942 and in 1944 through 1945.

Most broadly, what is involved between India and China is an attempt to define their respective status in Asia. Both countries are led by proud nationalist elites, determined to restore their countries to the respected position to which they feel history entitles them. China's belief in its special role in Asia makes it very difficult for it to concede South Asia as an Indian sphere of influence. Should India insist on this and attempt to impose it by military means, China could well feel compelled to respond.

NOTES

1. J. Malcolm MacKintosh, "The Soviet Generals' View of China in the 1960s," in *Sino-Soviet Military Relations*, Raymond L. Garthoff, ed., New York: Praeger, 1966, 183–92.

2. Thomas M. Gottlieb, *Chinese Foreign Policy Factionalism and the Origins of the Strategic Triangle*, R-1902-NA, Santa Monica, Calif.: Rand Corporation, November 1977, 34–35, 50–51.

3. Several analysts stress the impact of the Czech intervention on Chinese policy. Allen S. Whiting, "The Sino-American Detente: Genesis and Prospects," in *China and the World Community*, Ian Wilson, ed., Sydney: Australian Institute of International Affairs, 1973, 70–89; Robert G. Sutter, *China Watch: Toward Sino-American Reconciliation*, Baltimore: Johns Hopkins University Press, 1978.

4. Studies of the Zhenbao clash include Thomas W. Robinson, "The Sino-Soviet Border Dispute: Background, Development and the March 1969 Clashes," *American Political Science Review*, vol. lxvi, no. 4 (December 1972), 1175; Harold Hinton, *Bear at the Gate: Chinese Policymaking Under Soviet Pressure*, Stanford, Calif.: Hoover Institute Press, 1971; Harold C. Hinton, "Conflict on the Ussuri: A Clash of Nationalisms," *Problems of Communism*, vol. 20, no. 1 and 2 (January–April 1971), 48–59; Roger G. Brown, "Chinese Politics and American Policy: A New Look at the Triangle," *Foreign Policy*, no. 23 (Summer 1976), 3–23; Neville Maxwell, "The Chinese Account of the 1969 Fighting at Chen Bao," *China Quarterly*, no. 56 (October–December 1973), 730–39; Thomas M. Gottlieb, *Chinese Foreign Policy Factionalism*.

5. Harold C. Hinton, *Bear at the Gate*; John W. Garver, *China's Decision for Rapprochement with the United States, 1968–1971*, Boulder, Colo.: Westview, 1982, 54–71.

6. Cited in Garver, *China's Decision*, 69.

7. Arkady Shevchenko, *Breaking with Moscow*, New York: Ballantine, 1985, 165–68.

8. Cited in Garver, *China's Decision*, 75.

9. Lu Yung-shu, "Preparations for War in Mainland China," paper presented at First Sino-American Conference on Mainland China, Taibei: Institute of International Relations, 1970; Janice Hinton, *Civil Defense in the People's Republic of China: Coming to Terms with the "Paper Tiger"*, M.A. Thesis, Fletcher School of Law and Diplomacy, June 1977.

10. Garver, *China's Decision*, 75–76; Jonathan Pollack, "Chinese Attitudes Towards Nuclear Weapons, 1964–1969," *China Quarterly*, no. 50 (April–June 1972), 244–71.

11. Regarding China's nuclear deterrent in 1969, see John W. Lewis and Xue Litai, *China Builds the Bomb*, Stanford, Calif.: Stanford University Press, 1988, 206–07, 244–45; *The Chinese War Machine*, Ray Bonds, ed., London: Salamander Books, 1979, 131, 134, 144–45, 171. The 1969 issue of the authoritative *Strategic Survey* also contains valuable information, although it incorrectly concluded that "there is no evidence that China yet has an operational nuclear force to deploy," London: International Institute for Strategic Studies, 1969, 72. During the 1969 crisis, Western journalists speculated about so-called exotic means of delivery, such as disassembly of atomic weapons, infiltration of the components by commandos, and reassembly and detonation in the vicinity of an appropriate target. In fact, Chinese nuclear weapons in 1969 were far too crude for such tactics.

12. Regarding Sino-Soviet relations in the 1970s, see Kenneth G. Lieberthal, *Sino-Soviet Conflict in the 1970s: Its Evolution and Implications for the Strategic Triangle*, R-2342-NA, Santa Monica, Calif.: Rand Corporation, July 1978, 79–95; Robert Sutter, *Chinese Foreign Policy After the Cultural Revolution*, Boulder, Colo., Westview, 1978, 15–32; Harry Gelman,

"The Sino-Soviet Dispute in the 1970s: An Overview," in *The Sino-Soviet Conflict: A Global Perspective*, Herbert J. Ellison, ed., Seattle: University of Washington Press, 1982, 355–72.

13. Lieberthal, *Sino-Soviet Conflict*, 79–95.

14. Studies of the Sino-Vietnam rift include Nayan Chandra, *Brother Enemy: A History of Indochina Since the Fall of Saigon*, New York: Macmillan, 1988; Robert S. Ross, *The Indochina Tangle: China's Vietnam Policy, 1975–1979*, New York: Columbia University Press, 1988; William J. Duiker, *China and Vietnam: The Roots of Conflict*, Indochina Research Monograph, Berkeley: Institute of East Asian Studies, 1986; Eugene K. Lawson, *The Sino-Vietnamese Conflict*, New York: Praeger, 1984.

15. "Memorandum Outlining Vice Premier Li Xiannian's Talks with Premier Pham Van Dong on 10 June 1977," Xinhua, March 22, 1979. Quoted in Chandra, *Brother Enemy*, 93. Regarding the territorial dispute, see Pao-min Chang, *The Sino-Vietnamese Territorial Dispute*, New York: Praeger, 1985.

16. Regarding the ethnic Chinese issue, see Gareth Porter, "Vietnam's Ethnic Chinese and the Sino-Vietnamese Conflict," *Bulletin of Concerned Asian Scholars*, vol. 12, no. 4 (October–December 1980), 55–60; Pao-min Chang, "The Sino-Vietnamese Dispute Over the Overseas Chinese," *China Quarterly*, no. 90 (June 1982), 195–230.

17. Regarding Cambodia, see Pao-min Chang, *Kampuchea Between China and Vietnam*, Singapore: Singapore University Press, 1985; Joseph J. Zasloff and MacAlister Brown, "The Passion of Kampuchea," *Problems of Communism*, vol. 28, no. 1 (January–February 1979), 28–43; Ben Kierman, *How Pol Pot Came to Power: A History of Communism in Kampuchea, 1930–1975*, New York: Routledge, Chapman, and Hall, 1985. Regarding Sino-Cambodian relations in the 1950s and 1960s, see Michael Leifer, *Cambodia: The Search for Security*, New York: Praeger, 1967.

18. Regarding Soviet-Vietnam relations, see Robert C. Horn, *Alliance Politics Between Comrades: The Dynamics of Soviet-Vietnamese Relations*, Los Angeles: UCLA Center for the Study of Soviet International Behavior, 1987; Douglas Pike, *Vietnam and the Soviet Union: Anatomy of an Alliance*, Boulder, Colo.: Westview, 1987. Some analysts have argued that Chinese pressure on Vietnam pushed Hanoi into closer alignment with Moscow, and that this is proof that China's leaders must not have been overly concerned with the possibility of a Soviet military presence in Vietnam. Had they been, so this argument runs, they would not have attacked Vietnam. Gareth Porter, "The Great Power Triangle in Southeast Asia," *Current History*, vol. 79, no. 461 (December 1980), 161–64, 195; Gareth Porter, "Vietnam's Soviet Alliance: A Challenge to U.S. Policy," *Indochina Issues*, no. 6 (May 1980), 2–3; Gareth Porter, "The China Card and U.S. Indochina Policy," *Indochina Issues*, no. 11 (November 1980), 2.

19. Analyses of Chinese policy at this juncture include Jonathan Pollock, "Chinese Global Strategy and Soviet Power," *Problems of Communism*, vol. 30, no. 1 (January–February 1981), 54–69; William G. Hyland, "The Sino-Soviet Conflict: A Search for New Security Strategies," and Richard H. Solomon, "American Defense Planning and Asian Security: Policy Choices for a Time of Transition," in *Asian Security in the 1980s: Problems and Policies for a Time of Transition*, Richard H. Solomon, ed., R-2492-ISA, Santa Monica, Calif.: Rand Corporation, November 1979, 1–35, 39–53; William R. Heaton, *A United Front Against Hegemonism: Chinese Foreign Policy into the 1980s*, Washington, D.C.: National Defense University Press, March 1980; Banning Garrett and Bonnie Glaser, *War and Peace: The Views from Moscow and Beijing*, Berkeley: Institute of International Studies, 1984.

20. Studies of the 1979 war include King C. Chen, *China's War Against Vietnam, 1979: A Military Analysis*, Occasional Papers/Reprints Series in Contemporary Asian Studies, School of Law, University of Maryland, no. 5, 1983; Harlan W. Jenks, "China's Punitive War Against Vietnam, A Military Assessment," *Asian Survey*, vol. 19, no. 8 (August 1979), 801–15; Hemen Ray, *China's Vietnam War*, New Delhi: Radiant, 1983; Daniel Tretiak, "China's Vietnam War and Its Consequences," *China Quarterly*, no. 80 (December 1979), 740–67; James B. Linder and James A. Gregor, "The Chinese Communist Air Force in the 'Punitive' War Against Vietnam," *Air University Review*, vol. 32, no. 6 (September–October 1981), 67–77.

21. John W. Garver, "Chinese-Indian Rivalry in Nepal: The Clash over Chinese Arms Sales," *Asian Survey*, vol. xxxi, no. 10 (October 1991), 956–75.

Part Six

China in the Twenty-First Century

Chapter Fifteen

The Future
of Chinese Power

CHINA AND THE WORLD CRISIS OF SOCIALISM

The upheaval in China in early 1989 and the subsequent violent repression of that upheaval in June, the collapse of socialism in Eastern European countries later that year, and the deepening crisis of socialism in the Soviet Union and the final collapse of the USSR in December 1991 have all cast new uncertainties on China's future role in the world. During its modern history China was repeatedly swept by the waves of ideological movements emanating from the west. The question thus arises of whether socialism and communist rule in China will suffer the same fate as in the west.

China shares many of the problems endemic to socialist systems that undermined socialism in Europe and the Soviet Union. There is a huge gulf between the ordinary people and the party apparatchik who monopolize power and enjoy a wide range of special perquisites. A large part of the people, including the overwhelming portion of the intelligentsia, no longer believe in the Marxist-Leninist ideology that justifies apparatchik rule. Exposure to the West has brought into question the putative superiority of the socialist system. China's centrally planned and bureaucratically controlled economic system also involves massive inefficiency and waste. In spite of tinkering with incentive systems in order to stimulate individual initiative and responsibility, within the planned state sector there are few incentives to use resources efficiently, innovate, or take risks. Vast amounts of capital are still poured into state enterprises with little regard for efficiency, opportunity costs, or demand for the products produced. It was such gross inefficiency and irrationality that underlay the Soviet Union's slide into economic stagnation in the 1970s and 1980s. While a centrally planned economy worked fairly well in China in the early stages of extensive industrialization, as the economy became larger and more complex, rates of capital and labor productivity declined. Many of China's economic reforms of the 1980s were designed to reverse that decline by suffusing Chinese socialism with market indicators and individual incentives. China's post–June 4, 1989 conservative rulers were skeptical of these market-oriented reforms and many seemed to favor a reinvigoration of central economic controls. Had these Stalinist conservatives succeeded in dominating China's policy process, China could well have slid gradually into the same sort of economic stagnation experienced by the Soviet Union under Leonid Brezhnev.

Immediately after the repression of June 1989 many believed that a major return to central planning was likely. This did not occur. Although many hundreds of thousands of private and collective enterprises were closed down or forced to merge with state enterprises, many others survived and continued to grow. Especially in Guangdong and its surrounding provinces, private and collective enterprises operating outside the state plan continued to prosper. This allowed Guangdong to continue the explosive growth that had begun in the mid 1980s and that strongly resembled the growth achieved by Taiwan, Korea, and Japan in earlier decades. By 1992 half of the PRC GNP was produced by non-state enterprises much more responsive to market forces. China's mammoth state enterprises continued to lumber along, subsidized heavily by state banks and other state agencies for both ideological reasons and to avoid the unrest that would be produced by plant closures and unemployment.

There are other reasons why the eventual crisis of Chinese socialism is not likely to be as acute as in Eastern Europe and the Soviet Union. Politically, the Chinese Communist Party enjoys a good deal of legitimacy among the rural population arising from the fact that it led an indigenous revolution and carried out land reform. Eastern European socialism, by contrast, was imposed by Soviet occupying forces after World War II. Economically, China's agricultural sector is much stronger than was the case in any of the European socialist countries. After 1977, Chinese agriculture underwent de facto decollectivization, which unleashed the tremendous productive energy of China's peasantry. After June 1989 China's conservative rulers tinkered with the post-1977 family-based agricultural system, but did not fundamentally alter it. In the Soviet Union, agriculture was a critical weak link, while China's de facto privatized agricultural sector is a source of considerable vitality. There are also important differences in terms of extent of economic interaction with the outside world. China's economy was, and remains, much more open to foreign influences and much more linked to world markets than were the economies of Eastern Europe and the Soviet Union when they slid into crisis in the 1980s. By the 1990s, China was a good ten years ahead of the ex–Soviet-bloc countries in terms of mastering the intricacies of international business and breaking into highly competitive foreign markets. To some degree these extensive foreign contacts have counteracted the stultifying effects of central planning in China.

The disintegration of the USSR at the end of 1991 also had the effect of bolstering CCP rule. The breakup of the former Soviet superpower along ethnic lines, the precipitous decline of the Soviet economy and consequent widespread hardship, and the eruption of local civil wars in various regions of the ex-Soviet realm seemed to many Chinese an example of the sort of national catastrophe that could befall China. The CCP seized on the fate of the USSR, claiming that this proved the correctness of the repression of the challenge to CCP power in June 1989. Had the challenge to CCP power not been crushed, Party propagandists contended, events would have led to a comparable national catastrophe in China. These arguments were accepted, often grudgingly, by many Chinese. Even those who have reached the conclusion that capitalism is a better economic system than socialism and that the CCP is an isolated and increasingly corrupt elite, frequently believe that that elite offers the best chance for guiding China to a better future.

One scenario often advanced by such disaffected but obedient Chinese is that another ten to twenty years of continued economic reform will give rise to a vital civil society beyond the Party's domination. The importance of private and collective enterprise will steadily increase, while that of state enterprises will steadily decline. Market forces will increasingly dominate the economy, and the government will rely increasingly on indirect, market-conforming techniques of economic control. Independent professional and social associations will proliferate. A middle class of entrepreneurs and self-employed professionals will gradually emerge with desires to play a greater political role. Then, when the generation of Long March veterans is well out of the way, the question of ideology and political power can again be raised. A gradual, peaceful devolution of power from the Communist party might then be possible. Thus, a national catastrophe such as befell the USSR would be avoided, while China would arrive at the goal of a prosperous and liberal emerging democracy.

No one in China or in the outside world knows what will happen when Deng Xiaoping and the other remaining Long March era veterans die. Within the CCP all groups are maneuvering to position themselves for the succession struggle that is certain to occur. As of mid-1992, following Deng Xiaoping's southern tour earlier that year, a consensus seems to have solidified around continued economic reform and opening to the outside world. This could be illusory, however, and economic neo-stalinists could well emerge from the woodwork once Deng dies.

A resurgence of Chinese isolation and a turn inward cannot be ruled out. To China's embattled neo-stalinist leaders, the world has become an extremely dark and threatening place. They attribute the failure of socialism elsewhere in the world, as they do China's own upheaval of 1989, not to intrinsic shortcomings of socialism, but to deliberate, systematic subversion by U.S. imperialism. Given these perceptions, and the very real internal challenges faced by the CCP regime, China's leaders could be tempted to turn inward, once again isolating China from the world and clamping tight, totalitarian controls on what the Chinese people are permitted to hear, see, and think. Internal dissent could also be repressed without regard to negative Western reaction. Such a retreat into isolationism would obviously be at great cost to China's technological, scientific, and economic advance. But China's hard-line rulers could conclude that this was the only way to preserve socialism, and their own power. There is little question that those rulers believe their oft-repeated assertion that "only socialism can save China," and they might conclude that only totalitarian isolationism could save socialism in China.

One way or another, however, increased regional autonomy seems likely. The coastal provinces, which have benefited most from the market-oriented autonomy of the post-1978 period, will resist efforts to recentralize authority. Indeed, this was probably a major factor thwarting trends toward a reversal of earlier decentralizing reforms in the months after June 1989. Were Beijing to attempt to override such local sentiment and move forcefully toward a recentralization of economic authority, the possibility of a rebellion against the central government in which a section of the PLA remained neutral or joined the rebels could not be ruled out. This is a possibility Chinese leaders took quite seriously in the early 1990s. Given continued economic reform, such a provincial revolt is unlikely. But the consequences of continued reform will be that the provinces, especially the southern coastal provinces, will become steadily less dependent on Beijing for economic inputs and develop vested interests in maintaining foreign economic relations that may conflict with central policies.

Were there to be upheaval or civil war in China, the first and most certain result would be large waves of Chinese emigration, perhaps numbering in the millions. For geographic and cultural reasons, Southeast Asia would probably be the primary destination of these destitute hordes. Given the delicate ethnic balance and the strong anti-Chinese sentiments common at the grassroots of many of the Southeast Asian countries, this immigration could destabilize the reluctant "host" countries. Were the governments of those host countries to adopt harsh measures to deal with this immigration, Beijing might be tempted to respond forcefully. As we have seen, protection of the overseas Chinese communities in Southeast Asia is an important Chinese objective. An embattled Chinese government might also conclude that forceful moves to protect ethnic Chinese in Southeast Asia would be a good way to rally patriotic opinion about the government. Forceful foreign policy measures might be adopted partially or largely for the sake of strengthening China's internal unity.

CHINA: A FUTURE SUPERPOWER?

Barring disintegration of central authority in China, Chinese power will probably grow steadily into the twenty-first century. The conservative, stability-oriented development policies favored by China's post–June 1989 leaders will not produce the rapid growth that characterized the 1980s. Nonetheless, even under continued conservative policies, China will probably achieve annual GNP growth on the order of 5 percent to 8 percent. Projected to the year 2010, that will give China a mammoth aggregate GNP of between 1.2 trillion and 2.3 trillion 1987 U.S. dollars. China's scientific and technological level will also advance steadily—at least barring a return to isolationism. China's sustained, systematic, and vigorous efforts to acquire and master advanced foreign technology will boost its technological level. Many of the Chinese students who have flooded the science and engineering programs of top U.S. universities will not return home, but enough will to make important contributions to China's technological advance. It is virtually certain that a substantial portion of China's enhanced national wealth will be used as instruments of national power, from construction of a blue-water navy and other military force projection capabilities to extension of foreign economic assistance.

The immediate goals sought by these instruments of national power will have to do with the final obliteration of China's "national humiliation" and its "reestablishment" as a great power. The vision of a fully "restored" China is impressive. The integration of the dynamic economies of Taiwan and Hong Kong into the PRC would contribute substantially to China's technological and organizational sophistication. The size of Taiwan's economy is over seven times that of Shanghai, one of China's current economic dynamos. Incorporation of Taiwan would give it, all things being equal, the equivalent of seven Shanghais. Taiwan's vast store of capital and its businessmen's understanding of modern management and international trade would help energize the PRC economy. Incorporation of Taiwan would ipso facto transform the PRC from the world's fourteenth- to the seventh-ranked exporter of goods and services. Including Hong Kong with the PRC and Taiwan would boost China to the world's fourth-largest exporter, ranking only behind Germany, the United States, and Japan.[1]

A restored China would also control the entire South China Sea. Chinese warships and aircraft would exercise effective control over these vast "territorial waters" and the substantial petroleum resources that lie below them. Some of the most important commercial sea lanes in the world would cross China's southern "territorial sea," and the waters of that sea would lap on the shores of the Philippines, Malaysia, Indonesia, and Brunei. Just beyond China's territorial sea would lie the dynamic and largely Chinese city-state of Singapore. All of this could strengthen China's influence in Southeast Asia. It would also increase Southeast Asian fears of China.

According to China's vision of its fully restored self, a "restored" China would be respected by its neighbors. The countries of Southeast and South Asia especially would understand China's power and the fact that opposing it on fundamental issues (for example, by aligning with extra-regional powers hostile to China) would impose very heavy costs on them, while cooperation with China would lead to effective Chinese help in dealing with security and development problems. China will continue to provide substantial economic development assistance to friendly neighbors. With others it will maintain quasi-alliance relations. Pakistan will probably continue to be China's major regional ally, but relations with Thailand may evolve in this direction. China's security links with Thailand, the recession of Soviet power from Indochina, and the improvement of Sino-Vietnamese relations that began in 1989 may allow China to emerge as the arbiter of relations between Thailand and Vietnam. Cambodia, especially one in which the Khmer Rouge played a significant role, might also look to China for protection against its two ancient nemeses, Thailand and Vietnam. This, combined with China's position in the South China Sea, would go a long way toward establishing a pax Sinica over continental Southeast Asia.

China's national power will, of course, be relative to that of other countries. In this regard, China faces stiff competition. By the mid-1980s, Japan had emerged as the second-largest economy in the world and the financial center of East Asia. Asian trade and capital flows were increasingly oriented about Tokyo. Japan's technological prowess was already very impressive and gave every indication of becoming even more so. By the late 1980s, Japan was also the world's largest dispenser of foreign economic development assistance. Asian leaders and pundits were increasingly attracted by the Japanese development model and looked to Tokyo for advice in dealing with their development problems. Japan's political culture and constitutional system have thus far prevented it from fully translating its economic might into military power, but even with Japanese defense spending limited to just over 1 percent of GNP, Japan's aggregate defense budget ranks third in the world, well behind the United States and the Soviet Union, but well ahead of the fourth-ranking spender. In 1990, Japan's nominal defense spending was over six times that of China. Comparisons of nominal expenses mean little, of course, since costs are extremely high in Japan, while China's defense costs are greatly understated. But while relatively small in terms of numbers of aircraft, warships, and other military equipment, Japan's military is by far the most technologically sophisticated in Asia.

By the early 1990s, China had begun openly to express anxiety over the further growth of Japanese power. Ostensibly these apprehensions are rooted in the experience of Japanese aggression in the 1930s. These recollections undoubtedly are real and do play a role. But perhaps equally important are the concerns of China's leaders regarding their future capability to "restore" China's position in the world. It is not difficult to imagine ways in which Japan might use its economic and military power to thwart Chinese foreign policy objectives. Keeping alive Japanese contrition about its past aggression against China and limiting Japan's military power are good ways of preventing this.

India is China's other rival for Asian preeminence. Here the economic contest is more equal. Militarily too, China and India are roughly balanced, considering the geographic circumstances of any likely battlefield between the two countries. India perceives South Asia as its security zone, in which the right of self-defense entitles it to exclude the military presence of extra-regional powers. Except for the United States, this has meant primarily China. This runs counter to Chinese aspirations. China has sought to develop multifaceted, cooperative relations with all the countries of South Asia on the basis of the Five Principles of Peaceful Coexistence. In Beijing's view, military relations are part of normal state-to-state relations between two countries which the governments of any two sovereign countries may decide to establish or terminate, increase or diminish, as they wish. This is part of the sovereign right of independent nations. Yet India has repeatedly used its substantial regional power to exclude a Chinese military presence from the region. During the mid-1980s, New Delhi forced China to suspend military relations with Sri Lanka. Then in 1989 and 1990, it forced Nepal to renounce such ties. In private conversations and classified documents, Chinese analysts use the term "hegemony" to describe India's attitude toward the South Asian region. As of the early 1990s, Chinese resentment over Indian efforts to exclude a Chinese military presence from South Asia remained subordinate to a desire for cordial relations with India. When push came to shove, Beijing disengaged and retreated. Someday this might change. It deeply rankles Beijing that with China's defeat of first American and then Soviet efforts to contain China, latter-day regional hegemonists such as India have now picked up the same cause [2].

Aside from the pursuit of goals linked to China's nationalist agenda, it is unclear just how China will use its enhanced national power. One major uncertainty is whether China will embrace a new messianic national mission. Will China be satisfied to be just another great power, using instruments of power to protect and promote its own particular and perhaps mundane interests? Or will Chinese foreign policy be influenced and perhaps occasionally driven by a sense of overriding mission? Chinese pride in their cultural achievements and in China's historic role in East Asia suggests that China will not be satisfied with a mundane, run-of-the-mill role. The revolutionary messianism of the first three decades of the PRC also suggests a need for a sense of mission in China's national character. Leading the world's working people to liberation must have satisfied some deep needs in the modern Chinese character. It is unclear, however, just what China's self-assigned mission might be in the twenty-first century. While Chinese culture undoubtedly does evoke respect abroad, that culture definitely is not transferable. The Marxist-Leninist-Maoist doctrine and social-political institutions derived from it have few non-Chinese followers in the 1990s. The Maoist model of development, which evoked some enthusiasm outside of China in the 1960s and 1970s, has been superseded by the successes of the Asian NICs and by post-1978 revelations of China's continuing backwardness and poverty. The future definition of China's national mission remains an open question. PRC history suggests that modern Chinese feel that China must stand for something. The question is, "What?"

Champion of the developing world is the most obvious answer. The tone of China's foreign propaganda and analysis of world affairs frequently suggests that China sees itself in this fashion. There are serious problems with this approach, however. China's development record, while quite respectable, is not stellar. China's Stalinist ideology and society appeal to few people today. There is also increasing differentiation among developing countries, ranging from the oil-rich countries of the Middle East, to the NICs of East and Southeast Asia, to the economic regression of sub-Saharan Africa. To which "Third World" is China to appeal? Perhaps the most serious problem is that for the foreseeable future China will not be able to provide amounts of development assistance approaching the levels dispensed by Japan, the United States, or Western Europe. This means that developing countries searching for practical help with problems of economic development are likely to look to capitals other than Beijing.

The weakness of China's economic instruments and the virtual nonexistence of its ideological appeal could combine with a determination to play a major role to lead Beijing to rely on military instruments. Confronted with Japanese, American, and European economic superpower, saddled with a repugnant Stalinist ideology, and yet determined that China's interests would not be ignored or violated, Beijing might resort increasingly to military means. China might find itself in a situation comparable to that of the USSR in the 1970s: determined to play a major role and expand its national influence, but confronted with situations in which the only effective instrument it possessed was the military.

QUEST FOR THE "RECOVERY" OF TAIWAN

Were upheaval in China to bring assertive nationalists to the fore, the Taiwan question would be a prime candidate for forceful nation-unifying foreign policy moves. Even without the added impetus of domestic disunity, integration of Taiwan into the PRC will remain high on Beijing's foreign policy agenda.

China's leaders feel that time is running out on the Taiwan question. Since Sino-U.S. normalization in 1978, Beijing has hoped to persuade the KMT to enter into a "patriotic" partnership with the CCP, accepting titular PRC sovereignty over Taiwan in exchange for a guarantee of continued KMT rule over Taiwan. This has failed. Not only did the KMT reject offers that Beijing felt were extremely generous, but it gradually accommodated Taiwanese pro-independence sentiment. Beijing watched with dismay as Taiwan's political liberalization and democratization brought pro-independence sentiment to the surface and the KMT permitted increasingly open expressions of such traitorous sentiments. Beijing also believed that a major obstacle to KMT embrace of pro-independence ideas was the elderly KMT veterans who had been raised on the mainland and who still wielded great influence on the KMT Central Executive Committee. These elders were dying off, however, and power was passing to a younger generation raised on Taiwan and deeply influenced by Japanese and American cultures. Notions of a liberal, democratic "Republic of Taiwan" are extremely attractive to this younger generation. Again, time seems to be running out.

In 1978, Beijing unilaterally announced that it hoped to settle the Taiwan question peacefully. Certain developments, however, would make this impossible, according to Beijing. Chief among these was declaration of independence by Taiwan. By the end of the 1980s, Beijing had added continued KMT refusal to negotiate with the PRC to the list of situations justifying use of force against Taiwan.

Were Beijing to decide to use force to facilitate the "return of

Taiwan to the motherland," the most likely scenario would involve low-level military moves closely geared to political developments within Taiwan. Large-scale military action would be too costly, provoking all-out resistance from Taiwan which, even if overcome and subdued, could destroy a large part of China's air and naval forces. As importantly, large-scale military action would increase the risks of U.S. intervention.

A safer, less costly strategy would stress development of political assets within Taiwan. The CCP has always placed great emphasis on the integration of military and political actions, and on the construction of a "broad united front" to undermine and isolate its opponents. There is every reason to believe that efforts to recover Taiwan will follow these lines. Following Taiwan's relaxation of restrictions on travel between Taiwan and the mainland in November 1987, large numbers of Taiwanese visited the PRC—1.5 million by February 1991. Indirect trade between Taiwan and the mainland topped $4 billion in 1990, and Taiwanese businessmen have invested more than $1 billion in at least 1,000 factories in the mainland.[3] Virtually every locality in China has a "united front" office charged with welcoming and courting these "Taiwan compatriots." Presumably a few have succumbed to some combination of patriotic appeal and material enticement, and agreed to work for the reunification of the motherland.

Taiwan's political liberalization, together with the increasing sophistication of its economy and labor force, has also led to a demand for cheap, unskilled labor. This demand has been met, in part, by illegal immigration—61,000 as of December 1990.[4] Many of these illegal immigrants are from the Chinese mainland. Some special agents may have joined the ranks of poor job-seekers making their way to Taiwan. Finally, there are some people in Taiwan who consciously embrace the incorporation of Taiwan into the PRC for reasons of socialist or nationalist ideology. Military moves against Taiwan would probably be preceded by assiduous preparation of networks of influence among these constituencies.

Initial military moves would probably be of low level, designed to precipitate a political crisis in Taiwan. The objective would be to force Taibei to open negotiations with Beijing on reunification as a way of defusing the military confrontation. Beijing might, for example, announce that it would begin inspecting foreign ships approaching Taiwan's harbors to ensure that they carried no sophisticated military technology injurious to China's sovereignty or to efforts to achieve peaceful unification. As uncertainty mounted in commercial maritime circles, and as debate intensified within Taiwan over how to respond, pressure might be stepped up a bit, perhaps by authorizing a clash between PRC and Taiwanese warships or aircraft. Uncertainty in Taiwan would mount and might begin to snowball with emigration or flight of capital. Agents of influence within Taiwan would seek to increase confusion and encourage those calling for negotiation with Beijing as a way of defusing the crisis. Once negotiations were begun, this would become proof that the Chinese people were solving their own internal problems peacefully and that foreign powers should stay out of the issue lest they undermine negotiations and chances for a peaceful solution. Were Taibei to break off negotiations, this would serve as justification for renewal of military pressure.

THE FUTURE OF SINO-AMERICAN RELATIONS

Future cooperative and amicable relations between the United States and the People's Republic of China must be founded on common interests and realistic mutual assessments. Since the early 1970s, Chinese analysts have foreseen and applauded the replacement of the post-1945 bipolar international system with a multipolar system made up of China, Japan, Western Europe, the Soviet Union, and the United States. Chinese analysts viewed the emergence of such a multipolar system positively because they believed it would reduce the influence of the two superpowers that had confronted and threatened the PRC since its founding. Moreover, a multipolar system would allow the PRC greater room for maneuver, perhaps enabling it to exploit contradictions between Europe, Japan, and the United States as the Western alliance dissolved.

The explosive development of Japanese economic power during the 1970s and 1980s led to some rethinking of the consequences of multipolarity. As it became clear that Japanese industrial, financial, and technological power would become the dominant, organizing force in the emerging East Asian economy, Beijing began to reevaluate the consequence of a recession of U.S. power and influence in East Asia. This reevaluation began as early as 1973, when Beijing dropped its earlier objection to the U.S.-Japanese alliance. Two objectives underlay that reevaluation. First and most important in the 1970s was a desire to check the expansion of Soviet power. Second, and more long-range, Beijing wanted to prevent Japan from rapidly expanding its military capabilities and staking out independent security objectives in Asia. The decline of Soviet power in the early 1990s, coinciding with the further growth of Japanese power, may cause Beijing to further rethink the implications of true multipolarity via an uncoupling of the Japan-U.S. alliance.

China's broader interests in East and South Asia would not be served by a further decline of U.S. influence, much less a U.S. withdrawal. The result of either would probably be consolidation of Japan's leadership role in East Asia and India's dominant role in South

Asia. While U.S. and Chinese interests may clash on specific issues such as Taiwan, Korea, or Pakistan, their broader regional interests are parallel. China has an interest in keeping the United States engaged and influential in East and South Asia.

In the early 1990s, the conclusion of a U.S.-Canadian free-trade agreement in 1989, the movement toward Western European economic unification in 1992, and growing Japanese economic power linked with mounting Japanese-U.S. economic friction all led to increasing speculation about the possible emergence of three global economic blocs based on Western Europe, North America, and Japan. The emergence of such a system could be a major setback for China. If China gravitated toward Japan's Asian bloc, it would become Tokyo's junior partner and could easily become dependent on Japan. It might also become subject to discrimination by members of the American and European blocs, and lose leverage with countries of those regions once it became identified as a member of the East Asian bloc. Yet refusal to participate in the emerging Tokyo-based system might deprive China of the benefits of participating intimately in what could be the world's most dynamic economic region. And whether or not China participated in the East Asian bloc, it could be faced with the evolution of a Japan-organized international system virtually dooming Beijing's aspirations of preeminence in Asia. Such considerations will probably lead Beijing to uphold the existing international trade system and to oppose the movement toward global economic regions. This converges with U.S. interests, at least as this author interprets those interests.

Sober-minded mutual understanding is the other essential basis of future Sino-American amity. Americans have had a tendency to see in China what they wanted to see, to either romanticize or vilify China, rather than realistically appraising China on its own terms. Americans must avoid stereotypes of "exotic China," which reduce China to strange but simple dimensions. We must be aware of the profound cultural and intellectual differences between the Western tradition and that of China, and must avoid viewing China through the prism of American values. But we must simultaneously avoid the insidious notion that Chinese are so fundamentally different as human beings that standards of basic human rights are not applicable to them, and do not entitle them, as much as any people anywhere, to the solicitous concern of international public opinion when commonly recognized fundamental rights are violated. Americans must understand the experiences that have shaped Chinese perceptions and must attempt to view the world from the standpoint of China's leaders, but they need not romanticize China or the leaders who speak in its name. The hope for future cooperative relations between the United States and China must be founded on mutual understanding, not upon any sort of illusion.

NOTES

1. International Monetary Fund, *Direction of Trade Statistics Yearbook 1990*, 3–7.

2. Regarding the clash of Indian and Chinese interests in the South Asian region see John W. Garver, "China-Indian Rivalry in Nepal: The Clash over Chinese Arms Sales," *Asian Survey*, vol. xxxi, no. 10 (October 1991), 956–75. John W. Garver, "Chinese-Indian Rivalry in Indochina," *Asian Survey*, vol. xxvii, no. 11 (November 1989), 1205–19. John W. Garver, "China and South Asia," *The Annals of the American Academy of Political and Social Science*, vol. 519 (January 1992), 67–85.

3. *Christian Science Monitor*, February 13, 1991, 10–11.

4. *FBIS,DRC*, December 12, 1990, 71.

Index